AT THE EXISTENTIALIST CAFÉ

AT THE EXISTENTIALIST CAFÉ

Freedom, Being and Apricot Cocktails

with

Jean-Paul Sartre
Simone de Beauvoir
Albert Camus
Martin Heidegger
Edmund Husserl
Karl Jaspers
Maurice Merleau-Ponty
and others

Sarah Bakewell

Chatto & Windus
LONDON

10

Chatto & Windus, an imprint of Vintage,
20 Vauxhall Bridge Road,
London SW1V 2SA

Chatto & Windus is part of the Penguin Random House group of
companies whose addresses can be found at
global.penguinrandomhouse.com

Penguin
Random House
UK

First published by Chatto and Windus in 2016

www.vintage-books.co.uk

A CIP catalogue record for this book is available from the British Library

ISBN 9780701186586

Typeset by Palimpsest Book Production Ltd, Falkirk, Stirlingshire
Printed and bound by Clays Ltd, St Ives plc

Penguin Random House is committed to a sustainable future for our
business, our readers and our planet. This book is made from
Forest Stewardship Council®-certified paper

For Jane and Ray

CONTENTS

Sir, What a Horror, Existentialism!

In which three people drink apricot cocktails, more people stay up late talking about freedom, and even more people change their lives. We also wonder what existentialism is.

It is sometimes said that existentialism is more of a mood than a philosophy, and that it can be traced back to anguished novelists of the nineteenth century, and beyond that to Blaise Pascal, who was terrified by the silence of infinite spaces, and beyond that to the soul-searching St Augustine, and beyond that to the Old Testament's weary Ecclesiastes and to Job, the man who dared to question the game God was playing with him and was intimidated into submission. To anyone, in short, who has ever felt disgruntled, rebellious, or alienated about anything.

But one can go the other way, and narrow the birth of modern existentialism down to a moment near the turn of 1932–3, when three young philosophers were sitting in the Bec-de-Gaz bar on the rue du Montparnasse in Paris, catching up on gossip and drinking the house speciality, apricot cocktails.

The one who later told the story in most detail was Simone de Beauvoir, then around twenty-five years old and given to watching the world closely through her elegant hooded eyes. She was there with her boyfriend, Jean-Paul Sartre, a round-shouldered twenty-seven-year-old with down-turned grouper lips, a dented complexion, prominent ears, and eyes that pointed in different directions, for his almost-blind right eye tended to wander outwards in a severe exotropia or misalignment of the gaze. Talking to him could be disorienting for the unwary, but if you forced yourself to stick with the left eye, you would invariably find it watching you with warm intelligence: the eye of a man interested in everything you could tell him.

Sartre and Beauvoir were certainly interested now, because the third person at the table had news for them. This was Sartre's debonair old school friend Raymond Aron, a fellow graduate of the École normale supérieure. Like the other two, Aron was in Paris for his winter break. But whereas Sartre and Beauvoir had been teaching in the French provinces – Sartre in Le Havre, Beauvoir in Rouen – Aron had been studying in Berlin. He was now telling his friends about a philosophy he had discovered there with the sinuous name of phenomenology – a word so long yet elegantly balanced that, in French as in English, it can make a line of iambic trimeter all by itself.

Aron may have been saying something like this: traditional philosophers often started with abstract axioms or theories, but the German phenomenologists went straight for life as they experienced it, moment to moment. They set aside most of what had kept philosophy going since Plato: puzzles about whether things are real or how we can know anything for certain about them. Instead, they pointed out that any philosopher who asks these questions is *already* thrown into a world filled with things – or, at least, filled with the appearances of things, or 'phenomena' (from the Greek word meaning 'things that appear'). So why not concentrate on the encounter with phenomena and ignore the rest? The old puzzles need not be ruled out forever, but they can be put in brackets, as it were, so that philosophers can deal with more down-to-earth matters.

The phenomenologists' leading thinker, Edmund Husserl, provided a rallying cry, 'To the things themselves!' It meant: don't waste time on the interpretations that accrue upon things, and especially don't waste time wondering whether the things are real. Just look at *this* that's presenting itself to you, whatever *this* may be, and describe it as precisely as possible. Another phenomenologist, Martin Heidegger, added a different spin. Philosophers all through history have wasted their time on secondary questions, he said, while forgetting to ask the one that matters most, the question of Being. What is it for a thing to *be*? What does it mean to say that you yourself *are*? Until you ask this, he maintained, you will never get anywhere. Again, he recommended the phenomenological method: disregard intellectual clutter, pay attention to things and let them reveal themselves to you.

'You see, *mon petit camarade*,' said Aron to Sartre – 'my little comrade', his pet name for him since their schooldays – 'if you are a phenomenologist, you can talk about this cocktail and make philosophy out of it!'

Beauvoir wrote that Sartre turned pale on hearing this. She made it sound more dramatic by implying that they had never heard of phenomenology at all. In truth, they had tried to read a little Heidegger. A translation of his lecture 'What Is Metaphysics?' had appeared in the same issue of the journal *Bifur* as an early Sartre essay in 1931. But, she wrote, 'since we could not understand a word of it we failed to see its interest'. *Now* they saw its interest: it was a way of doing philosophy that reconnected it with normal, lived experience.

They were more than ready for this new beginning. At school and university, Sartre, Beauvoir and Aron had all been through the austere French philosophy syllabus, dominated by questions of knowledge and endless reinterpretation of the works of Immanuel Kant. Epistemological questions opened out of one another like the rounds of a turning kaleidoscope, always returning to the same point: I think I know something, but how can I *know* that I know what I know? It was demanding, yet futile, and all three students – despite excelling in their exams – had felt dissatisfied, Sartre most of all. He hinted after graduation that he was now incubating some new 'destructive philosophy', but he was vague about what form it would take, for the simple reason that he had little idea himself. He had barely developed it beyond a general spirit of rebellion. Now it looked as though someone else had got there before him. If Sartre blanched at Aron's news about phenomenology, it was probably as much from pique as from excitement.

Either way, he never forgot the moment, and commented in an interview over forty years later, 'I can tell you that knocked me out.' Here, at last, was a real philosophy. According to Beauvoir, he rushed to the nearest bookshop and said, in effect, 'Give me everything you have on phenomenology, now!' What they produced was a slim volume written by Husserl's student Emmanuel Levinas, *La théorie de l'intuition dans la phénoménologie de Husserl*, or *The Theory of Intuition in Husserl's Phenomenology*. Books still came with their leaves uncut. Sartre tore the edges of Levinas's book open without waiting to use a paperknife, and began reading as he walked down the street. He could have been Keats, encountering Chapman's translation of Homer:

> Then felt I like some watcher of the skies,
> When a new planet swims into his ken;
> Or like stout Cortez when with eagle eyes
> He star'd at the Pacific – and all his men
> Look'd at each other with a wild surmise –
> Silent, upon a peak in Darien.

Sartre did not have eagle eyes and was never good at being silent, but he was certainly full of surmises. Aron, seeing his enthusiasm, suggested that he travel to Berlin in the coming autumn to study at the French Institute there, just as he had done. Sartre could study the German language, read the phenomenologists' works in the original, and absorb their philosophical energy from near at hand.

With the Nazis just coming to power, 1933 was not the perfect year to move to Germany. But it was a good time for Sartre to change the direction of his life. He was bored with teaching, bored with what he had learned at university, and bored with not yet having developed into the author of genius he had been expecting to become since childhood. To write what he wanted – novels, essays, everything – he knew he must first have Adventures. He had fantasised about labouring with dockers in Constantinople, meditating with monks on Mount Athos, skulking with pariahs in India, and battling storms with fisherman off the coast of Newfoundland. For now, just not teaching schoolboys in Le Havre was adventure enough.

He made the arrangements, the summer passed, and he went to Berlin to study. When he returned at the end of his year, he brought back a new blend: the methods of German phenomenology, mixed with ideas from the earlier Danish philosopher Søren Kierkegaard and others, set off with the distinctively French seasoning of his own literary sensibility. He applied phenomenology to people's lives in a more exciting, personal way than its inventors had ever thought to do, and thus made himself the founding father of a philosophy that became international in impact, but remained Parisian in flavour: modern existentialism.

The brilliance of Sartre's invention lay in the fact that he did indeed turn phenomenology into a philosophy of apricot cocktails – and of the waiters who served them. Also a philosophy of expectation, tiredness, apprehensiveness, excitement, a walk up a hill, the passion for a desired lover, the revulsion from an unwanted one, Parisian gardens, the cold autumn sea at Le Havre, the feeling of sitting on overstuffed upholstery, the way a woman's breasts pool as she lies on her back, the thrill of a boxing match, a film, a jazz song, a glimpse of two strangers meeting under a street lamp. He made philosophy out of vertigo, voyeurism, shame, sadism, revolution, music and sex. Lots of sex.

Where philosophers before him had written in careful propositions and arguments, Sartre wrote like a novelist – not surprisingly, since he was one. In his novels, short stories and plays as well as in his philosophical treatises, he wrote about the physical sensations of the world and the structures and moods of human life. Above all, he wrote about one big subject: what it meant to be free.

Freedom, for him, lay at the heart of all human experience, and this set humans apart from all other kinds of object. Other things merely sit in place, waiting to be pushed or pulled around. Even non-human animals mostly follow the instincts and behaviours that characterise their species, Sartre believed. But as a human being, I have no predefined nature at all. I create that nature through what I choose to do. Of course I may be influenced by my biology, or by aspects of my culture and personal background, but none of this adds up to a complete blueprint for producing me. I am always one step ahead of myself, making myself up as I go along.

Sartre put this principle into a three-word slogan, which for him defined existentialism: 'Existence precedes essence'. What this formula gains in brevity it loses in comprehensibility. But roughly it means that, having found myself thrown into the world, I go on to create my own definition (or nature, or essence), in a way that never happens with other objects or life forms. You might think you have defined me by some label, but you are wrong, for I am always a work in progress. I create myself constantly through action, and this is so fundamental to my human condition that, for Sartre, it *is* the human condition, from the moment of first consciousness to the moment when death wipes it out. I am my own freedom: no more, no less.

This was an intoxicating idea, and once Sartre had fully refined it – that is, by the last years of the Second World War – it had made him a star. He was feted, courted as a guru, interviewed, photographed, commissioned to write articles and forewords, invited on to committees, broadcast on the radio. People often called on him to pronounce on subjects outside his expertise, yet he was never lost for words. Simone de Beauvoir too wrote fiction, broadcasts, diaries, essays and philosophical treatises – all united by a philosophy that was often close to Sartre's, though she had developed much of it separately and her emphasis differed. The two of them went on lecture and book tours together, sometimes being set up on throne-like chairs at the centre of discussions, as befitted the king and queen of existentialism.

Sartre first realised what a celebrity he had become on 28 October 1945, when he gave a public talk for the Club Maintenant (the 'Now Club') at the Salle des Centraux in Paris. Both he and the organisers had underestimated the size of the crowd that would show up for a talk by Sartre. The box office was mobbed; many people went in free because they could not get near to the ticket desk. In the jostling, chairs were damaged, and a few audience members passed out in the unseasonable heat. As a photo-caption writer for *Time* magazine put it, 'Philosopher Sartre. Women swooned.'

The talk was a big success. Sartre, who was only about five foot high, must have been barely visible above the crowd, but he delivered a rousing exposition of his ideas, and later turned it into a book, *L'existentialisme est un humanisme*, translated as *Existentialism and Humanism*. Both lecture and book culminated in an anecdote which would have sounded very familiar to an audience fresh from the experience of Nazi Occupation and Liberation. The story summed up both the shock value and the appeal of his philosophy.

One day during the Occupation, Sartre said, an ex-student of his had come to him for advice. The young man's brother had been killed in battle in 1940, before the French surrender; then his father had turned collaborator and deserted the family. The young man became his mother's only companion and support. But what he longed to do was to sneak across the border via Spain to England, to join the Free French forces in exile and fight the Nazis – red-blooded combat at last, and a chance to avenge his brother, defy his father, and help to free his country. The problem was, it would leave his mother alone and in danger at a time when it was hard even to get food on the table. It might also get her into trouble with the Germans. So: should he do the right thing by his mother, with clear benefits to her alone, or should he take a chance on joining the fight and doing right by many?

Philosophers still get into tangles trying to answer ethical conundrums of this kind. Sartre's puzzle has something in common with a famous thought experiment, the 'trolley problem'. This proposes that you see a runaway train or trolley hurtling along a track to which, a little way ahead, five people are tied. If you do nothing, the five people will die – but you notice a lever which you might throw to divert the train to a sidetrack. If you do this, however, it will kill one person, who is tied to that part of the track and who would be safe if not for your action. So do you cause the death of this one person, or do you do nothing and allow five to die? (In a variant, the 'fat man' problem, you can only derail the train by throwing a hefty individual off a nearby bridge onto the track. This time you must physically lay hands on the person you are going to kill, which makes it a more visceral and difficult dilemma.) Sartre's student's decision could be seen as a 'trolley problem' type of decision, but made even more complicated by the fact that he could not be sure either that his going to England would actually help anyone, nor that leaving his mother would seriously harm her.

Sartre was not concerned with reasoning his way through an ethical calculus in the traditional way of philosophers, however – let alone 'trolleyologists', as they have become known. He led his audience to think about it more personally. What is it like to be faced with such a choice? How exactly does a confused young man go about dealing with such a decision about how to act? Who can help him, and how? Sartre approached this last part by looking at the question of who could *not* help him.

Before coming to Sartre, the student had thought of seeking advice from the established moral authorities. He considered going to a priest – but priests were sometimes collaborators themselves, and anyway he knew that Christian ethics could only tell him to love his neighbour and do good to others, without specifying which others

– mother or France. Next, he thought of turning to the philosophers he had studied at school, supposedly founts of wisdom. But the philosophers were too abstract: he felt they had nothing to say to him in his situation. Then, he tried to listen to his inner voice: perhaps, deep in his heart, he would find the answer. But no: in his soul, the student heard only a clamour of voices saying different things (perhaps things like: I must stay, I must go, I must do the brave thing, I must be a good son, I want action, but I'm scared, I don't want to die, I have to get away. I will be a better man than Papa! Do I truly love my country? Am I faking it?). Amid this cacophony, he could not even trust himself. As a last resort, the young man turned to his former teacher Sartre, knowing that from him at least he would not get a conventional answer.

Sure enough, Sartre listened to his problem and said simply, 'You are free, therefore choose – that is to say, invent.' No signs are vouchsafed in this world, he said. None of the old authorities can relieve you of the burden of freedom. You can weigh up moral or practical considerations as carefully as you like, but ultimately you must take the plunge and do something, and it's up to you what that something is.

Sartre doesn't tell us whether the student felt this was helpful, nor what he decided to do in the end. We don't know whether he existed, or was an amalgam of several young friends or even a complete invention. But the point Sartre wanted his audience to get was that each of them was as free as the student, even if their predicaments were less dramatic. You might think you are guided by moral laws, he was saying to them, or that you act in certain ways because of your psychological make-up or past experiences, or because of what is happening around you. These factors can play a role, but the whole mixture merely adds up to the 'situation' out of which you must act. Even if the situation is unbearable – perhaps you are facing execution, or sitting in a Gestapo prison, or about to fall off a cliff – you are still free to decide what to make of it in mind and deed. Starting from where you are now, you choose. And in choosing, you also choose who you will be.

If this sounds difficult and unnerving, it's because it is. Sartre does not deny that the need to keep making decisions brings constant anxiety. He heightens this anxiety by pointing out that what you do really *matters*. You should make your choices as though you were choosing on behalf of the whole of humanity, taking the entire burden of responsibility for how the human race behaves. If you avoid this responsibility by fooling yourself that you are the victim of circumstance or of someone else's bad advice, you are failing to meet the demands of human life and choosing a fake existence, cut off from your own 'authenticity'.

Along with the terrifying side of this comes a great promise: Sartre's existentialism implies that it *is* possible to be authentic and free, as long as you keep up the effort. It is exhilarating to exactly the same degree that it's frightening, and for the same reasons. As Sartre summed it up in an interview shortly after the lecture:

> There is no traced-out path to lead man to his salvation; he must constantly invent his own path. But, to invent it, he is free, responsible, without excuse, and every hope lies within him.

It's a bracing thought, and was an attractive one in 1945, when established social and political institutions had been undermined by the war. In France and elsewhere, many had good reason to forget the recent past and its moral compromises and horrors, in order to focus on new beginnings. But there were deeper reasons to seek renewal. Sartre's audience heard his message at a time when much of Europe lay in ruins, news of Nazi death camps had emerged, and Hiroshima and Nagasaki had been destroyed by atom bombs. The war had made people realise that they and their fellow humans were capable of departing entirely from civilised norms; no wonder the idea of a fixed human nature seemed questionable. Whatever new world was going to arise out of the old one, it would probably need to be built without reliable guidance from sources of authority such as politicians, religious leaders, and even philosophers – the old kind of philosophers, that is, in their remote and abstract worlds. But here was a new kind of philosopher, ready to wade in and perfectly suited to the task.

Sartre's big question in the mid-1940s was: given that we are free, how can we use our freedom well in such challenging times? In his essay 'The End of the War', written just after Hiroshima and published in October 1945 – the same month as the lecture – he exhorted his readers to decide what kind of world they wanted, and make it happen. From now on, he wrote, we must always take into account our knowledge that we can destroy ourselves at will, with all our history and perhaps life on earth itself. Nothing stops us but our own free choosing. If we want to survive, we have to *decide* to live. Thus, he offered a philosophy designed for a species that had just scared the hell out of itself, but that finally felt ready to grow up and take responsibility.

The institutions whose authority Sartre challenged in his writings and talks responded aggressively. The Catholic Church put Sartre's entire works on its *Index of Prohibited Books* in 1948, from his great philosophical tome *Being and Nothingness* to his novels, plays and essays. They feared, rightly, that his talk of freedom might make people doubt their faith. Simone de Beauvoir's even more provocative feminist treatise *The Second Sex* was also added to the list. One would expect political conservatives to dislike existentialism; more surprisingly, Marxists hated it too. Sartre is now often remembered as an apologist for Communist regimes, yet for a long time he was vilified by the party. After all, if people insisted on thinking of themselves as free individuals, how could there ever be a properly organised revolution? Marxists thought humanity was destined to move through determined stages towards socialist paradise; this left little room for the idea that each of us is personally responsible for what we do. From different ideological starting points, opponents of existentialism almost all agreed that it was, as an article in *Les nouvelles littéraires* phrased it, a 'sickening mixture of philosophic pretentiousness, equivocal dreams, physiological technicalities, morbid tastes and hesitant eroticism . . . an introspective embryo that one would take distinct pleasure in crushing'.

Such attacks only enhanced existentialism's appeal for the young and rebellious, who took it on as a way of life and a trendy label. From the mid-1940s, 'existentialist' was used as shorthand for anyone who practised free love and stayed up late dancing to jazz music. As the actor and nightclubber Anne-Marie Cazalis remarked in her memoirs, 'If you were twenty, in 1945, after four years of Occupation, freedom also meant the freedom to go to bed at 4 or 5 o'clock in the morning.' It meant offending your elders and defying the order of things. It could also mean mingling promiscuously with different races and classes. The philosopher Gabriel Marcel heard a lady on a train saying, 'Sir, what a horror, existentialism! I have a friend whose son is an existentialist; he lives in a kitchen with a Negro woman!'

The existentialist subculture that rose up in the 1940s found its home in the environs of the Saint-Germain-des-Prés church on the Left Bank of Paris – an area that still milks the association for all it is worth. Sartre and Beauvoir spent many years living in cheap Saint-Germain hotels and writing all day in cafés, mainly because these were warmer places to go than the unheated hotel rooms. They favoured the Flore, the Deux Magots and the Bar Napoléon, all clustered around the corner of the boulevard Saint-Germain and the rue Bonaparte. The Flore was the best, for its proprietor sometimes let them work in a private room upstairs when nosy journalists or passers-by became too intrusive. Yet they also loved the lively tables downstairs, at least in the early days: Sartre enjoyed working in public spaces amid noise and bustle. He and Beauvoir held court with friends, colleagues, artists, writers, students and lovers, all talking at once and all bound by ribbons of cigarette or pipe smoke.

After the cafés, there were subterranean jazz dives to go to: in the Lorientais, Claude Luter's band played blues, jazz and ragtime, while the star of the club Tabou was the trumpeter and novelist Boris Vian. You could undulate to a jazz band's jagged parps and bleats, or debate authenticity in a dark corner while listening to the smoky voice of Cazalis's friend and fellow muse, Juliette Gréco, who became a famous chanteuse after her arrival in Paris in 1946. She, Cazalis and Michelle Vian (Boris's wife) would watch new arrivals at the Lorientais and

Tabou, and refuse entry to anyone who did not look suitable – although, according to Michelle Vian, they would admit anyone 'so long as they were interesting – that is, if they had a book under their arm'. Among the regulars were many of the people who had written these books, notably Raymond Queneau and his friend Maurice Merleau-Ponty, who both discovered the nightclub world through Cazalis and Gréco.

Gréco started a fashion for long, straight, existentialist hair – the 'drowning victim' look, as one journalist wrote – and for looking chic in thick sweaters and men's jackets with the sleeves rolled up. She said she first grew her hair long to keep warm in the war years; Beauvoir said the same thing about her own habit of wearing a turban. Existentialists wore cast-off shirts and raincoats; some of them sported what sounds like a proto-punk style. One youth went around with 'a completely shredded and tattered shirt on his back', according to a journalist's report. They eventually adopted the most iconic existentialist garment of all: the black woollen turtleneck.

In this rebellious world, just as with the Parisian bohemians and

Dadaists in earlier generations, everything that was dangerous and provocative was good, and everything that was nice or bourgeois was bad. Beauvoir delighted in telling a story about her friend, the destitute alcoholic German artist known as Wols (from Alfred Otto *Wolfgang Schulze*, his real name), who hung around the area living on handouts and scraps. One day, he was drinking with Beauvoir on the terrace of a bar when a wealthy-looking gentleman stopped to speak to him. After the man had gone, Wols turned to Beauvoir in embarrassment, and said, 'I'm sorry; that fellow is my brother: a banker!' It amused her to hear him apologise exactly as a banker might on being seen speaking to a tramp. Such topsy-turvydom may seem less odd today, following decades of such counter-cultural inversions, but at the time it still had the power to shock some – and to delight others.

Journalists, who thrived on salacious tales of the existentialist milieu, took a special interest in the love lives of Beauvoir and Sartre. The pair were known to have an open relationship, in which each was the primary long-term partner for the other but remained free to have other lovers. Both exercised this freedom with gusto. Beauvoir had significant relationships later in life, including with the American writer Nelson Algren and with Claude Lanzmann, the French film-maker who later made the nine-hour Holocaust documentary *Shoah*. As a woman, Beauvoir was judged more severely for her behaviour, but the press also mocked Sartre for his serial seductions. One story in *Samedi-soir* in 1945 claimed that he tempted women up to his bedroom by offering them a sniff of his Camembert cheese. (Well, good cheese was hard to get in 1945.)

In reality, Sartre did not need to dangle cheese to get women into his bed. One may marvel at this, looking at his photos, but his success came less from his appearance than from his air of intellectual energy and confidence. He talked enthrallingly about ideas, but he was fun too: he sang 'Old Man River' and other jazz hits in a fine voice, played piano, and did Donald Duck imitations. Raymond Aron wrote of Sartre in his schooldays that 'his ugliness disappeared as soon as he began to speak, as soon as his intelligence erased the pimples and swellings of his face'. Another acquaintance, Violette Leduc, agreed that his face could never be ugly because it was illuminated by the brilliance of his mind, as well as having 'the honesty of an erupting volcano' and 'the generosity of a newly ploughed field'. And when the sculptor Alberto Giacometti sketched Sartre, he exclaimed as he worked, 'What density! What lines of force!' Sartre's was a questioning, philosophical face: everything in it sent you somewhere else, swirling from one asymmetrical feature to another. He could wear people out, but he wasn't boring, and his clique of admirers grew and grew.

For Sartre and Beauvoir, their open relationship was more than a personal arrangement; it was a philosophical choice. They wanted to *live* their theory of freedom. The bourgeois model of marriage had no appeal for them, with its strict gender roles, its hushed-up infidelities, and its dedication to the accumulation of property and children. They had no children, they owned little, and they never even lived together, although they put their relationship before all others and met almost every day to work side by side.

They turned their philosophy into the stuff of real life in other ways, too. Both believed in committing themselves to political activity, and put their time, energy and fame at the disposal of anyone whose cause they supported. Younger friends turned to them for help in starting their careers, and for financial support: Beauvoir and Sartre each maintained protégés. They poured out polemical articles and published them in the journal they established with friends in 1945, *Les Temps modernes*. In 1973, Sartre also co-founded the major left-wing newspaper *Libération*. This has undergone several transformations since, including moving towards a more moderate politics and nearly going bankrupt, but both publications are still going at the time I'm writing this.

As their status grew and everything conspired to tempt them into the Establishment, Sartre and Beauvoir remained fierce in their insistence on remaining intellectual outsiders. Neither became academics in the conventional sense. They lived by school-teaching or freelancing. Their friends did likewise: they were playwrights, publishers, reporters, editors or essayists, but only a handful were university insiders. When Sartre was offered the Légion d'honneur for his Resistance activities in 1945, and the Nobel Prize in Literature in 1964, he rejected them both, citing a writer's need to stay independent of interests and influences. Beauvoir rejected the Légion d'honneur in 1982 for the same reason. In 1949, François Mauriac put Sartre forward for election to the Académie française, but Sartre refused it.

'My life and my philosophy are one and the same', he once wrote in his diary, and he stuck to this principle unflinchingly. This blending of life and philosophy also made him interested in other people's lives. He became an innovative biographer, publishing around two million words of life-writing, including studies of Baudelaire, Mallarmé, Genet and Flaubert as well as a memoir of his own childhood. Beauvoir too collected the minutiae of her own experience and that of friends, and shaped it all into four rich volumes of autobiography, supplemented by one memoir about her mother and another about her last years with Sartre.

Sartre's experiences and quirks found their way even into his most serious philosophical treatises. This could make for strange results, given that his personal take on life ranged from bad mescaline flashbacks and a series of embarrassing situations with lovers and friends to bizarre obsessions with trees, viscous liquids, octopuses and crustaceans. But it all made sense according to the principle first announced by Raymond Aron that day in the Bec-de-Gaz: *you can make philosophy out of this cocktail.* The topic of philosophy is whatever you experience, as you experience it.

Such interweaving of ideas and life had a long pedigree, although the existentialists gave it a new twist. Stoic and Epicurean thinkers in the classical world had practised philosophy as a means of living well, rather than of seeking knowledge or wisdom for their own sake. By reflecting on life's vagaries in philosophical ways, they believed they could become more resilient, more able to rise above circumstances, and better equipped to manage grief, fear, anger, disappointment or anxiety. In the tradition they passed on, philosophy is neither a pure intellectual pursuit nor a collection of cheap self-help tricks, but a discipline for flourishing and living a fully human, responsible life.

As the centuries went by, philosophy increasingly became a profession conducted in academies or universities, by scholars who sometimes prided themselves on their discipline's exquisite uselessness. Yet the tradition of philosophy as a way of life continued in a sort of shadow-line alongside this, often conducted by mavericks who had slipped through the gaps in traditional universities. Two such misfits in the nineteenth century had a particularly strong influence on the later existentialists: Søren Kierkegaard and Friedrich Nietzsche. Neither was an academic philosopher: Kierkegaard had no university career, and Nietzsche was a professor of Greek and Roman philology who had to retire because of ill health. Both were individualists, and both were contrarians by nature, dedicated to making people uncomfortable. Both must have been unbearable to spend more than a few hours with. Both sit outside the main story of modern existentialism, as precursors, but had a great impact on what developed later.

Søren Kierkegaard, born in Copenhagen in 1813, set the tone by using 'existential' in a new way to denote thought concerning the problems of human existence. He included it in the unwieldy title of a work of 1846: *Concluding Unscientific Postscript to Philosophical Fragments: a mimical-pathetical-dialectical compilation: an existential contribution*. This eccentric title was typical of him: he liked to play games with his publications, and he had a good eye for the attention-grabbing phrase: his other works included *From the Papers of One Still Living*, *Either/Or*, *Fear and Trembling*, *The Concept of Anxiety*, and *The Sickness Unto Death*.

Kierkegaard was well placed to understand the awkwardness and difficulty of human existence. Everything about him was irregular, including his gait, as he had a twisted spine for which his enemies cruelly mocked him. Tormented by religious questions, and feeling himself set apart from the rest of humanity, he led a solitary life much of the time. At intervals, though, he would go out to take 'people baths' around the streets of Copenhagen, buttonholing acquaintances and dragging them with him for long philosophical walks. His companions would struggle to keep up as he strode and ranted and waved his cane. One friend, Hans Brøchner, recalled how, when on a walk with Kierkegaard, 'one was always being pushed, by turns, either in towards the houses and the cellar stairwells, or out towards the gutters'. Every so often, one had to move to his other side to regain space. Kierkegaard considered it a matter of principle to throw people off their stride. He wrote that he would love to sit someone on a horse and startle it into a gallop, or perhaps give a man in a hurry a lame horse, or even hitch his carriage to two horses who went at different speeds – anything to goad the person into seeing what he meant by the 'passion' of existence. Kierkegaard was a born goader. He picked quarrels with his contemporaries, broke off personal relationships, and generally made difficulties out of everything. He wrote: 'Abstraction is disinterested, but for one who exists his existing is the supreme interest.'

He applied the same argumentative attitude to the personnel of philosophical history. He disagreed, for example, with René Descartes, who had founded modern philosophy by stating *Cogito ergo sum*: I think, therefore I am. For Kierkegaard, Descartes had things back to front. In his own view, human existence comes first: it is the starting point for everything we do, not the result of a logical deduction. My existence is active: I live it and choose it, and this precedes any statement I can make about myself. Moreover, my existence is *mine*: it is personal. Descartes' 'I' is generic: it could apply to anyone, but Kierkegaard's 'I' is the 'I' of an argumentative, anguished misfit.

He also took issue with G. W. F. Hegel, whose philosophy showed the world evolving dialectically through a succession of 'forms of consciousness', each stage superseding the one before until they all rise up sublimely into 'Absolute Spirit'. Hegel's *Phenomenology of Spirit* leads us to a climax as grand as that of the biblical Book of Revelation, but instead of ending with everyone divided between heaven and hell, it subsumes us all into cosmic consciousness. Kierkegaard countered

Hegel with typically awkward questions: what if I don't choose to be part of this 'Absolute Spirit'? What if I refuse to be absorbed, and insist on just being *me*?

Sartre read Kierkegaard, and was fascinated by his contrarian spirit and by his rebellion against the grand philosophical systems of the past. He also borrowed Kierkegaard's specific use of the word 'existence' to denote the human way of being, in which we mould ourselves by making 'either/or' choices at every step. Sartre agreed with him that this constant choosing brings a pervasive anxiety, not unlike the vertigo that comes from looking over a cliff. It is not the fear of falling so much as the fear that you can't trust yourself not to throw yourself off. Your head spins; you want to cling to something, to tie yourself down – but you can't secure yourself so easily against the dangers that come with being free. 'Anxiety is the dizziness of freedom', wrote Kierkegaard. Our whole lives are lived on the edge of that precipice, in his view and also in Sartre's.

There were other aspects of Kierkegaard's thought that Sartre would never accept, however. Kierkegaard thought that the answer to 'anguish' was to take a leap of faith into the arms of God, whether or not you could feel sure that He was there. This was a plunge into the 'Absurd' – into what cannot be rationally proved or justified. Sartre did not care for this. He had lost his own religious beliefs early in life: apparently it happened when he was about eleven years old and standing at a bus stop. He just knew, suddenly, that God did not exist. The faith never came back, so he remained a stalwart atheist for the rest of his life. The same was true of Beauvoir, who rejected her conventional religious upbringing. Other thinkers followed Kierkegaard's theological existentialism in various ways, but Sartre and Beauvoir were repelled by it.

They found a philosophy more to their taste in the other great nineteenth-century existentialist precursor, Friedrich Nietzsche. Born in Röcken in Prussia in 1844, Nietzsche set out on his brilliant career in philology, but turned to writing idiosyncratic philosophical treatises and collections of aphorisms. He directed these against the pious dogmas of Christianity and of traditional philosophy alike: for him, both were self-serving veils drawn over the harsher realities of life. What was needed, he felt, was not high moral or theological ideals, but a deeply critical form of cultural history or 'genealogy' that would uncover the reasons why we humans are as we are, and how we came to be that way. For him, all philosophy could even be redefined as a form of psychology, or history. He believed that every great philosopher actually wrote 'a kind of involuntary and unconscious memoir' rather than conducting an impersonal search for knowledge. Studying our own moral genealogy cannot help us to escape or transcend ourselves. But it can enable us to see our illusions more clearly and lead a more vital, assertive existence.

There is no God in this picture, because the human beings who invented God have also killed Him. It is now up to us alone. The way to live is to throw ourselves, not into faith, but into our own lives, conducting them in affirmation of every moment, exactly as it is, without wishing that anything was different, and without harbouring peevish resentment against others or against our fate.

Nietzsche was unable to put his ideas into much effect in his own life, not because he lacked the courage, but because his body betrayed him. In his forties, he fell victim to a disease, possibly syphilis or a brain tumour, which destroyed his faculties. After a distraught episode on the streets of Turin in January 1889, during which (the story goes) he weepingly threw his arms around the neck of an abused horse, he fell into irreversible dementia and spent the rest of his life an invalid. He died in 1900, having no idea of the impact his vision of human existence would one day have on the existentialists and others. Probably it would not have surprised him: while his own time failed to understand, he always felt his day would come.

Nietzsche and Kierkegaard were the heralds of modern existentialism. They pioneered a mood of rebellion and dissatisfaction, created a new definition of existence as choice, action and self-assertion, and made a study of the anguish and difficulty of life. They also worked in the conviction that philosophy was not just a profession. It was life itself – the life of an individual.

*

Having absorbed these older influences, the modern existentialists went on to inspire their own and later generations in a similar way, with their message of individualism and nonconformity. Throughout the second half of the twentieth century, existentialism offered people reasons to reject convention and change their lives.

The most transformative existentialist work of all was Simone de Beauvoir's pioneering feminist study, *The Second Sex*, published in 1949. An analysis of women's experience and life choices, as well as of the whole history of patriarchal society, it encouraged women to raise their consciousness, question received ideas and routines, and seize control of their existence. Many who read it may not have realised they were reading an existentialist work (partly because the English-language translation obscured much of its philosophical meaning), but that was what it was – and when women changed their lives after reading it, they did so in existentialist ways, seeking freedom and a heightened individuality and 'authenticity'.

The book was considered shocking at the time, not least because it included a chapter on lesbianism – although few yet knew that Beauvoir herself had had sexual relationships with both sexes. Sartre too supported gay rights, although he always insisted that sexuality was a matter of choice, which put him at odds with the views of many gay people who felt that they were simply born that way. In any case, existentialist philosophy offered gay people encouragement to live in the way that felt right, rather than trying to fit in with others' ideas of how they should be.

For those oppressed on grounds of race or class, or for those fighting against colonialism, existentialism offered a change of perspective – literally, as Sartre proposed that all situations be judged according to how they appeared in the eyes of those most oppressed, or those whose suffering was greatest. Martin Luther King Jr was among the civil-rights pioneers who took an interest. While working on his philosophy of non-violent resistance, he read Sartre, Heidegger and the German–American existentialist theologian Paul Tillich.

No one could argue that existentialism was responsible for every social change in the mid-twentieth century. But, with its insistence on freedom and authenticity, it gave impetus to radicals and protesters. And when the waves of change rose and broke into the students' and workers' uprisings of 1968, in Paris and elsewhere, many of the slogans painted on city walls echoed existentialist themes:

- It is forbidden to forbid.
- Neither god nor master.
- A man is not 'intelligent'; he is free or he is not.
- Be realistic: demand the impossible.

As Sartre remarked, the demonstrators on the 1968 barricades demanded nothing and everything – that is to say, they demanded freedom.

By 1968, most of the torn-shirted, kohl-eyed night-owls of the late 1940s had settled down to quiet homes and jobs, but not Sartre or Beauvoir. They marched in the front line, joined the Paris barricades, and addressed factory workers and students on picket lines, even though they sometimes found themselves perplexed by the new generation's way of doing things. On 20 May 1968, Sartre spoke to a gathering of about 7,000 students who had occupied the Sorbonne's magnificent auditorium. Of all the eager intellectuals who had wanted to get involved, Sartre was the one chosen to be wired up to a microphone and led before the melee to speak – as always, so diminutive that he was hard to spot, but in no doubt about his qualification for the role. He appeared first at a window to address students in the courtyard outside, like the Pope on the Vatican balcony, before being led into the packed auditorium. The students had piled themselves everywhere inside, climbing over the statues – 'there were students sitting in the arms of Descartes and others on Richelieu's shoulders', wrote Beauvoir. Loudspeakers mounted on the columns in the hallways transmitted the speeches outside. A TV camera appeared, but the students shouted for it to be taken away. Sartre had to bellow to be heard even through the microphone, but the crowd slowly calmed down to listen to the grand old existentialist. Afterwards, they kept him busy with questions about socialism and about post-colonial liberation movements. Beauvoir worried that he'd never get out of the hall again. When he did, it was to find a jealous group of writers waiting in the wings, annoyed that he'd been the only 'star' (as Marguerite Duras allegedly grumbled) whom the students wanted to hear.

Sartre was then just short of his sixty-third birthday. His listeners were young enough to be his grandchildren. Few would have remembered the end of the war, let alone those early years of the 1930s when he had begun thinking about freedom and existence. They would have seen Sartre more as a national treasure than as truly one of themselves. Yet they owed even more to him than they could have realised, in a way that went beyond political activism. He formed a link between them and his own generation of dissatisfied students in the late 1920s, bored with their studies and longing for 'destructive' new ideas. Further back, he connected them to the whole line of philosophical rebels: Nietzsche, Kierkegaard and the rest.

Sartre was the bridge to all the traditions that he plundered, modernised, personalised and reinvented. Yet he insisted all his life that what mattered was not the past at all: it was the future. One must keep moving, creating what *will* be: acting in the world and making a difference to it. His dedication to the future remained unchanged even as, entering his seventies, he began to weaken, to lose what remained of his vision, and to become hard of hearing and confused in his mind – and eventually to succumb to the weight of years after all.

Twelve years after the Sorbonne occupation, the biggest crowd of all assembled for Sartre's final celebrity appearance: his funeral, on 19 April 1980. It was not a state ceremony, as his refusal of Establishment pomp was honoured to the end. But it was certainly a massive public occasion.

Excerpts from the television coverage are still viewable online: you can watch as the hospital doors open and a small truck slowly emerges, piled high with a mountain of floral sprays that teeter and wave like soft coral as the vehicle creeps into the mass of people. Helpers walk in front to clear the way. Behind the truck comes the hearse, inside which you see the coffin, and Simone de Beauvoir with other chief mourners. The camera focuses on a single rose which someone has tucked into the hearse's door handle. Then it picks out a corner of the black cloth draped over the coffin inside, decorated with a single letter 'S'. The hushed commentator tells us that some 50,000 people are attending; about 30,000 of these line the three kilometres or so of streets between here and the Montparnasse cemetery, while another 20,000 wait at the cemetery itself. Just like the 1968 students, some people inside the cemetery have climbed onto the laps or heads of memorial figures. Minor mishaps have occurred; one man reportedly fell into the open grave and had to be hauled out.

The vehicles arrive and halt; we see bearers extract the coffin and convey it to the graveside, struggling to push through while maintaining their dignified demeanour. One bearer removes his hat, then realises the others have not, and replaces it: a tiny awkward moment. At the graveside, they lower the coffin in, and the mourners are handed forward. Someone passes a chair for Simone de Beauvoir to sit on. She looks dazed and exhausted, a headscarf tied over her hair; she has been dosing herself with sedatives. She drops a single flower into the grave, and many more flowers are thrown in on top of it.

The film footage shows only the first of two ceremonies. In a quieter event the following week, the coffin was dug up and the smaller coffin inside it removed so that Sartre could be cremated. His ashes went to their permanent spot, in the same cemetery but less accessible to a large procession. The funeral was for the public Sartre; the second burial was attended only by those close to him. The grave, with Beauvoir's ashes interred next to him when she died six years later, is still there, kept well tidied and occasionally flowered.

With these ceremonies, an era ended, and so did the personal story that wove Sartre and Beauvoir into the lives of so many other people. In the filmed crowd, you see a diversity of faces, old and young, black and white, male and female. They included students, writers, people who remembered his wartime Resistance activities, trade-union members whose strikes he had supported, and independence activists from Indochina, Algeria and elsewhere, honouring his contribution to their campaigns. For some, the funeral verged on being a protest march: Claude Lanzmann later described it as the last of the great 1968 demonstrations. But many attended only out of curiosity or a sense of occasion, or because Sartre had made some small difference in some aspect of their lives – or because the ending of such an outsized life simply demanded some gesture of participation.

I have watched that brief film clip online a dozen or more times, peering into the low-definition images of the many faces, wondering what existentialism and Jean-Paul Sartre meant to each of them. I only really know what they meant to me. Sartre's books changed my life too, albeit in an indirect and low-key way. I somehow failed to notice the news of his death and funeral in 1980, although I was already a suburban existentialist by then, aged seventeen.

I had become fascinated by him a year earlier. On a whim, I spent some of my sixteenth-birthday money on his 1938 novel *Nausea*, mainly because I liked the Salvador Dalí image on the Penguin cover: a bile-green rock formation and a dripping watch. I also liked the cover blurb, which called *Nausea* 'a novel of the alienation of personality and the mystery of being'. I wasn't sure what alienation meant, although I was a perfect example of it at the time. But I had no doubt that it would be my kind of book. It was indeed: when I started

reading, I bonded at once with its gloomy outsider protagonist Antoine Roquentin, who spends his days drifting disconsolately around the provincial seaside town of 'Bouville' (modelled on Le Havre, where Sartre had been stuck as a teacher). Roquentin sits in cafés and listens to blues records instead of getting on with the biography he is supposed to be writing. He walks by the sea and throws pebbles into its grey, porridge-like depths. He goes to a park and stares at the gnarled exposed root of a chestnut tree, which looks to him like boiled leather and threatens to overwhelm him by the sheer opaque force of its being.

I loved all this and was intrigued to learn that this story was Sartre's way of communicating a philosophy called 'existentialism'. But what was all this about 'being'? I had never been overwhelmed by the being of a chestnut root, nor had I noticed that things *had* being. I tried going to the public gardens in my own provincial town of Reading and staring at one of the trees until my eyes blurred. It didn't work; I thought I saw something move, but it was just the breeze in the leaves. Yet looking at something so closely did give me a kind of glow. From then on, I too neglected my studies in order to *exist*. I had already been inclined to absenteeism; now, under Sartre's influence, I became a more dedicated truant than ever. Instead of going to school, I got myself an unofficial part-time job in a Caribbean emporium selling reggae records and decorative hash pipes. It provided a more interesting education than I had ever had in a classroom.

Sartre had taught me to drop out, an underrated and sometimes useful response to the world. On the other hand, he also made me want to study philosophy. That meant passing exams, so I reluctantly applied myself to the syllabus at the last moment and squeaked through. I went to Essex University, where I did a philosophy degree and read more Sartre, as well as other thinkers. I fell under the spell of Heidegger and started a PhD on his work – but then dropped out again, in my second such disappearing act.

In the interim, I had been transformed yet again by my student experience. I managed to spend my days and evenings more or less as the existentialists had in their cafés: reading, writing, drinking, falling in and out of love, making friends, and talking about ideas. I loved everything about it, and thought life would always be one big existentialist café.

On the other hand, I also became aware that the existentialists were already considered out of fashion. By the 1980s, they had given way to new generations of structuralists, post-structuralists, deconstructionists and postmodernists. These kinds of philosopher seemed to treat philosophy as a game. They juggled signs, symbols and meanings;

they pulled out odd words from each other's texts to make the whole edifice collapse. They searched for ever more refined and unlikely wisps of signification in the writers of the past.

Although each of these movements disagreed with each other, most were united in considering existentialism and phenomenology the quintessence of what they were *not*. The dizziness of freedom and the anguish of existence were embarrassments. Biography was out, because life itself was out. Experience was out; in a particularly dismissive mood, the structuralist anthropologist Claude Lévi-Strauss had written that a philosophy based on personal experience was 'shop-girl metaphysics'. The goal of the human sciences was 'to dissolve man', he said, and apparently the goal of philosophy was the same. These thinkers could be stimulating, but they also turned philosophy back into an abstract landscape, stripped of the active, impassioned beings who occupied it in the existentialist era.

For decades after my second dropping-out I dipped into philosophy books occasionally, but lost the knack of reading them with the deep attention they needed. My old favourites remained on the far reaches of my bookcase, making it look like a spice shelf in a demiurge's kitchen: *Being and Nothingness, Being and Time, Of Time and Being, Totality and Infinity*. But they rarely shifted their dust – until, a few years ago, I picked up a collection of essays by Maurice Merleau-Ponty, looking for one I vaguely remembered about the Renaissance writer Michel de Montaigne, whom I was researching at the time.

Merleau-Ponty was a friend of Sartre and Beauvoir (until they fell out), and a phenomenologist who specialised in questions of the body and perception. He was also a brilliant essayist. I became diverted from Montaigne into the volume's other essays, and then to Merleau-Ponty's main work *The Phenomenology of Perception*. I was amazed afresh at how adventurous and rich his thinking was. No wonder I used to love this sort of thing! From Merleau-Ponty, I went on to revisit Simone de Beauvoir – whose autobiography I'd discovered during a long student summer selling ice creams on a grey, dismal English beach. I now read the whole thing again. Then came Albert Camus, Gabriel Marcel, Jean-Paul Sartre. Eventually I returned to the monumental Heidegger.

As I went on, I got the eerie feeling of blending again with my twenty-year-old self, especially as my copies of the books were filled with that self's weirdly emphatic juvenile marginalia.

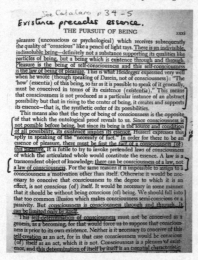

Yet my present-day self also watched over my responses, making critical or sardonic remarks from the sidelines. The two of me alternated as I read, sometimes quarrelling, sometimes being pleasantly surprised by each other, sometimes finding each other ridiculous.

I realised that, while I had changed in those twenty-five or so years, the world had changed too. Some of those fashionable movements that knocked existentialism out of the way have aged badly themselves, going into a decline of their own. The concerns of the twenty-first century are no longer the same as those of the late twentieth century: perhaps we are inclined to look for something different in philosophy these days.

If this is so, then there is a certain refreshment of perspective to be had from revisiting the existentialists, with their boldness and energy. They did not sit around playing with their signifiers. They asked big questions about what it means to live an authentic, fully human life, thrown into a world with many other humans also trying to live. They tackled questions about nuclear war, about how we occupy the environment, about violence, and about the difficulty of managing international relations in dangerous times. Many of them longed to change the world, and wondered what sacrifices we might or might not make for such an aim. Atheist existentialists asked how we can live meaningfully in the absence of God. They all wrote about anxiety and the experience of being overwhelmed by choice – a feeling that has become ever more intense in the relatively prosperous parts of the twenty-first-century world, even while real-world choices have shut down alarmingly for some of us. They worried about suffering, inequality and exploitation, and wondered whether anything could be done about these evils. As part of all these questions, they asked what individuals could do, and what they themselves had to offer.

They also asked what a human being *is*, given the last century's increasingly sophisticated understanding of brain physiology and body chemistry. If we are in thrall to our neurons and hormones, how can we still believe we are free? What distinguishes humans from other animals? Is it only a difference of degree, or are we truly set apart in some way? How should we think of ourselves?

Above all, they asked about freedom, which several of them considered the topic underlying all others, and which they interpreted both personally and politically. In the years following existentialism's decline, this topic went out of focus in parts of the world, perhaps because the great liberation movements of the 1950s and 1960s achieved so much in civil rights, decolonisation, women's equality and gay rights. It seemed as though these campaigns had got what they wanted, and that no point remained in talking about liberation politics. In a television interview in 1999, the French scholar Michel Contat looked back on the Sartre of the 1960s as someone who had given him and his generation 'a sense of freedom that directed our lives', but he immediately added that it was a topic few took much interest in any more.

But that was sixteen years ago, at the time I'm writing, and since then freedom has come into the spotlight again. We find ourselves surveilled and managed to an extraordinary degree, farmed for our personal data, fed consumer goods but discouraged from speaking our minds or doing anything too disruptive in the world, and regularly reminded that racial, sexual, religious and ideological conflict are not closed cases at all. Perhaps we are ready to talk about freedom again – and talking about it politically also means talking about it in our personal lives.

This is why, when reading Sartre on freedom, Beauvoir on the subtle mechanisms of oppression, Kierkegaard on anxiety, Camus on rebellion, Heidegger on technology, or Merleau-Ponty on cognitive science, one sometimes feels one is reading the latest news. Their philosophies remain of interest, not because they are right or wrong, but because they concern life, and because they take on the two biggest human questions: *what are we?* and *what should we do?*

In asking these two questions, most (not all) of the existentialists drew on their own life experience. But this experience was itself structured around philosophy. As Maurice Merleau-Ponty summed up this relationship, 'Life becomes ideas and the ideas return to life.' This connection became especially apparent when they talked ideas through with one another, which they did all the time. As Merleau-Ponty also wrote:

> A discussion is not an exchange or a confrontation of ideas, as if each formed his own, showed them to the others, looked at theirs, and returned to correct them with his own . . . Whether he speaks up or hardly whispers, each one speaks with all that he is, with his 'ideas', but also with his obsessions, his secret history.

Philosophical conversations between thinkers who had invested so much of themselves in their work often became emotional, and sometimes downright argumentative. Their intellectual battles form a long chain of belligerence that connects the existentialist story end to end. In Germany, Martin Heidegger turned against his former mentor Edmund Husserl, but later Heidegger's friends and colleagues turned their backs on him. In France, Gabriel Marcel attacked Jean-Paul Sartre, Sartre fell out with Albert Camus, Camus fell out with Merleau-Ponty, Merleau-Ponty fell out with Sartre, and the Hungarian intellectual Arthur Koestler fell out with everyone and punched Camus in the street. When the philosophical giants of each nation, Sartre and Heidegger, finally met in 1953, it went badly and they spoke mockingly of each other ever after.

Other relationships were extraordinarily close, however. The most intimate was that between Sartre and Beauvoir, who read each other's work and discussed their ideas almost every day. Beauvoir and Merleau-Ponty had also been friends since their teenage years, and Sartre and Beauvoir were charmed by Camus when they first met him.

When these friendships soured, it was generally because of ideas – most often political ideas. The existentialists lived in times of extreme ideology and extreme suffering, and they became engaged with events in the world whether they wanted to or not – and usually they did. The story of existentialism is therefore a political and a historical one: to some extent, it is the story of a whole European century. Phenomenology was first developed in the years before and during the First World War. Then Heidegger's philosophy emerged from the troubled situation of Germany between the wars. When Sartre went to Berlin in 1933, he saw Nazi marches and banners everywhere, and the mood of unease found its way into his work. His existentialism, and Beauvoir's, came of age during the Second World War, with the French experience of defeat and occupation, then went on to fill its sails with wild expectations for the post-1945 world. Existentialist ideas flowed into the widening stream of 1950s anti-conformism, and then into the full-blown idealism of the late 1960s. Through it all, the existentialists changed their thinking as the world changed; their constant shifts of direction kept them interesting, if not consistent – and not always on the right side, to say the least.

In short, the existentialists inhabited their historical and personal world, as they inhabited their ideas. This notion of 'inhabited philosophy' is one I've borrowed from the English philosopher and novelist Iris Murdoch, who wrote the first full-length book on Sartre and was an early adopter of existentialism (though she later moved away from it). She observed that we need not expect moral philosophers to 'live by' their ideas in a simplistic way, as if they were following a set of rules. But we can expect them to show how their ideas are lived *in*. We should be able to look in through the windows of a philosophy, as it were, and see how people occupy it, how they move about and how they conduct themselves.

Inspired both by Merleau-Ponty's mottos about lived ideas and by Iris Murdoch's 'inhabited philosophy', and triggered by my own eerie feelings on retracing my steps, I want to explore the story of existentialism and phenomenology in a way that combines the philosophical and the biographical. This is a mixture many of them were drawn to (although one repudiated it: Heidegger), and this too has fed my desire to try the same. I think philosophy becomes more interesting when it is cast into the form of a life. Likewise, I think personal experience is more interesting when thought about philosophically.

This will be a twentieth-century story, which is why there is very little more on the proto-existentialists Nietzsche and Kierkegaard. I'm also brief on theological existentialists and existentialist psychotherapists: they are fascinating but really need separate books to do them justice. On the other hand, people such as Iris Murdoch, the English 'new existentialist' Colin Wilson, the pugnacious Norman Mailer with his 'Existentialist Party', and the existentialist-influenced novelist Richard Wright have all found their way in, for various reasons. Some people are only here because they had an interesting role to play in the lives of the others: people like the ethical philosopher Emmanuel Levinas, the daring rescuer of manuscripts Herman Leo Van Breda, and the Czech phenomenologist Jan Patočka, who defied his country's regime and died for it.

The two gigantic figures in the story are inevitably Heidegger and Sartre – but those who know their *Being and Time* or *Being and Nothingness* may be surprised to find these masterworks chopped in shards and mixed up like chocolate chips in a cookie, rather than being dealt with by the whole bar, as it were. And they may not be the thinkers who, in the end, have the most to say.

These philosophers, together with Simone de Beauvoir, Edmund Husserl, Karl Jaspers, Albert Camus, Maurice Merleau-Ponty and others, seem to me to have participated in a multilingual, multi-sided conversation that ran from one end of the last century to the other. Many of them never met. Still, I like to imagine them in a big, busy café of the mind, probably a Parisian one, full of life and movement, noisy with talk and thought, and definitely an *inhabited* café.

When you peer in through the windows, the first figures you see are the familiar ones, arguing as they puff their pipes and lean towards each other, emphasising their points. You hear clinking glasses and rattling cups; the waiters glide between the tables. In the largest group in front, a dumpy fellow and an elegant woman in a turban are drinking with their younger friends. Towards the back, others sit at quieter tables. A few people are on a dance floor; perhaps someone is writing in a private room upstairs. Voices are being raised in anger somewhere, but there is also a murmuring from lovers in the shadows.

We can enter and take a seat: perhaps in the front, perhaps in an unobtrusive corner. There are so many conversations to overhear, one hardly knows which way to wag one's ears.

But first, before the waiter comes . . .

What is existentialism anyway?

Some books about existentialism never try to answer this question, as it is hard to define. The key thinkers disagreed so much that, whatever you say, you are bound to misrepresent or exclude someone. Moreover, it is unclear who was an existentialist and who was not. Sartre and Beauvoir were among the very few to accept the label, and even they were reluctant at first. Others refused it, often rightly. Some of the main thinkers in this book were phenomenologists but not existentialists at all (Husserl, Merleau-Ponty), or existentialists but not phenomenologists (Kierkegaard); some were neither (Camus), and some used to be one or both but then changed their minds (Levinas).

All the same, here is my attempt at a definition of what existentialists do. I put it here for reference, but by all means skip it and come back if the need or want arises.

– Existentialists concern themselves with *individual, concrete human existence*.

– They consider human existence different from the kind of being other things have. Other entities are what they are, but as a human I am whatever I choose to make of myself at every moment. I am *free* –

– and therefore I'm *responsible* for everything I do, a dizzying fact which causes

– an *anxiety* inseparable from human existence itself.

– On the other hand, I am only free within *situations*, which can include factors in my own biology and psychology as well as physical, historical and social variables of the world into which I have been thrown.

– Despite the limitations, I always want more: I am passionately involved in personal *projects* of all kinds.

– Human existence is thus *ambiguous*: at once boxed in by borders and yet transcendent and exhilarating.

– An existentialist who is also *phenomenological* provides no easy rules for dealing with this condition, but instead concentrates on *describing* lived experience as it presents itself.

– By describing experience well, he or she hopes to understand this existence and awaken us to ways of living more *authentic* lives.

So now let us return to 1933, and to the moment when Sartre went to Germany to learn about those new philosophers who called on him to pay attention to the cocktail on the table, and to everything else in life – in short, to the things themselves.

2

To the Things Themselves

In which we meet the phenomenologists.

Sartre's search for phenomenology took him to Berlin, but he would have found the heartland of the phenomenologists in a smaller city closer to home: Freiburg-im-Breisgau, in the south-west corner of Germany just over the French border.

With the Rhine separating it from France on the west, and the sombre Black Forest sheltering it on the east, Freiburg was a university city of about 100,000 people, a population often boosted by hikers or skiers passing through on their way to their holidays in the mountains – a fashionable pursuit in the 1920s and 1930s. They livened up Freiburg's streets with their hob-nailed boots and tanned knees and brightly embroidered braces, as well as their walking sticks studded with metal discs showing which routes they had already conquered. Beside them and the students, more traditional Freiburg residents carried on their lives surrounded by elegant university buildings and a tall cathedral, its sandstone tower perforated like lace and glowing a rosy colour in the evening sun. Further out, suburbs climbed over surrounding hills, especially the northern enclave of Zähringen where many university professors had houses on the steep streets.

It was a devoutly Catholic city and an intellectual one, with studious activity revolving around both its seminary and its university. The latter now featured an influential coterie in the philosophy department: the phenomenologists. Initially, this meant followers of Edmund Husserl, who took up Freiburg's chair of philosophy in 1916. He brought disciples and students with him, and recruited more, so that Freiburg remained a centre for his work long after his formal retirement in 1928. It was dubbed the 'City of Phenomenology' by one student, Emmanuel Levinas, the brilliant young Jewish Lithuanian whose book Sartre would later buy in Paris. Levinas's trajectory was typical of many phenomenology converts. He had been studying philosophy just over the French border in Strasbourg in 1928 when he saw someone in the town reading a Husserl book. Intrigued, he read it himself, and immediately arranged a transfer so he could study with Husserl in person. It changed his whole way of thinking. As he wrote, 'For the young Germans I met in Freiburg, this new philosophy is more than a new theory; it is a new ideal of life, a new page of history, almost a new religion.'

Sartre could have become a late joiner of this gang too. Had he gone to Freiburg, he might have taken up hiking and skiing, and become a lean mountain man instead of the 'real little Buddha' which he said he became during his year of Berlin beer and dumplings. Instead, he stayed in the capital's French Institute reading the phenomenologists' books, Husserl's above all, and learning the difficult German terms as he went. He spent the year formulating his ideas 'at Husserl's expense', as he later put it, but never met the master in person. Husserl probably never heard a word about him. Perhaps that was for the best, as he probably would have been unimpressed by the unfamiliar brew the young French existentialist would make of his ideas.

If we could do as disciples like Levinas did, and sign up for Husserl's classes in Freiburg back in the late 1910s and the 1920s, we might at first be disappointed. He neither looked nor sounded like a guru, or even the founder of a great philosophical movement. He was quiet, with round wire glasses and a delicate look. In youth, he had soft, curly blond hair, which soon receded to leave a bald-domed head over a moustache and neat beard. When he spoke, he accompanied his words with meticulous hand gestures: one person who attended a Husserl lecture said it reminded him of a 'watchmaker gone mad'. Another witness, the philosopher Hans-Georg Gadamer, noticed 'the fingers of the right hand circling the flat palm of the left hand in a slow, turning movement', as Husserl outlined each point – as if he were turning the idea round on his palm to look at it from different angles. In a very short surviving film clip of him as an elderly man in 1936, walking in a garden with his daughter, one can see him bobbing his hand up and down as he talks. Husserl himself was aware of his tendency to repetitive compulsions: he used to tell people that, as a boy, he was given a pocketknife as a present and was delighted, but sharpened it so obsessively that he wore the blade away entirely and was left with nothing but a handle. 'I wonder whether my philosophy is not unlike this knife', he mused.

It was by no means clear, in his boyhood, that his talents would lie in philosophy at all. Born on 8 April 1859 in the Moravian town of Prostějov (or Prossnitz, to a German-speaker such as himself; it is now in the Czech Republic), Husserl came from a Jewish family but converted to Lutheranism as a young man. His school career was undistinguished. One former schoolmate told a biographer that the young Husserl was 'in the habit of falling fast asleep during the lesson, and it was necessary for one of us to push him to wake him up. When the teacher called on him he would stand up sleepily, yawn and gape. Once he yawned so hard that his lower jaw remained stuck.' But this only happened when Husserl was not interested in the subject. He was more alert in his favourite class of the time, mathematics, and went on to study this at the University of Leipzig. But a fellow Moravian student there, Tomáš Masaryk (later the president of Czechoslovakia) persuaded Husserl to accompany him to the University of Vienna to take classes with a charismatic philosophy teacher named Franz Clemens Brentano. He spent two years in Vienna from 1884, and was so won over by Brentano that he resolved to devote his life to philosophy. From then on, there was no more sleeping on the job.

Brentano was the sort of teacher who could work such miracles. A former priest trained in Aristotelian philosophy, he had resigned from the priesthood and lost an earlier teaching job after questioning the Church's new doctrine of papal infallibility, which he considered indefensible. The unemployed Brentano spent a year travelling around Europe learning about other ideas, including those from the new field of experimental psychology, and decided that traditional philosophy needed reinvigorating from such sources. He then began teaching again in the more open-minded University of Vienna. There, he encouraged his students to break with tradition, criticise the great philosophers of the past, and think for themselves, while also taking care to be methodical. This was the combination that galvanized Husserl. Armed with Brentano's innovations, he embarked on his own philosophical work.

A long, difficult period ensued, in which Husserl slowly built his career as a *Privatdozent* or unpaid university tutor, surviving on free-lance fees – the usual route into German academic life. He soon had a family to support, marrying Malvine Steinschneider, another Jewish convert to Protestantism from his home town, and starting a family of three children. He meanwhile found time to publish increasingly innovative works of philosophy, notably *Logical Investigations* in 1900/1901 and *Ideas* in 1913. They made his name: he got a paid job in Göttingen and then, at last, took up the chair of philosophy in Freiburg, which would remain his home.

Husserl arrived in Freiburg in the middle of the First World War, in 1916, and it was a terrible year for his family. All three of the now-adult Husserl children joined the war effort: the daughter, Elli, worked in a field hospital, while the two sons fought on the front line. The elder, Gerhart, was severely wounded but survived. The younger son, Wolfgang, was killed at Verdun on 8 March 1916, aged twenty. Husserl, who was prone to episodes of depression, fell into one of his worst periods of despair.

Usually he got himself out of depression by furious work, sometimes writing major treatises in just a few weeks. This time it was harder. Yet he had a lot to distract him in Freiburg. Besides writing and teaching, he now managed an entourage of disciples who formed a sort of Husserlian laboratory. One pictures an array of white-coated phenomenologists tinkering at benches, but mostly their labours took the form of writing, teaching, and pursuing individual research projects. They edited a yearbook in which they published phenomenological texts, and taught basic university classes – 'phenomenological kindergarten', as one of the key assistants, Edith Stein, called it. Stein was struck by the extreme devotion Husserl expected from her and other colleagues. She was exaggerating only slightly when she joked to a friend, 'I am to stay with him until I marry; then I may only accept a man who will also become his assistant, and the same holds for the children.'

Husserl had to be possessive about his best followers, for only a few – Stein among them – mastered the art of reading his manuscripts. He used his own adaptation of a popular form of shorthand, the Gabelsberger system, and filled thousands of pages with this idiosyncratic script in a minuscule frenzy. Despite his precision of manner, he was not orderly about his writing. He would leave old projects discarded like shavings while he set off on new ones, which in turn he did not finish. His assistants worked to transcribe his drafts and tease out his arguments, but, each time they returned a document to him to revise, he would rewrite it as a new work. He always wanted to take his thought to some more puzzling and difficult place: somewhere not yet explored. His student (and later translator) Dorion Cairns recalled Husserl saying that his aim was always to work in whatever topic seemed the 'most distressing and uncertain' to him at any time – the ones that filled him with most anxiety and self-doubt.

Husserl's philosophy became an exhausting but exciting discipline in which concentration and effort must constantly be renewed. To practise it, he wrote, '*a new way of looking at things* is necessary' – a way that brings us back again and again to our project, so as 'to see what stands before our eyes, to distinguish, to describe'.

This was Husserl's natural style of working. It was also a perfect definition of phenomenology.

So what exactly *is* phenomenology? It is essentially a method rather than a set of theories, and – at the risk of wildly oversimplifying – its basic approach can be conveyed through a two-word command: *DESCRIBE PHENOMENA*.

The first part of this is straightforward: a phenomenologist's job is to *describe*. This is the activity that Husserl kept reminding his students to do. It meant stripping away distractions, habits, clichés of thought, presumptions and received ideas, in order to return our attention to what he called the 'things themselves'. We must fix our beady gaze on them and capture them exactly as they appear, rather than as we think they are supposed to be.

The things that we describe so carefully are called *phenomena* – the second element in the definition. The word *phenomenon* has a special meaning to phenomenologists: it denotes any ordinary thing or object or event *as it presents itself to my experience*, rather than as it may or may not be in reality.

As an example, take a cup of coffee. (Husserl liked coffee: long before Aron talked about the phenomenology of apricot cocktails, Husserl told students in his seminars, 'Give me my coffee so that I can make phenomenology out of it.')

What, then, is a cup of coffee? I might define it in terms of its chemistry and the botany of the coffee plant, and add a summary of how its beans are grown and exported, how they are ground, how hot water is pressed through the powder and then poured into a shaped receptacle to be presented to a member of the human species who orally ingests it. I could analyse the effect of caffeine on the body, or discuss the international coffee trade. I could fill an encyclopaedia with these facts, and I would still get no closer to saying what *this* particular cup of coffee in front of me is. On the other hand, if I went the other way and conjured up a set of purely personal, sentimental associations – as Marcel Proust does when he dunks his madeleine in his tea and goes on to write seven volumes about it – that would not allow me to understand this cup of coffee as an immediately given phenomenon either.

Instead, this cup of coffee is a rich aroma, at once earthy and perfumed; it is the lazy movement of a curlicue of steam rising from its surface. As I lift it to my lips, it is a placidly shifting liquid and a weight in my hand inside its thick-rimmed cup. It is an approaching warmth, then an intense dark flavour on my tongue, starting with a slightly austere jolt and then relaxing into a comforting warmth, which spreads from the cup into my body, bringing the promise of lasting alertness and refreshment. The promise, the anticipated sensations, the smell, the colour and the flavour are all part of the coffee as phenomenon. They all emerge by being experienced.

If I treated all these as purely 'subjective' elements to be stripped away in order to be 'objective' about my coffee, I would find there was nothing left of my cup of coffee as a phenomenon – that is, as it appears in the experience of me, the coffee-drinker. This experiential cup of coffee is the one I can speak about with certainty, while everything else to do with the bean-growing and the chemistry is hearsay. It may all be interesting hearsay, but it's irrelevant to a phenomenologist.

Husserl therefore says that, to phenomenologically describe a cup of coffee, I should set aside both the abstract suppositions and any intrusive emotional associations. Then I can concentrate on the dark, fragrant, rich phenomenon in front of me now. This 'setting aside' or 'bracketing out' of speculative add-ons Husserl called *epoché* – a term borrowed from the ancient Sceptics, who used it to mean a general suspension of judgement about the world. Husserl sometimes referred to it as a phenomenological 'reduction' instead: the process of boiling away extra theorising about what coffee 'really' is, so that we are left only with the intense and immediate flavour – the phenomenon.

The result is a great liberation. Phenomenology frees me to talk about my experienced coffee as a serious topic of investigation. It likewise frees me to talk about many areas that come into their own *only* when discussed phenomenologically. An obvious example, close to the coffee case, is expert wine-tasting – a phenomenological practice if ever there was one, and one in which the ability both to discern and to describe experiential qualities are equally important.

There are many such topics. If I want to tell you about a heart-rending piece of music, phenomenology enables me to describe it as a moving piece of music, rather than as a set of string vibrations and mathematical note relationships on which I have pinned a personal emotion. Melancholy music *is* melancholy; a sweet air *is* a sweet air; these descriptions are fundamental to what music is. Indeed, we do talk about music phenomenologically all the time. Even if I describe a sequence of notes as going 'up' or 'down', this has less to do with what the sound waves are doing (which is becoming more or less frequent, and longer or shorter) than with how the music plays out in my mind. I hear the notes climbing up an invisible ladder. I almost physically rise in my chair as I listen to Ralph Vaughan Williams's 'The Lark Ascending'; my very soul takes flight. That's not just me: it is what the music is.

Phenomenology is useful for talking about religious or mystical experiences: we can describe them as they feel from the inside without having to prove that they represent the world accurately. For similar reasons, phenomenology helps physicians. It makes it possible to consider medical symptoms as they are experienced by the patient rather than exclusively as physical processes. A patient can describe a diffuse or stabbing pain, or a sensation of heaviness or sluggishness, or the vague unease in a disturbed stomach. Amputees often suffer from 'phantom' sensations in the area of the lost limb; phenomenology allows these sensations to be analysed. The neurologist Oliver Sacks discussed such experiences in his 1984 book *A Leg to Stand On*, about his recovery from a severe leg injury. Long after the physical damage had healed, his leg felt separate from him, like a wax model: he could move it, but it did not feel like *his* from within. After much physiotherapy it returned to normal, but, had he not been able to convince his doctors that the feeling was phenomenologically important and that it belonged to the condition rather than being some personal oddity, he might not have received that therapy and might never have regained full control of his leg.

In all these cases, the Husserlian 'bracketing out' or *epoché* allows the phenomenologist to temporarily ignore the question 'But is it real?', in order to ask how a person experiences his or her world. Phenomenology gives a formal mode of access to human experience. It lets philosophers talk about life more or less as non-philosophers do, while still being able to tell themselves they are being methodical and rigorous.

The point about rigour is crucial; it brings us back to the first half of the command to *describe phenomena*. A phenomenologist cannot get away with listening to a piece of music and saying, 'How lovely!' He or she must ask: is it plaintive? is it dignified? is it colossal and sublime? The point is to keep coming back to the 'things themselves' – phenomena stripped of their conceptual baggage – so as to bail out weak or extraneous material and get to the heart of the experience. One might never finish adequately describing a cup of coffee. Yet it is a liberating task: it gives us back the world we live in. It works most effectively on the things we may not usually think of as material for philosophy: a drink, a melancholy song, a drive, a sunset, an ill-at-ease mood, a box of photographs, a moment of boredom. It restores this personal world in its richness, arranged around our own perspective yet usually no more noticed than the air.

There is another side effect: it ought in theory to free us from ideologies, political and otherwise. In forcing us to be loyal to experience, and to sidestep authorities who try to influence how we interpret that experience, phenomenology has the capacity to neutralise all the 'isms' around it, from scientism to religious fundamentalism to Marxism to fascism. All are to be set aside in the *epoché* – they have no business intruding on the things themselves. This gives phenomenology a surprisingly revolutionary edge, if done correctly.

No wonder phenomenology could be exciting. It could also be perplexing, and often it was a bit of both. A mixture of excitement and puzzlement was evident in the response of one young German who discovered phenomenology in its early days: Karl Jaspers. In 1913, he was working as a researcher at the Heidelberg Clinic of Psychiatry, having chosen psychology over philosophy because he liked its concrete, applied approach. Philosophy seemed to him to have lost its way, whereas psychology produced definite results with its experimental methods. But then he found that psychology was *too* workmanlike: it lacked philosophy's grand ambition. Jaspers was not satisfied by either. Then he heard about phenomenology, which offered the best from both: an applied method, combined with the soaring philosophical aim of understanding the whole of life and experience. He wrote a fan letter to Husserl, but in it admitted that he was not yet quite sure what phenomenology was. Husserl wrote back to him, 'You are using the method perfectly. Just keep it up. You don't need to know what it is; that's indeed a difficult matter.' In a letter to his parents, Jaspers speculated that Husserl did not know what phenomenology was either.

Yet none of this uncertainty could dim the excitement. Like all philosophy, phenomenology made great demands on its practitioners. It required 'a *different thinking*', Jaspers wrote; 'a thinking that, in knowing, reminds me, awakens me, brings me to myself, transforms me'. It could do all that, and also give results.

Besides claiming to transform the way we think about reality, phenomenologists promised to change how we think about ourselves. They believed that we should not try to find out what the human mind *is*, as if it were some kind of substance. Instead, we should consider what it *does*, and how it grasps its experiences.

Husserl had picked up this idea from his old teacher Franz Brentano, in Vienna days. In a fleeting paragraph of his book *Psychology from an Empirical Standpoint*, Brentano proposed that we approach the mind in terms of its 'intentions' – a misleading word, which sounds like it means deliberate purposes. Instead it meant a general reaching or stretching, from the Latin root *in-tend*, meaning to stretch towards or into something. For Brentano, this reaching towards objects is what our minds do all the time. Our thoughts are invariably *of* or *about* something, he wrote: in love, something is loved, in hatred, something is hated, in judgement, something is affirmed or denied. Even when I imagine an object that isn't there, my mental structure is still one of 'about-ness' or 'of-ness'. If I dream that a white rabbit runs past me checking its pocket watch, I am dreaming *of* my fantastical dream-rabbit. If I gaze up at the ceiling trying to make sense of the structure of consciousness, I am thinking *about* the structure of consciousness. Except in deepest sleep, my mind is always engaged in this *aboutness*: it has 'intentionality'. Having taken the germ of this from Brentano, Husserl made it central to his whole philosophy.

Just try it: if you attempt to sit for two minutes and think about nothing, you will probably get an inkling of why intentionality is so fundamental to human existence. The mind races around like a foraging squirrel in a park, grabbing in turn at a flashing phone-screen, a distant mark on the wall, a clink of cups, a cloud that resembles a whale, a memory of something a friend said yesterday, a twinge in a knee, a pressing deadline, a vague expectation of nice weather later, a tick of the clock. Some Eastern meditation techniques aim to still this scurrying creature, but the extreme difficulty of this shows how unnatural it is to be mentally inert. Left to itself, the mind reaches out in all directions as long as it is awake – and even carries on doing it in the dreaming phase of its sleep.

Understood in this way, the mind hardly *is* anything at all: it is its aboutness. This makes the human mind (and possibly some animal minds) different from any other naturally occurring entity. Nothing else can be as thoroughly *about* or *of* things as the mind is: even a book only reveals what it's 'about' to someone who picks it up and peruses it, and is otherwise merely a storage device. But a mind that is experiencing nothing, imagining nothing, or speculating about nothing can hardly be said to be a mind at all.

Husserl saw in the idea of intentionality a way to sidestep two great unsolved puzzles of philosophical history: the question of what objects 'really' are, and the question of what the mind 'really' is. By doing the *epoché* and bracketing out all consideration of reality from both topics, one is freed to concentrate on the relationship in the middle. One can apply one's descriptive energies to the endless dance of intentionality that takes place in our lives: the whirl of our minds as they seize their intended phenomena one after the other and whisk them around the floor, never stopping as long as the music of life plays.

Three simple ideas – description, phenomenon, intentionality – provided enough inspiration to keep roomfuls of Husserlian assistants busy in Freiburg for decades. With all of human existence awaiting their attention, how could they ever run out of things to do?

Husserlian phenomenology never had the mass influence of Sartrean existentialism, at least not directly – but it was his groundwork that freed Sartre and other existentialists to write so adventurously about everything from café waiters to trees to breasts. Reading his Husserl books in Berlin in 1933, Sartre developed his own bold interpretation of it, putting special emphasis on intentionality and the way it throws the mind *out* into the world and its things. For Sartre, this gives the mind an immense freedom. If we are nothing but what we think about, then no predefined 'inner nature' can hold us back. We are protean. He gave this idea a Sartrean makeover in a short essay which he began writing in Berlin, but published only in 1939: 'A Fundamental Idea of Husserl's Phenomenology: Intentionality'.

The philosophers of the past, he wrote, had been stuck in a 'digestive' model of consciousness: they thought that to perceive something was to draw it into our own substance, as a spider coats an insect in its own spittle to semi-dissolve it. Instead, with Husserl's intentionality, to be conscious of something is to burst out –

to wrest oneself from moist, gastric intimacy and fly out over there, beyond oneself, to what is not oneself. To fly over there, to the tree, and yet outside the tree, because it eludes and repels me and I can no more lose myself in it than it can dissolve itself into me: outside it, outside myself . . . And, in this same process, consciousness is purified and becomes clear as a great gust of wind. There is nothing in it any more, except an impulse to flee itself, a sliding outside itself. If, impossibly, you were to 'enter' a consciousness, you would be picked up by a whirlwind and thrown back outside to where the tree is and all the dust, for consciousness has no 'inside'. It is merely the exterior of itself and it is this absolute flight, this refusal to be substance, that constitute it as a consciousness. Imagine now a linked series of bursts that wrest us from ourselves, that do not even leave an 'ourself' the time to form behind them, but rather hurl us out beyond them into the dry dust of the world, on to the rough earth, among things. Imagine we are thrown out in this way, abandoned by our very natures in an indifferent, hostile, resistant world. If you do so, you will have grasped the profound meaning of the discovery Husserl expresses in this famous phrase: 'All consciousness is consciousness *of* something.'

For Sartre, if we try to shut ourselves up inside our own minds, 'in a nice warm room with the shutters closed', we cease to exist. We have no cosy home: being out on the dusty road is the very definition of what we are.

Sartre's gift for shocking metaphor makes his 'Intentionality' essay the most readable introduction to phenomenology ever written, and one of the shortest. It is certainly a better read than anything Husserl wrote. Yet Sartre was by then already aware that Husserl had later moved away from this outward-bound interpretation of intentionality. He had come to look at it a different way, as an operation that pulled everything back into the mind after all.

Husserl had long ago considered the possibility that the whole intentional dance could just as easily be understood as occurring *inside* a person's inner realm. Since the *epoché* suspended questions about whether things were real, nothing stood in the way of this interpretation. Real, not real; inside, outside; what difference did it make? Reflecting on this, Husserl began turning his phenomenology into a branch of 'idealism' – the philosophical tradition which denied external reality and defined everything as a kind of private hallucination.

What led Husserl to do this in the 1910s and 1920s was his longing for certainty. One might not be sure of much in the world, but one could be sure about what was going on in one's own head. In a series of lectures in Paris in February 1929, attended by many young French philosophers (though Sartre and Beauvoir missed it), Husserl laid out this idealist interpretation and pointed out how close it brought him to the philosophy of René Descartes, who had said 'I think, therefore I am' – an introspective starting point if ever there was one. Anyone who wants to be a philosopher, said Husserl, must at least once try to do as Descartes did: 'withdraw into himself' and start everything from scratch, on a certain foundation. He concluded his lectures by quoting St Augustine:

> Do not wish to go out; go back into yourself.
> Truth dwells in the inner man.

Husserl would later undergo another shift, turning again towards an outside arena shared with other people in a rich mixture of bodily and social experience. In his last years, he would say less about Descartes' and Augustine's inwardness, and more about the 'world' in which experience occurs. For now, however, he was almost entirely looking within. Perhaps the crises of the war years had intensified his desire for a private, untouchable zone, although the first stirrings did pre-date his son's death in 1916, and the last would continue for a long time after it. Debate continues to this day about how significant Husserl's changes of direction were, and how far his idealist turn went.

Husserl certainly turned idealist enough during his long reign in Freiburg to alienate a few key disciples. Among those to complain about it early on was Edith Stein, shortly after she finished her PhD thesis on the phenomenology of empathy – a subject that led her to look for connections and bonds between people in a shared exterior environment, not a withdrawn and solitary one. Early in 1917, she and Husserl had a long debate on the subject, with her sitting in the 'dear old leather sofa' where his favourites usually sat in his office. They argued for two hours without reaching agreement, and shortly afterwards Stein resigned as his assistant and left Freiburg.

She had other reasons for going: she wanted more time for her own work, which Husserl's demands made difficult. Unfortunately, she struggled to find another post. First she was blocked from one formal position at the University of Göttingen because she was a woman. Then, when another came up in Hamburg, she did not even apply because she felt sure that her Jewish origin would be a problem: the department already had two Jewish philosophers and that appeared to be the limit. She returned to her home town, Breslau (now Wrocław in Poland), and worked on her thesis there. She also converted to Christianity, after reading the autobiography of St Teresa of Ávila, and in 1922 become a Carmelite nun – a dramatic transformation. The Order gave her special dispensation to continue her studies and to send out for philosophy books.

Meanwhile, in Freiburg, her departure left a gap in Husserl's gang. In 1918 – still long before Sartre had heard of any of them or thought of going to Germany – that gap was filled by another impressive young phenomenologist. His name was Martin Heidegger, and he would prove far more trouble to the master than even the forthright and rebellious Edith Stein had been.

If Sartre had gone to Freiburg in 1933 and met both Husserl *and* Heidegger, his thinking might have got off to a different start indeed.

3

The Magician from Messkirch

*In which Martin Heidegger appears, and we
become perplexed about Being.*

Martin Heidegger's challenge to Husserl came in the opening lines of
a book, *Sein und Zeit* (*Being and Time*), which he published in Husserl's
own phenomenological *Yearbook* series in 1927. The first page contained
an innocuous-seeming quotation from Plato's dialogue *The Sophist*:

> For manifestly you have long been aware of what you mean
> when you use the expression '*being*'. We, however, who used to
> think we understood it, have now become perplexed.

Of all the perplexing things about '*being*', Heidegger goes on, the most
perplexing of all is that people fail to be sufficiently perplexed about it.
I say 'the sky *is* blue' or 'I *am* happy', as if the little word in the middle
were of no interest. But when I stop to think about it, I realise that it
brings up a fundamental and mysterious question. What can it mean to
say that anything *is*? Most philosophers had neglected the question; one
of the few to raise it was Gottfried von Leibniz, who in 1714 put it this
way: why is there anything at all, rather than nothing? For Heidegger,
this 'why' is not the sort of question that seeks an answer from physics
or cosmology. No account of the Big Bang or divine Creation could
satisfy it. The point of asking the question is mainly to boggle the mind.
If you had to sum up Heidegger's opening sally in *Being and Time* in one
word, that word might be 'wow!' It was this that led the critic George
Steiner to call Heidegger 'the great master of astonishment' – the person
who 'put a radiant obstacle in the path of the obvious'.

As a fresh starting point for philosophy, this 'wow!' is itself a kind of a Big Bang. It's also a big snub for Husserl. We are meant to understand that he and his followers are foremost among the people who fail to be astonished at being, because they have retreated into their navel-gazing inwardness. They have forgotten the brute reality on which all of us ought to be constantly stubbing our toes. Heidegger's book politely praises Husserl's phenomenological methods, and acknowledges him with a dedication 'in friendship and admiration'. But he also clearly implies that Husserl and his crew have lost themselves in their own heads, which is the very place of uncertainty and isolation from which intentionality had been supposed to rescue them. Wake up, phenomenologists! Remember being – out there, in here, under you, above you, pressing in upon you. Remember the things themselves, and remember your *own* being!

Oddly, Heidegger was first inspired to set off down this route by reading Franz Brentano – not Brentano's paragraph on intentionality, but his doctoral thesis, which concerned different meanings of the word 'being' in the works of Aristotle. The philosopher who led Heidegger to notice being was the same who led Husserl to intentionality, and thus to the inward turn.

Heidegger discovered Brentano's thesis when he was eighteen, living in his home town of Messkirch, not far from Freiburg but in the Upper Danube region of Swabia. It is a quiet Catholic town, dominated by a wildly over-the-top baroque church in the local style. Its interior, a riot of white-and-gold excess, with saints and angels and flying cherubs by the cloud, comes as a cheering surprise after the stern exterior and the solemn, dark forests around the town.

Martin, born on 26 September 1889, was the eldest child, with a younger sister, Marie, and a brother, Fritz. Their father, Friedrich, was the sexton of the church, and the family lived just opposite it: their steep-roofed house, the plain central one in a group of three, is still there. Martin and Fritz helped out with church duties from an early age, picking flowers for decoration and climbing the tower steps to ring its seven bells in the mornings. Each Christmas they began extra-early. After drinking milky coffee and eating cakes beside the Christmas tree at home, they would cross the little square to the church before 4 a.m. and began the *Schrecke-läuten* (fright-ringing) that woke all the townspeople. At Easter they stilled the bells and instead turned a handle to make small hammers hit wood, producing a rattling, pocking sound.

The sound of hammers striking wood or metal resonated through Martin's world, as his father was also the town's master cooper, making barrels and other ware. (A quick online search reminds us that coopers used to make 'casks, barrels, buckets, tubs, butter churns, hogsheads, firkins, tierces, rundlets, puncheons, pipes, tuns, butts, pins and breakers' – a beautiful list of objects that now sounds like a half-remembered dream.) The boys would go out in the nearby forest after woodcutters had passed by, collecting pieces which their father could use. Heidegger later wrote to his fiancée describing his memories of the cooper's workshop, and also of his grandfather, a shoemaker, who would sit on his three-legged stool hammering nails into soles, by the light of a glass globe. All this is worth dwelling on because, for Heidegger even more than for most writers, these childhood images remained important to him all his life; he never abandoned his allegiance to the world they evoked.

When the 'helpful son' jobs were done, Martin would run out past the church and through the park of the equally grandiose Messkirch castle into the forest, and sit with his homework on a rough-hewn bench at the side of a path in the deep woods. The bench and path helped him to think through any tangled text he was studying; later, whenever he was bogged down in a tough philosophical task, he would think back to the bench in the woods, and see his way out. His thoughts were always filled with images of dark trees, and dappled forest light filtering through the leaves to the open paths and clearings. He gave his books titles like *Holzwege* (forest paths) and *Wegmarken* (trailmarks). Their pages resound with the ringing of hammers and the serene tolling of village bells, with rustic crafts and the heft and feel of manual labour.

Even in his most rarefied later writing – or especially there – Heidegger liked to think of himself as a humble Swabian peasant, whittling and chopping at his work. But he was never exactly a man of the people. From boyhood, there was something set apart about him. He was shy, tiny, black-eyed, with a pinched little mouth, and all his life he had difficulty meeting people's eyes. Yet he had a mysterious power over others. In an interview for a BBC TV programme in 1999, Hans-Georg Gadamer recalled asking an old man in Messkirch if he had known Martin Heidegger as a boy. The man replied:

'Martin? Yes, certainly I remember him.'
'What was he like?'

'*Tscha* [Well],' answered the man, 'What can I say? He was the smallest, he was the weakest, he was the most unruly, he was the most useless. But he was in command of all of us.'

As he grew up, Heidegger attended seminary schools, then went to Freiburg where he studied divinity. But meanwhile, his encounter with Brentano's thesis led him to immerse himself in Aristotle, and to feel drawn towards philosophical rather than theological inquiry. He picked up the Freiburg university library's copy of Husserl's *Logical Investigations*, borrowed it and kept it in his room for two years. He was fascinated to see that Husserl's philosophy took no account of God. (Husserl, although a Christian, kept his faith separate from his work.) Heidegger studied Husserl's method of proceeding by close description and attention to phenomena.

He then followed Husserl in switching to philosophy, and building his career by scraping a living as an unsalaried *Privatdozent* for years. Also like Husserl, he acquired a family to support: he married Elfride Petri in March 1917, and they had two sons, Jörg and Hermann. Elfride was a Protestant, so they covered all bases by having a registry office wedding followed by two religious ones, Protestant and Catholic – after

which they both broke with their churches completely. Heidegger officially ceased to consider himself a believer, although signs of a yearning for sacred things are not hard to find in his work. Their marriage lasted, despite episodes of infidelity on both sides. Many years later, Hermann Heidegger revealed a secret he had heard from his mother long before: his real father was not Martin Heidegger, but a doctor with whom she had had an affair.

During Heidegger's early years studying and teaching in Freiburg,

Husserl was not yet based there; as soon as he arrived in 1916, Heidegger set out to court him. At first, Husserl responded in a vague and formal way. Then, as would happen to many others, he became enthralled by the strange young man. By the end of the war, Husserl was as keen as Heidegger was to *symphilosophein* – philosophise together, in the Greek word their circle liked to use.

At that time, Husserl was still in deep grief for the son killed in the war – and Heidegger was of a similar age to the Husserl children. (Unlike them, he had avoided the front line because he had a weak heart, and was instead given duties as a mail censor and weather-station assistant.) Having the young Heidegger around had an extraordinary effect on Husserl. 'O your youth – what a joy it is to me', he wrote. He became uncharacteristically gushy, adding three postscripts to one letter and then scolding himself for sounding like an old chatterbox. Husserl later looked back and marvelled at how infatuated he had let himself become, but it's not hard to see why it happened. At his sixty-first birthday party in 1920, Malvine Husserl jokingly called Heidegger the 'phenomenological child'. Heidegger cheerfully played up to the role of adoptee, sometimes beginning his letters 'Dear fatherly friend'. He once wrote a thank-you letter for the Husserls' hospitality by saying, 'I truly had the feeling of being accepted as a son.'

In 1924, Husserl helped Heidegger to get a paid job at the University of Marburg, not too far away. He stayed there for four years. In 1928, aged thirty-nine, he returned to Freiburg to take over the chair left vacant when Husserl retired – again with Husserl's helpful support. It was a relief to be back: Heidegger was never happy in Marburg, which he called a 'foggy hole', but it did give his career its first big push, and while there he also had an intoxicating affair with his student Hannah Arendt.

During the Marburg years, Elfride Heidegger used an inheritance to buy a plot of land just outside the Black Forest village of Todtnauberg, twenty-nine kilometres from Freiburg, overlooking the grand horseshoe sweep of village and valley. She designed a wood-shingled hut to be built on the site, wedged into the hillside. It was a gift for her husband: the family often went together, but Heidegger spent much time working there alone. The landscape, criss-crossed by paths to help him think, was even finer than that of his childhood. Then as now, it was frequented by skiers, sledders and hikers, but in evenings or out of season it was silent and tranquil, with the tall trees looking down like dignified grown-ups on the humans playing between them. When alone there, Heidegger would ski, walk, light a fire, cook simple meals, talk to the peasant neighbours, and settle for long hours at his desk, where – as he wrote to Arendt in 1925 – his writing took on the calm rhythm of a man chopping wood in a forest.

Increasingly, Heidegger imported the peasant image into his town job too. He started wearing a specially tailored version of traditional Black Forest dress: a brown farmer's jacket, with broad lapels and a high collar, set off by knee-length breeches. His students called it his 'existential' or 'one's ownmost' look, the latter a reference to one of his favourite phrases. They found him funny, but he did not share the joke because his sense of humour was somewhere between peculiar and non-existent. It didn't matter: his clothes, his rustic Swabian accent and his seriousness only heightened his mystique. His student Karl Löwith described how Heidegger's 'impenetrable' quality gave him a mesmerising hold over the class; you never knew where you were with him, so you hung on every word. Hans Jonas, who studied with both Husserl and Heidegger, remarked in a later radio interview that Heidegger was by far the more exciting of the two. Asked why, he replied that it was largely 'because he was much more difficult to understand'.

According to Gadamer, Heidegger's trademark style was to raise up a 'breathtaking swirl of questions' which would billow forth until, finally, he would roll them up into 'deep dark clouds of sentences from which the lightning flashed', leaving the students stunned. There was something occult about this, so the students created another nickname for him: the 'little magician from Messkirch'. Even amid the clouds and lightning, however, he usually focused his lectures on minutely close readings of the classical philosophers, demanding extreme concentration on the text. According to Hannah Arendt's memories of studying with him, Heidegger taught them to *think*, and thinking meant 'digging'. He worked his way down to the roots of things, she wrote, but rather than hauling them into the light he left them embedded, merely opening up exploratory routes around them – just as his beloved paths wound their way through the forest. Years later, and with a less sympathetic attitude, Daniel Dennett and Asbjørn Steglich-Petersen's satirical *Philosophical Lexicon* would define a 'heidegger' as 'a ponderous device for boring through thick layers of substance', as in, 'It's buried so deep we'll have to use a heidegger.'

Georg Picht, who attended Heidegger's courses as a student of eighteen, recalled the force of his thinking as something almost palpable. It could be felt as Heidegger entered the room, and he also brought with him an air of danger. His lectures were a form of theatre, 'masterfully staged'. Heidegger urged his students to think, but not necessarily to answer back. 'He thought that saying the first unthought-out thing that came to mind, which is called "discussion" today, was empty chit-chat.' He liked students to be respectful, but never syco-phantic. 'When a student once read out the minutes, peppered with Heidegger's own phraseology, he interrupted her: "We do not Heideggerize here! Let's move on to the matter in hand."'

Picht suspected that some of this Heideggerian rudeness was a defensive reaction: he felt threatened, both by others and from within himself. 'The history of Being could abruptly make its way into the personal, and the personal into what was to be thought.' Once, Picht felt he had a terrifying glimpse of what it might be like to *be* Heidegger: 'How can Heidegger the person be described? He lived in a thundery landscape. As we were taking a walk in Hinterzarten during a severe storm, a tree was uprooted ten meters in front of us. That touched me, as if I could then visualize what was going on inside him.'

Even as they made their nervous jests, the students around Heidegger knew they were privileged to be able to watch a great philosophy being developed piece by piece. All through the mid-1920s, as he taught courses on Plato, Aristotle or Kant, he would twist each text into some original and unusual interpretation, until the students felt that whole edifices built by previous philosophers might come crashing down in slabs about their heads. As Hannah Arendt summed it up: 'Thinking has come to life again; the cultural treasures of the past, believed to be dead, are being made to speak . . . There exists a teacher; one can perhaps learn to think.'

Of all the exciting moments they experienced, few could have rivalled one that occurred early in 1927. His student Hermann Mörchen remembered how Heidegger arrived at one of their seminars, and 'wordlessly, expectantly, like a child showing off his favourite toy, produced a galley-proof sheet straight from the printer'. It was the title page of his masterpiece, *Being and Time* – with that great opening call to amazement, followed by pages of strange text that could not be mistaken for anything written by any other philosopher, old or new.

So what *is* the being that Heidegger wants us to marvel at in *Being and Time*, and what are the beings that have it?

Heidegger's word *Sein* (being) cannot be easily defined, because what it refers to is not like other categories or qualities. It certainly is not an object of any kind. Nor is it an ordinary shared feature of objects. You can teach someone what a 'building' is by pointing to a lot of different structures from grass huts to skyscrapers; it may take a while but eventually they will get it. But you could go on forever pointing out huts, meals, animals, forest paths, church portals, festive atmospheres, and looming thunderclouds, saying each time, 'Look: being!', and your interlocutor is likely to become more and more puzzled.

Heidegger sums this up by saying that Being is not itself a being. That is, it is not a defined or delineated entity of any kind. He distinguishes between the German word *Seiende*, which can refer to any individual entity, such as a mouse or a church door, and *Sein*, which means the Being that such particular beings have. (In English, one way of signalling the distinction is by using the capital 'B' for the latter.) He calls it the 'ontological difference' – from 'ontology', the study of what is. It is not an easy distinction to keep clear in one's mind, but the ontological difference between Being and beings is extremely important to Heidegger. If we get confused between the two, we fall into errors – for example, settling down to study some science of particular entities, such as psychology or even cosmology, while thinking that we are studying Being itself.

Unlike beings, Being is hard to concentrate on and it is easy to forget to think about it. But one particular entity has a more noticeable Being than others, and that is myself, because, unlike clouds and portals, I am the entity who wonders about its Being. It even turns out that I have a vague, preliminary, non-philosophical understanding of Being already – otherwise I would not have thought of asking about it. This makes me the best starting point for ontological inquiry. I am both the being whose Being is up for question and the being who sort of already knows the answer.

I myself, then, will be the path. But Heidegger re-emphasises that this does not mean I should sign up for courses in human sciences such as biology, anthropology, psychology or sociology. These merely 'ontical' inquiries have nothing to contribute to an ontological investigation. Like the speculative debris cleared away by Husserl's *epoché*, they are likely only to get in the way by clogging up our inquiry with irrelevant ideas. If I want to know what a human being is, it's no good wiring one up to a EEG machine to measure brain waves, or analysing examples of behaviour. Just as Karl Jaspers had turned from psychology to phenomenology in order to practise 'a *different thinking*', Heidegger felt that the question of Being must be truly philosophical or it is nothing. Moreover, it should not be philosophical in the old-fashioned way, focused narrowly on questions of what we can know. A *new* new beginning is needed.

For Heidegger, this means not only starting with Being but ensuring constant vigilance and care in thinking. He generously helps us to achieve this by using a frustrating kind of language.

As his readers soon notice, Heidegger tends to reject familiar philosophical terms in favour of new ones which he coins himself. He leaves the German *Sein* or Being more or less as it is, but when it comes to talking about the questioner for whom its Being is in question (i.e. me, a human), he strenuously avoids talk of humanity, man, mind, soul or consciousness, because of the scientific, religious or metaphysical assumptions such words conceal. Instead, he speaks of 'Dasein', a word normally meaning 'existence' in a general way, and compounded of *da* (there) and *sein* (to be). Thus, it means 'there-being', or 'being-there'.

The effect is at once disconcerting and intriguing. Reading Heidegger, and feeling (as one often does) that you recognise an experience he is describing, you want to say, 'Yes, that's me!' But the word itself deflects you from this interpretation; it forces you to keep questioning. Just getting into the habit of saying Dasein takes you halfway into Heidegger's world. It is so important a term that English translators tend to leave it in the original German; an early partial French translation by Henry Corbin rendered it as '*réalité humaine*', which created another layer of confusion.

Why, one often wails, can't Heidegger speak plainly? His tangled and unnatural terms invite parody – as in Günter Grass's 1963 novel *Dog Years*, where a character falls under the influence of an unnamed philosopher and goes around calling underdone potatoes 'spuds forgetful of Being', and clearing rodents out of the kitchen's water pipes while wondering, 'Why rats and not other essents? Why anything at all rather than nothing?' One might think that, if Heidegger had anything worth saying, he could have communicated it in ordinary language.

The fact is that he does not want to be ordinary, and he may not even want to communicate in the usual sense. He wants to make the familiar obscure, and to vex us. George Steiner thought that Heidegger's purpose was less to be understood than to be experienced through a 'felt strangeness'. It is something like the 'alienation' or estrangement effect used by Bertholt Brecht in his theatre, which is designed to block you from becoming too caught up in the story and falling for the delusion of familiarity. Heidegger's language keeps you on edge. It is dynamic, obtrusive, sometimes ridiculous and often forceful; on a page of Heidegger, things are typically presented as surging or thrusting, as being thrown forward, lit up or broken open. Heidegger admitted that his way of writing produced some 'awkwardness', but he thought that a small price to pay for overturning the history of philosophy and bringing us back to Being.

For non-German readers, it should be added, some of the awkwardness is an artefact of translation. German welcomes monumental word constructions, but in English they tend to come out as long hyphenated lines, trundling along like mismatched railway carriages. The Question of Being, for example, is an elegant *Seinsfrage* in German. But even German cannot comfortably accommodate *Sich-vorweg-schon-sein-in-(der-Welt) als Sein-bei (innerweltlich begegnendem Seienden)*, or 'ahead-of-itself-already-being-in-(the-world) as being-together-with (beings encountered within the world)'.

One way of thinking about Heidegger is as a literary innovator, and perhaps even as a kind of Modernist novelist. I was well into working on this book when, via Janet Malcolm's study *Two Lives*, I came across excerpts from Gertrude Stein's experimental novel *The Making of Americans*. Stein sets out as if to relate a standard family saga, but abandons conventional ways of writing in order to say things like this about her characters:

I am always feeling each kind of them as a substance darker, lighter, thinner, thicker, muddier, clearer, smoother, lumpier, granularer, mixeder, simpler . . . and always I am feeling in each one of them their kind of stuff as much in them, as little in them, as all of a piece in them, as lumps in them held together sometimes by parts of the same sometimes by other kinds of stuff in them . . . [S]ome . . . are made of little lumps of one kind of being held together or separated from each other, as one comes to feel it in them, the lumps in them from each other by other kind of being in them, sometimes by other kind of being in them that is almost the complete opposite of the lumps in them, some because, the lumps are melting always in to the surrounding being that keeps the lumps from touching, in some because the kind of being in them is spread out so thin in them, that everything that they have learned, that they like to be in living, all reaction to everything interesting, in them, has really nothing to do in them with the thin spread being in them . . . Some are always whole ones though the being in them is all a mushy mass with a skin to hold them in and so make one.

The 'being' in them, she explains, 'can be slimy, gelatinous, gluey, white opaquy kind of thing and it can be white and vibrant and clear and heated and this is all not very clear to me'.

Heidegger would have disliked Stein's imprecision, but he might have appreciated the sight of a writer stretching language to its utmost to avoid the dulling effect of ordinary perceptions. He might also have recognised that her distinction between characters and the 'being' in them foreshadows his own notion of the ontological difference.

Thus, it can help to think of Heidegger as an experimental novelist, or a poet. Yet, even while rejecting the traditional philosophical virtue of clarity, he was adamant that he was a philosopher, and that there was nothing merely literary or playful about his language. His purpose was to overturn human thinking, destroy the history of metaphysics, and start philosophy all over again. A little violence done to language is to be expected, given an overall aim that is so extreme, and so violent.

The biggest overturning that *Being and Time* inflicts on old-school philosophy is to approach the question of Dasein and its Being in a way that Husserl had been supposed to do but did not make very evident: through everyday life.

Heidegger gives us Dasein in its weekday clothes, as it were: not in its Sunday best, but in its 'everydayness'. Other philosophers have tended to start with a human being in an unusual state, such as sitting alone in a room staring into the embers of a fire and thinking – which was how Descartes began. They then go on to use simple, everyday terms to describe the result. Heidegger does the opposite. He takes Dasein in its most ordinary moments, then talks about it in the most innovative way he can. For Heidegger, Dasein's everyday Being is right here: it is Being-in-the-world, or *In-der-Welt-sein*.

The main feature of Dasein's everyday Being-in-the-world right here is that it is usually busy doing something. I don't tend to contemplate things; I pick them up and act on them. If I hold a hammer, it is not normally to 'stare at the hammer-Thing', as Heidegger puts it. (He uses the lovely word *das Hammerding*.) It is to go to work hammering nails.

Moreover, I do my hammering in service of some purpose, such as building a bookcase for my philosophy tomes. The hammer in my hand summons up a whole network of purposes and contexts. It reveals Dasein's involvement with things: its 'concern'. He cites examples: producing something, using something, looking after something, and letting something go, as well as negative involvements such as neglecting something, or leaving it undone. These are what he calls 'deficient' forms, but they are still forms of concern. They show that Dasein's Being in general is one of 'care'. The distinction between 'care' and 'concern' (*Besorgen* and *Sorge*) is confusing, but both mean Dasein is in the world up to the elbows, and it is busy. We are not far from Kierkegaard and his point that I don't just exist, but have an interest or an investment in my existence.

My involvements, Heidegger continues, lead me to deploy 'useful things' or 'equipment' – items such as the hammer. These have a particular Being which Heidegger calls *Zuhandenheit*: 'readiness-to-hand' or 'handiness'. While I am hammering, the hammer has that kind of Being for me. If, for some reason, I lay down the hammer and gawp at it as a *Hammerding*, then it has a different kind: *Vorhandenheit* or 'presence-at-hand'.

For Heidegger, the philosophers' second-biggest mistake (after forgetfulness of Being) has been to talk about everything as though it was present-at-hand. But that is to separate things from the everyday 'concernful' way in which we encounter them most of the time. It turns them into objects for contemplation by an unconcerned subject who has nothing to do all day but gaze at stuff. And then we ask why philosophers seem cut off from everyday life!

By making this error, philosophers allow the whole structure of worldly Being to fall apart, and then have immense difficulty in getting it back together to resemble anything like the daily existence we recognise. Instead, in Heidegger's Being-in-the-world, everything comes already linked together. If the structure falls to pieces, that is a 'deficient' or secondary state. This is why a smoothly integrated world can be revealed by the simplest actions. A pen conjures up a network of ink, paper, desk and lamp, and ultimately also a network of other people for whom or to whom I am writing, each one with his or her own purposes in the world. As Heidegger wrote elsewhere, a table is not just a table: it is a family table, where 'the boys like to busy themselves', or perhaps the table where 'that decision was made with a friend that time, where that work was written that time, where that holiday was celebrated that time'. We are socially as well as equipmentally involved. Thus, for Heidegger, all Being-in-the-world is also a 'Being-with' or *Mitsein*. We cohabit with others in a 'with-world', or *Mitwelt*.

The old philosophical problem of how we prove the existence of other minds has now vanished. Dasein swims in the with-world long before it wonders about other minds. Others are those 'from whom, for the most part, one does *not* distinguish oneself – those among whom one is too'. *Mitsein* remains characteristic even of a Dasein that is shipwrecked on a desert island or trying to get away from everyone by living on the top of a pillar, since those situations are defined mainly by reference to the missing fellow Daseins. The Dasein of a stylite is still a Being-with, but it is (Heidegger loves this word) a 'deficient' mode of Being-with.

Heidegger gives an example that brings everything together. I am out for a walk, and I find a boat by the shore. What Being does the boat have for me? It is unlikely to be 'just' an object, a boat-thing which I contemplate from some abstract vantage point. Instead, I encounter the boat as (1) a potentially useful thing, in (2) a world which is a network of such things, and (3) in a situation where the boat is clearly useful for someone else, if not for me. The boat lights up equipment, world and *Mitsein* all at once. If I want to consider it a mere 'object', I can, but this does violence to everyday Being.

The surprising thing is that philosophy had to wait so long for someone to say these things. American pragmatists such as Charles Sanders Peirce, John Dewey and William James had explored human life as a practical, active affair, but they did not share Heidegger's grand philosophical vision, and were more inclined to use pragmatism to bring philosophy down to earth rather than to remind it of its greatest tasks and questions. Husserl did share Heidegger's scale of ambition, but he had relocated everything in his idealist cavern. For Heidegger, that was a fatal mistake: Husserl had bracketed out the wrong thing. He had bracketed out Being, the one thing that is indispensable.

Heidegger is philosophy's great reverser. In *Being and Time*, it is everyday Being rather than the far reaches of cosmology or mathematics that is most 'ontological'. Practical care and concern are more primordial than reflection. Usefulness comes before contemplation, the ready-to-hand before the present-at-hand, Being-in-the-world and Being-with-others before Being-alone. We do not hover above the great rich tangle of the world, gazing down from on high. We are already in the world and involved in it – we are 'thrown' here. And 'thrownness' must be our starting point.

Or, as his biographer Rüdiger Safranski has put it, Heidegger 'states the obvious in a way that even philosophers can grasp'.

Edmund Husserl did not fail to notice that, despite the words of dedication and praise, *Being and Time* was partly directed against him. He read it several times to be sure. After his first perusal he took it to Italy's Lake Como on holiday in the summer of 1929 and worked through it in detail, making incredulous notes in the margins: 'But that is absurd'. He made frequent use of '?', '!' and even '?!' But when he complained, Heidegger seemed to think his interpretation of the book as an attack on him was 'Nonsense!'

In private, Heidegger was becoming ever more dismissive about Husserlian philosophy. Even while Husserl was writing glowing letters of recommendation to help him get a job, Heidegger was telling other people that he considered his mentor 'ludicrous'. To Karl Jaspers, whom he had now befriended, Heidegger wrote in 1923, 'He lives with the mission of being the *founder of phenomenology*. No one knows what that is.' (Since Jaspers had long ago admitted that he did not know what phenomenology was, he could hardly help with that.) Their differences were clear by 1927. When Husserl and Heidegger tried to collaborate on an article on phenomenology for the *Encyclopaedia Britannica* early that year, they had to give up. For one thing, each felt that the other had problems expressing himself clearly. They were not wrong there. A more serious problem was that they now disagreed on almost every point in the definition of phenomenology.

Husserl took Heidegger's rebellion to heart. He had imagined it so differently! They had talked of how Heidegger might take over Husserl's *Nachlass* – his legacy of unpublished manuscripts – and carry his philosophy into the future. Having helped him to get the Marburg job, Husserl also helped him to take up his own job in Freiburg when he retired – hoping, as he admitted later, that this would bring Heidegger back into the fold. Instead, with Heidegger installed, Freiburg became the City of Two Phenomenologies. Husserl's version looked less and less exciting, while Heidegger's was becoming a cult.

Heidegger gave a long speech at Husserl's seventieth birthday celebrations on 8 April 1929, with slightly insulting subtexts in the guise
of a tribute, stressing how Husserl's philosophy ought to lend itself
to rethinking and changes of direction. In his speech of thanks, Husserl
said that it was true that he had set out to accomplish a task, but that
most of it was not completed. Another subtext there: he was on the
right path, despite what Heidegger thought, and everyone should join
him to get the job done.

Heidegger's behaviour was ignoble, but Husserl was expecting too
much. His desire to mould Heidegger into a mini-Husserl for the next
generation must have been suffocating. There was no reason to think
that Heidegger should follow him without question; that is never how
philosophy develops. In fact, the more revolutionary a philosophy is,
the more it is likely to be revolted against, precisely because it sets
dramatic challenges.

But Husserl did not see himself as some sort of old guard, from whom the new generation must naturally diverge and grow. On the contrary, he thought that *he* was becoming ever more radical while the youngsters were not keeping up. He saw himself as 'an appointed leader without followers, that is, without collaborators in the radical new spirit of transcendental phenomenology'.

For him, Heidegger's philosophical error was to remain on the level of the 'natural attitude' or 'common sense'. This seems an odd accusation: what could be wrong with that? But Husserl meant that Heidegger had not cast off the accumulated assumptions about the world that should have been set aside in the *epoché*. Obsessed with Being, he had forgotten to do a basic step in phenomenology.

For Heidegger, it was Husserl who was being forgetful. His turn inwards into idealism meant that he was still prioritising the abstract contemplative mind rather than dynamic Being-in-the-world. From the start of *Being and Time*, he makes it clear that he wants no theoretical investigation, no mere list of definitions and proofs, but a *concrete* investigation, starting from whatever Dasein is doing at the moment.

That's mere 'anthropology', retorted Husserl in a lecture of 1931. Starting with concrete worldly Dasein means giving up on the high aspirations of philosophy and its search for certainty. Husserl could not understand why Heidegger did not seem to get it – but Heidegger was less and less interested in what Husserl thought. He was now the more magnetic figure, drawing Husserl's protégés away.

Heidegger's *Being and Time* initially conjures up a seamless world of happy hammerers, communing with their fellows in their shared *Mitsein* while having a vague proto-understanding of Being which they never pause to think about in detail. If that were all there was to Heidegger, he probably would have inspired less passion – and if that were all there was to human life, we would hardly be interested in philosophy at all. Who would need philosophers in such a zipless world? Fortunately for the profession, zips get stuck; things break. And Heidegger analyses what happens next.

So I am hammering the bookcase; I am barely aware of the hammer at all, only of the nail sinking home and my general project. If I am typing a paragraph about Heidegger on the computer, I pay no attention to fingers, keyboard or screen; my concern streams through them to whatever it is I am trying to achieve. But then something goes wrong. The nail bends, or perhaps the whole hammerhead flies off the shaft. Or the computer freezes on me.

For a moment, I stand staring stupidly at the broken hammer, or, instead of looking *through* the computer, I stare angrily *at* the contraption and jab at its keys. What had been ready-to-hand flips into being present-at-hand: an inert object to be glared at. Heidegger sums up this altered state with the catchy phrase *das Nur-noch-vorhandensein eines Zuhandenen* – 'the Being-just-present-at-hand-and-no-more of something ready-to-hand'.

Examples of this crop up frequently in everyday life. In Nicholson Baker's novel *The Mezzanine*, a riveting phenomenological account of one man's lunch break, the protagonist pulls on a shoelace to tie it, but the lace snaps. Dumbly staring at the fragment in his hand, he flashes on similar incidents: the moment when one pulls on a thread to open a Band-Aid and the thread comes loose instead of tearing the paper, or the moment when one tries to use a stapler but, instead of biting through and closing the staple tightly on the other side, it 'slumps toothlessly', revealing itself as empty. (I read the book twenty years ago, and for some reason this little description stuck so fast that I rarely find a stapler out of staples without a murmur of 'It's slumped toothlessly' going through my mind.)

When such things happen, Heidegger says, they reveal 'the *obstinacy* of that with which we must concern ourselves'. This revelation lights up the project in a different way, together with the full context of my concern with it. No longer is the world a smoothly humming machine. It is a mass of stubborn things refusing to co-operate, and here I am in the middle of it, flummoxed and disoriented – which is just the state of mind Heidegger seeks to induce in us when we read his prose.

A small incident like a stapler running out of staples doesn't normally cause the collapse of our entire universe. After a skipped beat, the connections knit together again, and we carry on. But some-times a more comprehensive failure occurs – and it *is* possible that an empty stapler could be the catalyst for questioning my entire career and path in life.

A collapse of meanings on that scale was described by Austrian playwright and librettist Hugo von Hofmannsthal in a 1902 story translated as 'The Letter of Lord Chandos'. Masquerading as a genuine letter written in 1603 by an English aristocrat, it evokes Hofmannsthal's own experiences during a breakdown in which the whole structure of things and people around him fell to bits. Everyday items suddenly look to Chandos like things seen too closely through a magnifying glass, impossible to identify. He hears people gossiping about local characters and friends, but can make no coherent narrative out of what they are saying. Unable to work or look after his estate, Chandos finds himself staring for hours at a moss-covered stone, or a dog lying in the sun, or a harrow left abandoned in a field. The connections have gone. No wonder we call an experience like this a breakdown. It may sound familiar to anyone who has suffered depression, and it can also occur in various neurological disorders. For Heidegger, it would be an extreme case of the collapse of everyday Being-in-the-world, a collapse that makes everything obtrusive, disarticulated, and impossible to negotiate with our usual blithe disregard.

Heidegger gives us a different way of understanding why, some-times, it can be so disproportionately disheartening to have a nail bend under the hammer, and to feel everything turn against you. If you throw an apple core towards the bin and it misses, to borrow an example from the Philip Larkin poem 'As Bad as a Mile', it is not merely annoying because you have to get up and pick it off the floor. It can make *everything* feel awkward, questionable and uncomfortable. But it is in questions and discomfort that philosophy begins.

This was the sort of powerful, personal stuff that people craved from philosophy in troubled times: it was one reason why Heidegger acquired such influence. His starting point was reality in its everyday clothes, yet he also spoke in Kierkegaardian tones about the strangest

experiences in life, the moments when it all goes horribly wrong –
and even the moments when we confront the greatest wrongness
of all, which is the prospect of death. There can't be many people
who haven't experienced a taste of such moments in their lives,
even in peaceful, stable times. In the Germany of the 1920s, with
everything thrown into chaos and resentment after the First World
War, almost everyone could have recognised something in
Heidegger's vision.

By 1929, the Heidegger cult had spread beyond Freiburg and Marburg.
That spring, he spoke at a conference in the Alpine resort of Davos –
the setting for Thomas Mann's bestselling 1924 novel *The Magic
Mountain*, which Heidegger had read, and which included a battle of
ideas between the old-fashioned, rationalist Italian critic Luigi
Settembrini and the mystical ex-Jesuit Leo Naphta. It is tempting to
see parallels in the encounter that now occurred between the conference's two stars, as Heidegger was set against a great humanist scholar
of Kantian philosophy and the Enlightenment: Ernst Cassirer.

Cassirer was Jewish, tall, calm and elegant, with his white hair swept
up into a striking but antiquated bouffant style verging on a minor
beehive. Heidegger was short, evasive and compelling, with a pinched
moustache and hair combed severely flat. Their debates centred on
the philosophy of Kant, for their interpretations of that philosopher
differed dramatically. Cassirer saw Kant as the last great representative
of the Enlightenment values of reason, knowledge and freedom.
Heidegger, who had recently published *Kant and the Problem of
Metaphysics*, believed that Kant had dismantled those values by showing
that we can have no access to reality or true knowledge of any kind.
He also argued that Kant's main interest was not primarily in the
question of knowledge at all but in ontology: the question of Being.

Although no clear winner emerged from the debate, it seemed
natural to many observers to cast Cassirer as a throwback to a civilised
yet outmoded past, with Heidegger as the prophet of a dangerous yet
thrilling future. One person who interpreted the debate that way was
Emmanuel Levinas, who had now moved on from his days as Husserl's

student and was attending the conference as a fervent supporter of
Heidegger. As he said to an interviewer later, it was like seeing one
world end and another begin.

Toni Cassirer, Ernst's wife, found Heidegger vulgar. She remembered his arrival on the first evening: he literally turned heads, coming
in after the other delegates had assembled to listen to an after-dinner
speech. The door opened – rather as happens in *The Magic Mountain*,
where the slinky love-interest Clavdia Chauchat habitually enters the
dining room late and with a careless bang of the door. Toni Cassirer
looked round, and saw a beady-eyed little man. He looked to her like
one of the Italian workmen who were numerous in German lands
in those years, except that he was wearing his Black Forest garb. He
seemed 'as awkward as a peasant who had stumbled into a royal
court'.

She took an even dimmer view of his entourage later, after she
walked in on a performance put on by the students, satirically
re-enacting the debate. Levinas played Ernst Cassirer, dusting his
hair with white talc and twirling it into a high quiff like an ice-cream
cone. Toni Cassirer did not find him funny. Years later, Levinas
wished he had apologised to her for his irreverence; by then he had
abandoned his own adulation of Heidegger, as well as having
matured in general.

A few months after the Davos meeting, on 24 July 1929, Heidegger
followed it up with a brilliant inaugural lecture in Freiburg, under the
title 'What Is Metaphysics?' – the text Sartre and Beauvoir would see
in translation in 1931 without understanding it. This time Husserl
himself was among the huge crowd who gathered to hear the university's new professor perform. Heidegger did not disappoint. *What Is
Metaphysics?* was a crowd-pleaser, containing the most dramatic ideas
from *Being and Time* combined with some new ones. It even starts
with what sounds like a deadpan joke, a surprise coming from
Heidegger:

'What is metaphysics?' The question awakens expectations of a
discussion about metaphysics. This we will forego.

The rest of the lecture compares nothingness and Being, and contains a long discussion of 'moods' – another of Heidegger's key ideas. Dasein's moods can range from elation to boredom, or perhaps the diffuse sense of oppression and unease described by Kierkegaard as *Angst* – dread, or anxiety. Each mood reveals the world in a different light. In anxiety, the world shows itself to me as something 'uncanny' – the German word *unheimlich* here literally meaning 'not homely'. It reveals 'the total strangeness of beings'. In this unhomely, unfamiliar moment, the mood of anxiety opens up the first questioning movement of philosophy – particularly that big question, which forms the climax of Heidegger's lecture: 'Why are there beings at all, and why not rather nothing?'

Heidegger's performance was terrifying and darkly thrilling. It was also puzzling in places, which added to its effect. As he came to an end, at least one listener, Heinrich Wiegand Petzet, felt on the verge of falling to the ground in an ecstatic faint. 'The things of the world lay open and manifest in an almost aching brilliance', Petzet wrote. 'For a brief moment I felt as if I had had a glimpse into the ground and foundation of the world.'

Husserl, in the audience, was less ecstatic. He now feared the worst about Heidegger: he was no longer a protégé but a monstrous progeny. Shortly afterwards, he wrote to a colleague that he felt the need to reject Heidegger's work completely. In another letter looking back eighteen months later, he wrote of this moment: 'I arrived at the distressing conclusion that philosophically I have nothing to do with this Heideggerian profundity.' Heidegger's philosophy, Husserl decided, was of the kind that must be fought against at all costs. It was the sort of philosophy that he felt obliged to try to stamp out, and 'render impossible forever'.

4

The They, the Call

In which Sartre has nightmares, Heidegger tries to think, Karl Jaspers is dismayed, and Husserl calls for heroism.

Heidegger's magnetic performances in 1929 enhanced his philosophical appeal in a country that had emerged from war and a 1923 hyper-inflation crisis, only to sink into economic disaster again. Many Germans felt betrayed by the socialist government that had taken over in a kind of coup in the closing stages of the war. They muttered about Jews and Communists, and accused them of plotting to undermine the national cause. Heidegger seemed to share these suspicions. He too felt disillusioned and disoriented by the Germany of the 1920s.

Observers who visited the country during these years were shocked by its poverty, and by the way people were responding to it by turning to extremist parties of the left and right. When Raymond Aron first arrived in 1930, his shock immediately turned into a question: how could Europe avoid being drawn into another war? Two years later, the young French philosopher Simone Weil travelled through the country and reported back to a left-wing newspaper on how penury and unemployment were destroying the fabric of German society. Those who had jobs were haunted by the fear of losing them. People who could not afford homes became vagabonds or relied on relatives to put them up, which strained family relationships to their limits. Catastrophe could strike anyone: 'you see elderly men in stiff collars and bowler hats begging at subway exits or singing in cracked voices in the streets.' The old suffered, while the young, who had never known anything else, did not even have good memories to escape into.

The revolutionary potential of the situation was clear, but it was anyone's guess which way it would go: to the Communists or to Hitler's Nazis. Weil hoped it would be to the left, but she feared that, in desperate times, the severe uniforms and regimentation of the Nazi rallies would have more appeal than vague socialist dreams of equality. She was right. On 30 January 1933, a weak coalition government headed by President Paul von Hindenburg gave in to pressure and appointed Adolf Hitler as chancellor. Once a fringe figure of ridicule, Hitler now controlled the country and all its resources. Elections on 5 March increased his party's majority. On 23 March, a new Enabling Act gave him near-total power. He consolidated it through the summer. Thus, between Aron's invitation to Sartre after the apricot-cocktail conversation and Sartre's actual move to Berlin, the country was altered out of all recognition.

The first changes came quickly that spring, and they affected private life in the most basic and intrusive ways. In March, the Nazis awarded themselves new powers to arrest suspects and search homes at will. They created laws that allowed phone-tapping and mail surveillance – areas of privacy previously considered sacred. In April, they announced 'boycotts' of Jewish businesses, and removed all public employees deemed Jewish or having anti-Nazi affiliations from their jobs. Trade unions were banned on 2 May. The first spectacular book-burning took place on 10 May. All political parties other than the National Socialists were officially banned on 14 July 1933.

Many Germans, as well as other people around Europe, watched this rapid sequence of events in horror but felt unable to do much about it. Beauvoir later marvelled at how little she and Sartre worried in the early 1930s about the rise of Nazism in Germany – and this from two people who later became fiercely political. They read the papers, she said, but in those days they were more interested in murder stories or tales of psychological oddity, such as the Papin sisters' killing of the employer for whom they worked as maids, or a case in which a conventional couple brought home another couple for a sexual foursome then committed suicide the next day. Such incidents were curiosities of individual human behaviour, whereas

the rise of fascism seemed an abstract matter. Sartre and Beauvoir
did have a disturbing encounter with its Italian form in the summer
of 1933, just before Sartre's move to Berlin. They travelled to Rome
with a discount offer from the Italian railways and, walking around
the Colosseum late one evening, found themselves pinned by a spotlight and shouted at by men in black shirts. It shocked them, but did
not politicise them greatly.

Then came Sartre's year in Berlin, but for most of it he was so
absorbed in his reading of Husserl and others that at first he barely
noticed the outside world. He drank with his classmates and went for
long walks. 'I rediscovered irresponsibility', he recalled later in a notebook. As the academic year went on, the red-and-black banners, the
SA rallies and the regular outbreaks of violence became more
disturbing. In February 1934, Beauvoir visited him for the first time,
and was struck mainly by how normal Germany seemed. But when
she went again in June and travelled back with him from Berlin through
Dresden, Munich and the Nazis' favourite city of Nuremberg, the
military marches and half-glimpsed brutal scenes on the streets made
them both eager to get out of the country for good. By this time,
Sartre was having nightmares about rioting towns and blood splat-
tering over bowls of mayonnaise.

The mixture of anxiety and unreality that Sartre and Beauvoir felt
was not unusual. Many Germans felt a similar combination, except
for those who were Nazi converts, or else who were firm opponents
or direct targets. The country was steeped in the sensation that
Heidegger called 'uncanniness'.

Sometimes the best-educated people were those least inclined to
take the Nazis seriously, dismissing them as too absurd to last. Karl
Jaspers was one of those who made this mistake, as he later recalled,
and Beauvoir observed similar dismissive attitudes among the French
students in Berlin. In any case, most of those who disagreed with
Hitler's ideology soon learned to keep their view to themselves. If a
Nazi parade passed on the street, they would either slip out of view
or give the obligatory salute like everyone else, telling themselves
that the gesture meant nothing if they did not believe in it. As the

psychologist Bruno Bettelheim later wrote of this period, few people will risk their life for such a small thing as raising an arm – yet that is how one's powers of resistance are eroded away, and eventually one's responsibility and integrity go with them.

The journalist Sebastian Haffner, a law student at the time, also used the word 'uncanny' in his diary, adding, 'Everything takes place under a kind of anaesthesia. Objectively dreadful events produce a thin, puny emotional response. Murders are committed like schoolboy pranks. Humiliation and moral decay are accepted like minor incidents.' Haffner thought modernity itself was partly to blame: people had become yoked to their habits and to mass media, forgetting to stop and think, or to disrupt their routines long enough to question what was going on.

Heidegger's former lover and student Hannah Arendt would argue, in her 1951 study *The Origins of Totalitarianism*, that totalitarian movements thrived at least partly because of this fragmentation in modern lives, which made people more vulnerable to being swept away by demagogues. Elsewhere, she coined the phrase 'the banality of evil' to describe the most extreme failures of personal moral awareness. The phrase attracted criticism, mainly because she applied it to the actively genocidal Adolf Eichmann, organiser of the Holocaust, who was guilty of a lot more than a failure to take responsibility. Yet she stuck by her analysis: for Arendt, if you do not respond adequately when the times demand it, you show a lack of imagination and attention that is as dangerous as deliberately committing an abuse. It amounts to disobeying the one command she had absorbed from Heidegger in those Marburg days: *Think!*

But what is it, to think? Or, as Heidegger would ask in the title of a later essay, *Was heisst denken?* This could be translated as 'What does one call thinking?' or 'What calls for thinking?' – a play on words in the German. One might expect that Heidegger, with his constant reminders to shake off forgetfulness and to question everyday reality, would be the best placed of all philosophers to think well, and to call his compatriots to the task of responsible alertness.

Indeed, that was what he believed he was doing. But he did not do it in the way Arendt, Jaspers, Husserl or most of his other later readers would have wished.

Being and Time contained at least one big idea that should have been of use in resisting totalitarianism. Dasein, Heidegger wrote there, tends to fall under the sway of something called *das Man* or 'the they' – an impersonal entity that robs us of the freedom to think for ourselves. To live authentically requires resisting or outwitting this influence, but this is not easy because *das Man* is so nebulous. *Man* in German does not mean 'man' as in English (that's *der Mann*), but a neutral abstraction, something like 'one' in the English phrase 'one doesn't do that', or 'they' in 'they say it will all be over by Christmas'. 'The they' is probably the best translation available, except that it seems to point to some group 'over there', separate from myself. Instead, for Heidegger, *das Man* is *me*. It is everywhere and nowhere; it is nothing definite, but each of us is it. As with Being, it is so ubiquitous that it is difficult to see. If I am not careful, however, *das Man* takes over the important decisions that should be my own. It drains away my responsibility or 'answerability'. As Arendt might put it, we slip into banality, failing to think.

If I am to resist *das Man*, I must become answerable to the call of my 'voice of conscience'. This call does not come from God, as a traditional Christian definition of the voice of conscience might suppose. It comes from a truly existentialist source: my own authentic self. Alas, this voice is one I do not recognise and may not hear, because it is not the voice of my habitual 'they-self'. It is an alien or uncanny version of my usual voice. I am familiar with my they-self, but not with my unalienated voice – so, in a weird twist, my real voice is the one that sounds strangest to me. I may fail to hear it, or I may hear it but not know that it's me calling. I might mistake it for something coming from afar, perhaps a thin and reedy keening like the unheard cries for help of the microscopic hero in the 1957 film *The Incredible Shrinking Man* – one of the best mid-century expressions of paranoia about the disappearing powers of authentic humanity. The idea of being called to authenticity became a major theme in later existentialism, the call being interpreted as saying something like 'Be yourself!', as opposed to being phony. For Heidegger, the call is more fundamental than that. It is a call to take up a self that you didn't know you had: to wake up to your Being. Moreover, it is a call to action. It requires you to *do* something: to take a decision of some sort.

You might think that the decision would be to defy the siren song of the they-self in the public realm, and thus to resist intimidation and the general tendency towards conformity. You might deduce that the authentic voice of Dasein would call on you *not* to raise your arm as the march passes by.

But that was not what Heidegger meant.

Rumours had been circulating about Heidegger's Nazi associations for a while. In August 1932, the writer René Schickele noted in his diary that Heidegger was said to be consorting 'exclusively with National Socialists'. Husserl was told that Heidegger had made anti-Semitic remarks. Hannah Arendt heard similar stories. She wrote to Heidegger during the winter of 1932–3 asking point-blank whether he was a Nazi sympathiser. He denied it, in an angry letter emphasising how helpful he had been to Jewish students and colleagues. She was unconvinced, and they lost contact for seventeen years.

Heidegger seemed able to hide his views when it suited him. Moreover, when he was in love with Arendt, her being Jewish didn't seem to disturb him; he later became close to Elisabeth Blochmann, also Jewish by origin. He had taught many Jewish students, and had shown no objection to working with Husserl earlier in his career. A certain amount of anti-Semitism was common in everyday speech at the time; so there could have been room for doubt that these rumours about Heidegger added up to much.

But as it turned out, Arendt was right to assume the worst of him. In April 1933, all doubts about Heidegger were blown away when he accepted the post of rector of Freiburg University, a job that required him to enforce the new Nazi laws. It also required him to join the party. He did so, and then he delivered rousing pro-Nazi speeches to the students and faculty. He was reportedly seen attending the Freiburg book-burning on 10 May, trooping through a drizzly evening by torchlight towards the bonfire in the square just outside the university library – almost on the steps of his own philosophy department. In private, meanwhile, he filled notebooks with philosophical thoughts alternating with Nazi-flavoured anti-Semitic remarks. When these 'Black Notebooks' were published in 2014, they provided yet more confirmation of something already known: Heidegger was a Nazi, at least for a while, and not out of convenience but by conviction.

One gets a feel for how he spoke and thought during this time by reading the inaugural address he gave as rector, to an assembly of university staff and party members in a hall adorned with Nazi banners on 27 May 1933. Most of what he said reflects the party line: he speaks of how German students must replace the old, so-called 'academic freedom' with new forms of labour, military and 'knowledge' service. But he adds distinctive Heideggerian touches, as when he explains that this knowledge service will make students place their existence 'in the most acute danger in the midst of overpowering Being'. As the German *Volk* in general confronts 'the extreme questionableness of its own existence', so must the students commit themselves 'to essential and simple questioning in the midst of the historical-spiritual world of the *Volk*'. Thus, Heidegger used his speech to travesty two of the most profound themes of existentialist philosophy: self-questioning and freedom. He stressed this so-called 'questioning' again in another address that November, this time to accompany his (obligatory) 'Declaration of Support for Adolf Hitler and the National Socialist State'. He also developed enthusiastic educational plans of his own, volunteering to host summer camps for faculty and students at his Todtnauberg hut. They were designed to combine physical training with seminar discussions – a kind of philosophical Nazi boot camp.

Heidegger's Nazism was significant because he was now in a position of real power over others' lives. He had developed from being the nutty professor in funny clothes, writing beautiful and barely comprehensible works of genius for the few, into the official whom every student and professor would have to court. He could ruin careers and endanger people's physical safety if he chose to. Heidegger had said that Dasein's call would be unrecognisable, but few people reading *Being and Time* could have imagined that it would sound so much like a call to Nazi obedience.

His position also led him into personal betrayals. Among the new regulations of April 1933, which Heidegger had to enforce and maintain, was one removing from public and university posts all those whom the Nazis identified as Jews. This affected Husserl: although he was retired, he lost his emeritus status and the associated privileged access to university facilities. Husserl's son Gerhart, who was a law professor at the University of Kiel, lost his job by the same regulation – Gerhart, who had been wounded in the First World War and whose brother had given his life for Germany. The new laws were a stupendous insult to a family who had given so much. The only help the Heideggers offered was to send a bouquet of flowers to Malvine Husserl, with a letter from Elfride emphasising the Husserls' record of patriotism. The letter was apparently designed for them to use in their own defence, should they ever need it. But its tone was cool, and Malvine, who was not the type to put up with insults meekly, took offence. In the same year, a new edition of *Being and Time* appeared; Heidegger's dedication of the book to Husserl had disappeared.

Another friend was watching Heidegger's new role in dismay: Karl Jaspers. He and Heidegger had become close after they met at Husserl's birthday party – the one at which Malvine referred to Heidegger as the 'phenomenological child'. As Jaspers lived in Heidelberg, they only travelled to see each other occasionally, but their correspondence and long-distance friendship were warm.

They had many points of philosophical contact. Following his early encounter with Husserl's ideas, Jaspers had gone on to develop his own work, building on his psychology background as well as on Kierkegaardian existentialism. He was especially interested in

Kierkegaard's studies of 'either/or' choices and of freedom: the ways in which we face up to dilemmas and decide what to do. Jaspers focused on what he called *Grenzsituationen* – border situations, or limit situations. These are the moments when one finds oneself constrained or boxed in by what is happening, but at the same time pushed by these events towards the limits or outer edge of normal experience. For example, you might have to make a life-or-death choice, or something might remind you suddenly of your mortality, or some event may make you realise that you have to accept the burden of responsibility for what you do. Experiencing such situations is, for Jaspers, almost synonymous with existing, in the Kierkegaardian sense. Although they are hard to bear, these are puzzles in our existence, and thus open the door to philosophising. We cannot solve them by thinking in the abstract; they must be lived, and in the end we make our choices with our entire being. They are *existential* situations.

Jaspers' interest in border situations probably had much to do with his own early confrontation with mortality. From childhood, he had

suffered from a heart condition so severe that he always expected to die at any moment. He also had emphysema, which forced him to speak slowly, taking long pauses to catch his breath. Both illnesses meant that he had to budget his energies with care in order to get his work done without endangering his life.

For all of this, he relied on his wife Gertrud, to whom he was very close. Like many philosophers' wives, she took charge of his schedule and helped him with paperwork, but she also collaborated on his work. Jaspers developed his ideas through his discussions with her, almost in the way that Sartre later worked with Beauvoir, with the major difference that Beauvoir had her own philosophical career. Heidegger was amazed to learn of Jaspers' work with Gertrud; he would never have thought of involving Elfride so closely in his intellectual life. For him, philosophy was for doing alone in the Todtnauberg hut – or, at best, hammering out with chosen disciples and students.

Jaspers, far more than Heidegger, believed in the value of shared thinking. Despite his shortness of breath, he loved talking with people. Hannah Arendt, a lifelong friend, later looked back on their conversations in the 1920s and 1930s: 'I think about your study . . . with the chair at the desk and the armchair across from it where you tied your legs in marvellous knots and then untied them again.' Heidelberg was renowned for its scholarly salons and social circles: the most famous revolved around the sociologist Max Weber, but Jaspers became the centre of another. He had an almost religious reverence for the ideal of the university as a focus for cultural activity, which made him scrupulous even with dull administrative tasks. His communicative ideal fed into a whole theory of history: he traced all civilisation to an 'Axial Period' in the fifth century BC, during which philosophy and culture exploded simultaneously in Europe, the Middle East and Asia, as though a great bubble of minds had erupted from the earth's surface. 'True philosophy needs *communion* to come into existence,' he wrote, and added, 'Uncommunicativeness in a philosopher is virtually a criterion of the untruth of his thinking.'

Jaspers' enthusiasm for philosophical talk drove him, after meeting Heidegger at Husserl's party, to invite him to Heidelberg for an initial bout of 'symphilosophising' in 1920, and then another eight-day stay in 1922. On this second occasion, Gertrud was away, so the two men played like children on a week-long philosophical sleepover. Jaspers became fired up by the idea of publishing a journal together – two editors, two contributors – to be called *The Philosophy of the Age*. It would be filled with short, clear, decisive essays on their times. This never happened, but their plans brought them closer as friends. Having begun by addressing one another as 'Professor' in letters, then as

'Herr Heidegger' and 'Herr Jaspers', they were hailing each other by late 1923 as 'Dear Jaspers' – 'Dear Heidegger'. Heidegger was more subdued; when they were together, he sometimes sank into silences, which made Jaspers even more inclined to talk, to fill the gap. Yet Heidegger also wrote to tell Jaspers that these first steps in friendship had given him an 'uncanny' feeling – high Heideggerian words of praise.

He and Jaspers both felt that philosophy needed a revolution, but they disagreed on what form it should take. They also disagreed about style. Heidegger thought Jaspers' mania for lists and columns in his work was boring, while Jaspers read drafts of *Being and Time* and found them opaque. There were other early signs of disharmony. Once, Jaspers was told that Heidegger had spoken badly of him behind his back, so he confronted him. Heidegger denied it, and added in a shocked tone, 'I have never experienced anything like this before.' That left Jaspers puzzled too. The challenge ended with both of them disoriented and affronted, but Jaspers let the matter go.

The confusion increased. With the rise of the Nazis, something 'estranging' entered their relationship, as Jaspers put it in private notes about Heidegger written years later. Jaspers had reason to feel estranged from his friend: he was not Jewish himself, but Gertrud was. Like many others, the couple tended to be dismissive about the Nazi threat at first. They weighed the usual considerations: surely these barbarians could not stay in power long? Even for an eminent professor, it would be hard to flee the country and start again elsewhere, separated from everything that had given context to his life. Besides, leaving always meant paying punitive 'Reich Flight' taxes, and obtaining visas. From 1933 on, Karl and Gertrud regularly considered the possibility of escaping, but did not do it.

An awkward moment occurred when Heidegger visited Jaspers in March 1933, just before beginning the rectorship. The subject of National Socialism came up, and Heidegger said, 'One must get in step.' Jaspers was too shocked to speak, and did not push him, not wanting to hear what more he might say. That June, Heidegger stayed with Jaspers again while in Heidelberg to give a rerun of his speech on the new regime and universities. In the audience, Jaspers was struck by the 'thunderous applause' with which students greeted Heidegger's words. As for himself, he wrote, 'I sat in front at the periphery with my legs stretched out before me, my hands in my pockets, and did not budge.' The long legs that made such an impression on Arendt now provided their own commentary on Heidegger's speech.

Afterwards, at his home, Jaspers began to remark to Heidegger, 'It is just like 1914 . . .', intending to go on to say, 'once again this deceitful mass intoxication'. But Heidegger agreed so enthusiastically to the first few words that Jaspers left the sentence in mid-air. Over dinner a little later, the topic of Hitler and his lack of education came up, and this time Heidegger said, bizarrely, 'Education is completely irrelevant, just look at his wonderful hands!' Coming from anyone else, this would sound purely eccentric. From Heidegger, with his emphasis on handiwork and the wielding of tools, it was significant. He seemed to be attracted less by Nazi ideology than by the idea of Hitler dextrously and firmly moulding the country into a new form.

Gertrud Jaspers had been dreading Heidegger's visit, but she tried to welcome him for her husband's sake. Before his arrival, she wrote to her parents: 'Now I must say to myself: you are a lady from the Orient, they know how to cultivate hospitality! And I must simply be kind and keep quiet!' She did just that, but Heidegger was rude to her on leaving: 'he hardly said good-bye at all', wrote Jaspers to Arendt later. For this, above all, Jaspers could not forgive him. Years later, Heidegger would claim he had done it because he was 'ashamed', meaning presumably that he was embarrassed about his Nazi episode, but Jaspers was sceptical about this explanation. Their correspondence dried up for a long time, and Heidegger never came to the Jaspers house again.

Jaspers later thought he might have erred in treating Heidegger too delicately. When Heidegger sent him a printed version of his rectorial address in 1933, Jaspers' reply was supremely diplomatic: 'It was nice to see it in its authentic version after reading about it in the paper.' Should he have been more critical, he wondered later? Perhaps he had failed 'this intoxicated and enthused Heidegger'. Heidegger perhaps needed what a later generation would call an 'intervention', to save him from himself. It was, Jaspers implied, a failure of engagement on his own part – and he linked this to a more general failure of tolerant, educated Germans to face up to the challenge of the time.

Of course, it is relatively easy for later generations (or for the same people later in life) to see what challenges a particular 'border situation' presented; no such retrospective view was available to those living through it. A natural human tendency is to try to continue with as ordinary and civilised a life as possible, for as long as one can. Bruno Bettelheim later observed that, under Nazism, only a few people realised at once that life *could not* continue unaltered: these were the ones who got away quickly. Bettelheim himself was not among them. Caught in Austria when Hitler annexed it, he was sent first to Dachau and then to Buchenwald, but was then released in a mass amnesty to celebrate Hitler's birthday in 1939 – an extraordinary reprieve, after which he left at once for America.

The importance of remaining open to events and seeing instantly when a decision is required was a theme also explored that year by another existentialist philosopher, this time a French one: Gabriel Marcel. A Christian thinker who made his name as a playwright, and who communicated his ideas mainly through essays or through get-togethers with students and friends in his Paris flat, Marcel developed a strongly theological branch of existentialism. His faith distanced him from both Sartre and Heidegger, but he shared a sense of how history makes demands on individuals.

In his essay 'On the Ontological Mystery', written in 1932 and published in the fateful year of 1933, Marcel wrote of the human tendency to become stuck in habits, received ideas, and a narrow-minded attachment to possessions and familiar scenes. Instead, he urged his readers to develop a capacity for remaining 'available' to situations as they arise. Similar ideas of *disponibilité* or availability had been explored by other writers, notably André Gide, but Marcel made it his central existential imperative. He was aware of how rare and difficult it was. Most people fall into what he calls 'crispation': a tensed, encrusted shape in life – 'as though each one of us secreted a kind of shell which gradually hardened and imprisoned him'.

Marcel's 'shell' recalls Husserl's notion of the accumulated and inflexible preconceptions that one should set aside in the *epoché*, so as to open up access to the 'things themselves'. In both cases, what is rigid is cleared away, and the trembling freshness of what is underneath becomes the object of the philosopher's attention. For Marcel, learning to stay open to reality in this way is the philosopher's prime job. Everyone can do it, but the philosopher is the one who is called on above all to stay awake, so as to be the first to sound the alarm if something seems wrong.

Heidegger believed in vigilance too: he was determined to shock people out of their forgetfulness. But for him, vigilance did not mean calling attention to Nazi violence, to the intrusion of state surveillance, or to the physical threats to his fellow humans. It meant being decisive and resolute in carrying through the demands history was making upon Germany, with its distinctive Being and destiny. It meant getting in step with the chosen hero.

For Heidegger in the early 1930s, it really *was* all about the Germans.

This aspect of his work is easy for us to forget; we are used to reading philosophy as offering a universal message for all times and places – or at least as aiming to do so. But Heidegger disliked the notion of universal truths or universal humanity, which he considered a fantasy. For him, Dasein is not defined by shared faculties of reason and understanding, as the Enlightenment philosophers thought. Still less is it defined by any kind of transcendent eternal soul, as in religious tradition. We do not exist on a higher, eternal plane at all. Dasein's Being is local: it has a historical situation, and is constituted in time and place.

At the very beginning of *Being and Time*, Heidegger promises that the book will take us to a grand finale in which he will make this ultimate point: that *the meaning of Dasein's Being is Time*. He never did this because he never finished the book: what we have is just the first part. But he showed clearly which way he was planning to go. If we are temporal beings by our very nature, then authentic existence means accepting, first, that we are finite and mortal. We will die: this all-important realisation is what Heidegger calls authentic 'Being-towards-Death', and it is fundamental to his philosophy.

Second, it also means understanding that we are historical beings, and grasping the demands our particular historical situation is making on us. In what Heidegger calls 'anticipatory resoluteness', Dasein discovers 'that its uttermost possibility lies in giving itself up'. At that moment, through Being-towards-death and resoluteness in facing up to one's time, one is freed from the they-self and attains one's true, authentic self.

These are the pages of *Being and Time* in which Heidegger sounds most fascistic. There can be little doubt that he was thinking in political terms when he wrote his passages on death and resoluteness. Yet, even here, Heidegger's basic concepts *could* have led to quite a different interpretation. Just as his ideas of the 'they' and authenticity could have led him to a case for resisting totalitarian brainwashing, so his ideas of resoluteness and the acceptance of mortality could have formed a framework for courageous *resistance* to the regime and its intimidation techniques. It could have been a manifesto for anti-totalitarian heroism. Instead, it is apparent that Heidegger intended a mass of highly charged political meanings to be visible in this text – though perhaps only to those who were already inclined to be sympathetic.

Hans Jonas, one of Heidegger's former students, remembered how such coded terms were present even in earlier lectures, although Jonas himself was oblivious to them at the time. He did not see them because he was not attuned that way, but in retrospect – he told an interviewer – he recognised the 'Blood-and-Soil' language of the lectures, and the '(how should I say it?) primitive nationalism' in Heidegger's talk of resoluteness and history, together with his occasional anti-French political asides and his emphasis on Black Forest rusticism. At the time, it seemed a mere eccentricity. Only after Jonas was told of Heidegger's rectorial address in 1933 did he re-evaluate his whole memory of the long-ago seminars he had taken. 'That was when I realised, for the first time, certain traits in Heidegger's thinking and I hit myself on the forehead and said: "Yes, I missed something there before."'

By Christmas of 1933, however, Heidegger was feeling less at home in the role of public National Socialist philosopher than he had expected to be. According to his own account, he spent that winter break coming to a decision: he would resign the rectorship at the end of the next semester. He did just that, dating his letter of resignation 14 April 1934. After this, he later claimed, he had nothing more to do with Nazism. He even ventured a small rebellion by putting the original dedication to Husserl back into the 1935 edition of *Being and Time*. The new stance came at a significant cost to himself, he asserted, because he was harassed and spied on by party functionaries from then until the end of the war.

Heidegger hated talking about this period, and none of his own explanations of what happened in 1933 were ever satisfactory. In 1945, he wrote just one short piece dealing with the matter, entitled 'The Rectorate 1933/34: facts and thoughts'. There he admitted that he briefly saw the party as offering 'the possibility of an inner self-collection and of a renewal of the people, and a path toward the discovery of its historical-Western purpose'. But then, he said, he saw his mistake and extricated himself. The message of the essay can be summed up as 'oops, I didn't mean to be a Nazi'. It suited Heidegger to make himself sound this naive. When, also in 1945, the French writer Frédéric de Towarnicki weakened Heidegger's defences with a bottle of good wine before asking him 'why?', Heidegger responded by leaning forward and saying, in the tone of someone solemnly confiding a secret, '*Dummheit.*' He repeated the word again, with emphasis. '*Dummheit.*' Stupidity. The implication was that his worst failing was unworldliness. He even convinced the ever-generous Jaspers, who after the war referred to the Heidegger of 1933 as a 'dreaming boy' – a child caught up in events too difficult for him to understand.

The truth is rather different. For one thing, Heidegger clearly retained Nazi sympathies long after his resignation. In August 1934, he submitted plans to the Ministry for Science and Education for their proposed philosophical academy in Berlin, a kind of urban version of the Todtnauberg camps in which teachers and students would live together and pursue 'scientific work, recreation, concentration, martial games, physical work, walks, sport, and celebrations', under the guidance of a director and professors who were 'politically safe' National Socialists. Heidegger's submission was rejected, but not for any lack of enthusiasm in his way of presenting it. Two years later, when he travelled to Rome in 1936 to give a lecture on the poet Friedrich Hölderlin, he still wore a Nazi pin on his lapel, and he kept it there even when he and his part-Jewish former student Karl Löwith took a day off to go sightseeing with their families. Löwith was disgusted: regardless of Heidegger's views, it would have been easy for him to remove the badge if only to make his friends feel comfortable.

That was not the only time Heidegger showed a rigid shell – an extreme form of Gabriel Marcel's 'crispation' – in dealing with people. The philosopher Max Müller, who studied with Heidegger and worked as his assistant, found himself in trouble with the regime in 1937 for writing political articles and working for a Catholic youth group. Freiburg's vice rector, Theodor Maunz, told Müller that Heidegger had been approached for a report on his student's politics, and had given him a generally good assessment 'as a human being, educator, and philosopher'. On the other hand, he had included an observation that Müller had a negative opinion of the state. A single sentence like that meant doom. 'Go to him,' Maunz told Müller. 'Everything else will be fine if he crosses out that sentence.'

Müller turned to Heidegger – but Heidegger pedantically stuck to his point, saying, 'I gave the only answer that corresponds to the truth. But I have wrapped it in a cover of justifiable, good things.'

'That won't help me,' replied Müller. 'The sentence is there.'

Heidegger said: 'As a Catholic, you should know that one must tell the truth. Consequently, I cannot cross out the sentence.'

Müller disputed the theology behind this, but Heidegger was unmoved: 'No, I will stick to what I was asked. I can't take back my whole report now and say I won't write one at all, because people already know that I have given one to the university to be passed on. Nothing can be done. Don't hold it against me.'

These final words were what astonished Müller most. All Heidegger seemed to care about was justifying his own actions, with no thought to the danger facing the other man. Fortunately, Müller escaped serious consequences on this occasion, but it was no thanks to Heidegger. He remembered his parting remark to Heidegger that day: 'The point is not that I might hold it against you, the point is my existence.' His feelings about his former mentor were different from then on: he could never forget his experience of 'a certain ambiguity in Heidegger's character'.

This word 'ambiguity' comes up again and again in describing Heidegger, and it applies not just to his character or actions, but to his philosophy. Ever since 1945, philosophers and historians have tried to work out whether Heidegger's thought is entirely invalidated by his Nazism, or whether it can be judged in isolation from his personal and political flaws. Some people have proposed trying to rescue certain aspects while discarding others, burying the dangerous bits like so much radioactive waste while holding up the occasional fragment deemed worthwhile. But this seems unsatisfying: Heidegger's phil-osophy forms a dense, complicated whole in which every aspect depends on every other. If you try to remove everything unpleasant from *Being and Time*, the structure collapses.

Moreover, almost every important thought in Heidegger holds some ambiguity *within* itself. The most dangerous ideas can also be the ones with most to offer – as in the passages calling us to authenticity and answerability. Most puzzling of all are the sections where he wrote about *Mitsein*, or being with others: he was the first philosopher to make this experience so central in a philosophical work. He wrote beautifully about 'solicitude' for others: about the moments when we 'leap in' for another person, out of concern and fellow feeling. Yet none of this enabled Heidegger to show any fellow feeling at all for those suffering or persecuted in Nazi Germany. He could write about *Mitsein* and solicitude, but he could not apply it to history, or to the predicaments of those around him, including those to whom he seemed close.

He certainly seemed to have no idea what he was putting his friends through. Many who knew him, especially Husserl, Jaspers and Arendt, were confused by Heidegger's ambiguity, and wounded by his actions and attitudes. They could not bring themselves to forget him, so they agonised over him. Their effort to figure him out gave them a glimpse into a void. It wasn't that Heidegger had a bad character, Hannah Arendt wrote to Jaspers in 1949; it was that he had *no* character. Sartre said a very similar thing in an essay of 1944, speaking of Heidegger's Nazism: 'Heidegger has no character; there's the truth of the matter.' It is as if there was something about everyday human life that the great philosopher of everydayness did not get.

Brooding up at the hut in Todtnauberg, Heidegger struggled on with his writing and thinking through the 1930s. In 1935, he wrote miserably of 'the darkening of the world, the flight of the gods, the destruction of the earth, the reduction of human beings to a mass, the hatred and mistrust of everything creative and free'. But this was ambiguous too: did he mean that the Nazis were responsible for this, or that the general darkening and massification of humanity had made Nazism necessary?

He may have felt some confusion himself during these years; he certainly had difficulty expressing his thoughts. In July 1935, he wrote to Jaspers saying that all he had been able to manage lately in his work was a 'thin stammering'. But he had been working on translations, and with the letter he enclosed some lines from Sophocles' *Antigone*, the chorus's 'Ode on Man' section. (He would also have this translation printed privately later, as a birthday gift to his wife in 1943.) It begins, in the published English translation of Heidegger's German:

The manifold uncanny holds sway
And nothing uncannier than man.

Heidegger's thought itself was now becoming more and more 'uncanny'. In his snowy forest, he began a long, slow reorientation which has become known as the 'turn' (*die Kehre*), although it can be pinned down to no single event. It was a process leading Heidegger towards a more earthy, more receptive, more poetical way of thinking, and away from talk of resoluteness and decisiveness.

His poeticising and communing with the forest also led to new decisions of his own, however. Around the time he was considering whether to continue the rectorship, he was also offered a university post in Berlin – an option which must have complicated the Freiburg decision. But he rejected the offer. He gave his reasons in a radio address, published in the Nazi-approved publication *Der Alemanne* on 7 March 1934.

The address did not openly deal with politics at all, though its implications were political. He said that he would not move to Berlin because it would take him away from his Black Forest environment – from 'the slow and deliberate growth of the fir-trees, the brilliant, simple splendour of the meadows in bloom, the rush of the mountain brook in the long autumn night, the stern simplicity of the flatlands covered with snow'. When a blizzard blows around the cabin on a deep winter's night, he wrote, 'that is the perfect time for philosophy'. And:

> When the young farm boy drags his heavy sled up the slope and guides it, piled high with beech logs, down the dangerous descent to his house, when the herdsman, lost in thought and slow of step, drives his cattle up the slope, when the farmer in his shed gets the countless shingles ready for his roof, my work is of the same sort.

When the offer first came through, said Heidegger, he sought advice from his Todtnauberg neighbour, a seventy-five-year-old farmer since identified as Johann Brender. Brender thought for a moment – one of those long, thoughtful moments that wise country people supposedly go in for. Then he replied, not with words but with a quiet shake of the head. And that was all it took. There would be no Berlin for Heidegger; no cosmopolitan urban life; no more flirting with the 'intoxication of power'. It was back to the south-west German forest, to the tall trees, to the wood-chopping, and to the rustic benches at the side of the pathways, where his thinking worked best – that is, where 'all things become solitary and slow'.

These were the scenes – which just happened to correspond to Nazi rural kitsch of the worst sort – which would guide the rest of Heidegger's philosophising.

Karl and Gertrud Jaspers were also wrestling with their own decision, and continued to do so through the 1930s: should they leave Germany? The Nuremberg Laws of 1935 severely restricted their lives: they stripped Jews of their citizenship and banned mixed marriages, although those already existing, like theirs, were officially tolerated for the moment. The following year, Jaspers lost his university position because of his marriage. Yet they still could not bring themselves to leave. Instead, they kept their heads down and lived cautiously, very much as Jaspers had learned always to breathe and move cautiously, for fear of damaging his vital organs.

Hannah Arendt, instead, left early on: she had the benefit of a powerful warning. Just after the Nazi takeover, in spring 1933, she had been arrested while researching materials on anti-Semitism for the German Zionist Organisation at Berlin's Prussian State Library. Her apartment was searched; both she and her mother were locked up briefly, then released. They fled, without stopping to arrange travel documents. They crossed to Czechoslovakia (then still safe) by a method that sounds almost too fabulous to be true: a sympathetic German family on the border had a house with its front door in Germany and its back door in Czechoslovakia. The family would invite people for dinner, then let them leave through the back door at night. From Prague, Arendt and her mother went on to Geneva, then to Paris, and finally to New York, where Arendt settled. She told a television interviewer later that everyone had known from the start how dangerous Nazi Germany was, but knowing it in theory was one thing, while acting on it and turning it into 'personal destiny' was very different. They survived.

Heidegger's former sparring partner at Davos, Ernst Cassirer, did not wait for a warning. Living in Hamburg, where he had taught since 1919, he saw how things were going as soon as the laws of April 1933 came in and left promptly with his family in May. He spent two years at Oxford University, then six years at Göteborg in Sweden; when it looked as though Sweden would fall under German control, he moved on to the United States, where he taught at Yale and then Columbia. He survived until just before the end of the war: on 13 April 1945, in New York, he died of a heart attack while out for a walk.

Emmanuel Levinas had left for France well before the Nazis came to power. He taught at the Sorbonne, became naturalised as a Frenchman in 1931, and signed up to fight when the war began.

The Husserls' children, Elli and Gerhart, emigrated to the United States. Edmund Husserl himself was offered a post at the University of Southern California in November 1933; he could have become a Californian. I find it strangely easy to imagine him there, as neat as ever in his suit, strolling with a cane beneath the palm trees and clear white sun – just as many other intellectual European émigrés did. But he was not prepared to leave the country that was his home. Malvine Husserl stuck by him, equally defiant.

Husserl continued his work in his own extensive private library. The student whose safety Heidegger jeopardised, Max Müller, was often sent on errands to his house by Heidegger, usually to keep Husserl up to date on who was doing what in the philosophy faculty and which dissertations were being written. Apparently Heidegger did not want Husserl to be entirely isolated, yet he never went to visit him personally. Müller was pleased to have this excuse to see the great phenomenologist. From what he saw, he concluded that Husserl was indeed rather cut off, mainly because he took little interest in outside affairs. 'He was a strongly monological type and, as he had entirely concentrated on his philosophical problems, he did not actually experience the time that had begun in 1933 as "hard", unlike his wife.'

Husserl was paying more attention to the world than was apparent, however. In August 1934, he applied to go to Prague for the Eighth International Congress of Philosophy, dedicated to the theme 'the mission of philosophy in our time'. He was denied a travel permit, so he sent a letter to be read out at the congress instead. It was a short but stirring document, in which Husserl warned that a crisis was threatening the European tradition of reason and philosophical inquiry. He called on scholars in every field to take up their responsibility – their 'answerability to themselves', or *Selbstverantwortung* – to counter this crisis, and especially to establish international networks that would bring thinkers together across borders.

He repeated a similar message in person in a lecture to the Cultural

Society in Vienna in May 1935, this time being allowed to travel. Scholars must unite, he said, to resist the current slide into dangerous, irrationalist mysticism. A 'heroism of reason' was Europe's only hope. In November 1935, he applied again to travel to Prague, and permission was granted, so he delivered another lecture making similar arguments. Throughout that year, he had been working his ideas into a longer project. He finished the first two sections in January 1936, and published them as *The Crisis of the European Sciences and Transcendental Phenomenology*. Since the anti-Jewish laws now forbade him to publish anything in Germany, the work appeared in *Philosophia*, an international yearbook based in Belgrade.

In August 1937, Husserl had a fall, and did not make a good recovery. That winter, his health declined. He continued to work with collaborators and visitors on a third section of the *Crisis*, but he did not finish it. His mind failed him in his last few months; he spoke little, but occasionally said things like 'I've made many mistakes, but it can still all turn out well,' or 'I'm swimming in the River of Lethe and have no thoughts.' Then, with a flash of his old ambition, he said, 'Philosophy has to be built up all over again from the beginning.' He died on 27 April 1938, aged seventy-nine. The nursing sister who attended him said afterwards, to Malvine, 'He died like a holy man.'

Edmund Husserl was cremated, because of the fear that a gravestone in a cemetery might be desecrated by vandals. Malvine remained in their home for now, guarding her husband's ashes, his magnificent library, and his archive of personal papers – all written in that distinctive shorthand script, and including his many unpublished and unfinished works, not least the last sections of the *Crisis*.

Pleading illness, Heidegger did not attend the funeral.

5

To Crunch Flowering Almonds

In which Jean-Paul Sartre describes a tree, Simone de Beauvoir brings ideas to life, and we meet Maurice Merleau-Ponty and the bourgeoisie.

In 1934, after his year of Husserl-reading in Berlin, Sartre returned to France filled with energy. He set to work devising his own spin on phenomenology, enlivening it with distinctively Sartrean takes on Kierkegaard and Hegel. He also drew on personal material: his childhood experiences, his youthful enthusiasms, and his wide range of interesting phobias and obsessions. Now that he was reunited with Simone de Beauvoir, he also involved her in his work, and she in turn brought her past and personality into her own writing and thinking. It became a complex blend.

Sartre had to return to teaching, initially in Le Havre again. In his spare time he became a missionary for phenomenology, urging all his friends to study it – including those, like Merleau-Ponty, who had already done so. Beauvoir, who could read German well (apparently better than Sartre, although he had been speaking and reading it all year), spent much of 1934 immersed in phenomenological texts.

Keen to get his ideas on paper, Sartre finished off the essay he had begun in Berlin, 'A Fundamental Idea of Husserl's Phenomenology: Intentionality' – the piece that so memorably explained intentionality as an exile from the cosy digestive chambers of the mind out into the dusty world of being. He also worked on a study of the phenomenology of the imagination, of which a shortened version was published in 1936 as *L'imagination*, and a reworked full version in 1940 as

L'imaginaire or *The Imaginary*. Both works explored the phenomen-ological puzzle of how dreams, fantasies or hallucinations can be thought of in terms of the structure of intentionality, even when their objects are non-existent or absent in reality.

To extend his research in these areas, Sartre decided he should experience some hallucinations of his own, so he asked the physician Daniel Lagache, an old school friend, to help him try the drug mesca-line, which had first been synthesised in 1919. Intellectuals were falling over each other to get their hands on mescaline in the mid-century; the trend culminated in 1953 with *The Doors of Perception*, Aldous Huxley's famous phenomenological study of what it felt like to view paintings and listen to music while tripping. An existentialist experi-menter of the 1950s, the English writer Colin Wilson, described having an encounter with raw Being that was 'like waking up on a train and finding a stranger with his face within an inch of your own'. Long before then, Sartre sought his own face-to-face with Being. Dr Lagache injected him with the drug, then supervised the trip while Sartre, always the good phenomenologist, observed the experience from within and took notes.

The results were dramatic. While Huxley's drug adventure would be mystical and ecstatic, and one of Dr Lagache's assistants had enjoyed prancing through imaginary meadows with exotic dancers, Sartre's brain threw up a hellish crew of snakes, fish, vultures, toads, beetles and crustaceans. Worse, they refused to go away afterwards. For months, lobster-like beings followed him just out of his field of vision, and the facades of houses on the street stared at him with human eyes.

He put relatively little of his drug experience into his studies of the imagination, perhaps because it made him fear for a while that he was losing his mind. But he did use it in other works, including the 1937 story 'The Room' and the later 1959 play *The Condemned of Altona*, both of which feature young men under siege by hallucinatory monsters, as well as a semi-fictional 1938 piece called 'Foods'. This drew both on the mescaline imagery and a 1936 trip to Italy. The narrator, walking alone around Naples on a very hot day, observes

terrible things: a child on crutches picks a slice of watermelon crawling
with flies out of a gutter, and eats it. Through an open doorway, he sees
a man kneeling beside a little girl. While she says, 'Daddy; my daddy,'
the man lifts up her dress and bites into her buttocks as one might into
a loaf of bread. Sartre's narrator is overwhelmed by nausea – but with
it comes an insight: that nothing in the world happens with any necessity. Everything is 'contingent', and it could all have happened a
different way. The revelation horrifies him.

Sartre's own insight about 'contingency' must have come earlier,
as he had been collecting notes about it for a while, initially in a suit-
ably random blank notebook which he said he found on a Métro train
and which had an advertisement for 'Midi Suppositories' on the cover.
These notes evolved in Berlin into the draft of a novel, to which he
gave the working title *Melancholia*. This in turn became the novel that
I would encounter when I was sixteen: *Nausea*, the story of the writer
Antoine Roquentin and his driftings in Bouville.

Roquentin has initially come to this dull seaside town to research
the life of an eighteenth-century courtier, the Marquis de Rollebon,
whose papers are in the local library. Rollebon's career amounted to
a series of wild adventures and would be a gift to any biographer,
except that Roquentin now can't find a way to write about them. He
has discovered that life is nothing like these swashbuckling stories,
and he does not want to falsify reality. In fact, it is Roquentin himself
who has come adrift. Lacking the routine or family which lend structure to most people's lives, he spends his days in the library, or
wandering about, or drinking beer in a café that plays ragtime music
on the record player. He watches the townspeople doing their bourgeois, ordinary-folk things. Life resembles a lump of featureless dough,
characterised only by contingency, not by necessity. This realisation
comes in regular episodes, like waves, and each time it fills Roquentin
with a nausea that seems to attach to objects themselves – to the
world out there. He picks up a pebble to throw into the sea, but it
feels like a disgusting globular mass in his hand. He enters a room,
and the doorknob becomes a weird bulbous lump. In the café, his
usual beer glass with its bevelled edges and bright brewer's coat of

arms turns horrible and contingent on him. He tries to capture these experiences phenomenologically in a diary: 'I must say how I see this table, the street, people, my packet of tobacco, since *these* are the things which have changed.'

Eventually, while looking at the 'boiled leather' of a chestnut tree in the local park and feeling the nausea again, Roquentin realises that it is not just the tree but the *Being* of the tree that is bothering him. It is the way in which, inexplicably and pointlessly, it simply sits there refusing to make sense or tone itself down. This is what contingency is: the random, outrageous *thisness* of things. Roquentin realises he can no longer see the world as he used to, and that he will never complete his Rollebon biography because he cannot spin adventure stories. For the moment, he can't do much at all:

I slumped on the bench, dazed, stunned by that profusion of beings without origin: blooming, blossoming everywhere, my ears were buzzing with existence, my very flesh was throbbing and opening, abandoning itself to the universal burgeoning.

He does have some moments of respite, and these occur when his favourite café plays the record of a woman (probably Sophie Tucker) singing a melancholy, bluesy number called 'Some of These Days'. It begins with a delicate piano intro, which segues into the singer's warm voice; for the next few minutes, all is right with Roquentin's world. Each note leads to the next: no note could be otherwise. The song has necessity, so it bestows necessity on Roquentin's existence too. Everything is poised and smooth: when he lifts the glass to his lips, it moves on an easy arc, and he can set it down without spilling it. His movements flow, like those of an athlete or musician – until the song ends, and everything goes to pieces again.

The novel ends with Roquentin finding his way out through this vision of art as a source of necessity. He resolves to leave for Paris, in order to write – not a biography, but a different kind of book that will be 'beautiful and hard as steel and make people ashamed of their existence'. Later, Sartre reflected that this solution was a bit too easy; can art really save us from the chaos of life? But it gave Roquentin somewhere to go in what might otherwise have been an endless, unresolved novel, 'blooming, blossoming' in all directions. As we shall see later, anything that enabled Sartre to finish a book is to be applauded.

Sartre had incorporated many of his own experiences into his writing: the out-of-season seaside town, the hallucinations, the insight about contingency. Even the obsession with the chestnut tree was personal: his work is full of trees. In his autobiography, he recalled being terrified as a child by a ghost story in which a young woman, ill in bed, suddenly screams, points out of the window at the chestnut tree outside, then falls dead on her pillow. In Sartre's own story 'Childhood of a Leader', the protagonist Lucien becomes horrified by a chestnut tree because it sits there unresponsively when he kicks it. Sartre later told his friend John Gerassi that his apartment in Berlin looked out over a fine big tree – not a chestnut, but one similar enough to keep the memory of his Le Havre trees alive in his mind while he wrote.

Trees meant many things for Sartre: Being, mystery, the physical world, contingency. They were also a handy focus for phenomenological description. In his autobiography he also quotes something his grandfather once said to him: 'It's not just a question of having eyes, you have to learn how to use them. Do you know what Flaubert did to the young Maupassant? He sat him down in front of a tree and gave him two hours to describe it.' This is correct: Flaubert apparently did advise Maupassant to consider things 'long and attentively', saying,

> There is a part of everything that remains unexplored, for we have fallen into the habit of remembering, whenever we use our eyes, what people before us have thought of the thing we are looking at. Even the slightest thing contains a little that is unknown. We must find it. To describe a blazing fire or a tree in a plain, we must remain before that fire or that tree until they no longer resemble for us any other tree or any other fire.

Flaubert was talking about literary skill, but he could have been talking about phenomenological method, which follows exactly that process. With the *epoché*, one first discards second-hand notions or received ideas, then one describes the thing as it directly presents itself. For Husserl, this ability to describe a phenomenon without influence from others' theories is what liberates the philosopher.

The connection between description and liberation fascinated Sartre. A writer is a person who describes, and thus a person who is free – for a person who can exactly describe what he or she experiences can also exert some control over those events. Sartre explored this link between writing and freedom again and again in his work. When I first read *Nausea*, I suspect this was part of its appeal for me. I too wanted to be able to see things fully, to experience them, to write about them – and to gain freedom. That was how I came to stand in a park trying to see the Being of a tree, and how I came to study philosophy.

In *Nausea*, art brings liberation because it captures things as they are *and* gives them an inner necessity. They are no longer bulbous and nauseating: they make sense. Roquentin's jazz song is the model for this process. Actually, Beauvoir tells us in her memoirs that Sartre got the idea while watching a film rather than listening to music. They were keen cinemagoers, and had a particular fondness for the comedies of Charlie Chaplin and Buster Keaton, both of whom made films filled with balletic grace, as elegant as any song. I love the idea that Sartre's philosophical epiphany about the necessity and freedom of art might have come from the Little Tramp.

Sartre drew on his own experience too for the other side of Roquentin's obsession: his horror of anything fleshy, sticky or slimy. At one point, Roquentin even feels disgusted by the saliva inside his own mouth, and by his lips and his body in general – 'wet with existence'. In *Being and Nothingness*, published in 1943, Sartre went on to give us many more pages about the physical quality of *viscosité*, or *le visqueux* – 'viscosity' or 'gluey sliminess'. He wrote about the way honey pools as it is poured from a spoon, and evoked (with a shudder) the 'moist and feminine sucking' that occurs when a sticky substance adheres to one's fingers. Sartre would not have liked, I suspect, the face-sucking alien in Ridley Scott's film *Alien*, or the gelatinous 'cuddle

sponge' in Philip K. Dick's novel *Flow My Tears, The Policeman Said* –
which kills in precisely the way its name suggests – or the Great Boyg
in Ibsen's *Peer Gynt*, a 'slimy, misty' being of no distinct form. Still
less would he enjoy meeting the life form glimpsed at the end of
H. G. Wells' *The Time Machine*: a blob heaving itself around on a
beach, its tentacles trailing. Sartre's horror of such things is, literally,
visceral. He made so much of this imagery that, if a viscous pool or
splat of anything appears on a page of philosophy, you can be fairly
sure you are reading Sartre – although Gabriel Marcel claimed the
credit for first giving him the idea of writing about it in a philosophical way. Viscosity is Sartre's way of expressing the horror of
contingency. It evokes what he called 'facticity', meaning everything
that drags us down into situations and inhibits us from flying free.

Sartre's talent for combining personal gut responses with philosophical reasoning was one he cultivated deliberately. It sometimes
took work. In a TV interview of 1972, he admitted that he had
never spontaneously experienced nausea in the face of contingency
himself. Another interviewee was sceptical, saying that he once saw
Sartre staring at fronds of algae in water with a disgusted expression. Wasn't that 'nausea'? Perhaps the truth was that Sartre was
staring at the algae precisely so as to whip up the feeling and observe
what it was like.

Sartre built his ideas out of his life, but his reading found its way
into the mix too. It is not hard to spot signs of Heidegger in *Nausea*,
though perhaps not *Being and Time*, which Sartre had not yet read in
detail. The themes of *Nausea* are much closer to the ones in
Heidegger's 1929 lecture 'What Is Metaphysics?' – nothingness, being,
and the 'moods' that disclose how things are. This was the published
lecture that Beauvoir said they glanced at but had not been able to
understand.

I'm also struck by similarities to another work: Emmanuel
Levinas's essay 'De l'évasion' ('On Escape'), which appeared in
Recherches philosophiques in 1935 while Sartre was still working on
his drafts. Levinas there describes sensations that can come with
insomnia or with physical nausea, especially the oppressive feeling

that something is dragging you down and holding you prisoner – a heavy, solid, undifferentiated 'being' that weighs on you. Levinas calls this sense of heavy, blobbish being the '*il y a*', or the 'there is'. Later he would compare it to the rumbling, booming noise you hear when you put a shell to your ear, or when you are lying in an empty room as a child, unable to sleep. It feels 'as if the emptiness were full, as if the silence were a noise'. It is a nightmare sensation of total plenitude, leaving no space for thoughts – no inward cavern. In *Existence and Existents*, in 1947, Levinas described it as a state where beings appear to us 'as though they no longer composed a world', that is, devoid of their Heideggerian network of purposes and involvements. Our natural response to all this is to want to escape, and we find such escape in anything that restores our sense of structure and form. This could be art, music, or contact with another person.

I'm not aware of any allegation that Sartre copied this from Levinas or even that he had read the essay, though others have observed the interesting similarities. The most likely explanation is that both men developed their thoughts in response to Husserl and Heidegger. Sartre had given up on *Being and Time* for now, having discovered in Berlin that reading Husserl and Heidegger at the same time was too much for one brain. But in later years he found his way to Heidegger, whereas Levinas would head in the other direction, giving up all admiration for his former mentor because of his political choices. Levinas came to feel, unlike Heidegger, that people should never accept brute Being as it is. We become civilised by *escaping* the weight that presses on us in our nightmares, not by embracing it.

One sometimes has the feeling, reading Sartre, that he did indeed borrow from other people's ideas and even steal them, but that everything becomes so mixed with his own strange personality and vision that what emerges is perfectly original. He wrote in a state of almost trancelike concentration that lent itself to producing visionary experiences. His method was best summed up in an early letter that he wrote in 1926 to his then girlfriend Simone Jollivet, advising her on how to write. Focus on an image, he said, until you feel 'a swelling, like a bubble, also a sort of direction indicated to you'. This is your idea; afterwards you can clarify it and write it down.

This was essentially the phenomenological method – at least, a wildly colourful version of it, since Husserl would probably have disapproved of Sartre's weakness for anecdote and metaphor. While Heidegger turned Husserlian phenomenology into a kind of poetry, Sartre and Beauvoir made it novelistic, and hence more palatable for the non-professional. In her 1945 lecture 'The Novel and Metaphysics', Beauvoir observed that novels by phenomenologists were not as dull as those of some other philosophers because they described instead of explaining or putting things in categories. Phenomenologists take us to the 'things themselves'. One might say that they follow the creative-writing mantra, 'show, don't tell'.

Sartre's fiction is not always sparkling; it varies. So does Beauvoir's, but at her best she was a more natural fiction-writer than he was. She took more care over plot and language, and she subordinated raw ideas to the play of character and event more readily. She was also good at spotting where Sartre went wrong. As he struggled with revisions of the *Melancholia* manuscript in the mid-1930s, she read his drafts and urged him to inject some of the suspense they enjoyed so much in films and detective stories. He obeyed. He also appropriated this principle as his own, remarking in an interview that he had tried to make the book a whodunnit in which the clues lead the reader towards the guilty party – which was (and this is no great spoiler) 'contingency'.

He worked hard on improving the manuscript, and kept at it while it was rejected by a series of publishers. Eventually, it found one in Gallimard, which then remained faithful to him to the end. But Gaston Gallimard himself wrote to Sartre suggesting that he think of a better title. *Melancholia* wasn't commercial enough. Sartre suggested alternatives. Perhaps *Factum on Contingency*? (That had been the title of his earliest notes for the book in 1932.) Or how about *Essay on the Loneliness of the Mind*? When Gallimard recoiled from these, Sartre tried a new tack: *The Extraordinary Adventures of Antoine Roquentin*, to be combined with a blurb laboriously explaining the joke that there *are* no adventures.

In the end, Gallimard himself suggested the simple and startling *Nausea*. The book came out in April 1938 and was well received by critics, one of whom was Albert Camus. It made Sartre's name.

Meanwhile, Simone de Beauvoir too was beginning to sketch out her own first novel, though it would not be published until 1943: *L'invitée*, translated into English as *She Came to Stay*. She based it on a recent three-way love affair between herself, Sartre and one of her former students, Olga Kosakiewicz. In real life, this was a fraught love triangle that drew in more people until it became a love pentagon and eventually dissolved. By the time it ended, Olga was married to Sartre's former student Jacques-Laurent Bost, Sartre was sleeping with Olga's sister Wanda, and Beauvoir had retired to lick her wounds – and to conduct a long, secret affair with Bost. For the novel, Beauvoir removed a few of the complications, but added a philosophical dimension, as well as a melodramatic finale involving a murder. Sartre also later fictionalised the same events as one of several narrative threads in the first volume of his *Roads of Freedom* sequence.

The differences between their novels show differences in their philosophical and personal interests. Sartre's work was an epic exploration of freedom, in which the love affair takes its place among other threads. Beauvoir's interest was in the power lines of desire, observation, jealousy and control that connect people. She concentrated more on her central characters and excelled at exploring how emotions and experiences find expression through the body, perhaps in illness or in strange physical sensations, as when her protagonist's head feels unusually heavy as she tries to reason herself into feeling something she doesn't feel. Beauvoir won praise for these sections from Maurice Merleau-Ponty, who specialised in the phenomenology of embodiment and perception. He opened his 1945 essay 'Metaphysics and the Novel' with a dialogue quoted from *L'invitée*, in which the (Sartre-like) character Pierre tells the (Beauvoir-like) protagonist Françoise that he is amazed at the way a metaphysical situation can touch her in a 'concrete' way:

'But the situation is concrete,' replies Françoise, 'the whole meaning of my life is at stake.'

'I'm not saying it isn't,' says Pierre. 'Just the same, this ability of yours to put body and soul into living an idea is exceptional.'

This remark could apply to Beauvoir herself. Sartre bodied forth ideas in a fleshy way in *Nausea*, but never as plausibly as Beauvoir did, perhaps because she felt them more deeply. She had a kind of genius for being amazed by the world and by herself; all her life she remained a virtuoso *marveller* at things. As she said in her memoirs, this was the origin of fiction-writing: it began at those times when 'reality should no longer be taken for granted'.

Sartre envied her this quality. He tried to work himself up into the same state, looking at a table and repeating, 'It's a table, it's a table' until, he said, 'a shy thrill appeared that I'd christen joy'. But he had to force himself. It did not wash over him as it did Beauvoir. Sartre considered her talent for amazement at once the most 'authentic' kind of philosophy and a form of 'philosophical poverty', meaning perhaps that it did not lead anywhere and was insufficiently developed and conceptualised. He added, in a phrase that reflects his Heidegger-reading at the time, 'it's the moment at which the question transforms the questioner'.

Of all the things Beauvoir wondered at, one thing amazed her more than any other: the immensity of her own ignorance. She loved to conclude, after early debates with Sartre, 'I'm no longer sure *what* I think, nor whether I can be said to think at all.' She apparently sought out men who were brilliant enough to make her feel at a loss in this way – and there were few to be found.

Before Sartre, her foil in this exercise had been her friend Maurice Merleau-Ponty. They met in 1927, when they were both nineteen: she was a student at the Sorbonne, and Merleau-Ponty was at the École normale supérieure, where Sartre also studied. Beauvoir beat Merleau-Ponty in the shared examinations in general philosophy that year: he came third and she came second. They were both beaten by another woman: Simone Weil. Merleau-Ponty befriended

Beauvoir after this because, according to her account, he was keen
to meet the woman who had bested him. (Apparently he was less
keen on the rather formidable Simone Weil – and Weil herself
would prove unenthusiastic about Beauvoir, rebuffing her attempts
at friendliness.)

Weil's and Beauvoir's results were extraordinary considering that
they had not come through the elite École normale supérieure
system: it was not open to girls when Beauvoir began her tertiary
education in 1925. It had opened to female students for just one year,
in 1910, before closing the doors in 1911 and keeping them shut until
1927 – too late for her. Instead, she attended a series of girls' schools
which were not bad, but which had less exalted expectations. This
was just one of the many ways in which a woman's situation differed
from a man's in early stages of life; Beauvoir would explore such
contrasts in detail in her 1949 book *The Second Sex*. Meanwhile, all
she could do was study furiously, seek outlets in friendship, and rage
against the limitations of her existence – which she blamed on the
moral codes of her bourgeois upbringing. She was not the only one
to feel this way. Sartre, also a child of the bourgeoisie, rebelled just
as radically against it. Merleau-Ponty came from a similar background, but responded to it differently. He could enjoy himself quite
happily in the bourgeois milieu, while pursuing his independent life
elsewhere.

For Simone de Beauvoir, independence had come only after a battle.
Born in Paris on 9 January 1908, she grew up mostly in the city, but
in a social environment that felt provincial, since it hedged her
around with standard notions of femininity and gentility. Her
mother, Françoise de Beauvoir, enforced these principles; her father
was more relaxed. Simone's rebellion started in childhood, became
more intense in her teens, and still seemed to be going in adult-
hood. Her lifelong dedication to work, her love of travelling, her
decision not to have children, and her unconventional choice of
partner all spoke of total dedication to freedom. She presented her
life in those terms in the first volume of her autobiography, *Memoirs*

of a Dutiful Daughter, and reflected further on her bourgeois background later in her memoir of her mother's last illness, *A Very Easy Death*.

It was while she was first beginning to strike out alone as a student that she met Merleau-Ponty through a friend. She noted her impressions in her journal, calling him 'Merloponti'. He was attractive both in personality and in looks, she said, though she feared he was a little too vain about the latter. In her autobiography (where she gives him the pseudonym 'Pradelle'), she described his 'limpid, rather beautiful face, with thick, dark lashes, and the gay, frank laugh of a schoolboy'. She liked him at once, but that was not surprising, she added. *Everyone* always liked Merleau-Ponty as soon as they met him. Even her mother liked him.

Merleau-Ponty was just over two months younger than Beauvoir, born on 14 March 1908, and much more at ease with himself. He sailed through social situations with a relaxed self-possession which (as he himself thought) was probably the result of having had a very happy childhood. He had felt so loved and encouraged as a child, he said, never having to work hard for approval, that his disposition remained cheerful for life. He could be irritable sometimes, but he was, as he said in a radio interview in 1959, almost always at peace with himself. This makes him about the only person in this entire story who felt that way; a valuable gift. Sartre would later write, apropos Flaubert's lack of love in childhood, that when love 'is present, the dough of the spirits rises, when absent, it sinks'. Merleau-Ponty's childhood was always well buoyed up. Yet it cannot have all been as easy as he liked to imply, since he lost his father in 1913 to liver disease, so that he, his brother and his sister grew up with their mother alone. Where Beauvoir had a strained relationship with her mother, Merleau-Ponty remained utterly devoted to his for as long as she lived.

Everyone who knew Merleau-Ponty felt the glow of well-being emanating from him. Simone de Beauvoir was warmed by it at first. She had been waiting for someone to admire, and it seemed he would do. She briefly considered him as boyfriend material. But his relaxed attitude was disturbing to someone of her more combative disposition. She wrote in her notebook that his big fault was that 'he is not violent, and the kingdom of God is for violent people'. He insisted on being nice to everyone. 'I feel myself to be so different!' she cried. She was a creature of strong judgements, while he looked for multiple sides to any situation. He considered people a mixture of qualities, and liked to give them the benefit of the doubt, whereas in youth she saw humanity as consisting of 'a small band of the chosen in a great mass of people unworthy of consideration'.

What really irked Beauvoir was that Merleau-Ponty seemed 'perfectly adapted to his class and its way of life, and accepted bourgeois society with an open heart'. She would sometimes rant to him about the stupidities and cruelties of bourgeois morality, but he would calmly disagree. He 'got on perfectly well with his mother and sister and did not share my horror of family life', she wrote. 'He was not averse to parties and sometimes went dancing: why not? he asked me with an innocent air which disarmed me.'

In their first summer after becoming friends, they were much thrown on each other's company, as other students were away from Paris for the holidays. They went for walks, first in the gardens of the

École normale supérieure – an 'awe-inspiring place' for Beauvoir – and later in the Luxembourg Gardens, where they would sit 'beside the statue of some queen or other' and talk philosophy. Notwithstanding the fact that she had overtaken him in the exams, she found it natural to take on the role of philosophical novice beside him. In fact, she sometimes won their debates, almost by accident, but more often she was left happily exclaiming, 'I know nothing, nothing. I not only have no answer to give, but I haven't even found a satisfactory way of propounding the questions.'

She appreciated his virtues: 'I knew no one else from whom I could have learnt the art of gaiety. He bore so lightly the weight of the whole world that it ceased to weigh upon me too; in the Luxembourg Gardens, the blue of the morning sky, the green lawns and the sun all shone as they used to in my happiest days, when it was always fine weather.' But one day, after walking around the lake in the Bois de Boulogne with him, watching swans and boats, she exclaimed to herself, 'Oh, how untormented he was! His tranquillity offended me.' It was clear by now that he would never make a suitable lover. He was better as a brother figure; she only had a sister, so the role was vacant and perfectly suited to him.

He had a different effect on her best friend, Elisabeth Le Coin or Lacoin (called 'ZaZa' in Beauvoir's memoirs). Elisabeth too was unnerved by Merleau-Ponty's 'invulnerable' quality and his lack of anguish, but she fell for him passionately. Far from being invulnerable, she was prone to emotional extremes and wild enthusiasms, which Beauvoir had found intoxicating during their girlhood friendship. Elisabeth now hoped to marry Merleau-Ponty, and he seemed keen too – until he suddenly broke off the relationship. Only later did Beauvoir learn why. Elisabeth's mother, thinking Merleau-Ponty unsuitable for her daughter, had warned him to back off or else she would reveal an alleged secret about *his* mother: that she had been unfaithful, and that at least one of her children was not her husband's. To prevent a scandal engulfing both his mother and his sister, who was about to get married, Merleau-Ponty bowed out.

Beauvoir was even more disgusted after she learned the truth. How typical of the filthy bourgeoisie! Elisabeth's mother had shown a classic middle-class combination of moralism, cruelty and cowardice. Moreover, Beauvoir considered that the result literally proved lethal. Elisabeth had been very upset, and in the middle of the emotional crisis she caught a serious illness, probably encephalitis. She died of it, aged just twenty-one.

There was no causal connection between the two disasters, but Beauvoir always thought bourgeois hypocrisy had killed her friend. She forgave Merleau-Ponty his role in what had happened. Yet she never ceased to feel that he was too cosy and respected traditional values too much, and that this was a fault in him – a fault she swore never to allow into her own life.

A little after this, Beauvoir's 'violent' and opinionated side got all the satisfaction it craved when she met Jean-Paul Sartre.

Sartre too had a bourgeois childhood, born an adored only child two and a half years before Beauvoir, on 21 June 1905. Like Merleau-Ponty, he grew up without a father. Jean-Baptiste Sartre, a naval officer, died of tuberculosis when the infant Jean-Paul was just a year old. Throughout his early childhood, Sartre was doted on by his mother, Anne-Marie Sartre, and her parents, with whom they lived. Everyone loved his girlish curly hair and his delicate beauty. But he developed eye problems after an infection at the age of three. Under the bouncing curls, the results were barely noticeable – until his grandfather took him for a brutal haircut one day, and his damaged eye emerged into the light, together with his fishy lips and other disconcerting features. Sartre describes all this with high irony in his memoir *Words*, which recounts his early years. His amused tone becomes more intensely jaunty than ever when he discusses his looks, but he was genuinely hurt by the change in people's reactions to him. He remained obsessed with the topic of his ugliness – which he always referred to with this blunt term. It made him shy away from people for a while, but then he decided that he would not let it spoil his life. He would not sacrifice his freedom to it.

His mother married again, to a man Sartre didn't like, and they moved to La Rochelle, where he was bullied by bigger and rougher boys. It was a great crisis in his childhood: later he said that being a loner in La Rochelle had taught him all he ever needed to know 'about contingency, violence, the way things are'. Again, however, he would not be cowed. He got through it, and he blossomed again when the family moved to Paris and he was sent to a succession of good schools, culminating in the École normale supérieure. From being a pariah, he became the leader of the most fashionable, anarchic and formidable clique in the school. He always remained a sociable, alpha-type person, riddled with hang-ups, yet never hesitant about dominating a circle.

Sartre's group of iconoclasts and provocateurs, revolving around him and his best friend Paul Nizan, spent their days sitting in cafés, loudly slaughtering the sacred cows of philosophy, literature and bourgeois behaviour to anyone who ventured into their ambit. They attacked any topic that suggested delicate sensibilities, the 'inner life' or the soul; they created a stir by refusing to sit school examinations in religious knowledge, and they scandalised everyone by talking of human beings as bundles of fleshly urges rather than as noble souls. Beneath their brashness, they had the easy confidence of the impeccably educated.

It was during this era, in 1929, that Beauvoir met the Sartre clique through a friend named Maheu. She found them exciting and intimidating. They laughed at her because she took her studies so seriously – as of course she did, since being at the Sorbonne represented everything she had worked so hard to achieve. Education meant freedom and self-determination to her, whereas the boys took it for granted. But the group accepted her, and she and Sartre became friends. He and the others called her Castor, the Beaver, supposedly as a reference to her constant busy-ness, but also as a pun on her surname and the similar English word. Sartre had none of the offputting tranquillity of Merleau-Ponty: he was a loud-mouthed and uncompromising extremist. He was not demoted to being a brother; he became her lover, and soon they were even more important to each other than that. Sartre came to regard Beauvoir as his ally, his favourite conversationalist, the first and best reader of anything he wrote. He gave her the role that Raymond Aron had played in his earlier school days: that of the symphilosopher with whom he talked out all his ideas.

They considered marrying, but neither wanted a bourgeois marriage – or children, since Beauvoir was determined not to replay her own fraught relationship with her mother. Sitting on a stone bench in the Tuileries one evening, she and Sartre agreed a contract. They would be a couple for two years, after which they would decide whether to extend the contract, separate, or change their relationship in some way. Beauvoir admitted in her memoirs that this temporary arrangement frightened her at first. Her account of the conversation is filled with the imprinted details that come from strong emotion:

There was a kind of balustrade which served as a back-rest, a little way out from the wall; and in the cagelike space behind it a cat was miaowing. The poor thing was too big to get out; how

had it ever got in? A woman came and fed the cat some meat.
And Sartre said, 'Let's sign a two-year lease.'

Confinement, entrapment, distress, the tossing of charitable scraps:
this is terrifying imagery for a story supposedly about freedom. It
sounds like an ominous dream sequence. Did it really happen this
way, or did she flesh out the memory with symbolic detail?

In any case, the panic subsided, and the arrangement worked well.
They survived the two years, and became partners in a long-term but
non-exclusive relationship which lasted all their lives. It was perhaps
made easier by the fact that, after the late 1930s, it was no longer a
sexual one. (She wrote to her lover Nelson Algren, 'We dropped it
after about eight or ten years rather unsuccessful in this way.') They
also agreed two long-term conditions. One was that they must tell
each other everything about their other sexual involvements: there
must be honesty. They only partly kept to this. The other was that
their own relationship must remain primary: in their language, it
would be 'necessary' while other relationships could only be 'contingent'. They did stick to this, although it drove away some long-term
lovers who grew tired of being considered accidents. But that was the
deal, and everyone who became involved knew it from the start.

It has become common to express concern for Beauvoir's well-being
in this relationship, as if she (typical woman!) had allowed herself to
be bullied into something she did not want. The Tuileries scene does
suggest it might not have been her first choice when she was young,
and she suffered episodes of panic and jealousy at times. But a conventional bourgeois marriage would hardly have provided protection
against such feelings either.

I suspect that the relationship gave her exactly what she needed.
Had she and Sartre attempted a normal marriage, they would either
have split up or it would have ended in sexual frustration. Instead,
she had a great sex life – better than Sartre's, apparently, thanks to
his squeamishness. Beauvoir's memoirs attest to moods of 'languorous
excitement' and 'feelings of quite shattering intensity' in her youth,
and her later relationships were physically fulfilling. Sartre, if we

can judge by the vivid descriptions in his books, found sex a night-marish process of struggling not to drown in slime and gloop. (Before we mock him too much for this, let's remember that we know it only because he revealed it so candidly. Well, okay, let's mock him a little bit.)

The physical lusciousness of life was never a threat to Beauvoir: she could not get enough of it. As a child, she wanted to consume everything she saw. She would gaze greedily into the windows of sweet shops – 'the luminous sparkle of candied fruits, the cloudy lustre of jellies, the kaleidoscopic inflorescence of acidulated fruit-drops – green, red, orange, violet – I coveted the colours themselves as much as the pleasures they promised me'. She wished the whole universe could be edible, so it could be eaten as Hansel and Gretel ate from the gingerbread house. Even as an adult, she wrote, 'I wanted to crunch flowering almond trees, and take bites out of the rainbow nougat of the sunset.' Travelling to New York in 1947, she felt an urge to eat the neon signs, brightly arrayed against the night sky.

Her appetite extended to collecting things, including many gifts and souvenirs from her travels. When she finally moved from hotel rooms to a proper apartment in 1955, it quickly filled up with 'jackets and skirts from Guatemala, blouses from Mexico . . . ostrich eggs from the Sahara, lead tom-toms, some drums that Sartre had brought back from Haiti, glass swords and Venetian mirrors that he had bought in the rue Bonaparte, a plaster cast of his hands, Giacometti's lamps'. Her diary-keeping and memoir-writing also reflected an urge to acquire and relish everything that came into her grasp.

She explored the world with the same passion, travelling and walking fanatically. While living alone in Marseilles as a young school-teacher, she would pack buns and bananas on her days off, put on a dress and a pair of espadrilles, and set out at dawn to explore the mountainous countryside. Once, carrying bread, a candle and a water bottle full of red wine, she ascended Mont Mézenc and spent the night in a flint hut at the summit. She woke to find herself looking down on a sea of cloud, and ran down the path on rocks which, when the sun came out, heated up and burned her feet through the soles of her inappropriate shoes. On another walk, she got stuck in a gorge and barely managed to scramble out. Later, in the Alps in 1936, she fell down a sheer rock-face while out alone, but escaped with a few scratches.

Sartre was different. He would be persuaded to join her on walks, but didn't enjoy the sensation of fatigue. *Being and Nothingness* contains a marvellous description of slogging up a hill behind an unnamed companion, whom one pictures as Beauvoir (although the scene has something in common with Petrarch's famous ascent of Mont Ventoux). While this companion seems to be having fun, Sartre experiences the effort as a nuisance, something that intrudes on his freedom. He gives in quickly, throws down his knapsack and collapses at the roadside. The other person is tired too, but finds it blissful to forge on, feeling the glow of sunburn on the back of the neck and relishing the way the roughness of the path is revealed afresh by each trudging step. The whole landscape presents itself differently to the two of them.

Sartre preferred skiing, and that experience also found its way into *Being and Nothingness*. Walking over a snowfield is hard work, he pointed out, but skiing over it is a delight. The snow itself changes underneath you, phenomenologically speaking; instead of presenting itself as viscous and clinging, it becomes hard and smooth. It bears you up, and you slide flowingly over it, as easily as the notes of *Nausea*'s jazz song. He added that he was curious about waterskiing, a new invention which he had heard of but not tried. Even on snow, you left a line of ski-marks behind you; in water, you left nothing. That was the purest pleasure Sartre could imagine.

His dream was to pass through the world unencumbered. The possessions that delighted Beauvoir horrified Sartre. He too liked travelling, but he kept nothing from his trips. He gave away books after reading them. The only things he always kept by him were his pipe and his pen, and even these were not for getting attached to. He lost them constantly, he wrote: 'they're exiles in my hands'.

With people, he was generous to the point of obsession. He gave money away as fast as it came, in order to get it away from him, like a hand grenade. If he did spend it himself, he preferred not to use it on objects but 'on an *evening out*: going to some dancehall, spending big, going everywhere by taxi, etc. etc. – and in short, nothing must remain in place of the money but a memory, sometimes *less* than a memory'. His tips to waiters were legendary, as he took out the large wad of cash he carried everywhere and peeled off bills. He was equally generous with his writing, flinging out essays or talks or forewords for anyone who asked. Even words were not for hanging on to and eking out cautiously. Beauvoir was generous too, but her openness was two-way: she liked to gather as well as to dispense. Perhaps, in their divergent styles, one can see the two sides of phenomenological existentialism: the part that observes, collects and pores over phenomena, and the part that discards accumulated preconceptions in the Husserlian *epoché*, so as to be free.

With all these differences, they had a mutual understanding that no outsider seemed able to threaten. When Beauvoir's biographer Deirdre Bair was talking to her subject's friends, one of them, Colette Audry, summed it up by saying, 'Theirs was a new kind of relationship, and I had never seen anything like it. I cannot describe what it was like to be present when those two were together. It was so intense that sometimes it made others who saw it sad not to have it.'

It was also an extremely long relationship, lasting from 1929 to Sartre's death in 1980. For fifty years, it was a philosophical demonstration of existentialism in practice, defined by the two principles of freedom and companionship. Lest this sound too earnest, their shared memories, observations and jokes bound them together just as in any long marriage. A typical joke began soon after they met: visiting the zoo, they watched an enormously fat and tragic-looking sea elephant which sighed and raised its eyes to heaven as if in supplication while the keeper stuffed its mouth with fish. From then on, every time Sartre looked glum, Beauvoir would remind him of the sea elephant. He would roll up his eyes and heave comical sighs, and they would both feel better.

In later years, Sartre became more remote as his work took him away from their private duo, but he remained Beauvoir's constant reference point; someone she could lose herself in when she needed to. She knew she had a tendency to do this: it had happened with Elisabeth Le Coin in her schooldays, and she had tried it with Merleau-Ponty but been frustrated when his smiling and ironical manner deflected her. With Sartre, she could easily play at losing herself, without *actually* losing her real-world freedom as a woman or as a writer.

That was the most important element: it was a writers' relationship. Both Beauvoir and Sartre were compulsive communicators. They kept diaries, they wrote letters; they told each other every detail of their days. It is overwhelming even to think about the quantity of written and spoken words that flowed between them for half of the twentieth century. Sartre was always the first to read Beauvoir's work, the person whose criticism she trusted and who pushed her to write more. If he caught her being lazy, he would berate her: 'But Castor, why have you stopped thinking, why aren't you working? I thought you wanted to write? You don't want to become a housewife, do you?'

As the emotional dramas came and went, work remained the constant. Work! Work in cafés, work while travelling, work at home. Any time they were in the same city, they worked together, whatever else was going on in their lives. After Sartre moved into a proper apartment (with his mother) in 1946, at 42 rue Bonaparte, Beauvoir met him there every day so they could spend the morning or afternoon sitting side by side, at two desks, working. In a 1967 documentary made for Canadian TV, you can see them there, both smoking furiously, with no sound but the scratching of a pen. Beauvoir is writing in an exercise book, Sartre is reading over a manuscript. I find myself imagining this as a kind of endlessly looped video memorial. Perhaps it could have been installed on their shared grave in the Montparnasse cemetery. It's spooky to imagine them writing away there, all night, when the cemetery is closed, and all day as the visitors pass – but it would suit them better than a white grave, or any still image.

I Don't Want to Eat my Manuscripts

In which there occur a crisis, two heroic rescues, and the outbreak of war.

As titles go, that of Husserl's last unfinished work *The Crisis of the European Sciences and Transcendental Phenomenology* is not as arresting as *Nausea*. But the word at its head, 'crisis', perfectly sums up mid-1930s Europe. Mussolini's Fascists had been in power in Italy for over a decade, since 1922. In the Soviet Union, following Lenin's death in 1924, Stalin had manoeuvred himself into a position of control by 1929 and spent the 1930s starving, torturing, imprisoning and executing people in vast numbers. Hitler, having consolidated his first election victories in 1933, made his expansionist ambitions increasingly clear. In 1936, civil war broke out in Spain between the left-wing Republicans and the fascist Nationalists led by General Franco. Everything seemed to be conspiring to divide Europeans and lead them into another war. This was a prospect greatly feared, especially in France, where the First World War had killed around 1.4 million French soldiers in the trenches alone. The country itself was literally scarred by war, since so much of it had been fought on French soil, and no one wanted to see it happen again.

France did have some far-right organisations – Action française and the newer, more radical Croix-de-Feu or Iron Cross movement – but the general mood of pacifism kept their influence limited. The novelist Roger Martin du Gard voiced a common feeling when he wrote to a friend in September 1936, 'Anything rather than war! Anything! . . . Even Fascism in Spain! And don't push me, for I would say: yes . . . and "even Fascism in France!"' Beauvoir felt similarly, and said to

Sartre, 'Surely France at war would be worse than France under the Nazis?' But Sartre, who had seen the Nazis at close hand, disagreed. As usual, his imagination supplied lurid details: 'I have no wish to be made to eat my manuscripts. I don't want Nizan to have his eyes gouged out with teaspoons.'

By 1938, few dared hope for a reprieve. Hitler annexed Austria that March. In September he turned his attention to the strongly German Sudetenland area of Czechoslovakia, which included Husserl's homeland of Moravia. The British and French leaders Neville Chamberlain and Édouard Daladier agreed to his initial demands, and the Czechs had little choice but to accept. Hitler took this as encouragement to go further, so on 22 September he demanded the right to a full military occupation that would effectively open the doors to the rest of Czechoslovakia. There followed what became known as the Munich Crisis: a week during which people listened to their radios and read newspapers, fearing the announcement of war literally at any hour.

For a young existentialist of the individualist kind, war was the ultimate affront. It threatened to sweep away all those personal thoughts and concerns like toys from a table. As the English surrealist poet David Gascoyne, then living in Paris in a delicate state of mind, wrote in his journal during that week, 'What is so detestable about war is that it reduces the individual to complete insignificance.' Listening to his radio, Gascoyne tried to visualise bombers flying through the sky, and buildings falling. Similar visions of impending disaster haunt George Orwell's novel *Coming Up for Air,* published the following year: the advertising executive George Bowling walks down his suburban street imagining houses being smashed to the ground by bombs. Everything familiar seems about to disappear; Bowling fears that afterwards there will be only endless tyranny.

Sartre would try to capture the mood of the crisis in *The Reprieve,* the second volume of his *Roads of Freedom* sequence – not published until 1945, but set during the crucial week of 23–30 September 1938. Each of his characters struggles to adjust to the idea that their future may be curtailed and that nothing will be the same again. Sartre slips from one person's thoughts to another's, in a stream-of-consciousness method borrowed from the novels of John Dos Passos and Virginia Woolf. The young character Boris (based on Sartre's former student Jacques-Laurent Bost) calculates how long he is likely to survive in the army when war begins, and thus how many omelettes he can expect to eat before dying. In a crucial moment, as everyone gathers to hear Hitler speak on the radio, Sartre draws back from the scene to show us all of France, then all of Germany, and all of Europe. 'A hundred million free consciousnesses, each aware of walls, the glowing stump of a cigar, familiar faces, and each constructing its destiny on its own responsibility.'

Not all the book's experiments work, but Sartre captures the weird quality of a week in which millions of people were trying to get used to a different way of thinking about their lives – their projects or concerns, as Heidegger would have said. The book also reveals the first signs of a shift in Sartre's thought. In coming years, he would become ever more interested in the way human beings can be swept up by large-scale historical forces, while still each remaining free and individual.

As for Sartre personally, he found the answer for his anxieties of 1938 in, of all things, reading Heidegger. He embarked on the foothills of *Being and Time*, though he did not ascend the steeper slopes until two years later. Looking back from that later point, he recalled this as a year in which he craved 'a philosophy that was not just a contemplation but a wisdom, a heroism, a holiness'. He compared it to the period in ancient Greece, after the death of Alexander the Great, when Athenians turned away from the calm reasonings of Aristotelian science towards the more personal and 'more brutal' thinking of the Stoics and Epicureans – philosophers 'who taught them to live'.

In Freiburg, Husserl was no longer around to witness the events of that autumn, but his widow Malvine was still living in their fine suburban house, guarding his library and his huge *Nachlass* of manuscripts, papers and unpublished works. Living alone, seventy-eight years old, officially classed as Jewish despite her Protestant faith, she was vulnerable, but for the moment she kept danger away mainly by the sheer force of her defiant personality.

Earlier that decade, when her husband was still alive but after the Nazi takeover, they had discussed moving his documents to Prague, where it seemed they might be safer. A former student of Husserl, the Czech phenomenologist Jan Patočka, was willing to help arrange this. It did not happen, which was fortunate as the papers would not have been safe at all.

Prague had grown into something of a centre for phenomenology through the early twentieth century, partly because of Tomáš Masaryk – Czechoslovakia's president, and the friend who had persuaded Husserl to study with Franz Brentano. He died in 1937, and was spared seeing the disaster that befell his country, but in the meantime he had done much to encourage the development of phenomenology and had helped other former Brentano students to collect their teacher's papers in a Prague-based archive. In 1938, with the threat of a German invasion, Brentano's archives were in danger. Phenomenologists could only be relieved that the Husserl collection was not there with them.

But Freiburg was not safe either. If war came, the city might be among the first to see conflict, being near the French border. Already, Malvine Husserl was at the mercy of the Nazis: if they decided to storm the house she could not do much to protect its contents.

The situation of Husserl's *Nachlass*, and of his widow, attracted the attention of a Belgian philosopher and Franciscan monk named Herman Van Breda. He put together a proposal urging Louvain University's Institut Supérieur de Philosophie to support transcription of key Freiburg papers – work that could only be done by former assistants able to read Husserl's shorthand. With Edith Stein having become a Carmelite nun and Heidegger having gone his own way, this mainly meant two men who had been working with Husserl in recent years: Eugen Fink, originally from nearby Konstanz but now based in Freiburg, and Ludwig Landgrebe, currently in Prague.

Van Breda initially suggested financing the project *in situ* in Freiburg, but with the prospect of war this looked less advisable. He noted that

Malvine Husserl was determined to carry on 'as if the Nazi regime did not exist and without showing that she was its victim', which was admirable, but it might not be good for the papers. On 29 August 1938, as the Czech crisis began brewing, Van Breda travelled to Freiburg and met her and Eugen Fink; together they showed him the collection. He marvelled at the sheer visual impact of it: rows of folders containing around 40,000 pages of writings in Husserl's shorthand, plus another 10,000 typed or handwritten pages transcribed by his assistants, and in the library some 2,700 volumes collected over nearly sixty years and countless article offprints, many covered with Husserl's pencil notes.

Van Breda persuaded Malvine Husserl that something must be done. Returning to Louvain, he had another persuasion job to do: he talked his colleagues into agreeing to transfer and house the collection there, rather than funding a project remotely. This done, he went back to Freiburg, where Ludwig Landgrebe had now also arrived, leaving an unnerving situation in Prague. It was mid-September: it seemed that war might start in weeks or even days.

The immediate question was *how* to move the stuff. The manuscripts were more portable than the books, and more of a priority. But it certainly was not safe to drive for the border with thousands of sheets of paper, all written in what looked like an unreadable secret code.

A better idea was to take them to a Belgian embassy office and thence out of the country in a diplomatic pouch, guaranteeing immunity from interference. But the nearest office with an immunity agreement was in Berlin, a long way off in the wrong direction. Van Breda asked monks at a Franciscan monastery near Freiburg if they could hide the manuscripts or help smuggle them out, but they were reluctant. Then a Benedictine nun stepped in: Sister Adelgundis Jägerschmidt, from a nearby Lioba Sisters convent. She was another former student of phenomenology who had visited Husserl regularly in his last illness, in defiance of the rules against associating with Jews. She now volunteered to take the manuscripts herself to a small house owned by her fellow sisters in Konstanz, near the Swiss border. From there, she said, the nuns could carry the manuscripts bit by bit, in small packages, across to Switzerland.

It was a nerve-racking plan. If war broke out during the operation, the manuscripts could end up split between the two locations with the borders closed; some might be lost in the middle. The danger to the nuns was also obvious. It seemed the best option available, however, so on 19 September the heroic Sister Adelgundis loaded three heavy suitcases with 40,000 manuscript pages, and set off by train to Konstanz.

Unfortunately, although the sisters were willing to house the manuscripts temporarily, they considered smuggling them across the border too risky. Adelgundis left the suitcases with them and returned to give Van Breda the bad news.

He reverted to the idea of taking them to the Belgian embassy in Berlin. That now meant detouring via Konstanz to get them, and this time he went himself. So, on 22 September – the day Chamberlain

met Hitler and learned that Hitler had upped his demands on Czech
territory – Van Breda travelled to the convent. He collected the suitcases and continued to Berlin on a night train. One can imagine the
tension: war looming, three heavy suitcases packed with what looked
like coded secrets, a train rattling through a dark night. Arriving in
the city on the morning of Friday 23 September, Van Breda entrusted
the suitcases to a Franciscan monastery outside the centre, then went
to the embassy – to learn that the ambassador was away and no decisions could be taken. The junior officials did agree, however, to look
after the cases in the meantime.

So it was back to the Franciscans, and back to the embassy again
with the suitcases. At last, on Saturday 24 September, Van Breda saw
them locked away in the embassy safe. He travelled back to Freiburg,
then out of Germany to Louvain. He kept with him just a handful
of texts, so that the transcription project could start. To his relief, the
border guards waved him through without looking at the incomprehensible handwriting.

A few days later, the European crisis was resolved – temporarily. Benito
Mussolini brokered a meeting in Munich on 29 September, attended
by Hitler, Daladier and Chamberlain. No one from Czechoslovakia
was in the room when, in the early hours of 30 September, Daladier
and Chamberlain caved in to Hitler's increased demands. The next
day, German forces entered the Sudetenland.

Chamberlain flew back to Britain triumphant; Daladier flew back to
France ashamed and full of dread. Greeted by a cheering crowd as he
got off the plane, he reportedly muttered, *'Les cons!'* – the idiots! – at
least that was the story Sartre seems to have heard. Once the initial
relief passed, many in both France and Britain doubted that the agreement could last. Sartre and Merleau-Ponty were pessimistic; Beauvoir
preferred to hope that peace might prevail. The three of them debated
the matter at length.

As a side effect, the peace deal reduced the urgency about getting
Husserl's papers out of Germany. It was not until November 1938 that
the bulk of them were transported from Berlin to Louvain. When

they arrived, they were installed in the university library, which proudly organised a display. No one could know that in two years' time the German army would invade Belgium and the documents would be in danger again.

That November, Van Breda returned to Freiburg. Malvine Husserl had now decided to seek a visa so as to join her son and daughter in the US, but this took a long time, so in the meantime Van Breda arranged for her to move to Belgium. She arrived in Louvain in June 1939, joining Fink and Landgrebe, who had moved there in the spring and were getting to work. With her came a huge cargo: a container of her furniture, the full Husserl library in sixty boxes, her husband's ashes in an urn, and a portrait of him, which Franz Brentano and his wife Ida von Lieben had jointly painted as an engagement present before the Husserls' marriage.

Brentano's papers – still stored in an archive office in Prague – had meanwhile been through their own adventure. When Hitler moved on from the Sudetenland to occupy the rest of Czechoslovakia in March 1939, a group of archivists and scholars gathered most of them and spirited them out of the country on the very last civilian plane to leave. The papers ended up in the Houghton Library at Harvard University, and are still there today. The few files left behind were defenestrated through the office window by German soldiers, and mostly lost.

The Husserl archives survived the war and are mostly still in Louvain, with his library. They have kept researchers busy for over seventy-five years, and have generated a collected edition under the title *Husserliana*. So far, this comprises forty-two volumes of collected works, nine volumes of extra 'materials', thirty-four volumes of miscellaneous documents and correspondence, and thirteen volumes of official English translations.

One of the first to travel to Louvain to see the archive was Maurice Merleau-Ponty, who already knew Husserl's earlier work well, and had read about the unpublished manuscripts in an article in the *Revue internationale de philosophie*. In March 1939, he wrote to arrange a visit to Father Van Breda so as to pursue his special interest in the phenomenology of perception. Van Breda welcomed him, and Merleau-Ponty spent a blissful first week of April in Louvain, absorbed in the unedited and unpublished sections which Husserl had intended to add to *Ideas* and to *The Crisis of the European Sciences and Transcendental Phenomenology*.

These late works of Husserl's are different in spirit from the earlier ones. To Merleau-Ponty, they suggested that Husserl had begun moving away from his inward, idealist interpretation of phenomenology in his last years, towards a less isolated picture of how one exists in a world alongside other people and immersed in sensory experience. Merleau-Ponty even wondered whether Husserl had absorbed some of this from Heidegger – an interpretation with which not everyone agrees. Other influences might be seen too: from sociology, and perhaps from Jakob von Uexküll's studies of how different species experience their 'environment' or *Umwelt*. Whatever the source, Husserl's new thinking included reflections on what he called the *Lebenswelt*, or 'life-world' – that barely noticed social, historical and physical context in which all our activities take place, and which we generally take for granted. Even our bodies rarely require conscious attention, yet a sense of *being embodied* is part of almost every experience we have. As I move around or reach out to grasp something, I sense my own limbs and the arrangement of my physical self in the world. I feel my hands and feet from within; I don't have to look in a mirror to see how they are positioned. This is known as 'proprioception' – the perception of self – and it is an important aspect of experience which I tend to notice only when something goes wrong with it. When I encounter others, says Husserl, I also recognise them implicitly as beings who have 'their personal surrounding world, oriented around their living bodies'. Body, life-world, proprioception and social context are all integrated into the texture of worldly being.

One can see why Merleau-Ponty saw signs of Heidegger's philosophy of Being-in-the-world in this new interest of Husserl's. There were other connections too: Husserl's late works show him considering the long processes of culture and history, just as Heidegger did. But here there is a great difference between them. Heidegger's writings on the history of Being are suffused with a longing for some *home* time, a lost age or place to which philosophy should be traced, and from which it should be renewed. Heidegger's dream-home often calls to mind the forested Germanic world of his childhood, with its crafts-manship and silent wisdom. At other times, it evokes archaic Greek culture, which he considered the last period in which humanity had philosophised properly. Heidegger was not alone in being fascinated by Greece; it was a sort of mania among Germans at the time. But other German thinkers often focused on the flowering of philosophy and scholarship in the fourth century BC, the time of Socrates and Plato, whereas Heidegger saw that as the period in which everything had started going wrong. For him, the philosophers who truly connected with Being were pre-Socratics such as Heraclitus, Parmenides and Anaximander. In any case, what Heidegger's writings on Germany and Greece share is the mood of someone yearning to go *back* into the deep forest, into childhood innocence and into the dark waters from which the first swirling chords of thought had stirred. Back – back to a time when societies were simple, profound and poetic.

Husserl did not look for such a simple lost world. When he wrote about history, he was drawn to more sophisticated periods, especially those when cultures were encountering each other through travel, migration, exploration or trade. At such periods, he wrote, people living in one culture or 'home-world' (*Heimwelt*) meet people from an 'alien-world' (*Fremdwelt*). To those others, *theirs* is the home-world and the other is the alien-world. The shock of encounter is mutual, and it wakes each culture up to an amazing discovery: that their world is not beyond question. A travelling Greek discovers that the Greek life-world is just a Greek world, and that there are Indian and African worlds too. In seeing this, members of each culture may come to understand that they are, in general, 'worlded' beings, who should not take anything for granted.

For Husserl, therefore, cross-cultural encounters are generally good, because they stimulate people to self-questioning. He suspected that philosophy started in ancient Greece not, as Heidegger would imagine, because the Greeks had a deep, inward-looking relationship with their Being, but because they were a trading people (albeit sometimes a warlike one) who constantly came across alien-worlds of all kinds.

This difference highlights a deeper contrast of attitude between Husserl and Heidegger in the 1930s. During that decade's events, Heidegger turned increasingly to the archaic, provincial and inward-looking, as prefigured by his article about not going to Berlin. In response to the same events, Husserl turned outwards. He wrote about his life-worlds in a cosmopolitan spirit – and this at a time when 'cosmopolitan' was becoming recast as an insult, often interpreted as code for 'Jewish'. He was isolated in Freiburg, yet he used his last few talks of the 1930s, in Vienna and Prague, to issue a rousing call to the international scholarly community. Seeing the social and intellectual 'crisis' around him, he urged them to work together against the rise of irrationalism and mysticism, and against the cult of the merely local, in order to rescue the Enlightenment spirit of shared reason and free inquiry. He did not expect anyone to return to an innocent belief in rationalism, but he did argue that Europeans must protect reason, for if that was lost, the continent and the wider cultural world would be lost with it.

In his 1933 essay 'On the Ontological Mystery', Gabriel Marcel provided a beautiful image that sums up Husserl's view of what 'alien' encounters and international mingling can do for us. He wrote:

> I know by my own experience how, from a stranger met by chance, there may come an irresistible appeal which overturns the habitual perspectives just as a gust of wind might tumble down the panels of a stage set – what had seemed near becomes infinitely remote and what had seemed distant seems to be close.

A tumbling of stage sets and abrupt readjustment of perspectives characterise many of the surprise encounters seen so far in this book: Heidegger's boyhood discovery of Brentano, Levinas's discovery of Husserl in Strasbourg, Sartre's discovery of Husserl (and Levinas) via Raymond Aron at the Bec-de-Gaz – with more to come. Merleau-

Ponty's 1939 discovery of Husserl's late work was among the most fruitful of these moments of discovery. Largely out of that single week of reading in Louvain, he would develop his own own subtle and rich philosophy of human embodiment and social experience. His work, in turn, would influence generations of scientists and thinkers to this day, linking them to Husserl.

Husserl had perfectly understood the value to posterity of his unpublished works, unfinished, chaotic and barely legible though they were. He wrote to a friend in 1931, 'the largest and, as I actually believe, most important part of my life's work still lies in my manuscripts, scarcely manageable because of their volume'. The *Nachlass* was almost a life form in itself: the biographer Rüdiger Safranski has compared it to the giant conscious sea in Stanislaw Lem's science-fiction novel *Solaris*. The comparison holds up well, since Lem's sea communicates by evoking ideas and images in the minds of humans who come close to it. Husserl's archive exerted its influence in much the same way.

The whole hoard would have been lost without the heroism and energy of Father Van Breda. It would never have existed at all had Husserl not persisted in refining and developing his ideas long after many thought he had simply retired and gone into hiding. Moreover, none of it would have survived without a bit of sheer luck: a reminder of the role contingency plays in even the most well-managed human affairs.

Merleau-Ponty's visit to Louvain took place during the last few months of peace, in 1939. This was the year, as Beauvoir later described it, when history would take hold of them all and never again let them go.

Beauvoir and Sartre spent that August on holiday in a villa in Juan-les-Pins, with Paul Nizan and Jacques-Laurent Bost. They watched the papers and listened to the radio, hearing with fear and disgust of the Nazi–Soviet pact on 23 August, which meant that the Soviet Union would increase their own power and put up no opposition should Germany advance. This came as a particular blow for anyone who had been supporting Soviet Communism as the great counterweight to Nazism, as Nizan certainly had, and to some extent Sartre and Beauvoir too. If the Soviets would not stand up to the Nazis, who would? Once again, war seemed likely to start at any moment.

As they sunned themselves at the villa, one subject again dominated the friends' conversations. 'Was it preferable to come back from the front blinded, or with your face bashed in? Without arms, or without legs? Would Paris be bombed? Would they use poison gas?' Similar debates went on in another villa in southern France, where the Hungarian writer Arthur Koestler was staying with his friend Ettore Corniglion; the latter remarked that the shifts of emotion during that August reminded him of how his grandmother 'used to cure his chilblains by making him put his feet alternately in a bucket of cold and in a bucket of hot water'.

Sartre knew that he would not be posted to the front because of his eye problems. As a young man he had done his standard military service in a weather station, which meant he would be deployed in similar work now – the same thing Heidegger had done in the First World War. (Raymond Aron too would be posted to a weather station that year; it seems to have been the philosophers' posting.) Such a role would not involve combat, but it would still be dangerous. For Bost and Nizan the dangers would be greater: they were able-bodied and could both expect to be called up and sent to fight.

The French holiday season ended on 31 August, and many Parisians went home that day from their country breaks. Sartre and Beauvoir also returned to Paris, Sartre ready to collect the kit bag and army boots stored in his hotel room and report to his unit. He and Beauvoir changed trains in Toulouse, but found the Paris train so crowded they could not get on. They had to wait another two and a half hours, in a dark station amid a mass of anxious people and an apocalyptic atmosphere. Another train came; they got on with difficulty and made it to Paris, arriving on 1 September – the day German forces invaded Poland. Sartre collected his kit. Beauvoir saw him off at the Gare de l'Est early the next morning. On 3 September, Britain and France declared war on Germany.

The US visa for Malvine Husserl had never materialised, so she was still in Louvain when the war began. She remained there, discreetly hidden in a nearby convent in Herent. The Husserl collection was moved from the main university library to the Institut Supérieur de Philosophie in January 1940 – just in time. Four months later, much of the university library was destroyed by bombs when the German invasion began. It was the second time the library had been lost: an older building and a priceless original collection of books and manuscripts had been wiped out in the First World War.

On 16 September 1940, Malvine's container of possessions, now stored in Antwerp, was hit in an Allied bomb raid. Incredibly, according to his own account, the ever-resourceful Van Breda managed to get to the wreckage and recover one valuable item, the urn of Husserl's ashes, which he kept in his monastery cell for the rest of the war. Everything else was torn to pieces, including the Brentano portrait. To spare Malvine distress, Van Breda delayed telling her what had happened. He moved the Husserl papers to various locations in Louvain, to keep them safe.

Another person caught in the Low Countries when war broke out was Husserl's former assistant, Edith Stein. Having completed her thesis on empathy, converted to Christianity, taken orders as a Carmelite nun and become Sister Teresa Benedicta, she had moved in 1938 from a community in Cologne to one in Echt in the Netherlands, which at the time appeared to be safer. Her sister Rosa went with her.

In 1940, the Germans occupied the Netherlands along with the other countries of the region. They began deporting Jews to their deaths in 1942. The Carmelites tried to get the two sisters transferred to another community in Switzerland, but by this time it was impossible to get exit visas. For a brief period, Christian converts were exempted from the deportations, but this soon changed and the Nazis began raids on all Dutch monastic communities in July, searching for anyone non-Aryan. In Echt, they found Edith and Rosa. The two women were taken, along with many other converts of Jewish origin, to a transit camp and then to the camp of Westerbork. Early in August, they were sent on to Auschwitz. On the way, their train passed through their home town of Wrocław. A postal employee working at the station recalled seeing a train paused there for a while; a woman in a Carmelite

habit looked out and said that this was her home town. Red Cross
records show the two sisters arriving at Auschwitz on 7 August 1942.
On 9 August, they were murdered in the Birkenau gas chamber.

Edith Stein had continued her philosophical work all through her
years in the convent, and so she too left behind a collection of papers
and unpublished works. The nuns guarded this as long as they could.
When the Germans were retreating through the area in January 1945,
however, amid chaotic scenes, they had to flee and could not take the
papers with them.

In March, with the Germans gone, a couple of the sisters returned,
and with them came Herman Van Breda. They found many papers
still lying scattered in the open, and, with help from local townspeople,
gathered up everything of Stein's that they could rescue. Van Breda
took the papers to the Husserl Archives. In the 1950s, the scholar Lucy
Gelber took them to her own home to laboriously piece together the
scattered texts. She published them in instalments, as a collected
edition.

Edith Stein was beatified in 1987, and canonised by Pope John Paul
II in 1998. In 2010, in a deliberate move to redefine the Germanic
notion of 'hero', a marble bust of her was added to Ludwig I's Bavarian
Valhalla, a hall of heroes high in the forest overlooking the Danube.
She joined Frederick the Great, Goethe, Kant, Wagner and many
more, including another anti-Nazi, Sophie Scholl, who had been
executed in 1943 for her resistance activities.

Malvine Husserl lived out the whole war in Louvain. Only after it
ended, in May 1946, aged eighty-six, did she manage to join her children in America for her last few years of life. She died on 21 November
1950. Her body was returned to Germany, and she was buried in the
cemetery of Günterstal, just outside Freiburg. Edmund Husserl's ashes,
which she had kept with her in America, were interred with her. They
lie there today, with their son Gerhart, who died in 1973, and a memorial
stone for his younger brother Wolfgang, the one who died in the First
World War. Today one can still walk around the cemetery's green,
quiet paths, and use one of the little watering cans hanging on hooks
nearby to water the grave.

7

Occupation, Liberation

In which the war continues, we meet Albert Camus, Sartre discovers freedom, France is liberated, the philosophers throw themselves into engaged activity, and everyone wants to go to America.

In 1939, having seen Sartre off at the Gare de l'Est with his army kit and boots, Beauvoir could only wait for his news; for a long time she did not even know where he was posted. She walked around Paris on the first day after war was declared, and marvelled at how normal everything seemed. There were just a few oddities: policemen were on the streets with gas masks in little pouches, and when evening fell, many cars had headlights glowing like blue gemstones in the dark, their covers having been tinted as a blackout precaution.

This eerie state of affairs would continue for months, in the 'phony war', as it was known in English. To the French it was the *drôle de guerre* or 'funny war', to the Germans the *Sitzkrieg* or 'sitting war', and to the invaded Poles the *dziwna wojna*, or 'strange war'. There was much nervousness but little action, and none of the feared gas or bomb attacks. In Paris, Beauvoir collected a gas mask from the Lycée Molière where she was teaching, wrote entries in her diary, and tidied her room manically: 'Sartre's pipe, his clothes.' She and Olga Kosakiewicz both lived in rooms at the same hotel (the Hotel Danemark on the rue de Vavin – it's still there). Together they blacked out the windows with a disgusting-sounding mixture of blue dye, oil and suntan lotion. Paris in late 1939 was a city of many blue half-lights.

Beauvoir settled into work, still drafting and redrafting *L'invitée*. She found time to have affairs with a couple of her students, Nathalie Sorokine and Bianca Bienenfeld; both young women later became involved with Sartre too. Biographers have been hard on Beauvoir for what looks like a case of sordid 'grooming' as well as unprofessional conduct. It is hard to tell what motivated her, since she seemed indifferent to both women for much of the time. Perhaps the explanation lay in the tense, debilitating atmosphere of phony-war Paris, which led many people to odd behaviour. Elsewhere in the city, Arthur Koestler was observing how everything seemed to be turning grey, as though a disease were attacking Paris's roots. The journalist and short-story writer Albert Camus, who had come to the city from his home in Algeria, holed himself up in a room and listened to the street sounds outside his window, wondering why he was there. 'Foreign, admit that I find everything strange and foreign', he wrote in his notebook in March 1940. 'No future', he added in an undated note. Yet he did not let this mood stop him from working on literary projects: a novel, *L'étranger* (*The Stranger* or *The Outsider*), a long essay, *The Myth of Sisyphus*, and a play, *Caligula*. He called these his 'three absurds', because they all dealt with the meaninglessness or absurdity of human existence, a theme that seemed to come naturally during this time.

Meanwhile Sartre, whose meteorological posting turned out to be in Brumath, in Alsace near the German border, found himself with little to do but read and write. Between sending up balloons and peering through binoculars, or sitting in the barracks listening to the pocking sound of his fellow soldiers playing ping-pong, he managed to work on his own projects for up to twelve hours a day. He kept his diary, and wrote long daily letters, among them many affectionate outpourings to Simone de Beauvoir – for their letters finally got through, and they were back in contact. He jotted down the notes that would later evolve into *Being and Nothingness*, and produced the first drafts of his novel sequence *Roads of Freedom*. The first volume was scribbled out by 31 December 1939, so he immediately started on volume two. 'If the war goes on at this slow lulling rhythm I'll have written three novels and 12 philosophical treatises by peacetime', he told Beauvoir. He begged her to send him books: Cervantes, the

Marquis de Sade, Edgar Allan Poe, Kafka, Defoe, Kierkegaard, Flaubert, and Radclyffe Hall's lesbian novel *The Well of Loneliness*. His interest in the latter was probably sparked by Beauvoir's tales of her adventures, since, in accordance with their agreement, she told him everything.

Sartre could have gone along happily like this for years – but the funny war was a joke with a punchline. In May 1940, Germany abruptly overran Holland and Belgium, then attacked France. Fighting on the front, Bost was wounded, and would receive the Croix de guerre. Paul Nizan, Sartre's old friend and recent holiday companion, was killed near Dunkirk on 23 May, shortly before the great evacuation of Allied troops there. Merleau-Ponty was posted as an infantry officer to Longwy on the front line. He later recalled one long night during which he and his unit listened to the calls for help of a German lieutenant who had been shot and was stuck in the barbed wire: 'French soldiers, come get a dying man.' They had orders not to go to him, as the cries could have been a ploy, but the next day they found him dead on the wire. Merleau-Ponty would never forget the sight of 'the narrow chest which the uniform barely covered in that near-zero cold, . . . the ash-blond hair, the delicate hands'.

The fighting was brave but brief. With memories of the First World War so fresh, French commanders and politicians favoured an early surrender, avoiding futile loss of life – a rational view, although, like other seemingly rational calculations in the Nazi era, it came at a psychological cost. Raymond Aron's unit retreated without ever seeing the enemy, and joined groups of civilians fleeing on the roads; being Jewish, he knew the danger he faced from the Germans, and got himself quickly to Britain where he would work throughout the war as a journalist for the Free French forces. Merleau-Ponty was evacuated and remained for a while in a military hospital at Saint-Yrieix. Sartre too was captured.

Beauvoir lost contact with him again, and had no more news of him or anyone else for a long time. She too joined the refugee civilians, all fleeing south-west with no clear objective except avoiding what was advancing on them from the north-east. She left with Bianca Bienenfeld's family in a car filled with people and suitcases. A bicycle strapped to the front blocked the beam of their headlights as the overloaded car inched along in the traffic. Once free of the city, they parted ways. Beauvoir caught a bus to stay with friends in Angers for several weeks. After that, she returned to Paris, as many others did, and for part of the return journey she even got a lift on a German truck.

She found the city uncannily normal – except that now there were Germans strolling everywhere, some seeming arrogant, others perplexed or abashed. Even half a year later, in January 1941, the diarist Jean Guéhenno was observing, 'It seems to me I can read their embarrassment on the faces of the occupying forces . . . They don't know what to do on the streets of Paris or whom to look at.' Beauvoir resumed her habit of writing in cafés, but had to get used to the sight of groups of uniformed Nazis enjoying their coffees and cognacs at nearby tables.

She also set about adjusting to the small frustrations and compromises that became necessary for Parisians. To keep her teaching job at the school, she had to sign a document stating that she was neither a Jew nor a Freemason. It was 'repugnant', but she did it. Finding black-market produce or fuel for the coming winter became almost a full-time occupation as supplies dwindled in the city. Anyone who had friends in the countryside – as she did – would depend gratefully on their sending parcels of fresh food. Sometimes these took too long to arrive, however: the first package Beauvoir received contained a beautifully cooked joint of pork, crawling with maggots. She scraped them off and salvaged what she could. Later she devised ways of washing smelly meat in vinegar, then stewing it for hours with strong herbs. Her room had no heating, so she went to bed wearing ski trousers and a woolly sweater, and sometimes taught her classes in the same outfit. She took to wearing a turban, to save on hairdressers, and found that it suited her. 'I aimed at simplification in every sphere,' she wrote in her memoirs.

One necessary adjustment was learning to put up with the idiotic and moralistic homilies emanating every day from the collaborationist government – reminders to respect God, to honour the principle of the family, to follow traditional virtues. It took her back to the 'bour-geois' talk she had so hated in her childhood, but this time backed by a threat of violence. Ah – but perhaps such talk was *always* backed by hidden threats of violence? She and Sartre later made this belief central to their politics: fine-sounding bourgeois values, for them, were never to be trusted or taken at face value. They may have learned this attitude during the regime of humbug that was Occupied France.

Beauvoir still did not know whether Sartre was alive. To keep herself calm (and warm) she started going every afternoon, after a morning's teaching or writing, to the Bibliothèque nationale or the library of the Sorbonne, where she read her way through Hegel's *Phenomenology of Spirit*. The effort of sustained attention was comforting, and so was Hegel's stately vision of human history progressing through inevitable sequences of thesis, antithesis and synthesis towards sublimation in Absolute Spirit. She would leave the library each afternoon feeling a radiant sense of the rightness of all things – a feeling that lasted for about five minutes before the city's grubby reality brought it down. It was then that Kierkegaard had more to offer. She read him as well – that awkward, anguished, irreverent anti-Hegelian. Reading both at once must have been disorienting, yet somehow, like just the right combination of uppers and downers, it gave her what she needed. Both philosophies found their way into her gradually evolving novel *L'invitée*. They would become two key sources for her and for exis-tentialism in general: Kierkegaard with his insistence on freedom and choice, and Hegel with his vision of how history plays out on an epic scale, swallowing up individuals.

Meanwhile, at Trier in the Rhineland near the Luxembourg border, Sartre was alive and well and imprisoned in a POW camp, Stalag 12D. He too was immersing himself in reading a difficult book: *Being and Time*. Heidegger's work had already answered to his need for comfort in 1938. Now, as Sartre read him in a closer and more sustained way, he found him to be the perfect inspiration for a nation in defeat. Heidegger's philosophy had grown partly out of the humiliation of Germany in 1918; now it spoke to a humiliated France after June 1940. As Sartre read it, he also worked on his own philosophical notes, which were growing into a book. In one of the many brief letters he tried to send Beauvoir, on 22 July 1940, he added as a postscript, 'I've begun to write a metaphysical treatise.' This would become his greatest work: *L'être et le néant* (*Being and Nothingness*). The very day he mentioned this, to his relief, he received a backlog of seven letters from Beauvoir. His letters then began reaching her too, and they were back in contact at last. Then Sartre escaped.

It wasn't a very swashbuckling escape, but it was simple and it worked. He had been suffering a great deal from his eye problems, thanks to all the reading and writing – which were mostly done one-eyed. Sometimes both eyes were so sore that he tried to write with them closed, his handwriting wandering over the page. But his eyes gave him his escape route. Pleading the need for treatment, he procured a medical pass to visit an ophthalmologist outside the camp gates. Amazingly, he was then allowed to walk out, showing the pass, and he never went back.

Sartre's eyes had in fact saved his life several times over. First they exempted him from front-line combat, then they saved him from forced Nazi labour; now they gave him his ticket out of the Stalag. This blessing came at a cost in the long term: exotropia can cause a degree of tiredness and difficulty in concentrating that may have contributed to his destructive tendency to self-medicate with stimulant drugs and alcohol in later times.

But now he was free. He headed for Paris, and arrived both pleased with himself and disoriented. For months, he had been stuck with other prisoners all day and all night, and had discovered to his surprise that it was comforting to be so merged in solidarity and sameness with his fellow men. There was no fighting for personal space in the camp. As he wrote later, his own skin was the boundary of the space he had, and even as he slept he could always feel someone's arm or leg against his own. Yet it did not disturb him: those others were part of himself. He had never found physical proximity easy before, so this was a revelation. Now, coming back to Paris, he found himself putting off the moment of going back to his former haunts:

On my first night of freedom, a stranger in my native city, not having yet reached my friends of former days, I pushed open the door of a café. Suddenly, I experienced a feeling of fear – or something close to fear. I could not understand how these squat, bulging buildings could conceal such deserts. I was lost; the few drinkers seemed more distant than the stars. Each of them was entitled to a huge section of bench, to a whole marble table . . . If these men, shimmering comfortably within their tubes of rarefied gas, seemed inaccessible to me, it was because I no longer had the right to place my hand on their shoulder or thigh, or to call one of them 'fat-head'. I had rejoined bourgeois society.

It seemed that Sartre would rarely be as relaxed and happy again as he had been as a prisoner of war.

Beauvoir was briefly jubilant at seeing Sartre, then frankly pissed off by the way he began passing judgement on everything she had been doing to survive. He interrogated her: did she buy things on the black market? 'A little tea occasionally', she said. And what of that paper certifying that she was not a Jew or a Freemason? She should not have signed that. To Beauvoir, this only showed how sheltered Sartre's life had become in the camp. He had enjoyed swearing undying fraternity with his comrades while rubbing up against their thighs and shoulders, but life in Paris was different – not as 'bourgeois' as he seemed to imagine, and more psychologically tough. Unusually, Beauvoir sounds critical of Sartre at this point in her memoirs. But he unbent quickly. He proved happy to eat her black-market stews, and he too made the adjustments necessary to get on with life, and even to be published under Nazi censorship.

On the other hand, he was adamant that he had come back to *do* something. He assembled a dozen friends into a new Resistance group under the name 'Socialisme et liberté' and wrote a manifesto for them. The group spent most of its time writing or discussing manifestos and polemical articles, but even this was dangerous enough. They had a bad scare when one member, Jean Pouillon, lost a briefcase filled with incriminating pamphlets together with the group members' names and addresses. They all faced arrest, torture, death. Luckily, the person who found the briefcase turned it in to a lost-property office. The incongruity of this – the threat of Gestapo torture coexisting with the decent civic tradition of the lost-property office – captures the strangeness of life under Occupation.

The group foundered eventually – 'of not knowing what to do', wrote Sartre later. But being involved had a positive effect on their morale, as did other attempts at resistance, even those that seemed fey or futile. There was much encouragement to be found in miniature rebellions such as those of Jean Paulhan – one of their group – who left small anti-collaborationist poems signed only with his initials lying around on café tables or post-office counters. Other Parisians made similar gestures: forbidden to fly tricolour flags on Bastille Day, for example, people would find ways of bringing red, white and blue together, perhaps on a colourful scarf, or by wearing a red jacket together with a blue purse and white gloves. It all mattered.

Merleau-Ponty was now back in Paris too, and he founded a Resistance group called 'Sous la botte' (Under the Boot), which then merged with Sartre's. He married Suzanne Berthe Jolibois towards the end of 1940, and they had a daughter, to whom they gave the patriotic name Marianne – an Occupation baby who was also a sign of hope for the future. He taught at the Lycée Carnot, where, despite his own activities, he urged his students to be cautious. When he found, one day, that they had taken the obligatory portrait of Marshal Pétain down from the wall, he ordered them to put it back, not from any collaborationist sentiment but to protect their safety. Everyday life required constantly negotiating this balance between submission and resistance, as well as between ordinary activity and the extraordinary underlying reality.

It was even possible to have holidays from the Germans: Beauvoir and Sartre made several cycling trips in the 'free' zone of southern France, where the Vichy puppet government was in charge. They sent their bikes over in advance, then sneaked across the border through forests and fields at night with a guide, all clad in dark clothes. After spending a few weeks wheeling around the roads of Provence, and visiting other writers whom they vaguely hoped to coax into working for the Resistance (including André Gide and André Malraux), they crossed back again, refreshed by the taste of partial freedom. At least there was more food in the south, although they could not afford to buy much of it. Lack of good nutrition made them weak and accident-prone. Sartre once somersaulted over his handlebars, and Beauvoir collided with another bike, falling hard on her face and sustaining a swollen eye and a lost tooth. Weeks later, back in Paris, she squeezed a boil on her chin and felt a hard white nubbin emerge. It was her tooth, which had buried itself in the flesh of her jaw.

Back in Paris, it was important to stay mindful of how dangerous the occupiers were – something easy to forget if you were not among their direct targets. Sartre wrote of how the Germans 'gave up their seats to old ladies in the Métro, they showed affection to children and stroked their cheeks'. What's more, he added, 'do not go imagining that the French showed them a crushing air of contempt' – though they did venture small discourtesies when they could, as a way of preserving self-respect. Jean Guéhenno's diary recorded times when he deliberately failed to give directions on the street to Germans, or gave them rudely, in a way he would never normally do. Merleau-Ponty noted the difficulty he had in overcoming the rules of good manners that he had learned in childhood, but he too forced himself to be rude as a patriotic duty. For someone as naturally affable and well brought up as he, it took a decided effort.

Jews, and anyone actively suspected of Resistance activity, had a grimmer sense of what the Occupation really meant – but they too could be blithe for too long. When the regulation came in on 29 May 1942 that Jews must wear the yellow star, many of Sartre's and Beauvoir's Jewish friends ignored it. They also defied the bans on using restaurants, cinemas, libraries and other public places. As each new rule was announced, a few took it as their cue to flee if they could, usually via Spain to Britain or America, but others stayed. It seemed possible to live with the insults and threats – until it wasn't.

At the most unexpected times, terrifying holes could open up in the fabric of things. Sartre described it with his usual cinematic sense:

> You would phone a friend one day and the telephone would ring and ring in the empty apartment; you would ring his doorbell and he wouldn't come to the door; if the concierge broke in, you would find two chairs drawn up together in the hallway with German cigarette ends between the legs.

It was as if the pavements of the city opened occasionally, he wrote, and a tentacled monster reached up to drag someone down. The cafés, always filled with familiar faces, also became an index to disappearances. Beauvoir wrote of how two attractive Czech women, regulars at the Café Flore, were suddenly not there one day. They never came back. It was unbearable to see their empty places: 'it was, precisely, a *nothingness*'.

Cafés such as the Flore continued to be a focus for Parisian life. For a start, they were the best places to keep warm, certainly better than the sparse, cheap hotels in which many lived without heating or proper cooking facilities. Even after the war, the American writer James Baldwin would observe in the 1950s, 'The moment I began living in French hotels I understood the necessity of French cafés.' They also became places to talk, to conspire a little, to keep one's mind alive. They certainly governed Beauvoir's and Sartre's social lives, being the places where they saw ever-increasing circles of new acquaintances: poets, playwrights, journalists, artists like Pablo Picasso and Alberto Giacometti, and avant-garde writers such as Michel Leiris, Raymond Queneau and Jean Genet. The latter, a former thief and prostitute now gaining fame as a writer, simply marched up to Sartre one day in the Flore and said *bonjour*. This was one of many relationships forged at wartime café tables.

They met Albert Camus in a similarly abrupt way, but at the Théâtre Sarah-Bernhardt, where he introduced himself one day in 1943 while Sartre's play *The Flies* was in rehearsal. He and Sartre already knew a lot about each other: Camus had reviewed *Nausea* and Sartre had just been writing a piece on Camus' *The Outsider*. They immediately got on well. Beauvoir later said that she and Sartre found Camus 'a simple, cheerful soul', often funny and bawdy in conversation, and so emotional that he would sit down in the snow in the street at 2 a.m. and pour out his love troubles.

Since his lonely interlude in Paris in 1940, Camus had travelled to and from Algeria a few times. His wife Francine was still there, having become stuck in the country when Allied forces captured it – Albert being near Lyons at the time, receiving treatment for a bout of the tuberculosis from which he suffered throughout life. He had now finished the 'absurds' he had been working on three years earlier; these spoke above all of his dislocated experience as a French Algerian, caught between two countries and never fully at home in either. They also reflected his early experience of poverty: the Camus family had never been well off, but their situation had become dire after Camus' father Lucien died in the first year of the First World War. (Being recruited into an Algerian regiment, he was sent into battle wearing a picturesque colonial uniform of red trousers and a bright blue waistcoat, fatally inappropriate for the grey mud of northern France.) Albert, born on 7 November 1913, was then less than a year old. He grew up in a sordid apartment in Algiers with his brother, his grieving illiterate and deaf mother, and his grandmother, who was both illiterate and violent.

Thus, while the bourgeois young Sartre had his dreams of literary derring-do, and Merleau-Ponty had his happiness at being unconditionally loved, and Beauvoir had her books and sweet-shop windows, Camus grew up into a world of silence and absences. His family had no electricity, no running water, no newspapers, no books, no radio, few visitors at home, and no sense of the wider 'life-worlds' of others. He did manage to escape, to a *lycée* in Algiers and then to a career as a journalist and writer, but his childhood marked him. The very first entry of his first diary, written when he was twenty-two, contains the remark, 'A certain number of years lived without money are enough to create a whole sensibility.'

Camus went on to spend much of his life in France, but he always felt an outsider there, lost without the brilliant-white Mediterranean sun that had been the one compensation in his early life. The sun became almost a character in his fiction, especially in his first novel, *The Outsider*. This tells of a French-Algerian called Meursault (his first name is never given), who gets into a confrontation on a beach with a knife-wielding 'Arab' – whose name is never given at all. Meursault, who happens to have a friend's gun, shoots the man almost absent-mindedly while dazzled by the light glancing off the sea and the knife blade. Arrested and put on trial, he confusedly tells the judge that he did it because of the sun. As this shows, Meursault does not put his defence case well, and his lawyer is not much better. The court's attention is allowed to move away from the actual killing and on to Meursault's apparent lack of remorse for it, or indeed of an appropriate emotional response to anything at all, including his mother's recent death. Found guilty, he is sentenced to execution by guillotine: a killing just as cold and inhuman as Meursault's own crime, although no one points this out to the judge. The novel ends with Meursault in his cell awaiting death. He is afraid, yet finds a perverse consolation as he looks up at the sky and opens himself 'to the tender indifference of the world'.

It may seem odd that the man Beauvoir described as warm, funny and gushingly emotional should have been able to write so well about a man who is an affectless blank – or who, at least, cannot express emotion in the ways society expects. It is not hard to find possible reasons in his background: his father's pointless death, his own recurrent life-threatening illness, and his whole family's silence and disconnection. Yet the novel also captures something of the French wartime experience in general: again there is that seemingly bland surface, under which the abyss lurks.

In the same year as publishing *The Outsider*, 1942, Camus developed his ideas further in *The Myth of Sisyphus*. This too was short, though it would have been longer had he not agreed to drop a chapter on Franz Kafka because the censors would not accept material about a Jew. Camus, like Sartre and many others, learned to make compromises. Later, in a preface to the English translation in 1955, he would remark that *Sisyphus* owed much to his discovery, while working on the book during the French defeat, that 'even within the limits of nihilism it is possible to find the means to proceed beyond nihilism'.

The book's title refers to a story from Homer's *Odyssey*. King Sisyphus, having arrogantly defied the gods, is punished by being condemned to roll a boulder endlessly up a hill. Each time it gets near the top, it slips out of his grasp and rolls down, so he has to plod back and begin again. Camus asks: if life is revealed to be as futile as the labour of Sisyphus, how should we respond?

Like Sartre in *Nausea*, he points out that mostly we don't see the fundamental problem of life because we don't stop to think about it. We get up, commute, work, eat, work, commute, sleep. But occasionally a breakdown occurs, a Chandos-like moment in which a beat is skipped and the question of purpose arises. At such moments, we experience 'weariness tinged with amazement', as we confront the most basic question of all: why exactly do we go on living?

In a way, this is Camus' variant on Heidegger's Question of Being. Heidegger thought the questionable nature of existence looms up when a hammer breaks; Camus thought similarly basic collapses in everyday projects allow us to ask the biggest question in life. Also like Heidegger, he thought the answer took the form of a decision rather than a statement: for Camus, we must decide whether to give up or keep going. If we keep going, it must be on the basis of accepting that there is no ultimate meaning to what we do. Camus concludes his book with Sisyphus resuming his endless task while resigning himself to its absurdity. Thus: 'One must imagine Sisyphus happy.'

The main influence on Camus here was not Heidegger but Kierkegaard, especially in the 1843 essay *Fear and Trembling*. This too used a story to illuminate the 'Absurd': Kierkegaard chose the Bible tale in which God commands Abraham to sacrifice his beloved son Isaac rather than the more usual goat or sheep. Rather to God's surprise, it seems, Abraham travels to the sacrifice site with Isaac, making no complaint. At the last moment, God lets him off, and Abraham and Isaac go home. What astounds Kierkegaard is neither the obedience nor the reprieve, but the way in which Abraham and Isaac seem able to return to the way things were before. They have been forced to depart entirely from the realm of ordinary humanity and fatherly protection, yet somehow Abraham is still confident in his love for his son. For Kierkegaard, the story shows that we must make this sort of impossible leap in order to continue with life after its flaws have been revealed. As he wrote, Abraham 'resigned everything infinitely, and then took everything back on the strength of the absurd'. This was what Camus thought his modern readers needed to do, but in his case without any involvement of God. Here, too, one can see connections to life in Occupied France. Everything has been compromised, everything lost – yet there it all still seems to be. It is the *sense* that has gone. How do you live without sense? The answer offered by both Camus and Kierkegaard amounted to something like the motto in the British morale-boosting poster: Keep Calm and Carry On.

Camus' 'absurds' proved lastingly popular, although the third of the trio is less well known today: *Caligula*, a play recreating Suetonius' story of that depraved first-century emperor as a case study in freedom and meaninglessness pushed to their limits. *The Outsider* and *Sisyphus* remained bestsellers, appealing to readers for generations afterwards – including those grappling with nothing more unbearable than discontentment in suburbia. I was in that category when I first read them, at around the same time I read Sartre's *Nausea*, and I took all these books in a similar spirit, although I felt myself to be much more of an ill-at-ease Roquentin than a cool blank Meursault.

What I didn't realise was that important philosophical differences divided the work of Camus and Sartre. Much as they liked Camus personally, neither Sartre nor Beauvoir accepted his vision of absurdity. For them, life is *not* absurd, even when viewed on a cosmic scale, and nothing can be gained by saying it is. Life for them is full of real meaning, although that meaning emerges differently for each of us.

As Sartre argued in his 1943 review of *The Outsider*, basic phenomenological principles show that experience comes to us already charged with significance. A piano sonata *is* a melancholy evocation of longing. If I watch a football match, I see it *as* a football match, not as a meaningless scene in which a number of people run around taking turns to apply their lower limbs to a spherical object. If the latter is what I'm seeing, then I am not watching some more essential, truer version of football; I am failing to watch it properly as football at all.

Sartre knew very well that we can lose sight of the sense of things. If I am sufficiently upset at how my team is doing, or undergoing a crisis in my grasp of the world in general, I might stare hopelessly at the players as though they were indeed a group of random people running around. Many such moments occur in *Nausea*, when Roquentin finds himself flummoxed by a doorknob or a beer glass. But for Sartre, unlike for Camus, such collapses reveal a pathological state: they are failures of intentionality, not glimpses into a greater truth. Sartre therefore wrote in his review of *The Outsider* that Camus 'is claiming to render raw experience and yet he is slyly filtering out all the mean- ingful connections which are also part of the experience'. Camus, he said, was too influenced by David Hume, who 'announced that all he could find in experience was isolated impressions'. Sartre thinks life only looks pointillist like that when something has gone awry.

For Sartre, the awakened individual is neither Roquentin, fixating on objects in cafés and parks, nor Sisyphus, rolling a stone up the mountainside with the bogus cheerfulness of Tom Sawyer white- washing a fence. It is a person who is engaged in doing something purposeful, in the full confidence that it means something. It is the person who is truly free.

Freedom was *the* great subject of Sartre's philosophy, above all – and this is no accident – during the period when France was not free. It is central to almost everything he wrote then: *The Flies* (the play that was in rehearsal when he met Camus), the *Roads of Freedom* novels, his many essays and lectures, and above all his masterwork *Being and Nothingness*, which he developed from his years of note-taking and published in June 1943. It seems extraordinary that a 665-page tome mainly about freedom could come out in the midst of an oppressive regime without raising an eyebrow among the censors, but that was what happened. Perhaps the title put them off closer inspection.

That title was, of course, a nod to Heidegger's *Being and Time*, which *Being and Nothingness* resembles in size and weight. (Its American reviewer William Barrett would describe the published version at nearly 700 pages as 'a first draft for a good book of 300 pages'.) Still, it is a rich and mostly stimulating work. It combines Sartre's readings of Husserl, Heidegger, Hegel and Kierkegaard with a wealth of anecdotes and examples, often based on real-life incidents involving Simone de Beauvoir, Olga Kosakiewicz and others. The mood of Paris in wartime haunts it, with mini-scenes set in bars and in cafés, as well as in Parisian squares and gardens, and on the staircases of sleazy hotels. The atmos- phere is often one of tension, desire or mistrust between people. Many key incidents could be scenes from a *noir* or *nouvelle vague* film.

Being and Nothingess shares something else with *Being and Time*: it is unfinished. Both works end by dangling the prospect of a second part which will complete the argument of the book. Heidegger promises to demonstrate his ultimate point: that the meaning of Being is Time. Sartre promises to provide a foundation for existentialist ethics. Neither keeps the promise. What we do get in *Being and Nothingness* is an extended examination of human freedom, precisely worked out on the basis of a simple vision. Sartre argues that freedom terrifies us, yet we cannot escape it, because we *are* it.

To make this point, he begins by dividing all of being into two realms. One is that of the *pour-soi* ('for-itself'), defined only by the fact that it is free. This is us: it is where we find human consciousness. The other realm, that of the *en-soi* ('in-itself'), is where we find everything else: rocks, penknives, bullets, cars, tree roots. (Sartre does not say much about other animals, but they too, from sponges to chimpanzees, seem mostly to be in this group.) These entities have no decisions to make: all they have to do is to be themselves.

For Sartre, the in-itself and the for-itself are as opposed as matter and anti-matter. Heidegger at least wrote about Dasein as a kind of being, but for Sartre the for-itself is not a being at all. Gabriel Marcel memorably described Sartre's nothingness as an 'air-pocket' in the midst of being. It is a 'nothingness', a vacuum-like hole in the world. It is, however, an active and specific nothingness – the sort of nothingness that goes out and plays football.

The notion of a specific nothingness sounds odd, but Sartre explains it with a story of Parisian café life. Let's imagine, he suggests, that I have made an appointment to meet my friend Pierre at a certain café at four o'clock. I arrive fifteen minutes late and look around anxiously. Is Pierre still here? I perceive lots of other things: customers, tables, mirrors and lights, the café's smoky atmosphere, the sound of rattling crockery and a general murmuring hubbub. But there is no Pierre. Those other things form a field against which one item blares out loud and clear: the Absence of Pierre. One thinks of those Czech women who disappeared from the Flore: their absence is much more eloquent and glaring than their habitual presence ever was.

Sartre also offers a more lightweight example: I look in my wallet and see 1,300 francs inside. That seems positive. But if I expected to find 1,500 francs, what looms up at me from the wallet is the non-being of 200 francs. A nice joke, adapted from an old one told in the Ernst Lubitsch film *Ninotchka*, illustrates the point. (Apologies to the adaptor, whom I haven't been able to trace.) Jean-Paul Sartre walks into a café, and the waiter asks what he'd like to order. Sartre replies, 'I'd like a cup of coffee with sugar, but no cream.' The waiter goes off, but comes back apologising. 'I'm sorry, Monsieur Sartre, we are all out of cream.' How about with no milk?' The joke hinges on the notion that the Absence of Cream and the Absence of Milk are two definite negativities, just as Cream and Milk are two definite positivities.

It is peculiar idea – but what Sartre is trying to get at is the structure of Husserlian intentionality, which defines consciousness as only an insubstantial 'aboutness'. My consciousness is specifically mine, yet it has no real being: it *is* nothing but its tendency to reach out or point to things. If I look into myself and seem to see a mass of solidified qualities, of personality traits, tendencies, limitations, relics of past hurts and so on, all pinning me down to an identity, I am forgetting that none of these things can define me at all. In a reversal of Descartes' 'I think, therefore I am', Sartre argues, in effect, 'I am nothing, therefore I am free.'

Not surprisingly, this radical freedom makes people nervous. It is difficult enough to think of oneself as free at all, but Sartre goes further by saying that I *am* literally nothing beyond what I decide to be. To realise the extent of my freedom is to be plunged into what both Heidegger and Kierkegaard called 'anxiety' – *Angst* or, in French, *angoisse*. This is not a fear of anything in particular, but a pervasive unease about oneself and one's existence. Sartre borrows Kierkegaard's image of dizziness: if I look over a cliff and feel vertigo, it tends to take the form of the sickening sensation that I might, compulsively and inexplicably, throw myself off the edge. The more freedom of movement I have, the worse this anxiety becomes.

In theory, if someone tied me down securely near the edge, my vertigo would disappear, for I would know that I *could* not throw myself off and could therefore relax. If we could try a similar trick with the anxiety of life in general, everything would seem a lot easier. But it is impossible: whatever resolutions I make, they can never tie me down like real ropes can. Sartre gives the example of a gambling addict who has long ago resolved never to yield to the addiction. But if this man finds himself near a casino and feels the pull of temptation, he has to renew his resolution all over again. He cannot just refer back to the original decision. I may choose to follow certain general directions in my life, but I can't force myself to stick to them.

To avoid this problem, many of us try to convert our long-term decisions into real-world constraints of some kind. Sartre uses the example of an alarm clock: it goes off, and I roll out of bed as if I had no choice but to obey it, rather than freely considering whether I really want to get up or not. A similar idea lies behind more recent software applications that block you from helplessly watching videos of cats and puppies when you would rather be getting on with work. You can set it either to limit your time on particular sites, or to lock you out of the internet altogether. With a nod to paradox, the most popular of these programs is called 'Freedom'.

All these devices work because they allow us to pretend that we are not free. We know very well that we can always reset the alarm clock or disable the software, but we arrange things so that this option does not seem readily available. If we didn't resort to such tricks, we would have to deal with the whole vast scope of our freedom at every instant, and that would make life extremely difficult. Most of us therefore keep ourselves entangled in all kinds of subtle ways throughout the day. Sartre gives examples: 'I have an appointment this evening with Pierre. I must not forget to reply to Simon. I do not have the right to conceal the truth any longer from Claude.' Such phrases imply that we are boxed in, but for Sartre they are 'projections' of my choices. They are, in his great vertiginous turn of phrase, 'so many guard rails against anguish'.

To show how deeply such pretences are woven into everyday life, Sartre describes a waiter – a skilful, supercilious Parisian waiter, weaving between tables, balancing his tray, 'putting it in a perpetually unstable, perpetually broken equilibrium which he perpetually re-establishes by a light movement of the arm and hand'. As a human being, he is a free 'for-itself' like me, but he moves as though he were a beautifully designed mechanism, enacting a predefined role or game. What game is he playing? 'We need not watch long before we can explain it: he is playing *at being* a waiter in a café.' He does this as efficiently as the thief in G. K. Chesterton's Father Brown story 'The Queer Feet', who slips by unnoticed in a gentleman's club by moving like a waiter when the club members are around, and like a club member when the waiters are around. A waiter playing a waiter performs his actions so gracefully that the effect is like the sequence of musical notes in *Nausea*'s ragtime song: it seems absolutely *necessary*. He tries to be a work of art called *Waiter*, whereas in truth, like the rest of us, he is a free, fallible, contingent human being. In thus denying his freedom, he enters what Sartre calls *mauvaise foi*, or 'bad faith'. There is nothing exceptional about this: most of us are in bad faith most of the time, because that way life is liveable.

Most bad faith is harmless, but it can have darker consequences. In the short story 'The Childhood of a Leader', written in 1938, Sartre examined a character, Lucien, who shores up an identity for himself as an anti-Semite mainly in order to *be something*. He is pleased when he hears someone else say of him, 'Lucien can't stand Jews.' It gives him the illusion that he simply is the way he is. Bad faith here makes an entity out of a nonentity. Sartre developed this thought further in *Reflexions sur la question juive* (translated as *Anti-Semite and Jew*), begun in 1944 and published in 1946. He does not argue that all anti-Semitism comes down to bad faith (that would be a hard thesis to defend), but he uses the notion of bad faith to make a connection between two things that no one had put together quite so neatly: the fear of freedom, and the tendency to blame and demonise others.

For Sartre, we show bad faith whenever we portray ourselves as passive creations of our race, class, job, history, nation, family, heredity, childhood influences, events, or even hidden drives in our subconscious which we claim are out of our control. It is not that such factors are unimportant: class and race, in particular, he acknowledged as powerful forces in people's lives, and Simone de Beauvoir would soon add gender to that list. Nor did he mean that privileged groups have the right to pontificate to the poor and downtrodden about the need to 'take responsibility' for themselves. That would be a grotesque misreading of Sartre's point, since his sympathy in any encounter always lay with the more oppressed side. But for each of us – for *me* – to be in good faith means not making excuses for myself. We cannot say (to quote more examples from Sartre's 1945 lecture) 'I have never had a great love or a great friendship; but that is because I never met a man or a woman who were worthy of it; if I have not written any very good books, it is because I had not the leisure to do so.' We do say such things, all the time; but we are in bad faith when we do it.

None of this means that I make choices in a completely open field or void. I am always in some sort of pre-existing 'situation', out of which I must act. I actually need these 'situations', or what Sartre calls 'facticity', in order to act meaningfully at all. Without it, my freedom would be only the unsatisfying freedom of someone floating in space – perhaps a high jumper who makes a great leap only to find herself drifting off in zero gravity, her jump counting for nothing. Freedom does not mean entirely unconstrained movement, and it certainly does not mean acting randomly. We often mistake the very things that enable us to be free – context, meaning, facticity, situation, a general direction in our lives – for things that define us and take away our freedom. It is only *with* all of these that we can be free in a real sense.

Sartre takes his argument to an extreme point by asserting that even war, imprisonment or the prospect of imminent death cannot take away my existential freedom. They form part of my 'situation', and this may be an extreme and intolerable situation, but it still provides only a context for whatever I choose to do next. If I am about to die, I can decide how to face that death. Sartre here resurrects the ancient Stoic idea that I may not choose what happens to me, but I can choose what to make of it, spiritually speaking. But the Stoics cultivated indifference in the face of terrible events, whereas Sartre thought we should remain passionately, even furiously engaged with what happens to us and with what we can achieve. We should not expect freedom to be anything less than fiendishly difficult.

The difficulty of being free was the theme of the play Sartre was rehearsing when Camus introduced himself: *The Flies*. It opened on 3 June 1943, Sartre's first real play, if you do not count skits written for his fellow POWs in Stalag 12D. He later called it a drama 'about freedom, about my absolute freedom, my freedom as a man, and above all about the freedom of the occupied French with regard to the Germans'. Again, nothing about this seemed to faze the censors. This time it may have helped that he gave the play a classical setting – a ploy other writers also used during this time. Reviewers made little comment about its political message, although one, Jacques Berland in *Paris-Soir*, complained that Sartre seemed too much of an essayist and not enough of a playwright.

Camus had his Sisyphus; Sartre took his parable from the story of Orestes, hero of the *Oresteia* plays of Aeschylus. Orestes returns to his home town of Argos to find that his mother Clytemnestra has conspired with her lover Aegisthus to kill her husband, Orestes' father King Agamemnon. Aegisthus now rules as a tyrant over the oppressed citizenry. In Sartre's version, the populace is too paralysed by humiliation to be capable of rebelling. A plague of flies swarming over the city represents their demoralisation and shame.

But now Orestes the hero enters the scene. As in the original, he kills Aegisthus and (after a passing scruple) his own mother. He has successfully avenged his father and liberated Argos – but he has also done something terrible, and must take on a burden of guilt in place of the townspeople's burden of shame. Orestes is hounded out of town by the flies, who now represent the classical Furies. The god Zeus appears and offers to drive the Furies away, but Sartre's Orestes refuses his help. As an existentialist hero, rebelling against tyranny and taking on the weight of personal responsibility, he prefers to act freely and alone.

The parallels with the French situation in 1943 were clear to see. Sartre's audience would have recognised the debilitating effects of the compromises most of them had to make, and the humiliation that came from living under tyranny. As for the guilt factor, everyone knew that joining the Resistance could bring risks to one's friends and family, which meant that any act of rebellion brought a real moral burden. Sartre's play may not have bothered the censors, but it did have a subversive message. It also went on to have a long and equally provocative afterlife in other countries and other times.

Beauvoir was now exploring similar themes in her work. She wrote the only play of her career, not put into production until after the war (and then to bad reviews). *Useless Mouths* is set in a mediaeval Flemish city under siege; the city's rulers initially propose to sacrifice the women and children so as to conserve food for warriors. Later they realise that it is a better tactic to bring the whole population together to fight in solidarity. It is a clunky tale, so the bad reviews are not surprising, although Sartre's play was hardly any subtler. After the war, Beauvoir would publish her much better 'resistance novel' *The Blood of Others*, which weighed the need for rebellious action against the guilt that comes from putting people in danger.

Beauvoir also wrote an essay called 'Pyrrhus and Cineas' during this time, which takes the principle of bold action beyond war into more personal territory. The story comes from another classical source, Plutarch's *Lives*. The Greek general Pyrrhus is busying himself winning a series of great victories, knowing that there will be many more battles to come. His adviser, Cineas, asks him what he intends to do when he has won them all and taken control of the whole world. Well, says Pyrrhus, then I will rest. To this, Cineas asks: why not just rest now?

This sounds a sensible proposal, but Beauvoir's essay tells us to think again. For her, a man who wants to stop and navel-gaze is not as good a model as the one who commits himself to keep going. Why do we imagine that wisdom lies in inactivity and detachment, she asks? If a child says, 'I don't care about anything,' that is not a sign of a wise child but of a troubled and depressed one. Similarly, adults who withdraw from the world soon get bored. Even lovers, if they retreat to their private love-nest for too long, lose interest in each other. We do not thrive in satiety and rest. Human existence means 'transcendence', or going beyond, not 'immanence', or reposing passively inside oneself. It means constant action until the day one runs out of things to do – a day that is unlikely to come as long as you have breath. For Beauvoir and Sartre, this was the big lesson of the war years: the art of life lies in getting things done.

A related but different message emerges from Camus' 'resistance novel', again published only after the war in 1947: *The Plague*. It is set in the Algerian town of Oran during an outbreak of that disease; the bacillus suggests the Occupation and all its ills. Everyone in the town reacts differently, as quarantine is imposed and claustrophobia and fear increase. Some panic and try to flee; some exploit the situation for personal gain. Others fight the disease, with varying degrees of effectiveness. The hero, Dr Bernard Rieux, pragmatically gets down to the work of treating patients and minimising infection by enforcing quarantine regulations, even when these seem cruel. Dr Rieux is under no illusion that humanity can overcome deadly epidemics in the long term. The note of submission to fate is still there, as in Camus' other novels – a note never heard in Beauvoir or Sartre. But Dr Rieux concentrates on damage limitation and on pursuing strategies to ensure a victory, if only a local and temporary one.

Camus' novel gives us a deliberately understated vision of heroism and decisive action compared to those of Sartre and Beauvoir. One can only do so much. It can look like defeatism, but it shows a more realistic perception of what it takes to actually accomplish difficult tasks like liberating one's country.

By early summer of 1944, as Allied forces moved towards Paris, everyone knew that freedom was near. The growing emotion was hard to take, as Beauvoir noted; it was like the painful tingling that comes when sensation returns after numbness. There was also much fear of what the Nazis might do as they retreated. Life continued to be hard: merely finding enough to eat became more difficult than ever. But the faint sound of bombs and artillery brought hope.

The sounds came closer and closer – and suddenly, one hot day in mid-August, the Germans had gone. Parisians were unsure at first what was happening, especially as they still heard gunfire scattered around the city. On Wednesday 23 August, Sartre and Beauvoir walked to the office of the Resistance journal *Combat* to meet Camus, now the paper's literary editor: he wanted to commission a piece about the Liberation from them. They had to cross the Seine to get there; halfway across the bridge they heard the crack of gunshots and ran for their lives. But tricolours were now flying from windows, and the next day broadcasts from the BBC announced that Paris was officially liberated.

Church bells pealed throughout the next night. Walking the streets, Beauvoir joined in with a group of people dancing around a bonfire. At one point, someone said they saw a German tank, so everyone scattered, then cautiously returned. It was amid such scenes of nervous excitement that peace began for France. The next day brought the

official Liberation parade along the Champs-Elysées to the Arc de Triomphe, led by the Free French leader returned from exile, Charles de Gaulle. Beauvoir joined the crowd, while Sartre watched from a balcony. At last, wrote Beauvoir, 'the world and the future had been handed back to us'.

The first act of the future was settling accounts with the past. Reprisals began against collaborators, with swift acts of brutal punishment at first, followed by a wave of more formal trials, some of which also ended in death sentences. Here, Beauvoir and Sartre found themselves again disagreeing with Camus. After an initial hesitancy, Camus came out firmly against the death penalty. Cold, judicial killing by the state was always wrong, he said, however serious the offence. Before the trial in early 1945 of Robert Brasillach, the former editor of a fascist magazine, Camus signed a petition calling for mercy in case of a guilty verdict. Sartre was not involved, as he was away at the time, but Beauvoir pointedly refused to sign the petition, saying that from now on it was necessary to make tough decisions in order to honour those who had died resisting the Nazis, as well as to ensure a fresh start for the future.

She was curious enough to attend Brasillach's trial, which took place on a freezing 19 January 1945 as Paris was covered in deep snow. As the court briefly deliberated and then handed down the death sentence, she was impressed to see how calmly Brasillach took it. Yet this did not change her view that the sentence was right. In any case, the petition made no difference, and he was shot on 6 February 1945.

From now on, Beauvoir and Sartre would invariably line up against Camus whenever such issues were at stake. After his bolder and more effective Resistance activity at *Combat* and elsewhere, Camus now drew clearer lines: he opposed execution, torture and other state abuses, and that was that. Beauvoir and Sartre were not exactly in favour of such things, but they liked to point to complex political realities and means-ends calculations. They would ask whether there really could be cases where harm by the state could be justifiable. What if something very great is at stake, and the future of a vast number of people requires some remorseless act? Camus just kept returning to his core principle: no torture, no killing – at least not with state approval. Beauvoir and Sartre believed they were taking a more subtle and more realistic view.

If asked why a couple of innocuous philosophers had suddenly become so harsh, they would have said it was because the war had changed them in profound ways. It had shown them that one's duties to humanity could be more complicated than they seemed. 'The war really divided my life in two', Sartre said later. He had already moved away from some of what he had said in *Being and Nothingness*, with its individualist conception of freedom. Now, he sought to develop a more Marxist-influenced view of human life as purposeful and social. This was one reason why he never managed to write the follow-up volume on existentialist ethics: his ideas on the subject had changed too much. He did write many draft pages, published after his death as *Notebooks for an Ethics*, but he could not give them a coherent shape.

Merleau-Ponty too, having been radicalised by the war, was still desperately trying to be less nice. Having mastered the art of being beastly to Germans, he now far outdid Beauvoir and Sartre in writing fervent arguments for an uncompromising Soviet-style Communism. In an essay of 1945, 'The War Has Taken Place', he wrote that the war had ruled out any possibility of living a merely private life. 'We are in the world, mingled with it, compromised with it', he wrote. No one could rise above events; everyone had dirty hands. For a while, 'dirty hands' became a buzz term in the existentialist milieu. It went with a new imperative: get down to work, and do something!

Thus, now that the war in France was safely over, Sartre's gang raced out like greyhounds from opened racetrack gates. Sartre wrote a series of essays arguing that writers had a duty to be active and committed; these appeared in periodical form in 1947, and then separately in 1948 as *What Is Literature?* Authors had real power in the world, he said, and they must live up to it. He called for a *littérature engagée* – a politically committed literature. Beauvoir recalled how urgent all such tasks seemed: she would read of some incident that fired her up, think at once, 'I must answer that!', and rush out an article for publication. She,

Sartre, Merleau-Ponty and other friends produced so much writing so quickly that they got together to launch a new cultural journal in 1945: *Les Temps modernes*. Sartre was the journal's figurehead, and most people assumed he wrote all its editorials, although in fact Merleau-Ponty put in more work than anyone and wrote many uncredited pieces. The name *Modern Times* was taken from Charlie Chaplin's manic 1936 film about worker exploitation and industrialisation, a film Sartre and Beauvoir had enjoyed so much when it came out that they sat through two showings in succession. Their pace of literary production matched that lampooned in Chaplin's film, and over the coming decades *Les Temps modernes* became one of the great engines of intellectual debate in France and beyond. It is still being published today. It was in *Les Temps modernes* that Sartre's essay on 'committed literature' first appeared, and it set the tone for the years that followed.

The flow of existentialist fiction and drama continued, too. Beauvoir's *The Blood of Others* appeared in September 1945. Sartre published the first two volumes of his *Roads of Freedom* novel sequence, both written years earlier and set in 1938. They show his main character Mathieu Delarue progressing from a naive view of freedom as a mere do-as-thou-wilt selfishness towards a better definition, in which he faces up to the demands made by history. By the time the third volume appeared in 1949, *La mort dans l'âme* (variously translated as *Iron in the Soul*, *The Defeat* or *Troubled Sleep*), we see Mathieu bravely defending a village bell tower as France falls. He uses his freedom to better ends now, but the defeat appears to be the end of him. A projected fourth volume was meant to show him surviving after all, and finding real freedom through solidarity with comrades in the Resistance. Unfortunately, as generally happened when Sartre planned a grand conclusion for a project, the volume was never finished. Only a few fragments appeared, many years later. Just as the ethics question was left hanging in *Being and Nothingness*, the freedom question remained hanging in *Roads of Freedom*. In neither case was the problem to do with Sartre losing interest: it was because of his tendency to keep changing his mind philosophically and politically.

In all these 1940s novels, stories and essays, the dominant mood was not so much one of post-traumatic exhaustion as of excitement. The world had fallen to pieces, but for that very reason almost anything could now be done with it. It made for a thrilling and frightening mixture – which was just the combination of emotions that characterised the first wave of post-war existentialism in general.

It was a combination engendered in places far from Paris, too. In a 1959 study of war experiences, the American Heideggerian scholar J. Glenn Gray recalled travelling through the Italian countryside with his unit towards the end of the war there. One evening he stopped to exchange a few words in broken Italian with an elderly man smoking a pipe outside a hut. The encounter saddened Gray, since this traditional world and its age-old calm seemed about to be lost forever. Yet along with the premonition of loss he felt exhilaration and a sense of promise. Whatever happened next, Gray thought that evening, one thing was certain: the philosophers he had studied in college could have little to offer the post-war world. It would be a new reality, so new philosophers would be needed.

And here they were.

Thus began existentialism's year of marvels and mania, with all the wild experimentation we sneakily previewed in Chapter 1. Sartre's rousing lecture in October 1945 ended in mayhem and a big news story. Talk of his philosophy spread through Paris, and beyond. In 1946, Gabriel Marcel wrote, 'Hardly a day goes by without my being asked what is existentialism.' He added, 'Usually it is a society lady who asks for this information, but tomorrow it may be my charwoman or the ticket-collector on the Métro.' Every fashionable person wanted to learn about it, every Establishment institution fretted about it, and almost every journalist seemed to be using it to make a living.

Sartre's friend Boris Vian spoofed the craze in his 1947 novel *L'écume des jours*, translated as *Froth on the Daydream* or *Mood Indigo*. This surreal and playful romance includes, as a side character, a famous philosopher called Jean-Sol Partre. When Partre gives a lecture, he arrives on an

elephant and mounts a throne, accompanied by his consort the
Countess de Mauvoir. An extraordinary radiance emanates from his
slender body. The audience is so enraptured that his words are drowned
out by the cheering, and at the end the hall collapses in rubble from
pressure of numbers. Partre watches, delighted to see everyone
committing themselves with such engagement. The real Simone de
Beauvoir enjoyed Vian's satire, and called it a work of 'enormous
tenderness'.

The trumpet-playing Vian was the leader of the festive element
of the existentialist scene, which found its home in the Saint-
Germain-des-Prés area of the Left Bank. He had already pioneered
the trend for hosting jazz parties in private apartments towards the
end of the Occupation, with curfew-dodging youngsters known as
'zazous' – who avoided the banned hours by simply not going home
until the next day. With the war over, Vian played in the new cellar
clubs. He also mixed bizarre cocktails behind their bars, and fired
off amusing, sensationalist or surrealistic novels according to mood.
Later he wrote a Saint-Germain-des-Prés 'manual', giving maps,
descriptions and pen portraits of the exotic cavern-dwelling 'troglo-
dytes' to be found in it.

In the cellars and bars, philosophers often went literally arm in arm with jazz stars, dancing the night away. Merleau-Ponty was especially popular among habitués of the Left Bank, being known for his good cheer and flirtatious charm. He was, Vian observed, 'the only one of the philosophers who will actually invite a girl out onto the dance floor'. When Merleau-Ponty took Juliette Gréco dancing, he would also, at her request, teach her a little philosophy as they gyrated round the floor.

Sartre and Beauvoir danced too, when they managed to evade the new hangers-on and journalists in the better-known haunts. They loved jazz. Sartre wrote the lyrics for one of Juliette Gréco's most successful songs, 'La rue des Blancs-Manteaux'. Another song sung by Gréco, a 'Marseillaise existentialiste', had lyrics jointly penned by Merleau-Ponty, Boris Vian and Anne-Marie Cazalis. This told the sorry but well-rhymed tale of someone who was too poor to get credit at the Flore, too free despite reading Merleau-Ponty, and who always ended up stuck in the same disaster, notwithstanding Jean-Paul Sartre.

The existentialist culture of the late 1940s seemed very Parisian to anyone looking in from the outside, but it was also driven by a love, or at least a fascination, for all things American. Paris itself was still full of Americans, including servicemen left behind from the Liberation forces as well as new arrivals. Few young Parisians could resist American clothes, American films or American music. The fact that all of this had been banned by the Occupation authorities added to its appeal – and the 'zazous' had been secretly dancing to American jazz for months. The importance of American music for a whole generation is summed up in a story told by Juliette Gréco. She had been arrested by the Gestapo in 1943, held in a cell, and then, to her surprise, freed again. She walked eight miles home through wintry streets in a thin cotton dress, and as she walked, she defiantly sang an American song at the top of her voice: 'Over the Rainbow'.

To go with the jazz, blues and ragtime after the war, people sought out American clothes, readily available in flea markets; there was a particular craze for plaid shirts and jackets. If your twenty-first-century time machine could take you back to a Parisian jazz club immediately after the war, you would not find yourself in a sea of existentialist black; you would be more likely to think you'd walked into a lumber-jacks' hoedown. An impression of the effect can be had from Jacques Becker's film *Rendezvous de juillet*, released in 1949, which features an exuberant dance scene in the Lorientais club: as Claude Luter's band plays on the cramped stage, the check-shirted crowd leaps around on the dance floor. The sleek black turtleneck arrived afterwards – and when Americans in turn adopted that fashion, few realised they were returning a sartorial compliment.

In the cinemas, meanwhile, people devoured American crime movies and, from the *bouquinistes* along the Seine, they bought American fiction. The most popular writers were the hardest-boiled ones: James M. Cain, Dashiel Hammett and Horace McCoy, whose despairing Depression-era novel *They Shoot Horses, Don't They?* came out in French from Gallimard in 1946. Camus had emulated the style of American *noir* novels in *The Outsider*, and Sartre and Beauvoir were also fans. They loved non-genre American authors too: Ernest Hemingway, William Faulkner, John Steinbeck and John Dos Passos – who was, according to Sartre, the greatest writer of the era. Many American books were translated by French publishers: 'traduit de l'americain' became a favourite phrase on covers. Not all books that looked like translations were the real thing, however. A book called *I Spit on Your Graves*, ostensibly by 'Vernon Sullivan' and translated by Boris Vian, was by Vian himself. Written on a kind of dare, it was a violent, sensationalist story about a black man who kills two white women to avenge the lynching of his brother, but is hunted down and eventually shot dead by the police. Vian made money from it, but got into trouble the following year when a man in Montparnasse strangled his girlfriend and shot himself, leaving a copy of the novel by his bed with the description of a strangling circled in ink in case anyone failed to notice the similarity.

Americans, able to visit Paris as tourists for the first time in five years, fell in love with the city all over again as they had in the 1920s. They sat in the Flore and Deux Magots, and ventured down the cellar stairs into nightclubs. They listened to the talk of *l'existentialisme* and *les existentialistes*, and passed it on to their friends back home. Cultured New Yorkers began to court the real existentialists: one by one, Sartre, Beauvoir and Camus were all invited to cross the Atlantic for visits and lecture tours. They all accepted.

The first to go was Sartre, in mid-January 1945: at Camus' suggestion, he joined a delegation of invited French journalists, representing *Combat* and *Le Figaro*. (This was why he was away for the Brasillach trial.) He travelled around for two months, meeting countless people, of whom one, Dolorès Vanetti, became a long-term lover. His poor English prevented him from talking as freely as he usually liked to, but he watched carefully and took notes, then wrote articles on his return. He focused on socialist questions, such as the matter of how American workers coped with the high-speed automation of American factories. At the time, few thought of technological appliances, consumerism or automated production techniques as widespread features of modern life: rather, they were considered distinctively American, and this added to the country's glamorous but alarming image in many European minds. Can one actually live with all that technology? What does it do to a person? Sartre observed with surprise that US workers seemed cheerful, despite being cogs in a Chaplinesque industrial machine driven to go constantly faster and faster by their bosses. The whole of America seemed to be such a machine, and Sartre wondered whether it could possibly go on like that.

He returned for further visits in the late 1940s, and became more comfortable communicating with people, although his English remained limited. By Sartre's third visit, in 1948, Lionel Abel – who met him at a *Partisan Review* evening – was amazed at his loquacity in a language he barely knew: there was little Sartre could say, yet he never shut up.

Albert Camus was the next to go, touring the US from March to May 1946. He travelled more nervously than Sartre, aware of being a stranger and troubled by the constant small difficulties of figuring out how things worked and what one was supposed to do. His unease made him a good observer of differences. He noted:

the morning fruit juices, the national Scotch and soda . . . the
anti-Semitism and the love of animals – this last extending from
the gorillas in the Bronx Zoo to the protozoa of the Museum
of Natural History – the funeral parlors where death and the
dead are made up at top speed ('Die, and leave the rest to us'),
the barber shops where you can get a shave at three in the
morning . . .

He was especially impressed by the billboard in Times Square where
a giant GI puffed real smoke from a Camel cigarette. The only place
that seemed comforting in its familiarity was New York's Bowery
district, then a derelict zone of cheap bars and run-down hotels, with
the elevated railway line running through it at second-storey level,
casting everything below into deep shadow. 'A European wants to say:
"Finally, reality."' Like Sartre watching the workers, Camus was
attracted and repelled. Above all, he could not understand the apparent
lack of anguish in America. Nothing was properly tragic.

In 1947, Simone de Beauvoir made her journey. Unlike Sartre, she
already spoke and read English; like Camus, she was astounded at the
bizarre devices and inventions. She kept a diary in which she boggled
at such phenomena as the way letters were posted in her hotel: next
to the elevator on each floor was a tiny chute into which you dropped
your envelope so that it fluttered down to a box at the bottom. The
first time she saw the white things flashing by, she took them for
hallucinations. Next she went to a newsagent and tried to work out
how to buy stamps from the machines, but the coins confused her.
She made many friends, however, and after coming to grips with New
York she set out on a country-wide lecture tour with diversions to
visit jazz clubs, and cinemas where she saw 'thrillings' and 'laffmovies'.
While in Chicago, she met Nelson Algren, a tough-guy novelist who
wrote about addicts and prostitutes and the seamy side of American
life. They began an affair and she fell in love; they would remain lovers
for three years, although they were able to meet only at long intervals
in the US or France.

Her response to America was the now usual mixture of wariness and bliss. She was seduced: America 'was abundance, and infinite horizons; it was a crazy magic lantern of legendary images'. It was the future – or at least one possible version of the future. A rival version was offered by the Soviet Union, which also attracted her. But the United States was undoubtedly the stronger, at the moment. It was more confident; it was wealthy, and it had the Bomb.

One element of American life unequivocally horrified Sartre, Beauvoir and Camus: its racial inequalities, and not only in the South. After his first trip, Sartre wrote in *Le Figaro* of how black 'untouchables' and 'unseeables' haunted the streets, never meeting your gaze; it was as if they saw no one, and you were not supposed to see them either. A later visit inspired him to write a play about US racism, *The Respectful Prostitute*, based on a real-life case in which two black men were convicted of raping two white prostitutes and executed, despite an insufficiency of evidence against them. Beauvoir was also shocked by her encounters, or rather the lack of them, since the two worlds rarely mixed. She walked up to Harlem by herself, defying white New Yorkers' nervous warnings that it could be dangerous for her. Other French visitors also refused to get used to the separation of spheres that seemed natural to many white Americans. When Juliette Gréco had an affair with the jazz musician Miles Davis in 1949 and visited him in New York, he had to warn her that they should not go round together as openly as they did in Paris. People would call her 'a black man's prostitute', and her career would be ruined.

Conversely, many black Americans who found themselves in Paris after the war appreciated the experience of being treated with basic human respect. They were more than respected; they were often idolised, as French youngsters so loved black American music and culture. Some decided to stay on, and a few were drawn to existentialism, finding much to recognise in its philosophy of freedom.

The great example of this was Richard Wright, who had made his name in the US with the novels *Native Son* (1940) and *Black Boy* (1945). While still in New York he met both Sartre and Camus, and he and his wife became particularly good friends with Simone de Beauvoir, who stayed with them in 1947. He wrote in his journal that year, 'How those French boys and girls think and write; nothing like it exists anywhere on earth today. How keenly they feel the human plight.' In return, his French visitors loved his gritty, semi-autobiographical writing about life as a black man growing up in America. Camus arranged to have his books translated for Gallimard; Sartre commissioned him to write for *Les Temps modernes*. Wright managed, with difficulty, to get a visa to visit France himself, and was instantly converted. Just as the details of America had amazed the French, the peculiarities of Paris delighted Wright: 'The knobs were in the center of the doors!' He arranged further sojourns, and eventually settled in the city.

Even though the Europeans were puzzled by American ways, they loved being received so warmly: the US was (and still is) a tremendously hospitable country for new ideas, and for potential celebrities too. The year after Sartre's photo appeared in *Time* magazine with the caption 'Women swooned', Beauvoir was hailed in the *New Yorker* as 'the prettiest Existentialist you ever saw'. Articles on existentialism appeared in newspapers and cultural periodicals: the *New York Post*, the *New Yorker*, *Harper's Bazaar*, and the *Partisan Review* – favourite reading of intellectuals – which published essays on Sartre, Beauvoir and Camus, with translated excerpts from their works. The French exile Jean Wahl wrote 'Existentialism: a Preface' for the *New Republic* in October 1945. Along with the primers and prefaces came some gentle satire. In 1948, the *New York Times Magazine* reprinted an existentialist spoof by Paul F. Jennings from the British weekly the *Spectator*, called 'Thingness of Things'. It described a philosophy of 'resistentialism' propounded by one Pierre-Marie Ventre, dedicated to understanding why things resist and frustrate human beings at every turn, as when they trip us up underfoot, or decline to be found when lost. Ventre's slogan is '*Les choses sont contre nous*' – 'Things are against us'.

One thing about the existentialists seriously bothered American intellectuals, and that was their low taste in American culture – their love of jazz and blues, their interest in the sleazy murders of the Deep South, and their fondness for potboilers about hit men and psychopaths. Even their more elevated choices in American fiction were suspect, since cultured Americans were less inclined to appreciate their own modern novelists than the filigree meanderings of Proust – whom Sartre abhorred. William Barrett, an early existentialist populariser, wrote in the *Partisan Review* that Sartre's novels stood as 'grim reminders that one cannot read Steinbeck and Dos Passos as great novelists with impunity'. All such books, with their 'banal and meaningless conversations, characters wandering in and out, bars and dance-halls', were a bad influence. In the same issue, the critic F. W. Dupee concluded that the French taste for Faulkner was less a compliment to American literature than an indication of some terrible 'crisis in French taste and reason'.

A divergence also emerged in the American and French ways of thinking about existentialism. For the French in the 1940s, it tended to be seen as new, jazzy, sexy and daring. For Americans, it evoked grimy cafés and shadowy Parisian streets: it meant old Europe. Thus, while the French press portrayed existentialists as rebellious youths with outrageous sex lives, Americans often saw them as pale, pessimistic souls, haunted by dread, despair and anxiety à la Kierkegaard. This image stuck. Even now, especially in the English-speaking world, the word 'existentialist' brings to mind a *noir* figure staring into the bottom of an espresso cup, too depressed and anguished even to flick through the pages of a dog-eared *L'être et le néant*. One of the few to challenge this image early on was Richard Wright, who, after first meeting the existentialists, wrote to his friend Gertrude Stein that he could not understand why Americans insisted on seeing it as a gloomy philosophy: to him it meant optimism and freedom.

American readers in these early years had very little original material to go on if they wanted to judge existentialism for themselves, and if they did not read French. Only a few fragments of Sartre's and Beauvoir's work had so far been translated, and these did not include either *Nausea*, first translated by Lloyd Alexander as *The Diary of Antoine Roquentin* in 1949, or *Being and Nothingness*, translated by Hazel Barnes in 1956.

If it was hard to get accurate information about French existentialism, it was even harder to learn anything about the German thinkers who had started it all. One of the few who tried to correct this imbalance was Heidegger's former pupil and lover, Hannah Arendt, now based in the United States and working for Jewish refugee organisations. She wrote two 1946 essays, for the *Nation* and the *Partisan Review* respectively. One, 'French Existentialism', unpicked some of the myths about Sartre and the others. The other, 'What is Existenz Philosophy?', tried to plant existentialism back into its German roots, summarising the thought of Jaspers and Heidegger.

But this was a difficult moment to tell people that the prettiest existentialist you ever saw and the swoon-inducing Sartre owed their ideas to Germans. Few wanted to acknowledge this fact in France, either. And Heidegger was no ordinary German. If the magician of Messkirch could have magicked his own past away, everyone would have been happier.

8

Devastation

*In which Heidegger turns and is turned against, and some
awkward meetings occur.*

Germany in 1945 was a place where no one would want to be.
Survivors, isolated soldiers and displaced persons of all kinds roamed
the cities and countryside. Refugee organisations struggled to help
people get home, and occupying forces tried to impose order amid
near-total loss of infrastructure. Heaps of rubble often stank of dead
bodies buried inside. People searched for food, grew vegetables in
makeshift allotments, and cooked on open fires. Besides those killed,
around fourteen to fifteen million Germans had been made homeless
by firebombing and general destruction. The English poet Stephen
Spender, travelling the country after the war, compared the people he
saw wandering through the wreckage of Cologne and other places to
desert nomads who had stumbled across the ruins of a lost city. But
people, especially groups of *Trümmerfrauen* or 'rubble-women', did
begin working to clear the stones and bricks, supervised by occupying
soldiers.

Displaced persons from the camps often had to wait a long time
to go anywhere. Many German soldiers also remained missing; some
slowly made their way home, crossing whole countries by foot. They
were joined by well over twelve million ethnic Germans expelled from
Poland, Czechoslovakia and other Central and Eastern European countries; they too walked to Germany, pushing small wagons and trolleys
containing their possessions. The number of people simply trudging
around Europe at this time is astounding. The grandfather of a friend
of mine walked home to Hungary from a prison camp in Denmark.

When, in Edgar Reitz's 1984 film sequence *Heimat*, a young man turns up in his Rhineland village having walked all the way from Turkey, the scene is not as fanciful as it might seem. But many others remained stranded in far-off places for years, with relatives having no idea where they were.

Among those lost to communication in 1945 were the Heideggers' two sons, Jörg and Hermann. Both had been soldiers on the Eastern Front, and both were now in Russian POW camps. Their parents could only wait in uncertainty, not knowing whether either was alive.

Since his resignation from the Freiburg rectorship in 1934, Martin Heidegger had kept fairly quiet. The same heart condition that had kept him out of active service in the First World War had continued to prevent his being called up for service of any kind through most of the second. He taught at the university and spent as much time as possible in his Todtnauberg hut, feeling misunderstood and badly treated. A friend who saw him there in 1941, Max Kommerell, described him as having a good tan, a lostness in his eyes, and 'a delicate smile that is just a tiny, tiny bit crazy'.

With the Allies closing in by late 1944, the Nazi regime ordered the total mobilisation of all Germans, including those previously exempt. Heidegger, now fifty-five, was sent with other men to dig trenches near Alsace to ward off a French advance. This only lasted for a few weeks, but meanwhile he also took the precaution of hiding his manuscripts in safer places in case of invasion. Some were already stored in the vaults of the Messkirch bank where his brother Fritz worked; he squirrelled others away in a church tower in nearby Bietingen. In April 1945, he even wrote to his wife about a plan to put several volumes of writing into a secret cave which would be closed up and its location recorded on a treasure map, entrusted to just a few people. If this was ever done there is no evidence of it, but he did keep moving papers around. Heidegger's precautions were not irrational: Freiburg was badly damaged in air raids, and Todtnauberg was not large or secure enough to store much safely. He may also have feared that some items were incriminating.

He kept with him only a few manuscripts, including his recent work on Friedrich Hölderlin, whom Heidegger read obsessively. The great local poet of the Danube region, born in 1770 in Lauffen and suffering from bouts of insanity all his life, Hölderlin had set much of his visionary poetry in the local landscape, while also evoking an idealised image of ancient Greece – the very combination that had always fascinated Heidegger. The only other poet who would ever be so important to him was the even more disturbed Georg Trakl, an Austrian schizophrenic and drug addict who died aged twenty-seven in 1914. Trakl's eerie poems are filled with hunters, young women and strange blue beasts stepping through silent forests by moonlight. Heidegger immersed himself in both poets, and generally explored the question of how poetic language can summon forth Being, and open a space for it in the world.

In March 1945, the Allies arrived in Freiburg, and Heidegger moved out. He arranged for philosophers and students in his faculty to find refuge in Wildenstein, a spectacular castle perched high on a crag over the Danube near Beuron, not far from Messkirch (also, incidentally, not far from the castle of Sigmaringen where the Germans had herded members of the Vichy government for a grotesque *Decameron*-style

retreat after they fled France). Wildenstein's owners were the prince and princess of Sachsen-Meiningen; the princess had been Heidegger's lover. This is perhaps why Elfride Heidegger did not join them; she was left behind in Freiburg to mind the Heidegger house in the suburb of Zähringen. When the Allies arrived, they commandeered it, so that she would share the house for some time with a refugee from Silesia and the family of a French sergeant.

Meanwhile, the little band of university refugees – around ten professors and thirty students, mostly women – had cycled through the Black Forest, with Heidegger himself catching them up later on his son's bicycle. He stayed with the princess and her husband at a nearby forester's lodge which they used as their home, while the rest of the group ascended into the fairy-tale castle. Through May and June 1945, even after the French had arrived in the area, the philosophers helped to bring in hay from surrounding fields, and spent the evenings entertaining each other with lectures and piano recitals. At the end of June, they had their farewell party in the forester's lodge; Heidegger lectured them on Hölderlin. When the pleasant few months came to an end, the merry band returned home to Freiburg, no doubt ruddy-cheeked and fit. But Heidegger arrived in Freiburg to find his home full of strangers, the city under French administration, and a total ban against him teaching. His enemies had reported him as a suspected Nazi sympathiser.

Heidegger had spent that Danube spring of 1945 writing several new works, including a philosophical dialogue to which he gave the date 8 May 1945 – the day Germany's surrender became official. It is entitled 'Evening Conversation: in a prisoner of war camp in Russia, between a younger and an older man'. The two characters are German inmates of the POW camp, and when the dialogue opens they have just returned from their day of forced labour in the woods.

The younger man says to the older, 'As we were marching to our workplace this morning, out of the rustling of the expansive forest I was suddenly overcome by something healing.' What is this healing thing, he wonders? The older man says it may be something 'inexhaustible' that comes from that expanse. Their conversation continues, sounding very much like two Heideggers talking to one another:

YOUNGER MAN: You probably mean that the capacious, which prevails in the expanse, brings us to something freeing.

OLDER MAN: I do not only mean the capaciousness in the expanse, but also that this expanse leads us out and forth.

YOUNGER MAN: The capaciousness of the forests swings out into a concealed distance, but at the same time swings back to us again, without ending with us.

They go on trying to define the healing power, and to understand how it might free them from what the older man describes as the 'devastation that covers our native soil and its helplessly perplexed humans'.

'Devastation' (*Verwüstung*) becomes the key word of their conversation. It turns out that they are not only referring to recent events, but to a devastation that has been eating at the earth for centuries and turning everything into a 'desert' – *Wüste*, a word etymologically linked to *Verwüstung*. It has made its greatest gains in a certain workers' paradise (clearly the Soviet Union), and in a coldly calculating, technologically advanced rival land where 'everything remains overseeable and arranged and accounted for so as to be useful'. This, of course, is the United States; like Sartre and other Europeans in this era, Heidegger found it natural to associate it with technology and mass production. At the end of the dialogue, the younger man says that, rather than trying futilely to 'get over' universal devastation on such a scale, the only thing to do is to wait. So there they remain, a Germanic Vladimir and Estragon, waiting in their haggard landscape.

It is a typical Heideggerian document, filled with mutterings about capitalism, Communism and foreign lands that are up to no good – surely signs of what Hans Jonas called 'a certain "Blood and Soil" point of view'. Yet it also contains images that are moving and beautiful. It can't be read without thinking of the missing Heidegger sons, lost somewhere

to the East. It speaks eloquently of the ruins of Germany, and of the
German state of mind amid those ruins: a mixture of post-traumatic
distress, blankness, resentment, bitterness and cautious expectancy.

Having resumed his limbo life in Freiburg in the summer of 1945,
Heidegger set off one November day on a clandestine drive to recover
his hidden manuscripts from the countryside near Messkirch and Lake
Constance, or Bodensee. He was helped by the young French philosophy
enthusiast Frédéric de Towarnicki, who had called at Heidegger's house
and made friends with him. German civilians were not yet permitted
to travel without authorisation, so Towarnicki procured a driver and an
official-looking piece of paper in case they were stopped. Heidegger
installed himself in the back seat with an empty rucksack. They left in
the middle of the night, amid storm clouds and lightning flashes.

The car had gone barely twenty kilometres when one of the headlights flickered and went out. They continued, despite the difficulty
of seeing the road between black trees in the heavy rain. A French
patrol loomed out of the darkness, with its tricolour flag; the travellers had to stop and explain themselves. The guard scrutinised their
papers, pointed out that their rear lights were also broken, then waved
them on. They advanced cautiously. Twice, Heidegger asked the driver
to stop in front of a house in the middle of nowhere; both times he
got out with his backpack, went in, and came out smiling with the
bag loaded with documents.

The second headlight began to flicker too. Towarnicki tried to use
his electric torch to light the way, but it was not very effective. Then
the car swerved off the road and hit the embankment. Inspecting the
damage, the driver announced that they had a puncture. They all got
out while the driver tried to attach the spare wheel, which did not fit
the car correctly. Heidegger looked on, interested – one of his favourite
new philosophical topics was technology. He did not offer to help,
but wagged his finger with a mischievous air and said, 'Technik.' He
was clearly enjoying himself. Somehow the driver fixed the wheel and
they moved onwards to their last stop, Bietingen.

By now it was morning, and Heidegger settled himself in to stay at the house of his friends there. The long-suffering Towarnicki hitched back to Freiburg to arrange for a new car. He arrived to find Elfride glaring at him: what had he done with her husband? Still, the consensus was that he had done well by his friend: Heidegger later recalled the favour with gratitude, and gave Towarnicki an inscribed copy of his translation of the chorus from Sophocles' *Antigone*, with its passage on the strangeness of man. He wrote on it, 'In memory of our expedition to Constance.'

Heidegger's good cheer did not last long, as he now had to settle in for a long wait for judgement from the Denazification Committee and the university. Four years would pass before he was cleared to teach again, being finally declared a *Mitläufer* ('fellow traveller') in March 1949, after which he resumed teaching from 1950. The five years of uncertainty were difficult, and for the first year he also had the worry about his lost sons. In early 1946, he had a complete psychological breakdown, and in February was taken into the Haus Baden sanatorium in Badenweiler to recover. It must have looked for a while as though Heidegger was going the way of his heroes Hölderlin and Trakl. But, with treatment from psychiatrists who were already primed in his philosophical language and style of thought, he slowly improved. It helped when news came in March that the Heideggers' two sons were alive in Russia. A much longer wait ensued before they came home. Hermann was released in 1947, having fallen ill, but Jörg, the elder son, was still away in 1949.

Heidegger left the sanatorium in spring 1946, and convalesced in the Todtnauberg hut. The journalist Stefan Schimanski, who saw him there in June 1946 and October 1947, described the silence and isolation, and noted that Heidegger greeted him wearing heavy skiing boots even though it was summer. He seemed to want nothing but to be left alone to write. At the time of Schimanski's second visit, Heidegger had not been down to Freiburg for six months. 'His living conditions were primitive; his books were few, and his only relationship to the world was a stack of writing paper.'

Even before the war, Heidegger's philosophising had changed, as he gave up writing about resoluteness, Being-towards-death, and other bracing personal demands on Dasein, and shifted to writing of the need to be attentive and receptive, to wait and to open up – the themes that are woven through the prisoner-of-war dialogue. This change, known as Heidegger's *Kehre*, or 'turn', was not an abrupt whirl-around as the word suggests, but a slow readjustment, like that of a man in a field who gradually becomes aware of the movement of the breeze in the wheat behind him, and turns to listen.

As he was turning, Heidegger paid increasing attention to language, to Hölderlin and the Greeks, and to the role of poetry in thought. He also reflected on historical developments and on the rise of what he called *Machenschaft* (machination) or *Technik* (technology): modern ways of behaving towards Being which he contrasted with older traditions. By 'machination' he meant the making-machine-like of all things: the attitude that characterises factory automation, environmental exploitation, modern management and war. With this attitude, we brazenly challenge the earth to give up what we want from it, instead of patiently whittling or cajoling things forth as peasant smallholders or craftsmen do. We bully things into yielding up their goods. The most brutal example is in modern mining, where a piece of land is forced to surrender its coal or oil. Moreover, we rarely use what we take at once, but instead convert it to a form of abstract energy to be held in reserve in a generator or storehouse. In the 1940s and 1950s, even matter itself would be challenged in this way, as atomic technology produced energy to be held in reserve in power plants.

One might point out that a peasant who tills the land also challenges it to put forth grain, and then stores that grain. But Heidegger considered this activity quite different. As he argued in a lecture-essay first drafted in the late 1940s, 'The Question Concerning Technology', a farmer 'places the seed in the keeping of the forces of growth and watches over its increase'. Or rather, this is what farmers did until modern agricultural machinery came panting and chuffing along, promising ever greater productivity. In modern challenging-forth of this kind, nature's energy is not sown, tended and harvested; it is unlocked and transformed, then stored in some different form before being distributed. Heidegger uses military images: 'Everything is ordered to stand by, to be immediately at hand, indeed to stand there just so that it may be on call for a further ordering.'

It is a monstrous reversal – and for Heidegger humanity *has* become monstrous. Man is the terrible one: *deinos* in Greek (the word also featuring in the etymology of 'dinosaur', or 'terrible lizard'). This was the word that Sophocles had used when he wrote his chorus about the strange or uncanny quality unique to man.

This process even threatens the basic structure of intentionality: the way the mind reaches out to things as its objects. When something is placed 'on call' or in 'standing-reserve', says Heidegger, it loses its ability to be a proper object. It is no longer distinguished from us and cannot stand up to us. Phenomenology itself is thus threatened by modern humanity's challenging, devastating way of occupying the earth. This could lead to the ultimate disaster. If we are left alone 'in the midst of objectlessness', then we ourselves will lose our structure – we too will be swallowed up into a 'standing-reserve' mode of being. We will devour even ourselves. Heidegger cites the term 'human resources' as evidence of this danger.

For Heidegger, the threat of technology goes beyond the practical fears of the post-war years: machines running out of control, atom bombs exploding, radiation leaks, epidemics, chemical contamination. Instead, it is an ontological threat against reality, and against human being itself. We fear disaster, but the disaster may already be under way. There is hope, however. Heidegger reaches for his Hölderlin:

> But where danger is, grows
> The saving power also.

If we pay proper attention to technology, or rather to what technology reveals about us and our Being, we can gain insight into the truth of human 'belongingness'. From this point, we may find a way forward – which, Heidegger being Heidegger, turns out to mean going backwards into the origin of history, to find a long-forgotten source of renewal in the past.

He continued to work on this material for years. Most of the above thoughts came together in the full version of his 'The Question Concerning Technology', which he delivered as a lecture in Munich in 1953, to an audience including the atomic physicist Werner Heisenberg – a man who certainly knew about the challenging-forth of material energies.

At the same time, Heidegger continued to rework other writings begun in the 1930s, some of which offered a more positive vision of humanity's role on the earth. One was 'The Origin of the Work of Art', which appeared in a revised form in his *Holzwege* (*Off the Beaten Track*) in 1950. There he drew on a notion borrowed from the mediaeval German mystic Meister Eckhart: *Gelassenheit*, which can be translated as 'releasement' or 'letting-be'.

Letting-be became one of the most important concepts in the later Heidegger, denoting a hands-off way of attending to things. It sounds straightforward. 'What seems easier', asks Heidegger, 'than to let a being be just the being that it is?' Yet it is not easy at all, because it is not just a matter of turning indifferently away and letting the world get on with its business. We must turn *towards* things, but in such a way that we don't 'challenge' them. Instead, we allow each being to 'rest upon itself in its very own being'.

This is what modern technology does not do, but some human activities do have this character, and foremost among them is art. Heidegger writes of art as a form of poetry, which he considers the supreme human activity, but he uses the word 'poetry' in a broad sense to mean much more than arranging words into verses. He traces it to its Greek root in *poiēsis* – making or crafting – and he cites Hölderlin again, saying, 'poetically, man dwells on this earth'. Poetry is a way of being.

Poets and artists 'let things be', but they also let things come out and show themselves. They help to ease things into 'unconcealment' (*Unverborgenheit*), which is Heidegger's rendition of the Greek term *alētheia*, usually translated as 'truth'. This is a deeper kind of truth than the mere correspondence of a statement to reality, as when we say 'The cat is on the mat' and point to a mat with a cat on it. Long before we can do this, both cat and mat must 'stand forth out of concealedness'. They must un-hide themselves.

Enabling things to unhide themselves is what humans do: it is our distinctive contribution. We are a 'clearing', a *Lichtung*, a sort of open, bright forest glade into which beings can shyly step forward like a deer from the trees. Or perhaps one should visualise beings entering the clearing to dance, like a bower-bird in a prepared patch in the undergrowth. It would be simplistic to identify the clearing with human consciousness, but this is more or less the idea. We help things to emerge into the light by being conscious of them, and we are conscious of them *poetically*, which means that we pay respectful attention and allow them to show themselves as they are, rather than bending them to our will.

Heidegger does not use the word 'consciousness' here because – as with his earlier work – he is trying to make us think in a radically different way about ourselves. We are not to think of the mind as an empty cavern, or as a container filled with representations of things. We are not even supposed to think of it as firing off arrows of intentional 'aboutness', as in the earlier phenomenology of Brentano. Instead, Heidegger draws us into the depths of his Schwarzwald, and asks us to imagine a gap with sunlight filtering in. We remain in the forest, but we provide a relatively open spot where other beings can bask for a moment. If we did not do this, everything would remain in the thickets, hidden even to itself. To alter the metaphor, there would be no room for beings to emerge from their shell.

The astronomer Carl Sagan began his 1980 television series *Cosmos* by saying that human beings, though made of the same stuff as the stars, are conscious and are therefore 'a way for the cosmos to know itself'. Merleau-Ponty similarly quoted his favourite painter Cézanne as saying, 'The landscape thinks itself in me, and I am its conscious-ness.' This is something like what Heidegger thinks humanity contributes to the earth. We are not made of spiritual nothingness; we are part of Being, but we also bring something unique with us. It is not much: a little open space, perhaps with a path and a bench like the one the young Heidegger used to sit on to do his homework. But through us, the miracle occurs.

This is the sort of thing that enthralled me when I read Heidegger as a student – and I was most impressed by this post-'turn' Heidegger, difficult though he was to grasp. The more pragmatic *Being and Time*-era material about hammers and equipment was pretty good, but it didn't have this deeper, more perplexing beauty. The late Heidegger is writing a form of poetry himself, although he continues to insist, as philosophers do, that this is *how things are*; it is not only a literary trick. Rereading him today, half of me says, 'What nonsense!' while the other half is re-enchanted.

Beauty aside, Heidegger's late writing can also be troubling, with its increasingly mystical notion of what it is to be human. If one speaks of a human being mainly as an open space or a clearing, or a means of 'letting beings be' and dwelling poetically on the earth, then one doesn't seem to be talking about any recognisable *person*. The old Dasein has become less human than ever. It is now a forestry feature. There is glamour in thinking of oneself as a botanical or geological formation, or a space in the landscape – but can Dasein still put up a set of bookshelves? In the very period when Sartre was becoming *more* concerned with questions of action and involvement in the world, Heidegger was retiring almost entirely from consideration of those questions. Freedom, decision and anxiety no longer play much of a role for him. Human beings themselves have become hard to discern, and this is particularly disturbing coming from a philosopher who had not yet convincingly dissociated himself from those who perpetrated the twentieth century's worst crimes against humanity.

Besides, even the keenest Heideggerians must secretly feel that, at times, he talks through his hat. An oft-cited section in 'The Origin of the Work of Art' concerns, not a hat, but a pair of shoes. To convey what he means by art as *poiēsis*, Heidegger describes a Van Gogh painting which he claims depicts shoes belonging to a peasant woman. He goes off on a flight of fancy about what the painting poetically 'brings forth': the shoe-wearer's daily trudge through furrowed earth, the fields' ripening grain, the land's silence in winter, and the woman's fears of hunger and memories of the pains of childbirth. In 1968, the art critic Meyer Schapiro pointed out that the shoes were probably not a peasant's at all but Van Gogh's own. Schapiro kept investigating and, in 1994, found evidence that Van Gogh may have bought them second-hand as smart urban shoes in clean condition, only to then distress them with a long walk through the mud. He capped off his research by citing a note in Heidegger's own hand, admitting 'we cannot say with certainty where these shoes stand nor to whom they belong'. Perhaps it doesn't matter, but it seems clear that Heidegger read a great deal into the painting with very little justification, and that what he read in was a highly romanticised notion of peasant life.

It may be a personal matter: either Heidegger's thoughts on Van Gogh's painting speak to you, or they don't. To me they don't, yet there are other passages in the same essay which do move me. I always loved his description of an ancient Greek temple that seems to call forth the very earth and sky:

Standing there, the building rests on the rocky ground. This resting of the work draws up out of the rock the mystery of that rock's clumsy yet spontaneous support. Standing there, the building holds its ground against the storm raging above it and so first makes the storm itself manifest in its violence. The luster and gleam of the stone, though itself apparently glowing only by the grace of the sun, yet first brings to light the light of the day, the breadth of the sky, the darkness of the night. The temple's firm towering makes visible the invisible space of air.

I'm prepared for the possibility that someone else will find this boring or even odious. But Heidegger's idea that a human architectural construction can make even the *air* show itself differently has stayed somewhere behind my perceptions of buildings and art ever since I first read the essay.

I happily accept that it may have influenced me as a piece of literature rather than as philosophy but, if so, it must be said that this was not Heidegger's intention. He did not expect his readers to treat his work as an aesthetic experience, or to go away like visitors from an art gallery saying, 'I liked the temple – didn't think much of the shoes, though.' His work was supposed to bring us to what the young Karl Jaspers had called 'a *different thinking*, a thinking that, in knowing, reminds me, awakens me, brings me to myself, transforms me'. Besides, since Heidegger now saw all language as poetry, or even as the 'house of Being', he would think it totally infra dig to worry about whether a particular piece of language is best classified as poetry or philosophy.

Reading the late Heidegger requires a 'letting-go' of one's own usual critical ways of thinking. Many consider this an unacceptable demand from a philosopher, even though we are willing to do it for artists. In order to appreciate Wagner's *Ring* cycle or Proust's fiction one has to subscribe temporarily to the creator's own terms of entry or not attempt it at all. The same may be true of Heidegger's late works – and I have only quoted some relatively approachable sections here.

The greater difficulty may be to emerge from it intact afterwards. Heidegger himself found it hard to leave his own philosophical universe. Hans-Georg Gadamer remarked that he had seen Heidegger remain closed up in himself, seeming unhappy and unable to communicate at all until the other person 'came onto the way of thinking he had prepared'. That is a severely limited basis for conversation. Gadamer did add, however, that he became more relaxed after formal lessons were over and everyone enjoyed a glass of fine local wine together.

Several admirers who had previously followed Heidegger's path now turned away from him, appalled by both his Nazi past and the qualities of his late philosophy. Hannah Arendt wrote to Jaspers from America in 1949 describing Heidegger's post-'turn' lectures on Nietzsche as a 'quite awful' form of 'babbling'. She also disapproved of his hiding out in Todtnauberg to grumble about modern civilisation, safely remote from potential critics who did not bother to climb up a mountain just to reprimand him. 'Nobody is likely to climb 1,200 metres to make a scene', she claimed.

A few people did just that, however. One was his former student Herbert Marcuse, formerly an impassioned Heideggerian and now a Marxist. He made the journey in April 1947, hoping to get an explanation and an apology from Heidegger for his Nazi involvement. He did not get either. In August, he wrote asking Heidegger again why he would not make a clear disavowal of the Nazi ideology, when so many people were waiting for just a few words from him. 'Is this really the way you would like to be remembered in the history of ideas?' he asked. But Heidegger refused to oblige. He wrote on 20 January 1948 to thank Marcuse for a package he had sent, presumably of much-needed supplies, adding that he had distributed its contents only 'to former students who were neither in the Party nor had any other connections to National Socialism'. He then turned to Marcuse's questions, adding, 'Your letter shows me precisely how difficult it is to converse with persons who have not been in Germany since 1933.' He explained that he did not want to issue a facile statement of repudiation, because so many real Nazis had rushed to do just that in 1945, announcing their change of belief 'in the most loathsome way' without really meaning what they said. Heidegger did not want to join his voice to theirs.

One of the few ever to express sympathy for this response was Jacques Derrida, the great philosopher of deconstruction: in a talk of 1988, he turned the question of Heidegger's silence around by asking what would have happened if he *had* made a simple statement along the lines of 'Auschwitz is the absolute horror; it is what I fundamentally condemn.' Such an announcement would have satisfied expectations and closed the Heidegger file, as it were. There would be less to discuss and puzzle over. But then, said Derrida, we would feel 'dismissed from the duty' of thinking the question through and asking what Heidegger's refusal implied for his philosophy. By remaining silent, he left us a 'commandment to think what he himself did not think' – and for Derrida, this was more productive.

Marcuse was not willing to accept such an elaborate justification, and in any case Heidegger did not try to win him over. He ended his last letter to Marcuse with what sounds like a deliberate provocation, comparing the Holocaust to the post-war expulsion of Germans from Soviet-dominated zones of Eastern Europe – a comparison made by many other Germans at the time, but also a dig at Marcuse's Communist sympathies. Marcuse was so disgusted that he addressed his reply almost entirely to that point. If Heidegger was capable of presenting such an argument, did that not mean he must be considered 'outside of the dimension in which a conversation between men is even possible'? If Heidegger could not speak or reason, Marcuse could not see a way of attempting to speak or reason with him. With that, another silence descended.

Heidegger's philosophical 'turn' also brought a critical response from his old friend Karl Jaspers, with whom he had been out of contact for years.

Karl and Gertrud Jaspers had somehow managed to survive in Heidelberg throughout the war, in their cautious way, with Karl neither teaching nor publishing. It was a close thing, for it emerged later that their names were on a list of people due to be deported to concentration camps in April 1945; the US Army had occupied Heidelberg in March, just in time to save them. For now, the couple continued to live in Heidelberg, although in 1948 they came to the belated conclusion that they could no longer feel comfortable in Germany, and they moved to Switzerland.

In 1945, the denazification authorities at Freiburg University had approached Jaspers for his opinion on Heidegger: should he be allowed to resume teaching at the university? Jaspers submitted a characteristically thoughtful and balanced report that December. He concluded that Heidegger was a philosopher of the greatest importance who should be given all the university support he needed to pursue his own work – but who should *not* yet be allowed to teach. He wrote, 'Heidegger's mode of thinking, which seems to me to be fundamentally unfree, dictatorial and uncommunicative, would have a very damaging effect on students at the present time.'

While drafting the report, Jaspers re-established contact with Heidegger himself for the first time since before the war. Then, in 1949, he pointedly sent him a copy of his own 1946 book *Die Schuldfrage* (translated as *The Question of German Guilt*). Written in the context of the Nuremberg trials, this discussed the awkward question of how Germans should come to terms with their past and move towards the future. For Jaspers, the outcome of the various trials and denazification inquests was less important than the need for a change of heart in the Germans themselves, beginning with full acknowledgement of responsibility for what had happened, rather than turning away or making excuses as he felt many people were doing. Every German, he wrote, must ask the question 'how am I guilty?' Even people who had defied the Nazis or tried to help their victims still shared in some deep 'metaphysical' guilt, he thought, for, 'if it happens, and if I was there, and if I survive where the other is killed, I know from a voice within myself: I am guilty of being still alive'.

Jaspers' inner 'voice' calls to mind Heidegger's authentic voice of Dasein, calling from within and demanding answerability. But

Heidegger was now refusing answerability and keeping his own voice to himself. He had told Marcuse that he did not want to be one of those who jabbered out excuses, while carrying on as though nothing had changed. Jaspers similarly felt that facile or hypocritical excuses were no good. But he would not accept Heidegger's silence either. The language he considered necessary was not that of ritual disavowal, but that of genuine communication. Jaspers felt that Germans had forgotten how to communicate during the twelve years of hiding and silence, and had to relearn it.

This cut no ice with Heidegger, for whom communication was a long way down the list of what language could do. When he wrote back to Jaspers he made no comment on the contents of his *Schuldfrage*, but reciprocated by sending Jaspers some of his own recent writings. Jaspers was repelled. Picking out Heidegger's pet phrase describing language as 'the house of Being', he wrote back, 'I bristle, because all language seems to be only a bridge to me' – a bridge *between* people, not a shelter or home. Heidegger's next letter, in April 1950, made an even worse impression, filled with talk of the need to wait for the 'advent' of something that would take humans over, or appropriate them; the notions of advent and appropriation were also among Heidegger's post-'turn' concepts. This time, it was Jaspers who fell silent in response. When he at last wrote to Heidegger again, in 1952, it was to say that the new writing style reminded him of the mystical nonsense that had made fools of people for so long. It is 'pure dreaming', he said. He had already written calling Heidegger a 'dreaming boy' in 1950. That had seemed a generous interpretation of Heidegger's failings, but now he clearly felt it was time for Heidegger to wake up.

Jaspers retained his belief in the power of communication all his life, and put it into effect by doing popular radio talks and writing about current events in a way that would reach the widest audience possible. But Heidegger also addressed non-specialist audiences, especially while he was banned from teaching, since this became his only outlet. In March 1950, he delivered two lectures to residents and locals at the northern Black Forest sanatorium of Bühlerhöhe, as part of a

Wednesday-evening series of talks organised by the physician Gerhard Stroomann, who became a friend. Stroomann wrote afterwards, in enthusiastic Heideggerese, that the lectures were successful, but the Q&A sessions were unpredictable: 'when discussion begins, it contains the greatest responsibility and the ultimate danger. Practice is often lacking. One has to stay with the point . . . even if it is only a question.'

Heidegger kept trying. He presented early versions of his lecture on technology to, of all people, the members of the Bremen Club – mostly businessmen and shipping magnates, based in the Hanseatic town of that name. The lecture series was arranged by his friend Heinrich Wiegand Petzet, whose family lived there, and apparently it went down well. Perhaps Heidegger found it easier to get through to the general public than to philosophers, who would make more fuss if his points seemed to make no sense, rather than letting themselves be swept up in the mood of excitement.

Thus, all the time that Heidegger was obstinately resisting communication, his range of influence was growing. By the time he delivered the polished version of his technology lecture in Munich in 1953, his friend Petzet was able to note that the audience, puzzled though they were, responded to its closing words with an 'ovation like a storm breaking from a thousand throats that did not want to cease'. (He does not consider the possibility that they were applauding its being over.)

Even today, Jaspers, the dedicated communicator, is far less widely read than Heidegger, who has influenced architects, social theorists, critics, psychologists, artists, film-makers, environmental activists, and innumerable students and enthusiasts – including the later deconstructionist and post-structuralist schools, which took their starting point from his late thinking. Having spent the late 1940s as an outsider and then been rehabilitated, Heidegger became the overwhelming presence in university philosophy all over the European continent from then on. One Fulbright scholar who arrived in Heidelberg to study philosophy in 1955, Calvin O. Schrag, was surprised to see courses on many other contemporary philosophers, but none on Heidegger. Later his puzzlement disappeared. As he wrote: 'I quickly learned that *all* courses were on Heidegger.'

So who, in the end, was the better communicator?

After their failure of mutual comprehension, Heidegger and Jaspers never met again. There was no decision to make a final break; it just happened that way. Once, when Heidegger heard that Jaspers was passing through Freiburg in 1950, he asked for his train time so he could meet him on the platform, at least to shake hands. Jaspers did not reply.

They did resume a very occasional formal correspondence. When Jaspers turned seventy in 1953, Heidegger sent him greetings. Jaspers responded nostalgically, remembering their conversations back in the 1920s and early 1930s, the sound of Heidegger's voice, and his gestures. But, he added, if they met now, he would not know what to say. He told Heidegger that he regretted not having been stronger in the past – not having forced him to give a proper account of himself. 'I would have taken hold of you, so to speak; I would have relentlessly questioned you and made you take notice.'

Six and a half years later, Heidegger's own seventieth birthday came around, and Jaspers sent him good wishes. He ended his brief letter with a memory of an afternoon when he was about eighteen, on a winter holiday on the Feldberg, a skiing resort not far from Heidegger's part of the forest. Being delicate, not a strong skier like Heidegger, he had stayed close to the hotel and moved slowly on his skis, yet had still been amazed by the mountains' beauty, finding himself 'enchanted in a snowstorm at sunset', watching the changing light and colours on the hills. He closed the letter in the old affectionate way, 'Your Jaspers.' Jaspers' skiing story casts himself as the cautious one, hesitant and sceptical, aware of the attraction of distant vistas but disinclined to venture far towards them. Heidegger, he implies, is more daring, but he may be on the wrong path, in danger and too far gone to call back.

Jaspers was being modest. In reality, he was the one whose mind ranged widely across cultures and epochs, making connections and comparisons – while Heidegger never liked going far from his forest home.

Another former friend who turned against Heidegger was the young man who had playfully mocked Ernst Cassirer in Davos in 1929: Emmanuel Levinas.

Having moved to France before the war and acquired citizenship, Levinas had fought at the front and been captured when France fell. He was imprisoned in a unit reserved for Jewish prisoners of war in Stalag 11B, at Fallingbostel near Magdeburg. A harrowing five years followed, as he and his fellow inmates lived on watery soup and vegetable peelings while being worked to exhaustion chopping wood in the local forest. Their guards taunted them with the possibility that they might be shipped out to death camps at any moment. In fact, being in a POW camp probably saved Levinas's life. It gave him a degree of formal protection that he would not have had as a Jewish civilian at large, although his wife and daughter did also stay alive by hiding in a monastery in France, with help from friends. Back in his native country of Lithuania, the rest of his family did not survive. After Lithuania was occupied by Germany in 1941, all Levinas's relatives were confined to the ghetto with other Jews in their city, Kaunas. The Nazis assembled a large group one morning, among whom were Levinas's father, mother and two brothers. They took them into the countryside, and machine-gunned them to death.

Like Sartre during his interlude in the Stalag, Levinas wrote prolifically while he was incarcerated. He was able to receive writing paper and books, so he read Proust, Hegel, Rousseau and Diderot. He kept notebooks out of which grew his first major work of philosophy, *Existence and Existents*, published in 1947. Here he developed earlier themes, including that of the *'il y a'* ('there is') – the amorphous, undifferentiated, impersonal Being that looms over us in insomnia or exhaustion. This is Heidegger's Being presented as a terrible affliction, rather than as a mystical gift to be awaited in awe. Levinas had a particular horror for what Heidegger had called the ontological difference: the distinction between beings and their Being. If you take away

individual beings in order to be left with pure Being, Levinas felt, you
end up only with something terrifying and inhuman. This was one
reason why, as he wrote, his reflections – although initially inspired
by the philosophy of Heidegger – 'are also governed by a profound
need to leave the climate of that philosophy'.

Levinas turned away from the fog of Being, and went the other
way – towards individual, living, human entities. In his best-known
work, *Totality and Infinity*, published in 1961, he made the relationship
of Self with Other the foundation of his entire philosophy – as central
a concept for him as Being was for Heidegger.

He once said that this shift in thinking had its origin in an experience he had in the camp. Like the other prisoners, he had got used
to the guards treating them without respect as they worked, as if they
were inhuman objects unworthy of fellow feeling. But each evening,
as they were marched back behind the barbed-wire fence again, his
work group would be greeted by a stray dog who had somehow found
its way inside the camp. The dog would bark and fling itself around
with delight at seeing them, as dogs do. Through the dog's adoring
eyes, the men were reminded each day of what it meant to be acknowledged by another being – to receive the basic recognition that one
living creature grants to another.

As Levinas reflected on this experience, it helped to lead him to
a philosophy that was essentially ethical, rather than ontological
like Heidegger's. He developed his ideas from the work of Jewish
theologian Martin Buber, whose *I and Thou* in 1923 had distinguished
between my relationship with an impersonal 'it' or 'them', and the
direct personal encounter I have with a 'you'. Levinas took it further:
when I encounter *you*, we normally meet face-to-face, and it is through
your face that you, as another person, can make ethical demands on
me. This is very different from Heidegger's *Mitsein* or Being-with,
which suggests a group of people standing alongside one another,
shoulder to shoulder as if in solidarity – perhaps as a unified nation
or *Volk*. For Levinas, we literally face each other, one individual at a
time, and that relationship becomes one of communication and moral
expectation. We do not merge; we respond to one another. Instead

of being co-opted into playing some role in my personal drama of authenticity, you look me in the eyes – and you remain Other. You remain *you*.

This relationship is more fundamental than the self, more fundamental than consciousness, more fundamental even than Being – and it brings an unavoidable ethical obligation. Ever since Husserl, phenomenologists and existentialists had being trying to stretch the definition of existence to incorporate our social lives and relationships. Levinas did more: he turned philosophy around entirely so that these relationships were the *foundation* of our existence, not an extension of it.

This adjustment was so radical that Levinas, like Heidegger before him, had to perform contortions with his language to avoid slipping back into old ways of thought. His writing became more and more tortuous over the years, but this priority of the ethical relationship to the Other remained at its centre. As he grew older, his children made a joke of his most famous ideas. When his grandchildren fought over the biggest portions at the dinner table, someone would say of the one who got the lion's share, and thus who had obviously not prioritised the demands of others, 'He doesn't practise Grandpa's philosophy!'

It took courage to crack jokes with Levinas. As he went on, he became a formidable figure, prone to snapping at any Others he encountered at conferences or in classes who asked stupid questions or seemed to misunderstand him. In this, if nothing else, he still had something in common with his former mentor.

Other thinkers took radical ethical turns during the war years. The most extreme was Simone Weil, who actually tried to live by the principle of putting other people's ethical demands first. Having returned to France after her travels through Germany in 1932, she had worked in a factory so as to experience the degrading nature of such work for herself. When France fell in 1940, her family fled to Marseilles (against her protests), and later to the US and to Britain. Even in exile, Weil made extraordinary sacrifices. If there were people in the world who could not sleep in a bed, she would not do so either, so she slept on the floor. Some people lacked food, so she stopped eating almost entirely. She wondered in her journal whether one day someone might develop a form of human chlorophyll, so people could live on sunlight alone.

After a few years of self-starvation, Weil fell ill from tuberculosis complicated by malnutrition. She died in Ashford, Kent on 24 August 1943, of heart failure. All through these last years, she wrote copious philosophical studies of ethics and society, investigating the nature and limits of what human beings owed to one another. Her last work, *The Need for Roots*, argues, among other things, that none of us has rights, but each one of us has a near-infinite degree of duty and obligation to the other. Whatever the underlying cause of her death – and anorexia nervosa seems to have been involved – no one could deny that she lived out her philosophy with total commitment. Of all the lives touched on in this book, hers is surely the most profound and challenging application of Iris Murdoch's notion that a philosophy can be 'inhabited'. Indeed, Murdoch became an admirer of Weil's thinking, which pushed her to turn away from her early interest in Sartrean existentialism towards a more ethical philosophy based on 'the Good'.

Meanwhile, the Christian existentialist Gabriel Marcel was also still arguing, as he had since the 1930s, that ethics trumps everything else in philosophy and that our duty to each other is so great as to play the role of a transcendent 'mystery'. He too had been led to this position partly by a wartime experience: during the First World War he had worked for the Red Cross's Information Service, with the unenviable job of answering relatives' inquiries about missing soldiers. Whenever news came, he passed it on, and usually it was not good. As Marcel later said, this task permanently inoculated him against warmongering rhetoric of any kind, and it made him aware of the power of what is *unknown* in our lives.

One striking link between these radical ethical thinkers, all on the fringes of our main story, is that they had religious faith. They also granted a special role to the notion of 'mystery' – that which cannot be known, calculated or understood, especially when it concerns our relationships with each other. Heidegger was different from them, since he rejected the religion he grew up with and had no real interest in ethics – probably as a consequence of his having no real interest in the human. Yet every page of his late work suggests some direct experience of the ineffable or ungraspable. He too was a mystic.

The mystery tradition had roots in Kierkegaard's 'leap of faith'. It owed much to the other great nineteenth-century mystic of the impossible, Dostoevsky, and to older theological notions. But it also grew from the protracted trauma that was the first half of the twentieth century. Since 1914, and especially since 1939, people in Europe and elsewhere had come to the realisation that we cannot fully know or trust ourselves; that we have no excuses or explanations for what we do – and yet that we must ground our existence and relationships on something firm, because otherwise we cannot survive.

Even the atheistic Sartre showed a desire for a new way of thinking about values. He had been scathing about traditional ethics in *Nausea*, writing in Levinasian terms of how bourgeois types, professing to be well-meaning humanists, had 'never allowed themselves to be affected by the meaning of a face'. In *Being and Nothingness*, he went on to say that the placid old ethical principles based on mere tolerance did not go far enough any more. 'Tolerance' failed to engage with the full extent of the demands others make on us. It is not enough to back off and simply put up with each other, he felt. We must learn to give each other more than that. Now he went even further: we must all become deeply 'engaged' in our shared world.

The young French writer Frédéric de Towarnicki, having accompanied Heidegger on his quest to collect his manuscripts, next became keen to introduce him and Sartre to each other. He had already given Heidegger a series of articles on Sartrean existentialism by his fellow Frenchman Jean Beaufret. When they discussed these on a later visit, Heidegger marvelled at how Sartre managed to be at once philosopher, phenomenologist, dramatist, novelist, essayist and journalist. Elfride, who was also present, asked, *'Mais enfin, qu'est-ce que l'existentialisme?'* ('So what is this existentialism anyway?')

Next time he called, Towarnicki brought Heidegger a copy of *Being and Nothingness*. Heidegger playfully weighed its bulk in his hand and said that he had little time for reading at the moment – that time-honoured excuse. (On this occasion, as Towarnicki left, he showed him a treasure of his own, wrapped in sheets of silken paper inside his desk: a photograph of Nietzsche. 'He doesn't show that to everyone,' whispered Elfride.)

This was not encouraging, but Towarnicki did not easily give up on his hope of bringing Heidegger and Sartre together, either for a private meeting or a public debate. He tried to interest Camus too, but Camus wanted nothing to do with Heidegger. Sartre was more intrigued, but, like Heidegger, he kept telling Towarnicki that he was too busy to do anything at the moment. Instead, he invited Towarnicki to write up his own meetings with Heidegger for *Les Temps modernes*, which Towarnicki did.

Heidegger meanwhile found time to dip into *Being and Nothingness* after all. He told Towarnicki on his next visit that he appreciated Sartre's psychological acuity and his 'feeling for concrete things'. This, at least, was how Towarnicki reported it; since he was writing for *Les Temps modernes*, he may have been inclined to flatter its editor. Heidegger also gave him a courteous letter to deliver to Sartre. It included a remark that could be read in two ways: 'Your work is dominated by an immediate understanding of my philosophy the likes of which I have not previously encountered.'

To others, Heidegger was blunter in his response. When the American scholar Hubert Dreyfus saw *Being and Nothingness* on Heidegger's desk and remarked on it, Heidegger snapped, 'How can I even begin to read this *Dreck*!' – this rubbish. He began an extended essay in the form of a letter to Jean Beaufret, attacking the humanist version of existentialism that Sartre had presented to such acclaim in his 'Existentialism Is a Humanism' lecture, with its paean to freedom and individual action. Heidegger wanted nothing to do with this kind of philosophy. His piece, published in 1947 as 'Letter on Humanism' and filled with evocations of forest clearings and letting-be, stands as one of the key texts in his own decidedly anti-humanist new style of thinking. Sartre did not respond to it.

Heidegger's earlier letter to Sartre had invited him to come to Todtnauberg: 'In our little hut we could philosophise together, and go for skiing trips in the Black Forest.' According to Towarnicki, Heidegger had been impressed by Sartre's description of skiing in *Being and Nothingness* – which comes towards the end, suggesting that Heidegger had got well into the *Dreck* after all. It would be wonderful to imagine Sartre and Heidegger – and perhaps also Beauvoir, who was more athletic than Sartre – flying down the slopes, flush-cheeked, the wind whipping away their words, and Heidegger no doubt going much too fast for anyone to keep up, so as to show off. He liked to do this, judging by Max Müller's recollections of going out in the snow with him: 'When we were skiing, he laughed at me a number of times because I made turns and curves where he dashingly raced straight down.'

But the skiing trip never happened. Sartre was always busy; his diary was overflowing with appointments. After all, it would still be a little embarrassing for a Frenchman in 1945 to go off into the Black Forest snow with the former Nazi rector of Freiburg.

Early in 1948, Sartre and Beauvoir did travel to Germany to attend a Berlin production of Sartre's 1943 play about freedom, *The Flies*. In its original incarnation, the play had used the classical *Oresteia* story as a parable for the French situation under Occupation. Now, Jürgen Fehling's production at Berlin's Hebbel Theatre applied the same idea to the situation of Germany after the war, making the point clear with a grim stage set dominated by a temple in the shape of a bunker. The implication was that Germany was now similarly paralysed by its shame. Sartre's play had been designed to urge the French to shake off the past and act constructively for the future; perhaps this message could be reinterpreted to fit the German situation.

Sartre certainly thought so. In an article the year before, to mark a smaller production being performed in the French zone of Germany, he wrote that Germans shared a similar problem to the French a few years earlier:

> For the Germans, too, I think that remorse is pointless. I do not mean that they should simply wipe out past faults from their memory. No. But I feel sure that they won't earn the forgiveness they could get from the world just by being obligingly repentant. They will earn it rather by total, sincere commitment to a future of freedom and work, by their firm desire to build this future, and by the presence among them of as many men of goodwill as possible. Perhaps the play can – not lead them to this future – but encourage them to aim in that direction.

Not everyone in Germany agreed with this analysis, and the debate around the play attracted much attention. This in turn ensured full audiences: Simone de Beauvoir heard that some people were paying 500 marks for a ticket – over twice an average monthly salary. One person even paid two geese, a high price in a city where food was still scarce. Initially Beauvoir had been nervous about making the German trip, after fearing the German occupiers for so long in Paris, but she changed her mind on seeing the scale of the country's devastation in both the Heideggerian and ordinary senses of the word. It was then deepest winter; the temperature had been as low as −18°C for weeks, yet many Berliners went around without coats, and Beauvoir saw people pushing little trolleys so as to collect any useful item they saw on their walks. It was partly to keep warm that they were so keen on theatre-going, although it sometimes meant long journeys through the snow in inadequate shoes. Berlin was barely functioning, and it was awkwardly split between its Soviet, American, British and French administrative zones, the last three of which would unite to form West Berlin a few months later. It had certainly changed since Sartre saw it in 1933 and 1934. In a spare moment between his public appearances, he sought out the house where he had stayed back then, and found it just standing, but in a tumbledown state.

The main event was a debate hosted at the Hebbel Theatre itself on 4 February. Speaking in French with a translator, Sartre defended his play against speakers of both Christian and Marxist persuasions who believed it conveyed the wrong message for Germans. Its existentialist philosophy of liberation was all right for the French in 1943, they said, but it was wrong to urge Germans to move on just yet. The Nuremberg trials had barely finished; some of those who had committed crimes had never been held accountable at all. One speaker warned that many might seize on the play as a justification for disowning culpability for real past crimes, evading justice.

Sartre followed the discussions in German, before using the translator to respond. He argued that existentialist freedom was never

meant to be used as an excuse of any kind: that was the exact opposite of what it was about. In existentialism, there are no excuses.
Freedom comes with total responsibility.

His short speech prompted Christian writer Gert Theunissen to
shift to a more general attack on Sartre's conception of freedom. It
was just plain wrong to say 'existence precedes essence', Theunissen
said. Humans *do* have an essence, which is given to them by God, and
their job is to follow it. According to the transcript of the exchange,
this remark attracted 'loud approval in the room. Several whistles.
Hilarity.' Next Alfons Steiniger, head of the Society for the Study of
the Culture of the Soviet Union, came in from a Communist angle.
Sartre's play risked being taken 'as encouragement of triviality, of
nihilism, of pessimism', he said – these being the usual buzzwords
used by Communists to bash existentialism. In general, the discussion
rarely transcended this level. Not for the first or last time, Sartre was
stuck between two opponents who both hated him while having
almost nothing in common with each other.

Of course, they had a point. Just because existentialism was not
supposed to provide excuses did not mean that people would not try
to use it that way. It would not require great skill in sophistry to twist
The Flies into an argument for selective forgetfulness. Nor was it clear
that the parallels between the French situation of 1943 and the German
situation of 1948 went much beyond a feeling shared by much of the
rest of the world at this time, too: horror at the recent past, and
apprehension (mingled with hope) about the future.

Other aspects of *The Flies* would have resonated with Berliners in
1948, however, and these had more to do with current sufferings. The
stark landscape on stage looked a lot like the Berlin outside the door,
and even the theatrical device of the flies might have triggered memories – for, in the hot and terrible summer of 1945, German cities were
reportedly infested by an unpleasant large green fly species propagating
on the rotting bodies under the rubble.

Above all, Berlin was itself an occupied city. It was occupied by
anxiety and want, by the rival foreign powers, and especially by fear
of the Soviet Union. A couple of months after Sartre and Beauvoir

left, Soviet forces swooped and cut off all supplies coming into the western side of Berlin. In March 1948 they blocked the railway lines, and in June they cut off the roads. They set out to starve Berlin into submission, just as the Germans had starved Leningrad during the war.

To this, the Western powers responded with a bold remedy. They simply flew in everything that the city needed: food, coal, medicines. For over a year, absolutely everything necessary for survival came in by air, in an operation known as the Berlin Airlift. At one stage, a plane was landing in Berlin at a rate of one every minute, twenty-four hours a day. In May 1949, a deal was finally struck with the Soviets and the blockade was eased, but the planes kept flying in from the West until the end of that September. Berlin had no wall yet; that went up in 1961. But it was a divided city that would have to survive in a state of prolonged political emergency for the next forty years. Perhaps the drama of haunted, beleaguered Árgos had something to say to Berliners after all.

Sartre and Beauvoir had overcome their hesitation about going to Germany, but they still showed no sign of wanting to visit Heidegger. Sartre would not meet him until 1953 – and it would not go well.

The meeting occurred after Sartre travelled to the University of Freiburg for a lecture. The students were excited and the hall was crowded, but, as Sartre droned on for three hours in difficult French, their eagerness wilted. He probably noticed the drop in adulation levels by the end of the lecture, and this must have put him on the defensive even before he traipsed out to the suburb of Zähringen to meet Heidegger in his main home there. He did not go to Todtnauberg, and there was no skiing.

The two men had a conversation in German – Sartre's command of the language was just about up to this. Neither participant gave us a first-hand account of what was said, but Heidegger talked about it to Petzet, and Sartre talked about it to Beauvoir, after which both she and Petzet made notes. According to both, the dialogue quickly went haywire. Heidegger brought up the subject of *La dimension*

Florestan, a recent play by Gabriel Marcel which poked fun at an unnamed philosopher who holed himself up in a remote hut, emitting only the occasional incomprehensible pronouncement. Someone had told Heidegger about it, and, although he had not seen or heard the play himself, he had no difficulty in recognising its target and was unamused.

Sartre did his diplomatic duty as a Frenchman by apologising on Marcel's behalf. This was generous of him, considering that he had himself come under attack by Marcel several times, first in a review of *Being and Nothingness* in 1943 and then in a 1946 essay, 'Existence and Human Freedom'. Marcel had laid into Sartre's atheism, his lack of an ethical philosophy, and what he felt was Sartre's inability to accept 'grace' or gifts from others – notably, he implies, from God, but also from fellow humans. But Sartre showed considerable grace now in taking the flak from Heidegger for Marcel's satire.

After Heidegger had got the conversation off to a bad start by venting his feelings about this minor awkwardness, it was Sartre's turn to mount his hobby horse. He was burning to talk about the question of political engagement: the duty he felt writers and thinkers had to become involved with the politics of their time. This was, to say the least, an embarrassing topic for Heidegger, and not one he wanted to hear Sartre's views about. Sartre later told his secretary Jean Cau that, when he first brought it up, Heidegger looked at him 'with infinite pity'.

Actually, Heidegger's face was probably communicating something more like, '*Must* we talk about this?' Whatever his feelings, the result was more wasted time in a conversation that should have been far more interesting than it apparently was. If Heidegger and Sartre ever got onto discussing subjects such as freedom, Being, humanism, anxiety, authenticity or anything else of the sort, none of it was preserved. They spoke past one another.

Freiburg, the 'City of Phenomenology' that had haunted Sartre's work for two decades, had let him down, and in any case his own ideas had now departed a long way from Heidegger's. He left in a savage mood, annoyed even with the organisers of the lecture. When he got to the train and found that they had thoughtfully left a gift of roses in his compartment, perhaps a standard gesture for visiting celebrities, he considered it ridiculous. 'Bouquets of roses! Armfuls of them!' he said later to Cau, surely exaggerating somewhat. He waited until the train had left the station, then threw them out the window.

After his return, he marvelled to Beauvoir at how Heidegger was revered these days: 'Four thousand students and professors toiling over Heidegger day after day, just think of it!' From then on, he referred to Heidegger dismissively as the Old Man of the Mountain. The days had long passed when Sartre had seized on *Being and Time* as his only consolation during the days after France's defeat in 1940. But Sartre was not the only one who could not go backwards. The war had changed everything, for everyone.

9

Life Studies

In which existentialism is applied to actual people.

One day, somewhere around the time of the 1948 Berlin trip, Beauvoir was sitting with pen in hand, staring at a sheet of paper. Alberto Giacometti said to her, 'How wild you look!' She replied, 'It's because I want to write and I don't know what.' With the sagacity that came from its being someone else's problem, he said, 'Write anything.'

She did, and it worked. She took further inspiration from her friend Michel Leiris's experimental autobiographical writings, which she had recently read: these inspired her to try a free-form way of writing about her memories, basing them around the theme of what it had meant to her to grow up as a girl. When she discussed this idea with Sartre, he urged her to explore the question in more depth. Thus it is in relation to three men that Simone de Beauvoir describes the origin of her great feminist work, *The Second Sex*.

Perhaps the starting point had been a modest idea in need of masculine encouragement, but Beauvoir soon developed the project into something revolutionary in every sense: her book overturned accepted ideas about the nature of human existence, and encouraged its readers to overturn their own existences. It was also a confident experiment in what we might call 'applied existentialism'. Beauvoir used philosophy to tackle two huge subjects: the history of humanity – which she reinterpreted as a history of patriarchy – and the history of an individual woman's whole life as it plays itself out from birth to old age. The two stories are interdependent, but occupy two separate parts of the book. To flesh them out, Beauvoir combined elements of her own experience with stories gathered from other women she knew, and with extensive studies in history, sociology, biology and psychology.

She wrote quickly. Chapters and early versions appeared in *Les Temps modernes* through 1948; the full tome came out in 1949. It was greeted with shock. This freethinking lady existentialist was already considered a disturbing figure, with her open relationship, her child-lessness and her godlessness. Now here was a book filled with descriptions of women's sexual experience, including a chapter on lesbianism. Even her friends recoiled. One of the most conservative responses came from Albert Camus, who, as she wrote in her memoirs, 'in a few morose sentences, accused me of making the French male look ridiculous'. But if men found it uncomfortable, women who read it often found themselves thinking about their lives in a new way. After it was translated into English in 1953 – three years before *Being*

and Nothingness and nine years before Heidegger's *Being and Time* – *The Second Sex* had an even greater impact in Britain and America than in France. It can be considered the single most influential work ever to come out of the existentialist movement.

Beauvoir's guiding principle was that growing up female made a bigger difference to a person than most people realised, including women themselves. Some differences were obvious and practical. French women had only just gained the right to vote (with Liberation in 1944), and continued to lack many other basic rights; a married woman could not open her own bank account until 1965. But the legal differences reflected deeper existential ones. Women's everyday experiences and their Being-in-the-world diverged from men's so early in life that few thought of them as being developmental at all; people assumed the differences to be 'natural' expressions of femininity. For Beauvoir, instead, they were *myths* of femininity – a term she adapted from the anthropologist Claude Lévi-Strauss, and which ultimately derived from Friedrich Nietzsche's 'genealogical' way of digging out fallacies about culture and morality. In Beauvoir's usage, a myth is something like Husserl's notion of the encrusted theories which accumulate on phenomena, and which need scraping off in order to get to the 'things themselves'.

After a broad-brush historical overview of myth and reality in the first half of the book, Beauvoir devoted the second half to relating a typical woman's life from infancy on, showing how – as she said – 'One is not born, but rather becomes, a woman.'

The first influences begin in early childhood, she wrote. While boys are told to be brave, a girl is expected to cry and be weak. Both sexes hear similar fairy tales, but in them the males are heroes, princes or warriors, while the females are locked up in towers, put to sleep, or chained to a rock to wait to be rescued. Hearing the stories, a girl notices that her own mother stays mostly in her home, like an imprisoned princess, while her father goes off to the outside world like a warrior going to war. She understands which way her own role will lie.

Growing older, the girl learns to behave modestly and decorously.

Boys run, seize, climb, grasp, punch; they literally grab hold of the physical world and wrestle with it. Girls wear pretty dresses and dare not run in case they get dirty. Later, they wear high heels, corsets and skirts; they grow long fingernails which they have to worry about breaking. They learn, in countless small ways, to hesitate about damaging their delicate persons if they do anything at all. As Iris Marion Young later put it in 'Throwing Like a Girl', a 1980 essay applying Beauvoir's analysis in more detail, girls come to think of themselves as *positioned in* space' rather than as defining or constituting the space around them by their movements.

Adolescence brings a more heightened self-consciousness, and this is the age in which some girls become prone to self-harming, while troubled boys are more likely to pick fights with others. Sexuality develops, but small boys are already aware of the penis as something important, while the girl's genitals are never mentioned and seem not to exist. Early female sexual experiences may be embarrassing, painful or threatening; they may bring more self-doubt and anxiety. Then comes the fear of pregnancy. (This was written well before the Pill.) Even if young women enjoy sex, female sexual pleasure can be more overwhelming, and thus more disturbing, says Beauvoir. It is generally linked to marriage, for most women, and with this comes the repetitive and isolating labour of housework, which accomplishes nothing out in the world and is no real 'action'.

By now, all these factors have conspired to hold a woman back from establishing authority and agency in the wider world. The world is not a 'set of tools' for her, in the Heideggerian sense. Instead it is 'dominated by fate and run through with mysterious caprices'. This is why, Beauvoir believes, women rarely attain greatness in the arts or literature – although she makes an exception for Virginia Woolf, who showed, in her 1928 work *A Room of One's Own*, what disasters were likely to befall an imaginary sister of Shakespeare's born with the same talents. Beauvoir sees every element of women's situation as conspiring to box them in to mediocrity, not because they are innately inferior, but because they learn to become inward-looking, passive, self-doubting and over-eager to please. Beauvoir finds most female writers disappointing because they do not seize hold of the human condition; they do not take it up as their own. They find it difficult to feel *responsible* for the universe. How can a woman ever announce, as Sartre does in *Being and Nothingness*, 'I carry the weight of the world by myself'?

For Beauvoir, the greatest inhibition for women comes from their acquired tendency to see themselves as 'other' rather than as a transcendent subject. Here she drew on her wartime reading of Hegel, who had analysed how rival consciousnesses wrestle for dominance, with one playing 'master' and the other 'slave'. The master perceives everything from his own viewpoint, as is natural. But, bizarrely, so does the slave, who ties herself in knots trying to visualise the world from the master's point of view – an 'alienated' perspective. She even adopts his point of view on herself, casting herself as object and him as subject. This tormented structure eventually collapses when the slave wakes up to the fact that she has it all backwards, and that the whole relationship rests on the hard work that she is doing – on her labour. She rebels, and in doing so she becomes fully conscious at last.

Beauvoir found the Hegelian vision of human relationships as a protracted battle of gazes or perspectives a richly productive idea. She had been talking it through with Sartre for years. He too had been interested in the master–slave dialectic since the 1930s, and had made it a major theme in *Being and Nothingness*. Since his examples illustrating the battle of alienated gazes are particularly lively, let us detour away from Beauvoir for a few moments to visit them.

In his first example, Sartre asks us to imagine walking in a park. If I'm alone, the park arranges itself comfortably around my point of view: everything I see presents itself *to me*. But then I notice a man crossing the lawn towards me. This causes a sudden cosmic shift. I become conscious that the man is also arranging *his* own universe around himself. As Sartre puts it, the green of the grass turns itself towards the other man as well as towards me, and some of my universe drains off in his direction. Some of me drains off too, for I am an object in his world as he is in mine. I am no longer a pure perceiving nothingness; I have a visible outside, which I know he can see.

Sartre then adds a twist. This time he puts us in the hallway of a

Parisian hotel, peering through the keyhole of someone's door –
perhaps because of jealousy, lust or curiosity. I am absorbed in
whatever I'm seeing, and strain towards it. Then I hear footsteps in
the hall – someone is coming! The whole set-up changes. Instead of
being lost in the scene inside the room, I am now aware of myself
as a peeping tom, which is how I'll appear to the third party coming
down the hall. My look, as I peer through the keyhole, becomes 'a
look-looked-at'. My 'transcendence' – my ability to pour out of myself
towards what I am perceiving – is itself 'transcended' by the transcendence of another. That Other has the power to stamp me as a certain
kind of object, ascribing definite characteristics to me rather than
leaving me to be free. I fight to fend this off by controlling how that
person will see me – so, for example, I might make an elaborate
pretence of having stooped merely to tie my shoelace, so that he does
not brand me a nasty voyeur.

Episodes of competitive gazing recur throughout Sartre's fiction
and biographies, as well as in his philosophy. In his journalism, he
recalled the unpleasantness after 1940 of feeling oneself looked at as
a member of a defeated people. In 1944, he wrote a whole play about
it: *Huis clos*, translated as *No Exit*. It depicts three people trapped
together in a room: a military deserter accused of cowardice, a cruel
lesbian, and a flirtatious gold-digger. Each looks judgementally at at
least one of the others, and each longs to escape their companions'
pitiless eyes. But they cannot do so, for they are dead and in hell. As
the play's much-quoted and frequently misunderstood final line has
it: 'Hell is other people.' Sartre later explained that he did not mean
to say that other people were hellish in general. He meant that *after
death* we become frozen in their view, unable any longer to fend off
their interpretation. In life, we can still do something to manage the
impression we make; in death, this freedom goes and we are left
entombed in other's people's memories and perceptions.

Sartre's vision of living human relationships as a kind of intersub-
jective jiu-jitsu led him to produce some very strange descriptions of
sex. Judging by the discussion of sexuality in *Being and Nothingness*, a
Sartrean love affair was an epic struggle over perspectives, and thus

over freedom. If I love you, I don't want to control your thoughts directly, but I want you to love and desire me and to *freely* give up your freedom to me. Moreover, I want you to see me, not as a contingent and flawed person like any other, but as a 'necessary' being in your world. That is, you are not to coolly assess my flaws and irritating habits, but to welcome every detail of me as though no jot or tittle could possibly be different. Recalling *Nausea*, one might say that I want to be like the ragtime song for you. Sartre did realise that such a state of affairs is unlikely to last long. It also comes with a trade-off: you are going to want the same unconditional adoration from me. As Iris Murdoch memorably put it, Sartre turns love into a 'battle between two hypnotists in a closed room'.

Sartre derived this analysis of love and other encounters at least in part from what Simone de Beauvoir had made out of Hegel. They both pored over the implications of the master–slave dialectic; Sartre worked out his striking and bizarre examples, while Beauvoir made it the more substantial basis of her magnum opus. Her reading was more complex than his. For a start, she pointed out that the idea of love, or any other relationship, as a reciprocal encounter between two equal participants had missed one crucial fact: real human relationships contained differences of status and role. Sartre had neglected the different existential situations of men and women; in *The Second Sex*, she used Hegel's concept of alienation to correct this.

As she pointed out, woman is indeed 'other' for man – but man is not exactly 'other' for woman, or not in the same way. Both sexes tend to agree in taking the male as the defining case and the centre of all perspectives. Even language reinforces this, with 'man' and 'he' being the default terms in French as in English. Women try constantly to picture themselves as they would look to a male gaze. Instead of looking out to the world as it presents itself to them (like the person peering through the keyhole) they maintain a point of view in which they are the objects (like the same person after becoming aware of footsteps in the hall). This, for Beauvoir, is why women spend so much time in front of mirrors. It is also why both men and women implicitly take women to be the more sensual, the more eroticised, the more *sexual* sex. In theory, for a heterosexual female, men should be the sexy ones, disporting themselves for the benefit of her gaze. Yet she sees herself as the object of attraction, and the man as the person in whose eyes she glows with desirability.

Women, in other words, live much of their lives in what Sartre would have called bad faith, pretending to be objects. They do what the waiter does when he glides around playing the role of waiter; they identify with their 'immanent' image rather than with their 'transcendent' consciousness as a free for-itself. The waiter does it when he's at work; women do it all day and to a greater extent. It is exhausting, because, all the time, a woman's subjectivity is trying to do what comes naturally to subjectivity, which is to assert itself as the centre of the universe. A struggle rages inside every woman, and because of this Beauvoir considered the problem of how to be a woman the existentialist problem par excellence.

Beauvoir's initial fragments of memoir had by now grown into a study of alienation on an epic scale: a phenomenological investigation not only of female experience but of childhood, embodiment, competence, action, freedom, responsibility and Being-in-the-world. *The Second Sex* draws on years of reading and thinking, as well as on conversations with Sartre, and is by no means the mere adjunct to Sartrean philosophy that it was once taken to be. True, she successfully shocked one feminist interviewer in 1972 by insisting that her main influence in writing it was *Being and Nothingness*. But seven years later, in another interview, she was adamant that Sartre had nothing to do with working out Hegelian ideas of the Other and the alienated gaze: 'It was I who thought about that! It was absolutely not Sartre!'

Whatever had fed it, Beauvoir's book outdid Sartre's in its subtle sense of the balance between freedom and constraint in a person's life. She showed how choices, influences and habits can accumulate over a lifetime to create a structure that becomes hard to break out of. Sartre also thought that our actions often formed a shape over the long term, creating what he called the 'fundamental project' of a person's existence. But Beauvoir emphasised the connection between this and our wider situations as gendered, historical beings. She gave full weight to the difficulty of breaking out of such situations – although she never doubted that we remain existentially free despite it all. Women *can* change their lives, which is why it is worth writing books to awaken them to this fact.

The Second Sex could have become established in the canon as one of the great cultural re-evaluations of modern times, a book to set alongside the works of Charles Darwin (who re-situated humans in relation to other animals), Karl Marx (who re-situated high culture in relation to economics) and Sigmund Freud (who re-situated the conscious mind in relation to the unconscious). Beauvoir evaluated human lives afresh by showing that we are profoundly gendered beings: she re-situated men in relation to women. Like the other books, *The Second Sex* exposed myths. Like the others, its argument was controversial and open to criticism in its specifics – as inevitably happens when one makes major claims. Yet it was never elevated into the pantheon.

Is this further proof of sexism? Or is it because her existentialist terminology gets in the way? English-speaking readers never even saw most of the latter. It was cut by its first translator in 1953, the zoology professor Howard M. Parshley, largely on the urging of his publisher. Only later, reading the work, did his editor ask him to go easy with the scissors, saying, 'I am now quite persuaded that this is one of the handful of greatest books on sex ever written.' It was not just omissions that were the problem; Parshley rendered Beauvoir's *pour-soi* (for-itself) as 'her true nature in itself', which precisely reverses the existentialist meaning. He turned the title of the second part, 'L'expérience vécue' ('lived experience'), into 'Woman's Life Today' – which, as Toril Moi has observed, makes it sound like the title of a ladies' magazine. To make matters more confusing and further demean the book, English-language paperback editions through the 1960s and 1970s tended to feature misty-focus naked women on the cover, making it look like a work of soft porn. Her novels got similar treatment. Strangely, this never happened with Sartre's books. No edition of *Being and Nothingness* ever featured a muscle-man on the cover wearing only a waiter's apron. Nor did Sartre's translator Hazel Barnes simplify his terminology – although she notes in her memoirs that at least one reviewer thought she should have.

If sexism and the existentialist language were not to blame, another reason for *The Second Sex*'s intellectual sidelining might be that it presents itself as a case study: an existentialist study of just one particular type of life. In philosophy, as in many other fields, applied studies tend to be dismissed as postscripts to more serious works.

But that was never existentialism's way. It was always meant to be about real, individual lives. If done correctly, *all* existentialism is applied existentialism.

Sartre was just as interested as Beauvoir in seeing how existentialism could be applied to particular lives, and in his case it led him to biography. While Beauvoir traced a generic woman's life from babyhood to maturity, Sartre did the same with a series of individual men (and they *are* all men): Baudelaire, Mallarmé, Genet, Flaubert and himself, as well as subjects of shorter essays. In *Nausea*, he had Roquentin give up his biographical project so as not to impose a conventional narrative form on a life, but there is nothing conventional about Sartre's biographies. He abandons standard chronology and instead looks for distinctive shapes and key moments on which a life turns – those moments in which a person makes a choice about some situation, and thus changes everything. In these crux points, we catch a person in the very act of turning existence into essence.

The most important such moments tend to occur in childhood. Sartre's biographies all focus on his subjects' early years; *Words*, his own memoir, confines itself to them exclusively. This interest in childhood owes something to Freud, who also wrote psycho-biographies unpicking the dramas of a life, often tracing them to a 'primal scene'. Sartre liked to find primal scenes too, but by contrast with Freud they did not usually have to do with sex. Sartre thought sexual experiences took their power from more basic experiences to do with our very being. He sought out those experiences during which a child in a challenging situation took control and bent that situation his own way. In other words, he interpreted his subjects' lives in terms of their freedom. This happens above all in his book about the writer Jean Genet, which appeared in 1952 – three years after Beauvoir's *The Second Sex*, and visibly marked by her influence.

After first meeting Genet in the Café Flore during the war years, Sartre had followed his career with interest as Genet published erotic, poetic novels and memoirs based on his life in reform schools, prisons, and on the road as a thief and prostitute. His most provocative book, *Funeral Rites*, told of a French teenager who fights on the German side during the last days of the Occupation, even though the Germans are losing – or rather, because they are losing. Genet tended to sympathise with the defeated or despised in any situation; in 1944 that meant Germans and collaborators, not the triumphant *résistants*. He went on to support traitors, violent revolutionaries, Baader–Meinhof terrorists, Black Panthers and more or less anyone who was an outsider. He backed the student radicals of the 1960s, too, but remarked to William Burroughs, 'If they ever win, I'll turn against them.'

Sartre loved Genet's contrariness, as well as his way of poeticising reality. He was pleased when his publisher Gallimard asked him to write a foreword for a collected edition of Genet's works. But then Sartre's foreword grew to be 700 pages long. Rather than whacking Sartre over the head with the manuscript in a rage, Gallimard agreed to publish it as a separate book, under a title highlighting its theme of transfiguration: *Saint Genet*. This proved a good decision; it was as much a treatise of ideas as a biographical work. Sartre used elements of Marxist analysis, but mainly he approached Genet's life as a way of demonstrating his theory that 'freedom alone can account for a person in his totality'.

In doing this, he interpreted Genet above all as a *writer*, who took control of the contingencies of his life by writing about them. But where did Genet get this ability to transform the events of his life into art, asked Sartre? Was there a definite moment when Genet, a despised and abused child abandoned by his unmarried mother and taken in by an orphanage, began to turn into a poet?

Sartre found the moment he was looking for in an incident that occurred when Genet was ten years old and living with a foster family. Such a child was expected to be humble and grateful, but Genet refused to comply, and showed his rebellion by stealing small objects from the family and their neighbours. One day, he was sticking his hands in a drawer when a family member walked in on him and shouted, 'You're a thief!' As Sartre interpreted it, the young Genet was frozen in the gaze of the Other: he became an object slapped with a despicable label. Instead of feeling abashed, Genet took that label and changed its meaning by asserting it as his own. You call me a thief? Very well, I'll *be* a thief!

By adopting the other person's objectifying label as a substitute for his unself-conscious self, Genet was performing the same psychological contortion as the one Beauvoir had observed in women. She believed it put a strain on women all their lives, and made them hesitant and full of self-doubt. But Sartre saw Genet as performing the manoeuvre defiantly, reversing the effect: instead of keeping him down, his alienation gave him his escape. From then on, he *owned* his outsider identity as thief, vagrant, homosexual and prostitute. He took control of his oppression by inverting it, and his books take their energy from that inversion. The most degrading elements of Genet's experience – excrement, bodily fluids, bad smells, imprisonment, violent sex – become the ones held up as sublime. Genet's books turn shit into flowers, prison cells into sacred temples, and the most murderous prisoners into the objects of the greatest tenderness. This is why Sartre calls him a saint: where a saint transfigures suffering into sanctity, Genet transfigures oppression into freedom.

Sartre intuited all this largely because he was thinking at least as much of his own life as Genet's. His own bourgeois childhood had little in common with Genet's, yet he too had been through dark times. When his family moved to La Rochelle, the twelve-year-old Sartre had been confronted with a stepfather who intimidated him, and with life at a rough school where the other boys beat him, branded him a pariah, and sneered at him for being ugly. In his misery, Sartre decided on a ritual gesture that, he imagined, would make their violence a part of himself and turn it against them. He stole change from his mother's purse and used it to buy pastries for his tormenters. This seems a funny kind of violence – depending on what the pastries were like. But for Sartre it was a magical act. It was a transformation: his bullies had taken his possessions from him, so now he would *give* them something. Through his Genet-like theft and gift, he redefined the situation on his own terms and made a sort of artwork out of it. After that, as he told Beauvoir in later conversation, he was 'no longer someone who could be persecuted'. Interestingly, he remained a compulsive gift-giver for the rest of his life.

Like Genet, Sartre also had a more powerful way of taking control: he wrote books. For both of them, being a writer meant giving the world's contingencies the 'necessary' quality of art, just as the jazz singer in *Nausea* turns the chaos of being into beautiful necessity. All Sartre's biographies turn on this theme. In his 1947 study of Baudelaire, he shows us the young poet bullied at school but transforming his miseries into literature. The same thing happens in *Words*, which Sartre began drafting the year after publishing *Saint Genet*, in 1953. His driving question, he said in a later interview, was: 'how does a man become someone who writes, who wants to speak of the imaginary?' *Words* was his attempt to find out what makes a child like himself fall into the 'neurosis of literature'.

In fact, by the time he was writing *Words*, Sartre was worrying that something was ideologically wrong with this analysis of freedom and self-determination as modes of being enjoyed most fully by writers. Should one really spend one's life trying to take control of existence solely through art? Is this not self-indulgent? Perhaps one's energy should be used another way – such as marching shoulder to shoulder with the proletariat in the service of revolution. Working on *Words*, Sartre filled it with gleeful irony at his own expense – making it one of his most entertaining works by far. He then announced that it represented his 'farewell to literature'.

But Sartre's was never going to be the kind of farewell to literature that meant *stopping* writing, as the poet Rimbaud had done. It turned out to mean writing more and more, in an ever greater mania, while abandoning the attempt to revise and give careful shape to his thoughts. *Words* was, rather, Sartre's farewell to careful crafting and polishing – a process that may have been becoming more difficult for him, as his vision worsened. He managed to make it sound like a virtuous renunciation, but from the point of view of his readers it feels more like a declaration of war.

The next stage of Sartre's life-writing career would lead him to the work he thought would be his greatest achievement in the genre, and which instead is one of the world's impossible books. *The Family Idiot* is a multi-volume life of Gustave Flaubert, in which Sartre prioritised – as before – the question of what leads a writer to become a writer. But he approached it differently. Sartre traced Flaubert's way of writing to his childhood in a bourgeois family who had dismissed him as an 'idiot' because of his tendency to stare blankly into space for long periods, daydreaming or apparently thinking about nothing. In labelling him as idiot – a typical bourgeois act of exclusion – they cut him out of normal social intercourse. Sartre compares the infant Flaubert to a domestic animal, partly absorbed in human culture and partly separated from it, and haunted by what he is missing.

What he lacks, above all, is familial love, which would have drawn him into the realm of the fully human. Instead, Flaubert is left with what Sartre calls 'the acrid, vegetative abundance of his own juices, of the self. Mushroom: elementary organism, passive, shackled, oozing with abject plenitude.' This abandonment in the mushroom patch of the soul makes him confused about his own consciousness, and about the boundaries between self and other. Feeling 'superfluous', Flaubert does not know what his role in the world is supposed to be. Out of this comes his 'perpetual questioning' and a fascination with the fringes of conscious experience. As Sartre said to an interviewer who asked why he had wanted to write about Flaubert, it was because of these fringes: 'with him I am at the border, the barrier of dreams'.

The project took Sartre's own writing to the border too – the border of sense. He weaves together a Hegelian and a Marxist interpretation of Flaubert's life, with much emphasis on the social and economic, but he also brings in a quasi-Freudian notion of the unconscious. He often uses the term '*le vécu*', or 'the lived'. Beauvoir and others used this word too, but in Sartre's hands it becomes almost a substitute for 'consciousness'. It denotes the realm in which a writer like Flaubert manages to understand himself without being fully transparent to himself – or, says Sartre, in which 'consciousness plays the trick of determining itself by forgetfulness'. The idea is at once seductive and difficult. Perhaps the best way of putting it is to say that *The Family Idiot* is Sartre's attempt to show how a writer becomes a writer without ever becoming fully conscious.

Sartre himself struggled to manage his immense project. Having begun to write it in 1954, he ran out of steam and put the manuscript aside for a long time, then rolled up his sleeves again and rapidly finished three volumes, which came out in 1971 and 1972. These ran to an astonishing 2,800 pages, or about 2,000 pages longer than one might expect from even the most long-winded biography. Even now, he had not finished: this took the story only to Flaubert's writing of *Madame Bovary*. A fourth volume was projected, but never appeared. This makes it unsatisfying, but a greater problem is that the existing volumes are almost entirely unreadable.

One person enjoyed it, at least. Simone de Beauvoir read it in draft, as she did all Sartre's books. She read it *several times*. Then she wrote in her memoirs:

I do not know how many times I went through *L'idiot de la famille*, reading long sections out of sequence and discussing them with Sartre. I went right through it again from the first

page to the last during the summer of 1971 in Rome, reading for
hours on end. None of Sartre's other books has ever seemed to
me so delightful.

I wish I could see what Beauvoir saw. I have tried – I've rarely started
a book with such a *desire* to like it, but it was a desire thwarted. I am
saucer-eyed with awe at the achievement of the translator, Carol
Cosman, who spent thirteen years meticulously rendering the whole
work into English. I am less impressed with Sartre, who had clearly
decided that the very nature of the project ruled out revisions,
polishing or any kind of attempt at clarity.

The book has its moments, though. Occasional lightning flashes
strike the primordial soup, although they never quite spark it into life,
and there is no way to find them except by dredging through the bog
for as long as you can stand it.

In one such moment, while talking about the power of the gaze,
Sartre recalls being present at a scene in which a group of people
were talking about a dog – a variant on the scene described by Levinas
in his prison camp, where the dog looked joyfully at the humans. This
time, as the people look down at him, the dog realises they are paying
him attention, but cannot understand why. He becomes agitated and
confused, gets up, bounds towards them, stops, whines, and then
barks. As Sartre wrote, he seems to be 'feeling at his expense the
strange reciprocal mystification which is the relationship between man
and animal'.

Sartre rarely grants other animals the compliment of recognising
their forms of consciousness. Until now he had implicitly set them
all in the realm of the 'in-itself' along with trees and slabs of concrete.
But now it seems his view has shifted. Animals may not be fully
conscious – but perhaps humans are not either, and this may be what
Sartre means by taking us to the border of dreams.

Sartre's interest in his subjects' unconscious or semi-conscious minds
had developed well before the Flaubert book. Towards the end of
Being and Nothingness, he had explored the idea that our lives might

be arranged around projects that are genuinely ours, yet that we do not fully understand. He also called for a new practice of existentialist psychoanalysis, to be based on freedom and on worldly being. He never accepted Freud's picture of the psyche as being arranged in layers, from the unconscious upwards, as if it were a slice of baklava or a geological sediment to be studied; nor did he agree on the primacy of sex. But he did take an increasing interest in the more impenetrable zones of life, and in our mysterious motivations. He was particularly interested in the way Freud – like himself – had changed and refined his own ideas as he went on. Freud was a thinker built on the same monumental scale as himself; Sartre respected that – and of course he too was a writer above all.

In 1958, Sartre had a chance to explore Freud's life in more detail when the director John Huston commissioned him to write a screenplay for a biopic. Sartre took the job on partly because he needed the money: a huge tax bill had left him short. But, having agreed to do it, he threw himself into the job with his usual energy, and produced a screenplay that would have made a seven-hour film.

Huston did not want a seven-hour film, so he invited Sartre to come and stay in his house in Ireland while they worked together on cutting it down. Sartre proved to be an overwhelming guest, talking incessantly in rapid French which Huston could barely follow. Sometimes, after leaving the room, Huston would hear Sartre still raving on, apparently having failed to noticed his listener's departure. In fact, Sartre was just as puzzled by his host's behaviour. As he wrote to Beauvoir, 'suddenly in mid-discussion he'll disappear. Very lucky if he's seen again before lunch or dinner.'

Sartre obediently cut some scenes, but, while writing his new version, he could not resist adding new ones in their place and extending others. He presented Huston with a script that would no longer make a seven-hour film, but an eight-hour one. Huston now fired Sartre and used two of his regular screenwriters to script a much more conventional film, which duly appeared in 1962 with Montgomery Clift playing Freud. Sartre's name was never credited, apparently by his own request. Much later, his screenplay was published in its multiple versions, so that (if so inclined) one can now pore over all the variant passages and reflect on yet another of Sartre's non-standard contributions to literary biography.

Flaubert, Baudelaire, Mallarmé and Freud were not able to answer back to Sartre's interpretations, but Genet was. His response was mixed. Sartre enjoyed telling a story that Genet first threw the manuscript into the fireplace, then pulled it out just before the flames took hold – which may or may not have been true. Genet did comment to Jean Cocteau that it made him nervous to have been turned into a 'statue' by Sartre. Sartre must have noticed the irony of writing an interpretive study of how a man refused to accept the interpretive gaze of others. It was particularly awkward for the self-mythologising Genet to become a writer written about; he was more used to being on the other end of the pen, and he felt 'disgust' at being stripped of his artistic disguise.

On the other hand, he was also flattered to be an object of such attention, and it helped that he simply liked Sartre. After the remark about being disgusted, he told the same interviewer, 'It's very enjoyable to spend time with a guy who understands everything and laughs rather than judges . . . He's an extremely sensitive person. Ten or fifteen years ago I saw him blush a few times. And a blushing Sartre is adorable.'

One major point of disagreement between Sartre and Genet concerned Genet's homosexuality. Sartre interpreted it as part of Genet's creative response to being labelled a pariah – thus, a free choice of outsiderhood and contrariness. Instead, for Genet, it was a given fact, like having green or brown eyes. He argued this point with Sartre, but Sartre was adamant. In Saint Genet he even had the effrontery to comment, of Genet's more essentialist opinion, 'we cannot follow him in this'.

Many people now favour Genet's view over Sartre's, considering that regardless of other factors that may enter the mix, some of us simply are gay, or at least have a strong propensity in that direction. Sartre seemed to feel that, if we do not completely choose our sexuality, we are not free. But, to turn his own words back on him, 'we cannot follow him in this' – at least, I can't. Why should sexual orientation not be like other mostly innate qualities, such as being tall or short – or being extroverted or introverted, adventurous or risk-averse, empathetic or self-centred? Such tendencies seem at least partly inborn, yet even within the terms of Sartre's philosophy they do not make us unfree. They simply form part of our situation – and existentialism is always a philosophy of freedom *in situation*.

Beauvoir seemed more sensitive than Sartre was to these subtle interzones in human life. *The Second Sex* was almost entirely occupied with the complex territory where free choice, biology and social and cultural factors meet and mingle to create a human being who gradually becomes set in her ways as life goes on. Moreover, she had explored this territory more directly in a short treatise of 1947, *The Ethics of Ambiguity*. There, she argued that the question of the relationship between our physical constraints and the assertion of our freedom is not a 'problem' requiring a solution. It is simply the way human beings are. Our condition *is* to be ambiguous to the core, and our task is to learn to manage the movement and uncertainty in our existence, not to banish it.

She hastens to add that she does not believe we should therefore give up and fall back on a bland Sisyphus-like affirmation of cosmic flux and fate. The ambiguous human condition means tirelessly *trying* to take control of things. We have to do two near-impossible things at once: understand ourselves as limited by circumstances, and yet continue to pursue our projects as though we are truly in control. In Beauvoir's view, existentialism is the philosophy that best enables us to do this, because it concerns itself so deeply with both freedom and contingency. It acknowledges the radical and terrifying scope of our freedom in life, but also the concrete influences that other philosophies tend to ignore: history, the body, social relationships and the environment.

Beauvoir's brief sketch of these ideas in *The Ethics of Ambiguity* is one of the most interesting attempts I've read at describing the bizarre mixture of improbabilities that human beings are. It is here that she laid out the first foundations of *The Second Sex* and of her entire novelistic vision of life. Yet, disappointingly, she repudiated parts of *The Ethics of Ambiguity* later because it did not fit with her Marxist social theory. 'I was in error when I thought I could define a morality independent of social context', she wrote meekly. But perhaps we need not follow her in this.

IO

The Dancing Philosopher

In which Merleau-Ponty has a chapter to himself.

One thinker in Beauvoir's circle who shared her vision of the ambiguity of the human condition was her old friend Maurice Merleau-Ponty – the friend who, when they were both nineteen, had irritated her because of his tendency to see different sides of things, at a time when she was given to firm, instant judgements. They had both changed since then. Beauvoir could still be opinionated, but had become more attuned to contradiction and complexity. Merleau-Ponty had spent the war working himself into uncompromising attitudes that went against his grain. He adopted a dogmatic pro-Soviet position, which he maintained for several years after the war before dramatically abandoning it. He often changed his views in this way when his thinking took him in a new direction. But he always remained a phenomenologist at heart, dedicated to the task of describing experience as closely and precisely as he could. He did this in such an interesting way that he deserves a (short) chapter completely to himself in this book.

We have already met him earlier in life, while he was enjoying his happy childhood. After that, he pursued a conventional academic career while Beauvoir and Sartre were becoming media stars. No photographers or American fans chased Merleau-Ponty around the Left Bank. Journalists did not quiz him about his sex life – which is a shame, as they would have dug up some interesting stories if they had. Meanwhile, he quietly turned himself into the most revolutionary thinker of them all, as became clear on publication of his masterwork of 1945, *The Phenomenology of Perception*. He remains an influential figure in modern philosophy, as well as in related fields such as cognitive psychology. His vision of human life is best summed up by these brief remarks near the end of *The Phenomenology of Perception*:

> I am a psychological and historical structure. Along with existence, I received a way of existing, or a style. All of my actions and thoughts are related to this structure, and even a philosopher's thought is merely a way of making explicit his hold upon the world, which is all he is. And yet, I am free, not in spite of or beneath these motivations, but rather by their means. For that meaningful life, that particular signification of nature and history that I am, does not restrict my access to the world; it is rather my means of communication with it.

This bears reading twice. The aspects of our existence that limit us, Merleau-Ponty says, are the very same ones that bind us to the world and give us scope for action and perception. They make us what we are. Sartre acknowledged the need for this trade-off, but he found it more painful to accept. Everything in him longed to be free of bonds, of impediments and limitations and viscous clinging things. Heidegger recognised limitation too, but then sought something like divinity in his mythologising of Being. Merleau-Ponty instead saw quite calmly that we exist only through compromise with the world – and that this is fine. The point is not to fight that fact, or to inflate it into too great a significance, but to observe and understand exactly how that compromise works.

His own career was a case study in the art of compromise too, being balanced neatly between two disciplines that were often considered rivals: psychology and philosophy. Merleau-Ponty worked to bring them together for the benefit of both. Thus his doctoral thesis in 1938 was on behavioural psychology, but he then became professor of philosophy at the University of Lyons in 1945. In 1949, he took over as professor of psychology and pedagogy at the Sorbonne, succeeding Jean Piaget – but next became head of philosophy at the Collège de France in 1952. Throughout these changes of role, he made his psychological studies

intensely philosophical, while building his philosophy on psychological
and neurological case studies, including studies of effects of brain
injuries and other traumas. He was influenced especially by gestalt
theory, a school of psychology which explores how experience comes
to us as a whole rather than as separate bits of input.

What excited Merleau-Ponty in all of this was not existentialist talk
of anguish and authenticity. It was a simpler set of questions – which
turn out not to be simple at all. What happens when we pick up a
cup in a café, or sip our cocktail while listening to the hubbub around
us? What does it mean to write with a pen, or to walk through a
door? These actions are almost impossible to describe or understand
fully – yet most of us perform them with the greatest of ease, day
after day. This is the real mystery of existence.

In *The Phenomenology of Perception,* Merleau-Ponty starts with Husserl's
notion that we must philosophise from our own experience of

phenomena, but he adds the obvious point that this experience comes to us through our sensitive, moving, perceptive bodies. Even when we think of a thing that is not there, our minds construct that imaginary thing with colours, shapes, tastes, smells, noises and tactile qualities. In abstract thought, we similarly draw on physical metaphors or images – as when we talk of ideas as weighty, or discussions as heated. We are sensual even when we are being most philosophical.

But Merleau-Ponty also followed Husserl and the gestalt psychologists in reminding us that we rarely have these sense experiences 'raw'. Phenomena come to us already shaped by the interpretations, meanings and expectations with which we are going to grasp them, based on previous experience and the general context of the encounter. We perceive a multicoloured blob on a table directly *as* a bag of sweets, not as a collection of angles, colours and shadows that must be decoded and identified. The people we see running around in a field *are* a football team. This is why we fall for optical illusions: we have already seen a diagram as some expected shape, before looking again to realise that we have been fooled. It is also why a Rorschach blot comes to us as a picture of something, rather than as a meaningless design.

Of course we have to learn this skill of interpreting and anticipating the world, and this happens in early childhood, which is why Merleau-Ponty thought child psychology was essential to philosophy. This is an extraordinary insight. Apart from Rousseau, very few philosophers before him had taken childhood seriously; most wrote as though all human experience were that of a fully conscious, rational, verbal adult who has been dropped into this world from the sky – perhaps by a stork. Childhood looms large in Beauvoir's *The Second Sex* and in Sartre's biographies; Sartre wrote in his Flaubert book that 'all of us are constantly discussing the child we were, and are'. But his strictly philosophical treatises do not prioritise childhood as Merleau-Ponty's do.

For Merleau-Ponty, we cannot understand our experience if we don't think of ourselves in part as overgrown babies. We fall for optical illusions because we once *learned* to see the world in terms of shapes,

objects and things relevant to our own interests. Our first perceptions
came to us in tandem with our first active experiments in observing
the world and reaching out to explore it, and are still linked with those
experiences. We learned to recognise a bag of sweets at the same time
as we learned how good it is to devour its contents. After a few years
of life, the sight of sweets, the impulse to reach out for them, the
anticipatory salivation, the eagerness and the frustration if told to
stop, the joy of the crackling wrappers and the bright colours of the
candied concoctions catching the light all form part of the whole.
When the infant Simone de Beauvoir wanted to 'crunch flowering
almond trees, and take bites out of the rainbow nougat of the sunset',
it was because her growing mind was already a synaesthetic swirl of
appetite and experience. Perception remains this way, with all the
senses working together holistically. We 'see' the fragility and smooth-
ness of a pane of glass, or the softness of a woollen blanket. As
Merleau-Ponty writes: 'In the movement of the branch from which
a bird has just left, we read its flexibility and its elasticity.'

At the same time, perception is bound up with our own movements around the world: we touch and grasp and interact with things
in order to understand them. To discover the texture of a cloth, we
rub it between our fingers with a practised motion. Even our eyes
move constantly, rarely taking anything in with a single fixed stare.
And, unless we have lost vision in one eye, like Sartre, we judge
distance by seeing stereoscopically. The eyes work together, cali-
brating angles – but we don't 'see' these calculations. What we see
is the object out there: the thing itself. We rarely stop to think that
it is partly constituted by our own shifting gaze and our way of
paying attention or reaching out to things.

Our perceptions also tend to be accompanied by that strange sense
called 'proprioception' – the sense that tells us whether our legs are
crossed or our head is cocked to one side. My own body is not an
object like others; it is me. If I sit down with my knitting, says Merleau-
Ponty, I might have to hunt for my knitting needles but I don't hunt
for my hands and fingers. And if I rest my arm on the table, 'I will
never think to say that it is *next to* the ashtray in the same way that

the ashtray is next to the telephone.' Our proprioception is exquisitely sensitive and complex:

> If I stand in front of my desk and lean on it with both hands, only my hands are accentuated and my whole body trails behind them like a comet's tail. I am not unaware of the location of my shoulders or my waist; rather, this awareness is enveloped in my awareness of my hands and my entire stance is read, so to speak, in how my hands lean upon the desk. If I am standing and if I hold my pipe in a closed hand, the position of my hand is not determined discursively by the angle that it makes with my forearm, my forearm with my arm, my arm with my torso, and, finally, my torso with the ground. I have an absolute know-ledge of where my pipe is, and *from this* I know where my hand is and where my body is.

Proprioception can also operate through extensions of myself. If I drive a car, I develop a feel for how much space it takes up and what size gap it will fit through, without needing to get out and measure it each time. It starts to feel like part of me, rather than an external piece of machinery controlled by wheel and pedals. My clothes or the things I am carrying all become *me*: 'Without any explicit calculation, a woman maintains a safe distance between the feather in her hat and objects that might damage it; she senses where the feather is, just as we sense where our hand is.'

Normally, we take all these marvels for granted, but when they go wrong they reveal a lot about how ordinary experience works. Merleau-Ponty read case studies in the field, notably those based on a man called Johann Schneider, who, after a brain injury, could not feel what position his limbs were in, or where you were touching him if you laid your hand on his arm. Other studies concerned amputees' experiences of uncomfortable 'phantom' sensations where their lost limbs had been – tingling, pain or just the basic sense of having an arm or leg where there wasn't one. In more recent times, such sensations have been magicked away by using input from other senses: if an amputee 'moves' his or her phantom limb while watching a mirror reflection of the matching real limb on the other side, it can sometimes help to banish the illusion. Oliver Sacks, who in *A Leg to Stand On* described his own disorder of leg proprioception after an injury, elsewhere tried simple trickery with video goggles and fake rubber arms to create the feeling that he had a third arm, or even that he was embodied in something on the other side of the room. The experiments were fun, but the leg injury wasn't: Sacks felt an immense relief when normal proprioception came back to him and he had his whole, proper body back. It felt like getting back to his full self, having been forced to make do with an 'I' that was in part merely abstract, or Cartesian. His Merleau-Pontian embodied self was so much more *him*.

Another factor in all of this, for Merleau-Ponty, is our social existence: we cannot thrive without others, or not for long, and we need this especially in early life. This makes solipsistic speculation about the reality of others ridiculous; we could never engage in such speculation if we hadn't already been formed by them. As Descartes could have said (but didn't), 'I think, therefore *other people* exist.' We grow up with people playing with us, pointing things out, talking, listening, and getting us used to reading emotions and movements; this is how we become capable, reflective, smoothly integrated beings. Merleau-Ponty was especially interested in the way babies imitate those around them. If you playfully pretend to bite the fingers of a fifteen-month-old baby, he wrote, its response is to make its own biting movements, mirroring yours. (He may have tried this with his own baby, who was about that age while he was working on *The Phenomenology of Perception*.)

In general, Merleau-Ponty thinks human experience only makes sense if we abandon philosophy's time-honoured habit of starting with a solitary, capsule-like, immobile adult self, isolated from its body and world, which must then be connected up again – adding each element around it as though adding clothing to a doll. Instead, for him, we slide from the womb to the birth canal to an equally close and total immersion in the world. That immersion continues as long as we live, although we may also cultivate the art of partially with-drawing from time to time when we want to think or daydream.

For Merleau-Ponty, consciousness can never be a 'nothingness' radic-ally divided from being, as Sartre had proposed in *Being and Nothingness*. He does not even see it as a 'clearing', like Heidegger. When he looks for his own metaphor to describe how he sees consciousness, he comes up with a beautiful one: consciousness, he suggests, is like a 'fold' in the world, as though someone had crumpled a piece of cloth to make a little nest or hollow. It stays for a while, before eventually being unfolded and smoothed away.

There is something seductive, even erotic, in this idea of my conscious self as an improvised pouch in the cloth of the world. I still have my privacy – my withdrawing room. But I am part of the world's fabric, and I remain formed out of it for as long as I am here.

'Starting from there, elaborate an idea of philosophy', wrote Merleau-Ponty hastily to himself in later notes – for *The Phenomenology of Perception* was just the beginning of his research. He wrote much more, including an unfinished work later published as *The Visible and the Invisible*. He repeated the image of the folded cloth there, but he also tried a new image.

This was the idea of consciousness as a 'chiasm'. The word 'chiasm' or 'chiasmus' comes from the Greek letter *chi*, written χ, and it denotes exactly that crossed intertwining shape. In biology, it refers to the crossing of two nerves or ligaments. In language, it is the rhetorical device in which one phrase is countered by another inverting the same words, as when John F. Kennedy said, 'Ask not what your country can do for you, but what you can do for your country,' or when Mae West said, 'It's not the men in my life, it's the life in my men.' The inter-woven figure calls to mind two hands grasping each other, or the way a woollen thread loops back to grip itself in a knitting stitch. As Merleau-Ponty put it: 'the hold is held'.

For him, this was the perfect way of making sense of the connec-tion between consciousness and world. Each clasps the other, as if by criss-crossed, knitted links. Thus, I can see things in the world, but I can also *be seen*, because I am made of the world's own stuff. When I touch something with my hand, that thing touches my hand too. If this were not the case, I could neither see nor touch anything at all. I never peer into the world from a safe place outside it, like a cat looking into a fishtank. I encounter things because I am encounter*able* to others. He wrote: 'It is as though our vision were formed in the heart of the visible, or as though there were between it and us an intimacy as close as between the sea and the strand.'

Traditional philosophy has no name for this 'visibility', says Merleau-Ponty, so he uses the word 'flesh', meaning something much more than a physical substance. Flesh is what we share with the world. 'It is the coiling over of the visible upon the seeing body, of the tangible upon the touching body.' It is because I am flesh that I move and respond to things while I observe them. It is what makes me '*follow with my eyes* the movements and the contours of the things themselves'.

By the time of these works, Merleau-Ponty is taking his desire to describe experience to the outer limits of what language can convey. Just as with the late Husserl or Heidegger, or Sartre in his Flaubert book, we see a philosopher venturing so far from shore that we can barely follow. Emmanuel Levinas would head out to the fringes too, eventually becoming incomprehensible to all but his most patient initiates.

With Merleau-Ponty, the further he wades out into the mysterious, the closer he also comes to the basics of life: to the act of picking up a glass and drinking, or to the bounce of a branch as a bird flies away. This is what astonishes him, and for him there can be no question of banishing that puzzle by 'solving' it. The philosopher's task is neither to reduce the mysterious to a neat set of concepts nor to gaze at it in awed silence. It is to follow the first phenomenological imperative: to go to the things themselves in order to describe them, attempting 'rigorously to put into words what is not ordinarily put into words, what is sometimes considered inexpressible'. Such philosophy can be seen as an art form – a way of doing what Merleau-Ponty thought Cézanne did in his paintings of everyday objects and scenes: taking the world, making it new, and giving it back almost unchanged except in that it had been observed. As he wrote of Cézanne in a beautiful essay, 'Only one emotion is possible for this painter – the feeling of strangeness – and only one lyricism – that of the continual rebirth of existence.' In another essay, he wrote of how the Renaissance writer Michel de Montaigne put 'not self-satisfied understanding but a consciousness astonished at itself at the core of human existence'. One could say the same of Merleau-Ponty himself.

When, in 1952, Merleau-Ponty was made head of philosophy at the Collège de France, a journalist at *L'aurore* used the occasion to mock existentialism with an allusion to its popularity with the jazz-club crowd: 'It is only a cerebral way of dancing the boogie-woogie.' As it happened, Merleau-Ponty had a flair for the boogie-woogie too. While being the most academically eminent of the Left Bank thinkers, he was also their best dancer: Boris Vian and Juliette Gréco both commented on his talents.

Merleau-Ponty's jive and swing moves went along with a generally urbane manner and a perfect ease in company. He liked good clothes, but not flashy ones; English suits were his favourite at a time when they were admired for their high quality. He worked hard, but he spent part of each day in the Saint-Germain-des-Prés cafés near where he lived, popping in regularly for his morning coffee – usually on the late side as he didn't like early rising.

He combined his night life with being a devoted family man, with a very different domestic routine from that of Sartre or Beauvoir. He had just one daughter, Marianne Merleau-Ponty, who now looks back fondly on his way of playing, laughing or making funny faces to amuse her as a small child. It was sometimes difficult to be a philosopher's daughter: she recalls how galling it was to have the teacher say to her years later, after an oral exam in which she had fumbled a particular topic, 'You do realise that a certain Merleau-Ponty has written about this question?' It was never her favourite subject, but when she had to resit exams he helped her patiently, and inscribed copies of his books to 'Marianne, his favourite philosopher'. He seemed more alive than other philosophers, she says – more *in life* – but this was because philosophy and life were the same to him.

Despite the fun and games, he retained an elusive quality, especially by contrast with Sartre's tendency to be upfront and in-your-face. His self-possessed way of smiling off the most serious events could be frustrating, as Simone de Beauvoir found, but it was attractive too. Merleau-Ponty was aware of his appeal and was a noted flirt. He sometimes went beyond flirtation. According to second-hand gossip reported by Sartre in a letter to Beauvoir, he could come on a bit strong after too many drinks, trying his luck with several women over a single evening. They often turned him down, Sartre noted – 'not that they don't like him, he's just too hasty'.

Although his marriage remained unassailable, he did have a serious affair with at least one other woman: Sonia Brownell, later the wife of George Orwell. They met in 1946 when Sonia sought to commission a piece from him for Cyril Connolly's cultural review, *Horizon*, for which she was an assistant editor. They wrote playful letters to each other, then began their affair around Boxing Day 1947, when Merleau-Ponty went to London to spend a week with her. The week did not all go smoothly. Sonia was volatile, moody, and prone to outbursts; her wayward emotions had probably appealed to Merleau-Ponty at first; perhaps she even reminded him of his emotive long-ago girlfriend Elisabeth Le Coin. But his letters show him moving from pained puzzlement to a definite cooling of affection. The affair eventually ended when Sonia arrived in Paris one day, expecting to meet him, but instead found a polite note at her hotel from his wife Suzanne, informing her that her husband had left for southern France. Not long after this, on 13 October 1949, Sonia married the very ill George Orwell at his hospital bed.

Even before their relationship, Merleau-Ponty had been considering a move to England, and he asked his friend A. J. Ayer to help him get a post at University College London. This never happened. But he liked the country, and spoke and wrote good English – although after he wrote his first English letter to Sonia they switched to French, in which she was more fluent. He practised English by doing questionnaires in *Meet Yourself*, an eccentric self-help book compiled in 1936 by Prince Leopold Loewenstein Wertheim-Freudenberg and the novelist William Gerhardie. The book would have appealed to Merleau-Ponty's interest in psychology: it was designed to 'X-ray' the reader's character through a hypertextual mass of questions through which one took different routes depending on one's answers. Since Gerhardie was a writer with a distinctive sensibility of his own, the book's questions are sometimes quite weird: 'Do Mickey Mouse films or other animated cartoons of that sort frighten you?' 'Have you ever felt as though the world around you has suddenly become unreal and dreamlike? Do not answer yet. The sensations are hard to describe. They are very complex, but the most characteristic thing about them is an uncanny feeling as of having lost one's identity.'

In fact, Merleau-Ponty was almost unique among the existentialist milieu in *not* being prone to such attacks of uncanniness or anxiety. It was an important difference between him and the neurotic Sartre. Merleau-Ponty was not followed down the street by lobsters; he had no fear of chestnut trees, and was not haunted by the thought of other people staring at him and fixing him in their judgemental gaze. Rather, for him, looking and being looked at are what weave us into the world and give us our full humanity. Sartre acknowledged this interweaving, and he also acknowledged the importance of the body, but it all seemed to make him nervous. Some kind of *struggle* is always going on in Sartre's work – against facticity, against being devoured by the quicksand of Being, and against the power of the Other. Merleau-Ponty doesn't struggle much, and doesn't seem to fear dissolving into the syrupy or vaporous. In *The Visible and the Invisible*, he gives us some very un-Sartrean descriptions of erotic encounters, describing how one body embraces another along its length, 'forming tirelessly with its hands the strange statue which in its turn gives everything it receives; the body is lost outside of the world and its goals, fascinated by the unique occupation of floating in Being with another life.'

Sartre once remarked – speaking of a disagreement they had about Husserl in 1941 – that 'we discovered, astounded, that our conflicts had, at times, stemmed from our childhood, or went back to the elementary differences of our two organisms'. Merleau-Ponty also said in an interview that Sartre's work seemed strange to him, not because of philosophical differences, but because of a certain 'register of feeling', especially in *Nausea*, that he could not share. Their difference was one of temperament and of the whole way the world presented itself to them.

The two also differed in their purpose. When Sartre writes about the body or other aspects of experience, he generally does it in order to make a different point. He expertly evokes the grace of his café waiter, gliding between the tables, bending at an angle *just so*, steering the drink-laden tray through the air on the tips of his fingers – but he does it all in order to illustrate his ideas about bad faith. When Merleau-Ponty writes about skilled and graceful movement, the movement itself is his point. *This* is the thing he wants to understand.

Merleau-Ponty had even less in common with Heidegger, apart from their prioritising of Being-in-the-world. Heidegger is good on some bodily experiences, such as hammering a nail, but he has little to say about other kinds of physical sensation in Dasein's body. He avoids ambiguous realms in general. He argues that the meaning of Dasein's Being lies in Time, yet avoids the whole topic of development. He does not tell us whether there can be a toddler Dasein, just opening up its first 'clearing', or a Dasein with advanced Alzheimer's, for whom the forest is closing in. When he turns to other animals, it is to dismiss them as uninteresting beings that cannot make their own 'world', or that have only an impoverished one. The Heidegger scholar Richard Polt has listed a whole range of questions that Heidegger does not ask: 'How did Dasein evolve? When does a fetus or newborn enter the condition of Dasein? What conditions are necessary in the brain in order for Dasein to take place? Can other species be Dasein? Can we create an artificial Dasein using computers?' Heidegger avoids these ambiguous zones because he considers them 'ontical' matters, worth considering only by such disciplines as psychology, biology and anthropology – not by noble philosophy.

Merleau-Ponty does not make such distinctions. The edges and shadows of the discipline were what interested him most, and he welcomed anything ontical researchers could contribute. He based his philosophy on human beings who are in constant change from childhood onwards; he wanted to know what happened when faculties were lost, or when people were injured and damaged. By prioritising perception, the body, social life and childhood development, Merleau-Ponty gathered up philosophy's far-flung outsider subjects and brought them in to occupy the centre of his thought.

In his inaugural lecture at the Collège de France on 15 January 1953, published as *In Praise of Philosophy*, he said that philosophers should concern themselves above all with whatever is ambiguous in our experience. At the same time, they should think clearly about these ambiguities, using reason and science. Thus, he said, 'The philosopher is marked by the distinguishing trait that he possesses *inseparably* the taste for evidence and the feeling for ambiguity.' A constant movement is required between these two – a kind of rocking motion 'which leads back without ceasing from knowledge to ignorance, from ignorance to knowledge'.

What Merleau-Ponty is describing here is another kind of 'chiasm' – an X-like interweaving, this time not between consciousness and world, but between knowledge and questioning. We can never move definitively from ignorance to certainty, for the thread of the inquiry will constantly lead us back to ignorance again. This is the most attractive description of philosophy I've ever read, and the best argument for why it is worth doing, even (or especially) when it takes us no distance at all from our starting point.

II

Croisés comme ça

In which the existentialists fight about the future.

Merleau-Ponty observed in a lecture of 1951 that, more than any previous century, the twentieth century had reminded people how 'contingent' their lives were – how at the mercy of historical events and other changes that they could not control. This feeling went on long after the war ended. After the A-bombs were dropped on Hiroshima and Nagasaki, many feared that a Third World War would not be long in coming, this time between the Soviet Union and the United States. The two superpowers' wartime alliance had broken down almost instantly; they now stood glaring at each other from either side of a weakened, impoverished and self-doubting Western Europe.

If another war did start, it seemed possible that this time it might destroy civilisation and even life itself. At first only the United States had the A-bomb, but Soviet engineers and spies were known to be working on the problem, and people soon learned of the full dangers from radiation and environmental devastation. As Sartre wrote in response to Hiroshima, humanity had now gained the power to wipe itself out, and must decide every single day that it wanted to live. Camus also wrote that humanity faced the task of choosing between collective suicide and a more intelligent use of its technology – 'between hell and reason'. After 1945, there seemed little reason to trust in humanity's ability to choose well.

After this, each new bomb-test raised the anxiety level. When the Americans exploded a more powerful A-bomb in July 1946, Beauvoir heard a radio announcer say that it had already triggered a chain reaction, making matter itself disintegrate in a slow wave spreading across the planet. Within a few hours, everything on earth would be gone. Now *that's* a nothingness at the heart of being. Later that year came rumours that the Soviets were plotting to leave suitcases filled with radioactive dust in key US cities, with timers set to burst their seals and kill millions. Sartre lampooned this story in his play *Nekrassov* in 1956, but at the time few were sure what to believe. Radiation was all the more terrifying for being invisible and so easily deployed; the power of the universe itself could be packed into a few suitcases.

But, while some feared The End, others had equally dramatic hopes for a new beginning. Hölderlin had said that 'where danger is, grows / the saving power also'. Perhaps, some thought, the recent war's catastrophes would not bring disaster but a total transformation of human life, with war and other evils abolished forever.

One idealistic wish was for an effective world government that would resolve conflicts, enforce treaties, and render most wars impossible. Camus was among those sharing this hope. For him, the immediate lesson after Hiroshima was that humanity must develop 'a true international society, in which the great powers will not have superior rights over small and middle-sized nations, where such an ultimate weapon will be controlled by human intelligence rather than by the appetites and doctrines of various states'. To some extent, the United Nations fulfilled these aims, but it never became as broadly effective as hoped.

Others saw the American Way as the road ahead. The United States had a high stock of gratitude and goodwill in Europe after the war; it consolidated this in the late 1940s with the Marshall Plan, pouring billions of dollars into traumatised European countries to speed recovery, and to keep Communism contained within the parts of Central Europe which the Soviet Union had already enfolded in its repressive bear hug. The US even offered money to the Russians and other countries in their ambit, but Moscow made sure that those countries all refused. In Western Europe, some found it humiliating to accept American cash, but they had to admit that it was needed.

Alongside the internationalists and the pro-Americans, a third group in post-war Western Europe favoured putting their hope in the Soviet Union. This was, after all, the one major nation on earth that had actually tried to put into effect the great Communist ideal for humanity – the prospect that (at some far-off point when all the cleaning-up work was done) human beings would banish poverty, hunger, inequality, war, exploitation, fascism and other evils from existence forever, simply by an act of rational management. It was the most ambitious attempt to change the human condition ever attempted. If it failed the first time, it might never be tried again, so it seemed worth defending at all costs.

We are here talking about the events of just seven decades ago – a modest human lifespan – yet it has already become difficult to think ourselves sufficiently into that time to understand how this ideal swayed so many intelligent, sophisticated people in the West. Now, the conventional wisdom has become that Communism would never have worked in any possible world, and therefore that those who failed to see it as futile from the start were fools. Yet, to people who had been through the hardships of the 1930s and the Second World War, it could seem an idea worth believing in despite its acknowledged unlikeliness. People did not see it as a mere dream, of the kind you wake from with a vague impression that you've seen something marvellous but impossible. They thought it a practical goal, albeit one to which the path would be long and difficult, with many pitfalls along the way.

These pitfalls were not hard to spot. That list of beautiful, distant Communist goals was matched by an equally long list of grim realities: labour camps, intimidation, unjust imprisonments, killings, famines, shortages and a lack of personal freedom. The first major shock had come in the 1930s, when news emerged of the Moscow show trials in which disgraced party members 'confessed' to acts of sabotage or conspiracy before being sent to their deaths. In 1946, more information came out, some of it through a book called *I Chose Freedom*, by the Soviet defector Victor Kravchenko. When the book was translated into French in 1947, the Communist-supported journal *Les lettres françaises* dismissed it as a US government fabrication. Kravchenko's lawyers sued the journal, and the case was heard in Paris early in 1949, with witnesses brought in to rhapsodise about life in the Soviet Union, and to discredit the author. Kravchenko technically won, but was given a single franc in damages. The following year, another writer sued *Les lettres françaises*: David Rousset, a Buchenwald survivor who had been attacked by the journal after calling for an investigation into Soviet camps. He won his case. Both trials were contentious, but did much to raise awareness that the Soviet Union was not the Worker's Paradise it claimed to be – or not yet.

Even now, many insisted that it was more worthy of defence than the ultra-capitalist model of the United States. The US also lost some of its moral high ground after the government's extreme fear of Communism led it to crack down on any vaguely leftist organisation, and to surveil and harass its own citizens. Anyone suspected of being a 'Red' risked being fired, blacklisted, and denied a passport to travel. In 1951, the naive couple Ethel and Julius Rosenberg were sentenced to death for handing atomic secrets to the Russians. The executions, carried out in 1953, shocked many inside and outside the country. Sartre fired off an angry article for the newspaper *Libération*. In the States, Hannah Arendt wrote to Jaspers that she feared such incidents portended a national catastrophe comparable to the one seen in Germany. 'An unimaginable stupidity must have taken hold in the USA. It frightens us because we are familiar with it.'

If both great powers were falling short of their ideals, perhaps the only way to choose between them was to ask which ideals were more worth *trying* to attain. Leftists felt that, even if America stood for good things like jazz and freedom, it also stood for untrammelled personal greed, economic colonialism and worker exploitation. At least the Soviet Union represented a noble possibility, and for such a goal, what moral compromise might not be worth making?

Seventy years earlier, in *The Brothers Karamazov*, Dostoevsky had summed up a moral dilemma of this kind in a simple question. Ivan Karamazov asks his brother Alyosha to imagine that he has the power to create a world in which people will enjoy perfect peace and happiness for the rest of history. But to achieve this, he says, you must torture to death one small creature now – say, that baby there. This is an early and extreme variety of the 'trolley problem', in which one person must be sacrificed in order (it's hoped) to save many. So, would you do it, asks Ivan? Alyosha's answer is a clear no. Nothing can justify torturing a baby, in his view, and that is all there is to be said. No weighing of benefits changes this; some things cannot be measured or traded.

In 1940s Paris, the writer who followed Alyosha's position was Albert Camus. In his essay 'Neither Victims Nor Executioners' he wrote, 'I will never again be one of those, whoever they be, who compromise with murder.' Whatever the payoff, he would not support formal justifications for violence, especially by the state. He stuck to this position from then on, although he never ceased to meditate on it. His Dostoevskian play of 1949, The Just, features a group of Russian terrorists debating whether or not they might kill bystanders as collateral damage during a political assassination. Camus makes it clear that he thinks it wrong. He thought the same when independence struggles began in his own country, Algeria, in November 1954. Rebels planted bombs and killed innocents, while the French authorities inflicted tortures and executions. Camus' view was that neither could be justified. People will always do violent things, but philosophers and state officials have a duty not to come up with excuses that will justify them. His opinion made him controversial. In 1957, at a talk to mark his receiving the Nobel Prize in Literature, Camus was asked to explain his failure to support the rebels. He said, 'People are now planting bombs in the tramways of Algiers. My mother might be on one of those tramways. If that is justice, then I prefer my mother.' For Camus there could be no objective justification for either side's actions, so his own loyalties were the only possible source of guidance.

Sartre would train himself to see things differently – at least, he did eventually. Before the war, he could still sound like an Alyosha himself, or a Camus. Merleau-Ponty had once asked him what he would do if he had to choose between two events, one of which would kill 300 people and the other 3,000. What difference was there, philosophically speaking? Sartre replied that there was a mathematical difference, of course, but not a philosophical one, for each individual is an infinite universe in his or her own eyes, and one cannot compare one infinity with another. In both cases, the disaster of loss of life was literally incalculable. Relating this story, Merleau-Ponty deduced that Sartre was talking as a pure philosopher at the time, rather than adopting 'the perspective of heads of government'.

Later, both Sartre and Beauvoir moved away from this view, and would decide that one could and even must weigh and measure lives in a judicious way, and that the Alyosha position was an evasion of that duty. They came to feel that refusing to do the calculation – setting one baby now against millions of future babies – was merely selfish or squeamish. If this sounds like an antiquated argument advanced only by wild Communist dreamers, we might remind ourselves that apparently civilised countries have sought to justify tortures, imprisonments, killings and intrusive surveillance in the same way in our own time, citing unspecified future threats to an unspecified number of people.

Sartre, Beauvoir and (for now) Merleau-Ponty felt that they were being tougher and more honest than Camus, because they saw the need to get one's hands dirty – that favourite phrase again. Of course, the stain was the blood of other people conveniently far away. But Sartre also insisted that he would sacrifice himself if need be. At a writers' conference in Venice in 1956, the English poet Stephen Spender asked him what his wishes would be if he were wrongly persecuted and imprisoned by a Communist regime. Would he want his friends to campaign for his release, if that campaign damaged Communism's credibility and jeopardised its future? Or would he accept his fate for the greater good? Sartre reflected for a moment, then said that he would refuse the campaign. Spender disliked this answer: 'It seems to me that the only good cause has always been that of one person unjustly imprisoned,' he said. That, retorted Sartre, is the crux of the drama; perhaps in the modern world 'injustice against one person' is no longer the point. It had taken Sartre a while to talk himself out of his compunctions about this shocking notion, but by the mid-1950s he was there.

The imaginary scenario discussed by Sartre and Spender resembles the plot of *Darkness at Noon*, a novel by Arthur Koestler, an ex-Communist turned anti-Communist. The novel, published in English in 1940 and in French in 1946 as *Le zéro et l'infini*, was based on the case of Nikolai Bukharin, tried and executed during the Soviet purges in 1938. Koestler portrayed his fictionalised version as a man so loyal to the party that he signed a false confession and went voluntarily to his death for the good of the state. This was way too credulous as an interpretation of Bukharin's real-life case, since his confession was produced under duress. But Koestler gave the intellectuals a story to quarrel over: just how far might a person go to defend Communism? He raised similar questions in his essay 'The Yogi and the Commissar', which contrasted the 'commissar' type, prepared to do anything for a remote ideal goal, with the 'yogi' type, who sticks to present realities.

Merleau-Ponty, in the first flush of his commissar period, responded to Koestler's essay with a two-part attack in *Les Temps modernes* entitled 'The Yogi and the Proletarian'. He mainly used the rhetorical device sometimes known as 'what-aboutery': so the Soviet goal was flawed, but what about the many abuses of the West? What about capitalist greed, colonial repression, poverty and racism? What about the West's pervasive violence, which was merely better disguised than its Communist equivalent?

Koestler ignored Merleau-Ponty's piece, but his friend Camus was enraged. According to Beauvoir, Camus stormed into a party one evening at Boris Vian's, hurled invective at Merleau-Ponty, then stormed out again. Sartre ran after him. The scene ended in recriminations and resentment, and even Sartre and Camus fell out over it for a while, although on this occasion they made up.

Sartre, Beauvoir, Camus and Koestler had previously become good friends, debating political topics in high spirits during convivial, drunken evenings. During one of their wild nights out at an émigré

Russian nightclub around 1946, the question of friendship and political commitment came up. Could you be friends with someone if you disagreed with them politically? Camus said you could. Koestler said no: 'Impossible! Impossible!' In a sentimental buzz of vodka, Beauvoir took Camus' side: 'It *is* possible; and we are the proof of it at this very moment, since, despite all our dissensions, we are so happy to be together.' Cheered by this warm thought, they boozed on happily until after dawn, although Sartre still had to prepare a lecture for the next day on, of all things, the theme of 'The Writer's Responsibility'. They all thought this was hilarious. At dawn, they left each other in exuberant spirits. And Sartre did somehow get the lecture written in time, on almost no sleep.

During another late-night carousal in 1947, however, the friendship question came up again, and this time the mood was less good-humoured. Koestler clinched his side of it by throwing a glass at Sartre's head – not least because he got the idea, probably rightly, that Sartre was flirting with his wife Mamaine. (Koestler was known as an unscrupulous seducer himself, and an aggressive one to say the least.) As they all stumbled outside, Camus tried to calm Koestler by laying a hand on his shoulder. Koestler flailed out at him, and Camus hit him back. Sartre and Beauvoir dragged them apart and hustled Camus off to his car, leaving Koestler and Mamaine on the street. All the way home, Camus wept and draped himself on the steering wheel, weaving over the road: 'He was my friend! And he hit me!'

Sartre and Beauvoir eventually came to agree with Koestler about one thing: it was *not* possible to be friends with someone who held opposed political views. 'When people's opinions are so different,' said Sartre, 'how can they even go to a film together?' In 1950, Koestler mentioned to Stephen Spender that he'd bumped into Sartre and Beauvoir after a long gap and had suggested they have lunch. They responded with an awkward silence, and then Beauvoir said (according to Spender's second-hand version), 'Koestler, you know that we disagree. There no longer seems any point in our meeting.' She crossed her forearms in a big X, and said, 'We are *croisés comme ça* about everything.'

This time it was Koestler who protested, 'Yes, but surely we can remain friends just the same.'

To this, she responded with phenomenology. 'As a philosopher, you must realise that each of us when he looks at a *morceau de sucre* [sugar lump] sees an entirely different object. Our *morceaux de sucre* are now so different that there's no point in our meeting any longer.'

It's a saddening image: sweet confections on a table; philosophers peering at them from different sides. To each of them, the sugar presents itself differently. It catches the light from one side, but not from the other. To one, it looks bright and sparkly; to another, grey and matte. To one, it means a delicious addition to coffee. To another, it means the historical evils of slavery in the sugar trade. And the conclusion? That there is no point in even talking about it. This is a strange distortion of the phenomenological theme. The X of political cross-purposes also makes a nasty twist on Merleau-Ponty's all-reconciling 'chiasm' figure. The whole knotted mess ends in silence – and that in turn recalls the silence that descended over Marcuse and Heidegger around the same time, when Marcuse concluded that no dialogue was possible given the immensity of their difference.

The debate about friendship is really a variant of the debate about what sacrifices might be worth making for Communism. In both cases, you have to weigh abstract values against what is personal, individual and immediate. You have to decide what matters most: the person in front of you now, or the effects your choices might have on an undefined population of future people. Each of our thinkers resolved this conundrum differently – and sometimes the same person reached different conclusions at different times.

Sartre was the least consistent of them all, both on the Soviet question and on the question of friendship, for he did sometimes expect people to be loyal to him despite political differences. In October 1947, he expected loyalty from his old schoolmate Raymond Aron, but did not get it, and was so angry that he broke off contact completely.

That year was a difficult one for France – which was probably also why the Koestler quarrel had become so heated. The country was ruled by a centrist coalition government, but this had come under attack both from the Communist left and from the right-wing Rassemblement du peuple français, led by the wartime head of the French forces in exile, General Charles de Gaulle. Sartre felt that the Gaullist party had become almost fascist in style, indulging in mass rallies and whipping up a personality cult around the leader. But Aron, who had been with the Free French in London and knew de Gaulle well, had much more sympathy for his approach and had moved well to the right of Sartre.

The autumn saw a growing crisis, as the Gaullists' marches and the Communist Party's strikes and demonstrations (actively supported by the Soviet Union) both threatened the stability of the middle. People began to worry that there would be a civil war and even a revolution. Some found this prospect exciting. In a note to Merleau-Ponty, Sonia Brownell wrote that she'd just had lunch with some French writers in London who could not stop gabbling about the battles they intended to fight on Paris's streets, and the best way of making petrol bombs.

With this crisis at its height, Aron chaired a radio debate pitting Sartre, as a representative of the left, against a gang of Gaullists – who laid into him ferociously on air. Aron stayed out of it, and Sartre was dismayed at Aron's letting them gang up on him without attempting to support his old friend. Looking back on the incident, Aron claimed that he did not feel entitled to take sides since he was the chair of the discussion. Sartre suspected that the real reason was Aron's own Gaullist sympathies. For years, the two men did not speak.

Aron may not have realised how personally threatened Sartre felt during this period. He received menacing letters, one containing a picture of himself smeared with excrement. One night he heard that a gang of army officers was roaming the Left Bank looking for him; he sought refuge with friends and did not return to his well-known address above the Bar Napoléon for several days. This would not be the last time his outspoken political views put him in danger.

In truth, at this stage, Sartre was simultaneously opposed to the Gaullists *and* still critical of the Soviet Union; he thus drew the anger of both sides. French Communists had long disapproved of existentialism as a philosophy because of its insistence on personal freedom. A 1946 pamphlet by the Marxist sociologist Henri Lefebvre had summed up existentialism as 'a dreary, flabby mixture' leading to too much dangerous 'open-mindedness'. People were free, Sartre said – but Lefebvre demanded to know, 'what would a man who every morning chose between fascism and anti-fascism represent?' How can such a person be considered better than someone 'who had chosen, once and for all, the fight against fascism, or who had not even had to choose?' Lefebvre's point sounds reasonable until you think about what it implies. The party demanded the kind of commitment that means never having to think again, and this Sartre could not support – yet. Later, he tied himself in knots trying to resolve the conflict between his support for revolutionary politics and his basic existentialist principles, which ran counter to it.

In February 1948, he tried resolving the conundrum by joining a breakaway party, the Rassemblement démocratique revolutionnaire (RDR) or Revolutionary Democratic Assembly, which aimed at a non-aligned socialism. The party did not accomplish much except to make things more complicated, and Sartre resigned after a year and a half.

Meanwhile, in April 1948, he got himself into even more trouble with his new play called, naturally, *Dirty Hands*. This showed party members in Illyria, a fictional small country reminiscent of post-war Hungary, making moral compromises with their ideals and trying to come to terms with their prospects as they wait for a Soviet-style takeover. The Communists were not amused. The Soviet cultural commissar Alexander Fadayev called Sartre 'a hyena with a fountain pen' and Sartre went out of favour in all the Soviet bloc countries. The Czech writer Ivan Klíma, then a college student, listened to his teachers attacking Sartre for his 'decay and moral degeneration' – which immediately made Klíma desperate to read him.

Sartre was now under attack from all sides, politically confused, and overworking himself more than ever in an attempt to make it all add up. Much of his stress was self-inflicted, yet he was not prepared to make his life easier by simply keeping quiet occasionally. Beauvoir too was under strain from work, political tension and a personal crisis: she was trying to decide how to manage her long-distance relationship with Nelson Algren, who was not happy coming second to Sartre and wanted her to move to America. She and Sartre both tried to stave off their exhaustion with pills. Sartre became ever more addicted to his favourite drug Corydrane, a combined amphetamine and painkiller. Beauvoir took orthedrine for anxiety attacks, but it only made them worse. By the time she and Sartre set off for a Scandinavian holiday in the summer of 1948, she was suffering hallucinations in which birds swooped down at her and hands pulled her upwards by her hair. The calm of the northern forests helped her more than the pills did. She and Sartre saw beautiful things there: 'dwarf forests, earth the colour of amethysts planted with tiny trees red as coral and yellow as gold'. Beauvoir's pleasure in life gradually returned. But Sartre remained a tormented soul for the next few years.

On 29 August 1949, after years of espionage and development, the Soviet Union exploded an atom bomb. From now on, the threat of annihilation would be mutual. A few months later, on 1 October, Mao Tse-tung proclaimed the People's Republic of China and allied it with the Soviet Union, so that now two Communist superpowers faced the West. The fear level increased. American schoolchildren were put through drills in which they responded to a bomb warning by diving under desks with their hands covering their heads. The government poured money into further research, and on January 1950 announced that they were working on a much bigger weapon, the hydrogen or H-bomb.

That year, war broke out on the Korean peninsula, with both China and the Soviet Union backing the North against the US in the South. The consequences seemed incalculable: would the Bomb go off? Would the war spread to Europe? Would the Russians occupy France as the Germans had done? This last idea came remarkably quickly to French minds, which may seem odd when the war was on the other side of the world, but it reflected the still-recent memories of the last Occupation, and the alarming and unpredictable nature of the new conflict.

Camus asked Sartre if he'd thought about what would happen to him personally if the Russians invaded. Perhaps the 'hyena with a fountain pen' would not be allowed to have the last laugh. Sartre turned the question back on the questioner: what would Camus do? Oh, said Camus, he would do what he did during the German Occupation – meaning he would join the Resistance. Sartre responded piously that he could never fight against the proletariat. Camus pressed his point: 'You must leave. If you stay it won't be only your life they'll take, but your honour as well. They'll cart you off to a camp and you'll die. Then they'll say you're still alive, and they'll use your name to preach resignation and submission and treason; and people will believe them.'

Over dinner with Jacques-Laurent Bost, Olga Kosakiewicz and Richard Wright – the latter now living in Paris – Beauvoir and Sartre again discussed the subject: 'how to get away, where, when?' Nelson Algren had written offering to help them get into the United States, but they did not want this. If they had to leave France, it should be for a neutral country. Perhaps, Beauvoir wrote, they would go to Brazil, where the Austrian writer Stefan Zweig had found refuge during the last war. But Zweig had committed suicide there, unable to endure exile. And this time it would be to flee socialism! How could this be happening?

Merleau-Ponty likewise feared the worst for France should there be war, yet he too did not want to run away from Communists. Sartre noted that he now seemed exceptionally light-hearted – 'with that boyish air which I always knew him to assume when matters threatened to turn serious'. If the invasion came, joked Merleau-Ponty, he would go and become an elevator boy in New York.

Merleau-Ponty was more disturbed by events than he showed, and not just from personal fear. While the Korean conflict was building, he and Sartre had bumped into each other on holiday in Saint-Raphaël on the Côte d'Azur. They were happy to see one another, but then argued all day, first as they walked along the seafront, then on the terrace of a café, and then at the station where Sartre awaited his train. They had to thrash out a coherent editorial position on Korea for *Les Temps modernes*. But Merleau-Ponty had come to feel they should not fire off instant opinions on situations they did not understand. Sartre disagreed. If war is imminent, how can you keep silent? Merleau-Ponty took a gloomy view: 'Because brute force will decide the outcome. Why speak to what has no ears?'

The underlying disagreement was about more than editorial policy; it was about how far one should take one's belief in Communism. Merleau-Ponty had been shocked by North Korea's invasion of the South, and thought it showed the Communist world to be just as greedy as the capitalist world and just as inclined to use ideology as a veil. He had also been disturbed by the increasing publicity about Soviet camps. This represented a major change of perspective for the man who, until recently, had been the most pro-Communist of them all. Conversely, the once-wary Sartre was becoming more inclined to give Communist countries the benefit of the doubt.

No Soviet invasion of France came out of the Korean conflict, but the war, which continued until 1953, did change the global political landscape and spread a mood of paranoia and anxiety as the Cold War settled in. During these years, Merleau-Ponty continued to develop his doubts, while Sartre climbed off the fence. What really radicalised him was a bizarre event in France.

One evening, on 28 May 1952, a police road unit waved down the current leader of the French Communist Party, Jacques Duclos, and searched his car. Finding a revolver, a radio and a pair of pigeons in a basket, they arrested him, claiming that the birds were carrier pigeons intended for taking messages to his Soviet masters. Duclos replied that the pigeons were dead, and thus unsuitable for use as carriers. He had been taking them to his wife to cook for dinner. The police said that the birds were still warm and not yet stiff, and that Duclos could have hastily smothered them. They locked him up in a holding cell.

The next day, an autopsy was conducted on the pigeons, searching for microfilm hidden inside their persons. There followed a hearing at which three pigeon experts were brought in to give an opinion on the birds' ages, which they estimated at twenty-six and thirty-five days respectively, and on their exact breed – which they pointedly said they could not identify 'because the number and variety of known pigeon types, and the many cross-breeds that have been and still are being created by amateur breeders, makes identification difficult'. The experts concluded, however, that the pigeons were probably of the common domestic type found everywhere, and showed no signs of being bred to carry messages. All the same, Duclos was kept in prison for a month before being released. A huge campaign was mounted to support him, and the Communist poet Louis Aragon wrote a poem about the 'pigeon plot'.

This absurd affair seemed to Sartre the culmination of years of harassment and provocation of Communists in France. As he wrote later, 'after ten years of ruminating, I had come to the breaking point'. The pigeon plot drove him to make a commitment. As he wrote, 'In the language of the Church, this was my conversion.'

Perhaps, in the language of Heideggerianism, it was his *Kehre* – a 'turn' which required every point of Sartre's thought to be reconsidered according to new priorities. While Heidegger's turn had led him away from resoluteness into 'letting-be', Sartre's now led him to become more resolute, more *engagé*, more public, and less willing to compromise. Feeling at once that he had to 'write or suffocate', he wrote at top speed and produced the first part of a long essay called *The Communists and Peace*. He wrote it with rage in his heart, he said later – but also with Corydrane in his blood. Barely stopping for sleep, he produced pages of justifications and arguments in favour of the Soviet state, and published the result in *Les Temps modernes* in July 1952. A few months later, he followed it with another intemperate outburst, this time attacking his friend Albert Camus.

A confrontation with Camus had been building for a while. It was almost inevitable, considering how different their views had become. In 1951, Camus published an extended essay, *The Rebel*, in which he laid out a theory of rebellion and political activism that was very different from the Communist-approved one.

For Marxists, human beings are destined to progress through predefined stages of history towards a final socialist paradise. The road will be long, but we are bound to get there, and all will be perfect when we do. Camus disagreed on two counts: he did not think that history led to a single inevitable destination, and he did not think there was such a thing as perfection. As long as we have human societies, we will have rebellions. Each time a revolution overturns the ills of a society, a new status quo is created, which then develops its own excesses and injustices. Each generation has a fresh duty to revolt against these, and this will be the case forever.

Moreover, for Camus, true rebellion does not mean reaching towards an ecstatic vision of a shining city on a hill. It means setting a *limit* on some very real present state of affairs that has become unacceptable. For example, a slave who has been ordered around all his life suddenly decides he will take no more, and draws a line, saying 'so far but no further'. Rebellion is a reining in of tyranny. As rebels keep countering new tyrannies, a balance is created: a state of moderation that must be tirelessly renewed and maintained.

Camus' vision of endless self-moderating rebellion is appealing – but it was rightly seen as an attack on Soviet Communism and its fellow travellers. Sartre knew that it was directed partly against himself, and he could not forgive Camus for playing into the hands of the right at a delicate historical moment. The book clearly called for a review in *Les Temps modernes*. Sartre hesitated to rip his old friend to pieces, so he delegated the task to his young colleague Francis Jeanson – who ripped Camus to pieces, damning the *The Rebel* as an apology for capitalism. Camus defended himself in a seventeen-page letter to the editor, meaning Sartre, although he did not name him. He accused Jeanson of misrepresenting his argument, and added, 'I am beginning to become a little tired of seeing myself . . . receive endless lessons in effectiveness from critics who have never done anything more than turn their armchair in history's direction.'

This dig prompted Sartre to write his own response after all. It turned into an ad hominem tirade that was overemotional even by his own recent standards. That's it, said Sartre; their friendship was over. Of course he would miss Camus, especially the old Camus that he remembered from wartime Resistance days. But now that his friend had become a counter-revolutionary, no reconciliation was possible. Again, nothing could trump politics.

Camus never published a reply to Sartre's reply, although he did draft one. Again, the rest was silence. Well, not exactly, because ever since this famous quarrel occurred, a little industry of books and articles has flourished, analysing the confrontation to its last punctuation mark. It has come to be seen as a quarrel that defines a whole age and an intellectual milieu. It is often mythologised as a drama in which Sartre, a 'dreaming boy' chasing an impossible fantasy, meets his comeuppance in the form of a clear-sighted moral hero who also happens to be cooler and wiser and better-looking: Camus.

This makes a good story, but I think there are subtler ways to think about it, and that it helps if we make the effort to understand Sartre's motivation, and to ask why he reacted so intemperately. Pressurised about politics for years, taunted as a decadent bourgeois, Sartre had undergone a conversion experience which had made him see the whole world in a new light. He considered it his *duty* to renounce personal feeling for Camus. Individual sentiment was a self-indulgence, and must be transcended. Just like Heidegger in his *Being and Time* period, Sartre thought the important thing was to be resolute at all costs: to grasp what must be done, and do it. In the Algerian War, Camus would choose his mother over justice, but Sartre decided that it was not right to choose his friend if his friend was betraying the working class. Beauvoir, charmed though she had been by Camus in the past, took the same line: *The Rebel* was a deliberate gift to their enemies at a crucial point in history, and it could not be allowed to pass.

Camus was disturbed by the quarrel, which occurred at a difficult period for him. His personal life was soon to get worse, with marriage difficulties, writer's block, and the horror of war in his Algerian homeland. In 1956 his crisis would find expression in a novella, *The Fall*, whose hero is a 'judge-penitent': a former trial judge who has decided to sit in judgement on himself. In an Amsterdam bar, over several evenings, the judge relates his life to an unnamed narrator, culminating in a shocking story. One night in Paris, he saw a woman throw herself off a bridge, yet failed to jump in and save her. He cannot forgive himself. The judge acknowledges his sins, but on the other hand he seems to feel that this gives him moral authority to point out the sins of others. As he tells his interlocutor, and implicitly also us, his readers, 'The more I accuse myself, the more I have a right to judge you.' There is a lot of Camus in this remark.

Sartre and Beauvoir were not penitents like the protagonist of *The Fall*, but they were aware of stern eyes looking back at them from the future. 'We feel that we are being judged by the masked men who will succeed us', wrote Sartre in 1952, adding, 'our age will be an object for those future eyes whose gaze haunts us'. Beauvoir wrote in her last volume of memoirs that she had once felt superior to earlier writers because, by definition, she knew more history than they did. Then the obvious truth dawned: her generation too would one day be judged by future criteria. She saw that her contemporaries would suffer what historian E. P. Thompson later called 'the enormous conde-scension of posterity'.

Sartre still believed, however, that one must call the shots as one sees them at the time. If you fence-sit just because you are scared to make an error, then you are definitely making one. As Kierkegaard had said:

It is perfectly true, as philosophers say, that life must be under-stood backwards. But they forget the other proposition, that it must be lived forwards. And if one thinks over that proposition it becomes more and more evident that life can never really be understood in time because at no particular moment can I find the necessary resting-place from which to understand it.

There would never be a point of stillness and contemplation. For Sartre, in politics as in everything, the correct direction was always onwards – even if that onward road led you round U-turns, and even if you went too fast to be fully in control.

Sartre upset another old friend through his actions with *Les Temps modernes* in 1952: he printed his first *Communists and Peace* article without showing it to his co-editor Merleau-Ponty. This was a breach of manners which Sartre knew might cause offence. He also knew that Merleau-Ponty might object to the article or suggest toning it down, and in his passion Sartre could not bear any such delay.

By this time, Merleau-Ponty had moved closer to Camus' position, but with the major difference that he had once put his faith in the socialist utopia. Camus had never shared the 'dream', but Merleau-Ponty knew what it meant to be a believer. This made Merleau-Ponty an insightful critic after giving it up, but it did not make him any more able to save his relationship with Sartre.

The tension between the two men grew through 1952 and into early 1953. On 15 January that year, Sartre attended the Collège de France to hear Merleau-Ponty's inaugural lecture in his new role as its head. Merleau-Ponty used the lecture, among other things, to remind philosophers to remain vigilant about public affairs, and to be alert to ambiguities. Afterwards, Sartre failed to speak the conventional words of warm congratulation. According to Merleau-Ponty, Sartre said 'in a glacially cold tone' that the lecture was 'amusing', and added, waving at the *collège* with its Establishment air, 'I hope that you are going to subvert all this a little.' Sartre himself had refused all similar honours offered to him and would continue to do so – to the point that, a decade later, he would turn down the Nobel Prize. He always felt that Merleau-Ponty was too willing to become a cosy insider.

Merleau-Ponty had accepted the Collège de France role without a qualm, and was now hurt by Sartre's attitude. He let it pass, but that summer their disagreement blew up in letters while Sartre was on holiday in a sweltering Rome. Afterwards Sartre realised that the heat may have gone to his head. Also, as usual, he had been working too hard and obsessing about the future of humanity.

Sartre began by writing to tell Merleau-Ponty that a person who was no longer 'engaged' politically should not expect to criticise those who were. You are right, Merleau-Ponty replied. Indeed, *he* has now decided never again to issue hasty responses to events as they occur. After Korea, he has concluded that one needs a longer perspective to understand history. He no longer wishes to 'become engaged on every event, as if it were a test of morality' – a tendency which he describes as bad faith. This was a provocative thing to say to Sartre, of all people. Merleau-Ponty also complained about Sartre's cold treatment of him after the lecture, which was still rankling.

Sartre replied on 29 July, 'for God's sake, don't interpret my intonations or physiognomies as you do, that is, wholly askew and emotionally'. As to his tone, he now says, touchingly and plausibly, 'If I appeared glacially cold, it's because I always have a kind of timidity about congratulating people. I don't know how to do it, and I'm aware of this. It's certainly a character trait, and I admit it to you.'

This should have mollified Merleau-Ponty, but there was still an offensive tone in Sartre's letters, and the roots of their disagreement were profound. As usual, Merleau-Ponty smiled things off after Sartre's return, which annoyed Sartre even more. As Sartre himself admitted, his own tendency was to argue a question to the end, until he had either convinced the other person or the other had convinced him. Merleau-Ponty, instead, 'found his security in a multiplicity of perspectives, seeing in them the different facets of being'. How infuriating!

In reality, Merleau-Ponty too was disturbed by the quarrel. His daughter Marianne remembers hearing her parents discussing Sartre for hours. Also, he had to decide what to do about Les Temps modernes. For a long time he had done much of the actual work there, writing unsigned editorials and making sure each issue came out on time. But Sartre was the figurehead, and no one could work at Les Temps modernes without getting on with its star. As Sartre remembered it, Merleau-Ponty began turning up ever later to editorial meetings, and muttering asides instead of openly taking part in discussion. Sartre challenged him to say what he was thinking; Merleau-Ponty preferred not to.

By the end of 1953, Les Temps modernes was ready to explode – and then came the spark. They had taken on a strongly pro-Soviet piece, and Merleau-Ponty wrote an editorial remark to preface it, pointing out that the views it expressed were not those of Les Temps modernes. Seeing the text before publication, Sartre cut the remark without telling Merleau-Ponty.

When Merleau-Ponty realised this, he and Sartre had a long, strained telephone conversation. Sartre recalled it later; Marianne Merleau-Ponty also remembers overhearing it. After two hours on the phone, her father hung up, turned to her mother, and said, 'Alors, c'est fini' – 'Well, that's the end of it.' He probably meant that he had ended his involvement in Les Temps modernes, but it could equally be taken as referring to the end of the friendship. Afterwards, the two men spoke from time to time, and Merleau-Ponty would courteously say, 'I'll call you.' But, said Sartre, he never did.

The crisis with Sartre coincided with a greater trauma in Merleau-Ponty's life: his mother died in December 1953. Having grown up without a father, and being obliged to defend her against gossip, he had become exceptionally close to her. As Sartre recognised later, she had been the source of the happy childhood that had made such a difference in Merleau-Ponty's life; her death meant losing his connection to that golden age. Shortly afterwards, recalled Sartre, Merleau-Ponty met Beauvoir and said to her, 'casually, with that sad gaiety which masked his most sincere moments: "But I am more than half dead."' The break with Sartre was less significant than this bereavement, but it came at a bad time, and robbed him of the routine and the sense of mission that Les Temps modernes had brought to his life.

Sartre too may have been more upset by the break than he revealed. He overreacted, alleging that Merleau-Ponty's entire history at Les Temps modernes had been treacherous. He thought his co-editor had kept his profile low deliberately, not putting his name on the masthead so as to avoid committing himself to any definite perspective. Merleau-Ponty was as much in command as himself, but remained 'light and free as air', grumbled Sartre. If he did not like something he could walk away. In general, Merleau-Ponty resolved conflicts by seeking 'a living accord' rather than by exerting authority in a straightforward way. These seem strange complaints, but rather typical ones to hear about Merleau-Ponty, who was so amiable, and so damned elusive.

In 1955, Merleau-Ponty laid out his final rejection of Communist ideology in a book called Adventures of the Dialectic. This combined critiques of Georg Lukács and other Marxist theorists with a long chapter, 'Sartre and Ultrabolshevism', which took Sartre's recent political writings to task for their inconsistencies and lack of practicality. Beauvoir waded in with an essay attacking Merleau-Ponty, arguing that he had misunderstood aspects of Sartre's thought. Her old friendship with him had now also disappeared. But the combined ire of Sartre and Beauvoir was nothing compared to the torrent of real Communist hatred that descended on Merleau-Ponty's head from the party faithful in response to his book. A group of Communist intellectuals organised a meeting on 29 November 1955 entirely dedicated to anti-Merleau-Ponty speeches. It was attended by students, and featured denunciations by Henri Lefebvre and others. These were all collected and published in 1956, under a title playing on his own: *Mésaventures de l'anti-marxisme: les malheurs de M. Merleau-Ponty.*

Shortly after this, Merleau-Ponty and Sartre found themselves thrown together at a Venice writers' conference organised by the European Cultural Society – the same one at which Sartre told Spender that he would endure unjust imprisonment to save the Communist state. The conference brought together writers from both sides of the Iron Curtain to debate recent developments in the Soviet Union – which was now entering a post-Stalin 'thaw' period under Khrushchev – and also the question of a writer's duty to be politically committed. This was the very subject over which Merleau-Ponty and Sartre had fallen out. Thinking they would be pleased to see each other, the organisers placed them side by side on the podium. Sartre blanched when he saw the name card next to his, but it was all right: 'Someone was speaking, he came in behind me, on tiptoe, lightly touched my shoulder and when I turned around, he smiled at me.' They had other relaxed moments during the conference, too: Sartre remembered them exchanging amused looks about an English delegate – very likely Spender, who was inclined to make irreverent remarks about *littérature engagée*. But a single smile of complicity could not revive a friendship.

Both philosophers had now moved far beyond the positions they had adopted in 1945 and 1946, when they shared similar views on the need to get dirty and make 'difficult' decisions with other people's lives. They had crossed paths, and parted in opposite directions – another X. Sartre went through a period of doubt, then emerged from it radicalised and prepared to risk his life for the ideal state. Merleau-Ponty went deeply into Communist ideology, then gave it up in favour of a conviction that human life could never be forced to fit the lineaments of an ideal. He had, as he put it, woken up. When Communist 'nostalgia' is exorcised, he said, 'one leaves behind reveries and everything becomes interesting and new again'. In the Collège de France lecture, too, he spoke of philosophers as the people who are wakeful while others sleep.

Of course, Sartre thought he was the one who was awake. He later summed up their disagreement by saying, 'I thought that while I was being faithful to his thought of 1945 [i.e. Merleau-Ponty's Communist period], he was abandoning it. He thought he was remaining true to himself and I betraying him.'

Not only is this a remarkably fair-minded portrayal of what divided them, but it resonates with echoes of an earlier, quite different schism: the one that occurred between Edmund Husserl and Martin Heidegger in the late 1920s. They too each thought they were sailing into new and more exciting territory, leaving the other behind, lost, misled or becalmed.

During these dramas, Beauvoir kept notes with her usual spirit of tireless observation and reflection. In 1954, she turned the notes into *The Mandarins*, an epic novel tracing events and emotions from the end of the war and the fear of the Bomb to the discussions of Soviet camps and trials, the pros and cons of political commitment, the love affairs and the fights. She adjusted a few details, sometimes making her friends seem wiser and more prescient than they were, but it all grew into a hefty and surprisingly enjoyable portrait of an era and a milieu. It won the Goncourt Prize. With the royalties from increased sales, she bought an apartment on the rue Victor Schoelcher near the Montparnasse cemetery. This meant that she now lived quite a way from Sartre, who continued to live with his mother above the Bar Napoléon. But she strolled along to the Saint-Germain-des-Prés district most days, probably favouring the leafy route through the Jardin du Luxembourg, so as to see friends and to work side by side with Sartre as they always had.

A new lover moved in with her to the Montparnasse apartment, Claude Lanzmann. She had been won over by his passionate beliefs and his strong sense of who he was: she wrote that, to define himself, 'he said first of all: I'm a Jew'. Sartre had once criticised this kind of firm identity statement as an act of bad faith, since it implied presenting oneself as a fixed self rather than as a free consciousness. In truth, she and Sartre always had a weakness for people with uncompromising identities and attitudes. Lanzmann was in a permanent state of rage about what the Jews had suffered, wrote Beauvoir admiringly. He once told her, 'I want to kill, all the time.' He experienced his feelings physically – as she did. He would weep or vomit out of sheer anger. By contrast to the planetary figure of Sartre at the height of his fame, it must have been refreshing. It certainly made a contrast with her former friend Merleau-Ponty, who, with every rise in the pressure level, seemed only to smile more wryly and make more quips.

In a notebook entry written around 1954 after rereading old diaries, Sartre calmly listed recent quarrels and divergences: complete breaks with Koestler, Aron and several others, a relationship with Camus that meant speaking only briefly while 'avoiding essential subjects', and the split with Merleau-Ponty. (He added a diagram showing how several of them had also fallen out with each other.) He noted elsewhere that it did not bother him to lose friendships: 'A thing is dead – that's all.' Yet he would write generous obituary pieces a few years later for both Camus and Merleau-Ponty. Remembering Camus, he wrote wistfully of how they would laugh together: 'there was a side of him that smacked of the little Algerian tough guy, very much a hooligan, very funny'. He added: 'He was probably the last good friend I had.'

When it came to Raymond Aron, Sartre nursed a more lasting resentment, perhaps because they had been closer in schooldays and yet had gone on to diverge more starkly over politics. In 1955, Aron published *The Opium of the Intellectuals*, a direct attack on Sartre and his allies, accusing them of being 'merciless towards the failings of the democracies but ready to tolerate the worst crimes as long as they are committed in the name of the proper doctrines'. Sartre took revenge in May 1968, when Aron opposed the student rebellions: he accused Aron of being unfit to teach.

Very late in life, during an event in aid of refugees from Vietnam in the late 1970s, Sartre and Aron met and shook hands while photographers clicked away, excited at capturing what they took to be a major reconciliation. By this time, however, Sartre was ill and rather dazed, losing his vision and much of his hearing. Either because of this, or as a deliberate snub, Sartre did not reply in kind when Aron greeted him with their old term of endearment, 'Bonjour, mon petit camarade.' He responded only, 'Bonjour.'

One famous remark has come to be associated with Aron and Sartre, although it was not spoken by either one of them. In 1976, during an interview with Bernard-Henri Lévy, Aron opined that leftist intellectuals hated him not because he had pointed out the true nature of Communism, but because he had never shared their belief in it in the first place. Lévy replied, 'What do you think? Is it better, in that case, to be Sartre or Aron? Sartre the mistaken victor, or Aron defeated but correct?' Aron gave no clear answer. But the question was remembered, and converted into a simple and sentimental maxim: that it is better to be wrong with Sartre than right with Aron.

During the 1950s, determined to give his time and energy to any cause he thought needed him, Sartre overstretched himself alarmingly. This led to some of his most foolish and reprehensible moments, as when he travelled to the Soviet Union at the invitation of an organisation of Russian writers in May 1954, and afterwards published a series of articles suggesting, for example, that Soviet citizens did not travel because they had no desire to do so and were too busy building Communism. Later, he claimed that, having come home in a state of exhaustion, he had delegated the writing to his secretary, Jean Cau.

Cau did recall of this period that Sartre's fear of underproducing often drove him over the edge. 'There's no time!' he would cry. One by one, he gave up his greatest pleasures: the cinema, theatre, novels. He wanted only to write, write, write. This was when he convinced himself that literary quality control was bourgeois self-indulgence; only the cause mattered, and it was a sin to revise or even to reread. He filled sheets with ink while Beauvoir, a painstaking reviser herself, watched nervously. Sartre churned out essays, talks, philosophical works – occasionally with help from Cau, but mostly alone. His bibliographers Michel Contat and Michel Rybalka calculated that, over his entire life, he averaged twenty pages a day, and that was of completed work, not drafts. (By this stage, there *were* no drafts.) In Ireland, too, John Huston had been amazed each morning at breakfast to find that Sartre had been up for hours and had already written some twenty-five new pages of his Freud script. Sartre's biographer Annie Cohen-Solal used engine-room and turbine metaphors to describe his production from the late 1940s onwards, while Olivier Wickers wrote of his treating sleep as a military necessity: a bivouac, or the pit stop one must give a machine to keep it working.

Meanwhile, he continued overdosing on Corydrane. The recommended intake was one or two pills daily, but Sartre got through a whole tube. He combined it with heavy drinking, and even enjoyed the way the combination scrambled his brains: 'I liked having confused, vaguely questioning ideas that then fell apart.' Often, at the end of a day, he took downers to help him pass out. He did cut down on the Corydrane when writing something 'literary', because he knew it led to too much 'facility', as he put it. Writing a new scene for his *Roads of Freedom* series, for example, he found that every street his character Mathieu walked down generated a mass of fresh metaphors. When he mentioned this to Beauvoir in an interview, she added, with (one imagines) a shudder, 'I remember. It was dreadful.' The fatal 'facility' had already become evident in a

1951 notebook he kept in Italy, of which he said to Beauvoir in 1974 that there were some twenty pages 'about the plashing sound that gondolas make'. Of course, this could just be diligent phenomenology.

Very little of the overproduction came from either authorial vanity or from need of money. His Freud screenplay, taken on to pay a bill, was a rare exception. Mostly it came from his love of commitment and his desire to help friends by promoting their writing or campaigns. This generosity of purpose is an easily forgotten fact about Sartre. He expected himself to *do something* at every moment: to be engaged and active even when he had no time to think things through. More circumspect types stopped for reflection, but Sartre thought that was a bourgeois luxury too.

Merleau-Ponty once said in an interview that there was a simple fact about Sartre that few people know and that did not often come across in his books. It was this: '*il est bon*'. He is good. His 'goodness' was his fatal flaw: it led him to overwork, and more significantly it was what led him to believe that he must reconcile his existentialism with Marxism in the first place. That was an impossible and destructive task: the two just were incompatible. But Sartre thought the oppressed classes of the world required it from him.

Many years later, in an interview just before Sartre's death, his young assistant Benny Lévy challenged him – quite aggressively – to say who exactly it was that vanished when the pro-Soviet apologist in Sartre finally disappeared. Who died, he asked? 'A sinister scoundrel, a dimwit, a sucker, or a basically good person?'

Sartre answered, mildly, 'I'd say, a person who's not bad.'

Whatever goodness there had been in defending Soviet Communism earlier in the 1950s, it became harder to see in October and November 1956.

When Stalin died, the talk of a 'thaw' in the Soviet Union's policies had encouraged reformers in Hungary's Communist government to introduce a few signs of personal and political freedom. Demonstrators took to the streets demanding more. In response, the Soviet Union sent soldiers, and battles broke out around Budapest; the rebels seized the city's radio station and called on Hungarians to resist. An apparent truce held for a while, but on 1 November Russian tanks rolled across the border from Ukraine and lumbered on into Budapest. Tank troops demolished buildings where people were hiding. They fired on railway stations and public squares, and threatened to destroy the city's Parliament buildings. On Sunday 4 November, at noon, the radio rebels surrendered with their final broadcast: 'We are now going off the air. *Vive l'Europe! Vive la Hongrie!*' The rebellion was defeated.

For Communist sympathisers in the West, this demonstration of brute Soviet power was a great shock. Many tore up their Communist Party cards, and even the remaining believers wrung their hands and wondered how to incorporate the new development into their vision. Sartre and Beauvoir were among those most confused. In January 1957, they produced a special issue of *Les Temps modernes* condemning the Soviet action and giving space to many Hungarian writers to write about the events – but in private they continued to feel uneasy, and they disliked the way the right seized on the invasion to promote their own ideology.

Very soon after the Hungarian uprising, Sartre began to write a new work of vast extent, the *Critique of Dialectical Reason*. It was an attempt to create something on the scale of *Being and Nothingness*, but built around his new social thinking and the ideal of political commitment. Instead of emphasing consciousness, nothingness and freedom, he now brought everything back to concrete situations and the principle of concerted action in the world. Beauvoir considered the *Critique of Dialectical Reason* Sartre's ultimate response to the catastrophe of 1956. As if merging Marxism with existentialism were not acrobatic enough, he was now trying to adapt the result to a situation in which the Soviet Union had proved itself untrustworthy. As Sartre himself put it in 1975, 'The *Critique* is a Marxist work written against the Communists.' It could also be seen as an existentialist work written against the old, unpoliticised existentialism.

The book was formidably difficult to bring off. Sartre published the first volume, *Theory of Practical Ensembles*, in 1960; that alone reached nearly 400,000 words. The second volume – surprise! – was never finished. He made extensive notes but could not get it into shape. These notes were published posthumously in 1985.

By the time of giving up on the second volume, Sartre's attention had already turned away from the Soviet Union and towards new battles. He took an interest in Mao's China. He also began to see himself as an intellectual pioneer, not of Communism, but of a more radical rebellion – one that fit much better with the existentialist way of life.

12

The Eyes of the Least Favoured

*In which we meet revolutionaries, outsiders
and seekers after authenticity.*

If a lot of people with incompatible interests all claim that right is on
their side, how do you decide between them? In a paragraph of the
final part of *The Communists and Peace*, Sartre had sketched the outline
of a bold solution: why not decide every situation by asking how it
looks to 'the eyes of the least favoured', or to 'those treated the most
unjustly'? You just need to work out who is most oppressed and
disadvantaged in the situation, and then adopt their version of events
as the right one. Their view can be considered the criterion for truth
itself: the way of establishing 'man and society as they truly are'. If
something is not true in the eyes of the least favoured, says Sartre,
then it is *not true*.

As an idea, this is astoundingly simple and refreshing. At a stroke,
it wipes out the weasely cant indulged in by the advantaged – all those
convenient claims that the poor 'deserve' their fate, or that the rich
are entitled to the disproportionate wealth that accumulates upon
them, or that inequality and suffering should be accepted as inevitable
parts of life. For Sartre, if the poor and disadvantaged do not believe
such arguments, they are wrong arguments. This is similar to what
one might call the Genet Principle: that the underdog is always right.
From now on, like Jean Genet, Sartre submits himself joyfully to the
alienated, downtrodden, thwarted and excluded. He tries to adopt the
gaze of the outsider, turned against the privileged caste – even when
that caste includes himself.

No one could say that this is easy to do, and not only because (as

Beauvoir had pointed out in *The Second Sex*) borrowing someone else's perspective puts a strain on the psyche. Anyone who tries to do it also runs into a mass of logical and conceptual problems. Disagreements inevitably ensue about *who* exactly is least favoured at any moment. Each time an underdog becomes an overdog, everything has to be recalculated. Constant monitoring of roles is required – and who is to do the monitoring?

As Merleau-Ponty pointed out in his 'Sartre and Ultrabolshevism', Sartre himself did not stick to his own principle. Confronted with the gaze of those unfavoured in Stalin's prisons, he managed for a long time to take no account of their accusing eyes, giving reasons why they could be disregarded. But perhaps the 'gaze' idea was never intended to make consistent sense. Just as with Levinas's or Weil's ethical philosophies, in which the demands made on us by the gaze of the Other are theoretically infinite in extent, an ideal does not become any less inspiring just because it is impossible to stick to.

Sartre's 'eyes of the least favoured' idea is as radical as Levinas's Other-directed ethics, and more radical than Communism. Communists believe that only the party can decide what is right. To turn morality over to a mass of human eyes and personal perspectives is to invite chaos and lose the possibility of a real revolution. Sartre ignored the party line and revealed himself to be just as much of an old maverick as ever. He could not be a proper Marxist even when he was trying.

His new approach appealed more to activists who did not want to join any party but who were active in new-style liberation movements, especially the protests of the 1950s and 1960s against racism, sexism, social exclusion, poverty and colonialism. Sartre threw his weight behind these struggles, and did what he could to help – mostly with his favourite weapon, the pen. Writing forewords for younger authors' polemics gave him new subjects to be *engagé* about, and allowed him to feel that his philosophy was truly achieving something, a feeling that had eluded him after the Soviet project curdled.

As long ago as 1948, he had written an essay called 'Black Orpheus', originally published as the preface to Léopold Senghor's *Anthology of New Black and Malagasy Poetry*. Sartre there described how poetry by black and post-colonial writers often reversed the fixing, judging 'gaze' of their oppressors. From now on, he said, white Europeans can no longer coolly assess and master the world. Instead, 'these black men are looking at us, and our gaze comes back to our own eyes; in their turn, black torches light up the world and our white heads are no more than Chinese lanterns swinging in the wind'. (Sartre was still polishing his metaphors in those days.)

In 1957, he introduced Albert Memmi's double work *Portrait du colonisé* and *Portrait du colonisateur* (translated as *The Colonizer and the Colonized*), which analysed the 'myths' of colonialism in the same way that Beauvoir had analysed the myths of femininity in *The Second Sex*. After this, Sartre wrote an even more influential foreword to an epoch-defining 1961 work of anti-colonialism, Frantz Fanon's *The Wretched of the Earth*.

Fanon was a messianic thinker and an intellectual who had been influenced by existentialism himself, and who devoted his short life to questions of race, independence and revolutionary violence. Born in Martinique, of mixed African and European descent, he studied philosophy in Lyons – with Merleau-Ponty among others, although Fanon did not warm to Merleau-Ponty's calm style. When he published his own first book in 1952, it was impassioned rather than calm, but it was also highly phenomenological: *Black Skin, White Masks* explored the 'lived experience' of black people cast into a role of Other in a white-dominated world.

Next, Fanon moved to Algeria and became active in the independence movement, but was expelled for this in 1956 and went to live in Tunisia. While there, he was diagnosed with leukaemia. He had treatment in the Soviet Union, and gained a brief remission, but was once again gravely ill in 1961 when he began work on *The Wretched of the Earth*. Feverish and weak, he travelled to Rome, and was there introduced to Beauvoir and Sartre by Claude Lanzmann.

Sartre fell for Fanon immediately, and was delighted to write a foreword for *The Wretched of the Earth*. He already liked Fanon's work, and he liked him even better in person. Lanzmann later commented that he had never seen Sartre so captivated by a man as at that meeting. The four of them talked through lunch, then all through the afternoon, then all evening, until 2 a.m., when Beauvoir finally insisted that Sartre needed to sleep. Fanon was offended: 'I don't like people who hoard their resources.' He kept Lanzmann up until eight the next morning.

By this time, Fanon had only a few months to live. In his last weeks, he was flown to the United States to get the best available treatment, a trip arranged (surprisingly) by a CIA agent with whom he had become friends, Ollie Iselin. But nothing could be done, and he died in Bethesda, Maryland, on 6 December 1961, aged thirty-six. *The Wretched of the Earth* came out just afterwards, with the foreword by Sartre.

Beauvoir recalled Fanon saying in Rome, 'We have claims on you' – just the sort of thing they loved to hear. That burning intensity, and the willingness to make demands and to assign guilt if necessary, was what had attracted Beauvoir to Lanzmann. Now it thrilled Sartre too. Perhaps it took them back to their war years: a time when *everything mattered*. Sartre certainly embraced Fanon's militant arguments, which in this book included the notion that anti-imperial revolution must inevitably be violent, not just because violence was effective (though that was one reason) but because it helped the colonised to shake off the paralysis of oppression and forge a new shared identity. Without glorifying violence, Fanon considered it essential to political change; he had little sympathy for Gandhi's idea of of non-violent resistance as a source of power. In his contribution, Sartre endorsed Fanon's view so enthusiastically that he outdid the original, shifting the emphasis so as to praise violence for its own sake. Sartre seemed to see the violence of the oppressed as a Nietzschean act of self-creation. Like Fanon, he also contrasted it with the hidden brutality of coloni-alism. And, as in 'Black Orpheus', he invited his readers (presumed white) to imagine the gaze of the oppressed turned against them, stripping away their bourgeois hypocrisy and revealing them as monsters of greed and self-interest.

Sartre's foreword to *The Wretched of the Earth* provides a snapshot of what was at once most odious and most admirable about him in these militant years. His fetishising of violence is shocking, yet there is still something to be admired in his willingness to engage with the predicament of the marginalised and oppressed in such a radical way. Indeed, Sartre had by now become so used to taking radical stances that he hardly knew any longer how to be moderate. As his friend Olivier Todd commented, Sartre's beliefs changed, but his extremism never did. Sartre agreed. Asked in 1975 to name his worst failing, he replied, 'Naturally in the course of my life I have made lots of mistakes, large and small, for one reason or another. But at the heart of it all, every time I made a mistake it was because I was not radical enough.'

Being radical meant upsetting people, and this could include other radicals. Frantz Fanon's widow Josie Fanon was among those to take against Sartre: she disliked the fact that he also supported Zionism during this period, which she felt made him an enemy to most Algerians. Sartre's ability to engage with both causes speaks for his generous intentions. Yet it also shows another paradox in his 'least favoured' principle. More than one group can be considered unfavoured by history, so what happens if their claims are incompatible? Sartre's praise of violence held a worse paradox, too: who could be less 'favoured' than the victim of any violent attack, regardless of its motivation or context?

Sartre was aware that odd personal impulses underlay his interest in violence. He traced it to his childhood experience of bullying, and his decision to take on the bullies' aggression as part of himself. Talking about it with Beauvoir in 1974, he said that he had never forgotten the violence he had learned at the school in La Rochelle. He even thought it had influenced his tendency to put friendships on the line: 'I've never had tender relationships with my friends since then.' One suspects it also fed his desire for extremism in all things.

In the case of anti-colonial violence, or violence against whites, Sartre's own people were implicitly on the receiving end, but this only made him applaud it more. There was satisfaction to be had in reversing viewpoints and picturing himself standing in the gale of someone else's righteous rage. Beauvoir similarly celebrated news of uprisings against France's colonising forces around the word, feeling elated about anti-colonial attacks in Indochina in the 1950s. It was a matter of political conviction, of course, but her response seems more visceral than intellectual. This was a complex emotional state for someone whose own country had been occupied and oppressed just ten years earlier. Indeed, when the Algerian War began in 1954, she observed herself feeling just as disturbed by the sight of French uniforms in public as she had by German ones – except that now she shared the culpability herself. 'I'm French,' she would say to herself, and feel as though she were confessing to a deformity.

The years in which Algeria was fighting for self-determination, 1954 to 1962, were traumatic ones, bringing appalling suffering. The bloodshed found its way to Paris, as pro-independence demonstrators were killed in the heart of the city. French torture and executions of civilians in Algeria caused widespread dismay. Camus' loyalties were with his mother, but he opposed the authorities' abuses too. Sartre and Beauvoir were more single-minded in their support of the Algerian liberation movement; they campaigned actively, and both wrote eloquent contributions to books by and about tortured Algerians. Sartre wrote in his foreword to Henri Alleg's *The Question*: 'Anybody, at any time, may equally find himself victim or executioner' – an allusion to Camus' earlier essay 'Neither Victims Nor Executioners'. Had Sartre and Beauvoir not already fallen out with Camus, they might have done so now over the Algerian situation.

We could accuse Sartre and Beauvoir of cheering on the violence from the safety of the sidelines, but this time their position was not safe at all. Just as in 1947, Sartre received death threats. In October 1960, 10,000 French army veterans marched in an anti-independence demonstration shouting, among other slogans, 'Shoot Sartre!' When he signed an illegal petition urging French soldiers to disobey orders that they disagreed with, he faced prosecution and prison, until President Charles de Gaulle allegedly ruled this out with the remark, 'One does not imprison Voltaire.' Finally, on 7 January 1962, someone took the incitements to murder seriously. At 42 rue Bonaparte, where Sartre lived with his mother, a bomb was planted in the apartment above theirs. The explosion damaged both storeys and tore off the apartment doors; it was only by good luck that no one was injured. Camus had feared for his mother in Algeria, but it was Sartre's mother who now faced danger. He moved to a new apartment at 222 boulevard Raspail, renting a separate one for his mother nearby. Sartre was now closer to where Beauvoir lived, and further away from his old, well-known haunts in Saint-Germain-des-Prés, making him harder to find.

Sartre did not let the attack stop his campaigning: he and Beauvoir continued to speak at demonstrations, write articles, and give evidence in support of those accused of terrorist activity. According to Claude Lanzmann, they would get up in the middle of the night to make desperate phone calls seeking reprieve for Algerians due to be executed. In 1964, Sartre turned down the Nobel Prize in Literature, saying that he did not want to compromise his independence and that he deplored the committee's tendency to offer the prize only to Western writers or to anti-Communist émigrés, rather than to revolutionary writers from the developing world.

In effect, when offered the prize, Sartre had mentally consulted the 'least favoured', rather as Heidegger had sought the wisdom of the Todtnauberg 'peasant' next door when offered the Berlin job in 1934. In Heidegger's story, his neighbour silently shook his head. In Sartre's mind, the least favoured similarly gave him the authoritative headshake: *no*. But Heidegger's refusal was all about retreat and resignation from worldly complexities. Sartre's was a response to the demands of unjustly treated human beings – and it tied him more closely than ever to the lives of others.

Long before Sartre, others had written about the role of the 'gaze' in racism. In 1903, W. E. B. Du Bois had reflected in *The Souls of Black Folk* on black people's 'double-consciousness, this sense of always looking at one's self through the eyes of others, of measuring one's soul by the tape of a world that looks on in amused contempt and pity'. Later black American writers also explored the Hegelian battle for control of perspectives. In 1953, James Baldwin described visiting a Swiss hamlet where no one had seen a black person before, and where they gawped at him in amazement. He reflected that, in theory, he ought to feel as early white explorers did in African villages, accepting the stares as tribute to his marvellousness. Like the explorers, he was more widely travelled and sophisticated than the locals. Yet he could not feel that way; instead he felt humiliated and ill at ease.

As a black gay man, Baldwin had been through years of double marginalisation in the United States, where racial divisions were institutionalised and homosexuality was illegal. (The first state to decriminalise it was Illinois, in 1962.) He made his home for years in France – and there he joined his fellow novelist Richard Wright, who was now well settled in Paris.

After his discovery of and meetings with the existentialists in the 1940s, Wright had become more Francophile and more existentialist than ever. In 1952 he finished his existentialist novel *The Outsider*, the story of a troubled man named Cross Damon who flees to start a new life after he is confused with another man who dies in a subway crash. The white authorities are unable to tell one black man from another; Damon takes advantage of their error to flee a lawsuit for getting an underage girl pregnant. He then gets into worse difficulties, committing murders to conceal his identity. He also becomes involved with Communists, as Wright himself had. Having reinvented himself, Damon feels a great freedom, but also a dizzying responsibility to decide the meaning of his life. The story ends badly, as Damon is hunted down for his crimes and killed; in his dying moments, he says that he did it all to be free and to find out what he is worth. 'We're different from what we seem . . . Maybe worse, maybe better, but certainly different . . . We're strangers to ourselves.'

Wright applies the philosophies of Sartre and Camus to the black American experience. The result is an interesting book, yet it also had some weaknesses and could have benefited from editorial help to bring out its ideas more powerfully. Instead, Wright got an editor and an agent who preferred to relieve the book of ideas altogether, rather as happened with the English-language translation of Beauvoir's

The Second Sex. The publishing world expected something simple and raw from an author like Wright, not an intellectual reworking of the likes of *Nausea* and *The Outsider*. Reluctantly, he revised his work to trim down the philosophy. While he was doing this painful job, a new novel arrived in the post: *Invisible Man*, by Ralph Ellison. It too told of an alienated black man making a journey from invisibility to authenticity. *Invisible Man* had a lighter touch than Wright's novel, and contained no French philosophy. It sold better and won the National Book Award.

Wright wrote generously to Ellison, praising his work and inviting him to Paris – to which Ellison commented rudely, 'I am getting a little sick of American Negroes running over for a few weeks and coming back insisting that it's paradise.' He thought Wright had harmed himself by moving abroad: he had spoiled the freedom of his writing by seeking freedom in real life. Wright got this sort of remark a lot: his editor, Edward Aswell, thought he had won peace as an individual but lost literary momentum. Even James Baldwin wrote 'Richard was able, at last, to live in Paris exactly as he would have lived, had he been a white man, here, in America. This may seem desirable, but I wonder if it is.'

I wonder something different: why did Wright's Parisian existence attract such condemnation? Baldwin himself lived in France, and Ralph Ellison used a Prix de Rome fellowship to move to Italy for two years after the success of *Invisible Man* – although he did miss America, and returned to it. White writers moved abroad all the time; no one told them they would lose their ability to write if they did so. Wright believed his freedom was essential to him, to get perspective: 'I need to live free if I am to expand.' It seems a reasonable claim. The real objection, I suspect, was not that Richard Wright moved to France but that he wrote about French ideas.

True, Wright wrote no more novels after this. (Neither did Ellison.) He did write books of travel and reportage, notably *The Color Curtain*, about the great Bandung conference of developing countries in April 1955, and *White Man, Listen!*, in 1957, dedicated to Westernised individuals in Asia, Africa and the West Indies – those 'lonely outsiders who exist precariously on the clifflike margins of many cultures'. His sympathy for the existential misfit never declined; it merely migrated to non-fiction.

On 19 September 1956, Wright spoke at the First International Congress of Negro Writers and Artists at the Sorbonne. There, he was the only speaker to draw attention to the almost total absence of women in the debate. He pointed out how close the congress's key topics were to those Simone de Beauvoir had explored in *The Second Sex*: power struggles, the alienated gaze, self-consciousness, and the construction of oppressive myths. Feminist and anti-racist campaigners also shared the existentialist commitment to action: the 'can-do' belief that the status quo could be understood in intellectual terms, but should not be accepted in life.

*

The Second Sex had meanwhile been having ever more powerful effects on women around the world. The makers of a 1989 television programme and book called *Daughters of de Beauvoir* collected stories from women whose lives were changed by reading her work during the 1950s, 1960s and 1970s. These were women such as Angie Pegg, a housewife in a small Essex town who picked up *The Second Sex* at random in a bookshop, and read it until four in the morning. She plunged first into the chapter on how housework isolates women from the world, then went back to read the rest. Until that moment, Pegg had thought she was the only one to feel disconnected from life because of the way she spent her days; Beauvoir made her realise that she was not – and showed her *why* she felt that way. It was another of those life-changing book discoveries, like Sartre's or Levinas's when they read Husserl. By the morning, Pegg had decided on a change of direction in her life. She abandoned her mop and duster and went to university to study philosophy.

As well as *The Second Sex*, many women took inspiration from Beauvoir's four volumes of autobiography, which started in 1958 with *The Memoirs of a Dutiful Daughter* and continued until *All Said and Done*, in 1972. Margaret Walters, growing up in Australia, was thrilled by the confident tone and content of these books. They told the epic story of one woman seeking freedom – and finding it. Women living in traditional marriages were especially intrigued by Beauvoir's account of her open relationship with Sartre and other lovers. Kate Millett, who became an eminent feminist herself, remembered thinking: 'There she is in Paris, living this life. She's the brave, independent spirit, she's writ large what I would like to be, here in Podunk.' She also admired Beauvoir's and Sartre's joint political commitment. 'What both of them represented was the adventure of trying to lead an ethical life, trying to live according to a radical ethical politics, which isn't just the leftist bible – you have to invent situation ethics all the time. And that's an adventure.'

Simone de Beauvoir led women to make such drastic changes in their lives during these decades that, inevitably, some felt they had thrown away too much. One of the interviewees, Joyce Goodfellow, described abandoning her marriage and walking out on a steady but dull job. She ended up as a totally free woman – and a single mother, who struggled for years with poverty and solitude. 'What you read really does influence your life,' she said wryly.

What you read influences your life: the story of existentialism as it spread around the world in the fifties and sixties bears this out more than any other modern philosophy. By feeding feminism, gay rights, the breaking down of class barriers, and the anti-racist and anti-colonial struggles, it helped to change the basis of our existence today in fundamental ways. At the same time, many were inspired to head off in search of more personal forms of liberation. Sartre had called for a new existentialist psychotherapy, and this was established by the 1950s, with therapists seeking to treat patients as individuals struggling with questions of meaning and choice rather than as mere sets of symptoms. The Swiss psychiatrists Medard Boss and Ludwig Binswanger developed 'Daseinanalysis', based on Heidegger's ideas; later Sartre's ideas became more influential in the US and Britain. Rollo May and Irvin Yalom worked in an overtly existentialist framework, and similar ideas guided 'anti-psychiatrists' such as R. D. Laing as well as the 'logotherapist' Viktor Frankl, whose experiences in a Nazi concentration camp had led him to conclude that the human need for meaning was almost as vital as that for food or sleep.

These movements drew energy from a more general desire for meaning and self-realisation among the young, especially in America. After the war, many people had settled into as peaceful a life as they could manage, recognising the value of a steady job and a house in the suburbs with greenery and fresh air. Some veterans found it hard to adjust, but many wanted only to enjoy what was good in the world. Their children grew up with the benefits of this, but then, entering adolescence, wondered whether there was more to life than mowing the lawn and waving to the neighbours. They revolted against the narrow-minded political order of Cold War America, with its blend of comfort and paranoia. When they read J. D. Salinger's 1951 novel *The Catcher in the Rye*, they decided that, like its hero Holden Caulfield, the one thing they did not want to be was *phony*.

There followed a decade or so when literature, theatre and cinema were all abuzz with what we might call 'authenticity dramas'. They range from the Beat writers, with their riffs on restlessness or addiction, to films of generational disaffection such as *Rebel Without a Cause* (1955), or, in France, Jean-Luc Godard's *À bout de souffle* (1960). Existentialism was sometimes acknowledged, if only ironically. Marcel Carné's 1958 film *Les tricheurs* ('The Cheaters', translated as *Youthful Sinners*) was a fable in which two young Left Bank nihilists are so hip and polyamorous that they fail to notice they are falling in love and ought to have chosen a bourgeois marriage instead. In *Funny Face* (1957), Audrey Hepburn's character goes into a Parisian nightclub in search of a famous philosopher, becomes carried away by the music, and does a wild existentialist dance. But she too is safely married off – to an ageing Fred Astaire.

Other films and novels maintained a harder edge, refusing to settle for the old ways. A minor masterpiece of this period is Sloan Wilson's 1955 novel *The Man in the Grey Flannel Suit*. Its hero, a war veteran,

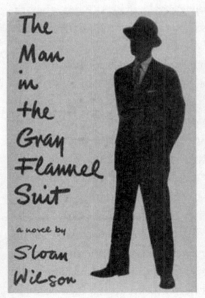

struggles to fit into his suburban environment and a corporate job in which he is supposed to work long hours on tasks that make no sense. In the end, he lights out for a more authentic way of life, rejecting security. The title became something of a catchphrase, especially after the book was made into a film starring Gregory Peck. As Sloan Wilson recalled, executives began wearing (identical) sports clothes to work instead of grey suits – just to prove that *they*, unlike all the other conformists, were free and authentic individuals.

George Orwell's *Nineteen Eighty-Four* of 1949 had made a key connection between conformist culture and technological control; other writers now picked up on this theme. David Karp's little-known 1953 novel *One* is set in a society that enforces complete psychological uniformity. The hero is arrested after the state detects signs of individualism in him so subtle that even he hadn't noticed them. He is gently but forcibly re-educated – a soothing, medicalised process rather than a confrontational one, and all the more terrifying for that.

Other dramas also linked the fear of technology with the fear that humans might be reduced to ant-like creatures of no power or worth. In an earlier Heidegger chapter, I mentioned one of my favourite films, *The Incredible Shrinking Man* of 1957 – which is a techno-horror as well as an existential drama. It begins when the hero is exposed to a cloud of radioactive fallout at sea. Back home, he begins to dwindle, losing size and dignity until he is the size of a dust speck. He cannot stop it happening, although he uses all the tools and devices at his disposal to survive, and ends as a tiny figure in the grass, looking out at the immensity of the universe. Other 1950s films similarly linked the twin Heideggerian terrors of lost authenticity and uncanny technology – including some, like *The Invasion of the Body Snatchers* (1956), that are more often read simply as expressions of Cold War anti-Communism. In movies such as *Godzilla* and *Them!* (both 1954), squid, leeches, scorpions, crabs, radioactive ants and other nightmare creatures pour out of a devastated, violated earth to take revenge. It is intriguing to read Heidegger's lecture 'The Question Concerning Technology' with its talk of the 'monstrous' and 'terrible' in man, the violation of the earth, and the stripping of resources, while musing on the fact that the published version came out in the same year as *Godzilla*.

Along with the fiction came a new kind of non-fiction from a new breed: the sociologist, psychologist or philosopher as existentialist rebel. David Riesman led the way with his study of modern alienation, *The Lonely Crowd*, in 1950. A flurry in 1956 included Irving Goffman's *The Presentation of Self in Everyday Life*, William Whyte's *Organization Man* and Paul Goodman's *Growing Up Absurd*. The most dramatic work of existentialist non-fiction was written a little later by a member of the old guard: Hannah Arendt. Her 1963 work *Eichmann in Jerusalem*, begun as a *New Yorker* article and developed into a book, concerned the Jerusalem trial of Adolf Eichmann, organiser of the Holocaust. Having attended the trial and observed his curiously blank responses, Arendt interpreted him as the ultimate Man in the Grey Suit. For her, he was a mindless bureaucrat so in thrall to the Heideggerian 'they' that he had lost all human individuality and responsibility, a phenomenon which she characterised as 'the banality of evil'. Her interpretation was controversial, as were other aspects of the book, but it fascinated an audience that was now in a moral panic, *not* about extreme beliefs, but about the very opposite: faceless, mindless conformism. Partly in response to Arendt's work, researchers such as Stanley Milgram and Philip Zimbardo perfected experiments exploring just how far people would go in obeying orders. The results were alarming: almost everyone, it seemed, was willing to inflict torture if a sufficiently authoritative figure commanded it.

Not all polemics against inauthenticity were so carefully thought out. The novelist Norman Mailer – the only major American author to identify explicitly as an existentialist – devoted his 1957 essay 'The White Negro' to a figure whom he lauded as:

> the American existentialist – the hipster, the man who knows that if our collective condition is to live with instant death by atomic war, relatively quick death by the State as *l'univers concentrationnaire*, or with a slow death by conformity with every creative and rebellious instinct stifled . . . if the fate of twentieth century man is to live with death from adolescence to premature senescence, why then the only life-giving answer is to accept the terms of death, to live with death as immediate danger, to divorce oneself from society, to exist without roots, to set out on that uncharted journey into the rebellious imperatives of the self. In short, whether the life is criminal or not, the decision is to encourage the psychopath in oneself.

Mailer apparently decided to put this into practice. Having announced a plan to run for mayor of New York City on an 'existentialist' ticket

in 1960, he had to give it up after drunkenly stabbing his wife Adele
at the party to launch the campaign. He ran for mayor again in 1969,
but not as an existentialist. His grasp of the philosophical theory never
seemed more than superficial. When the marginally better-informed
English writer Colin Wilson asked Mailer what existentialism meant
to him, he reportedly waved his hand and said, 'Oh, kinda playing
things by ear.' His biographer Mary V. Dearborn has suggested that
his knowledge of the subject derived, not from the as-yet-untranslated
Being and Nothingness as he liked to pretend, but from a Broadway
production of *No Exit* combined with a hasty reading of *Irrational Man*,
a popular guide published in 1958 by William Barrett – the philosophy
professor who had earlier written about Sartre for the *Partisan Review*.

William Barrett's book was good and very influential; it followed
another bestselling work edited by Walter Kaufmann in 1956,
Existentialism from Dostoevsky to Sartre. This collected excerpts from
Kierkegaard, Dostoevsky, Nietzsche, Jaspers, Heidegger, Sartre and
Camus, along with 'parables' by Franz Kafka and an editor's introduction which defined existentialism as a series of 'revolts against traditional
philosophy', by writers sharing a 'perfervid individualism'. Both
Kaufmann's book and Barrett's were bestsellers, and fed curiosity about
the original texts, now at last appearing in translation. Beauvoir's *The
Second Sex* came out in English in 1953. *The Myth of Sisyphus* appeared
in 1955, joining earlier translations of Camus' novels. In 1956 came the
big one: *Being and Nothingness*, translated by Hazel Barnes and showing
Sartre at his monumental best. Barnes followed it with books comparing
existentialist thought to other traditions, including Zen Buddhism –
another fashion of the era. She also presented a television series in
1961, *Self-Encounter: a study in existentialism*, explaining philosophical
ideas with help from mini-performances of excerpts from existentialist
plays. It was a great idea – although Barnes's memoirs relate that the
series was marked by a tragic incident. In one of the dramas, an actor
played a doctor who reflected on the theme of death. The day after
filming, the actor saw a kitten stuck up a telephone pole, and climbed
up to rescue it. He touched a live wire, and was killed.

*

Existentialism was all the rage in the United States by now, while on the other side of the Atlantic, Britain had been proceeding more cautiously. Professional philosophers in both countries had long since been put off by the logical positivist Rudolf Carnap, a German émigré based in the US, who had written a 1932 paper mocking such Heideggerian phrases as 'the nothing nothings' (*das Nichts nichtet*). His attack drew a line between 'Anglo-American' and 'Continental' philosophy that still exists today. Non-professional readers were not concerned about this, and found existentialism stimulating – but in England, they also had other cultural obstacles to overcome. As pointed out by Iris Murdoch, the country's first populariser of the topic, the English were used to ideas that emerged from a world in which 'people play cricket, cook cakes, make simple decisions, remember their childhood and go to the circus', whereas the existentialists came from a world in which people commit great sins, fall in love, and join the Communist Party. As the 1950s went on, however, English youngsters found that sin and politics could indeed be more fun than cakes.

Iris Murdoch encouraged them. She herself had been thrilled by her first encounter with Sartre, when she was working for the refugee organisation UNRRA in Brussels in 1945. She heard him lecture in the

city, had him sign her copy of *L'être et le néant*, and wrote to a friend, 'The excitement – I remember nothing like it since the days of discovering Keats & Shelley & Coleridge when I was very young.' Later she would mostly abandon existentialism, but for now she did much to publicise it. She gave talks, wrote the first book about Sartre in 1953, added existentialist flourishes to her own first novel, *Under the Net*, and even set her own example by indulging in free love with bisexual abandon.

Iris Murdoch's academic career in Oxford and her patrician tones (she always spoke of 'phlossofeh' and 'litch-cha') limited her appeal at a time when traditional English social structures were being under-mined from below by Angry Young Men with cheeky attitudes and regional accents. It was hard for pretentious Parisians to compete – until a very different English existentialist exploded onto the scene in 1956, that year of existentialist wonders.

His name was Colin Wilson; he came from Leicester in the Midlands, and had not been to university. His book was named *The Outsider*, in homage to Camus, and it took readers on a wild ride through alienated stranger or 'outsider' types in modern literature, from Dostoevsky, H. G. Wells, T. E. Lawrence and the outpourings of the disturbed dancer Vaslav Nijinsky to Sartre's Roquentin and

Camus' Meursault. The sources were eclectic, the tone bold, the ideas big, the challenge to traditional academia unmistakeable. The British book trade was taken by storm.

It helped that Wilson himself was a publicist's dream. Not yet twenty-five years old, he looked gorgeous, with abundant hair falling over one brow, a firm jaw, pouting lips and a chunky existentialist turtleneck. His background was gritty, although he had fled Leicester early on to mix with the poets and beatniks of 1950s London. He spent one penniless summer in 1954 sleeping on Hampstead Heath in a small tent with two sleeping bags, cycling down every day to the library of the British Museum to leave his backpack in the cloakroom and work on a novel in the round Reading Room. That winter, he rented a room in New Cross and passed a lonely Christmas Day reading Camus' *The Outsider.* Impressed by Meursault's life of 'smoking, making love and lounging in the sun', he decided to write a book about the 'outsiders' of modern life – all those young men brooding in the margins of philosophy and the arts, searching for meaning or else finding meaning in absurdity. When the museum reopened, Wilson ordered piles of books and wrote his manuscript in an inspired rush. He found a publisher in Victor Gollancz, who took Wilson to lunch to celebrate their deal and said (as Wilson recalled it), 'I think it possible that you may be a man of genius.' Wilson was delighted: 'It was a conclusion I had reached years before, but it was pleasant to hear it confirmed.'

The publishers were even more pleased to hear the Hampstead Heath story, and to promote the irresistible notion of a beautiful young vagrant sleeping under a tree by night and writing under the museum's venerable dome by day. When journalists ran away with the idea that Wilson had written *this* book while sleeping rough, no one corrected them, although in fact he was now settled in a flat in Notting Hill. The first print run of 5,000 copies sold out in a few hours. Critics raved. *Punch* ran a spoof which showed, 'with frequent quotations from books we have already read, as well as some that have not been written yet', how Lewis Carroll's Alice turns from an Outsider to an Insider by slipping into the looking-glass world. As she does so, 'Existentialism changes to Inexistentialism and, in the words of the Swami Oompah, the Many become More.'

Then came the backlash. A correspondent wrote to the *Times Literary Supplement* pointing out eighty-six major errors and 203 minor ones in Wilson's many quotations. Then the *Daily Mail* got hold of excerpts from his private journal, including the statement, 'I *am* the major

literary genius of our century.' The English public may take an occasional intellectual to its bosom, but it expects genteel self-deprecation
in return. What ensued was the unedifying sight of an outsider being
firmly reminded of his outsiderhood. Establishment critics booted
Wilson back into the wilderness. He fled to a quiet place in the country.

The Outsider is certainly an eccentric book, revealing hasty and
partial readings of its sources. Yet it has flair and conviction, and it
had a deep impact on many readers – especially on those who, like
Wilson himself, lacked the privileges of a canonical education but
were intelligent and newly confident, eager to explore cultural ideas
and to question the world. It was a book about outsiders *for* outsiders.
One such reader was my own father, a Midlands boy born in the same
year as Wilson and sharing all his curiosity and optimism. He tells me
that *The Outsider* was one of the few sources of light during a drab
period in post-war Britain.

Wilson encouraged his readers to take his writing personally. He
called his thinking 'the new existentialism', and gave it a life-affirming
and even an ecstatic spin. In an autobiography, he revealed that he
had once come close to suicide as a teenager, but decided not to go
through with it. At the moment of choosing to live, he had an overwhelming experience: 'I glimpsed the marvellous, immense richness
of reality, extending to distant horizons.' He tried to communicate
this sense of the sheer *worthwhileness* of life in his books, believing
that the old existentialists had made an error in assessing life too
glumly. In later books, this vision of human possibility led him to a
range of subjects united mainly by their total lack of intellectual
respectability: murder, the occult, sexuality. These did not help his
reputation, but they did bring him readers. He also wrote thrillers and
science fiction, although the most appealing of his novels remains his
autobiographical *Adrift in Soho* (1961), which tells of an innocent youth
falling in with London bohemians who take him to their parties, saying
things like, 'I can't be bothered to tell you everybody's name. Address
the men as daddy-o and the women as toots.'

Wilson lived a long and productive life, and never gave up writing
even when publishers joined reviewers in withdrawing their favour.

He became an angry ageing man, ranting against anyone who dared to doubt him – people such as Humphrey Carpenter, who visited him while researching a book on the Angry Young Men. To a more sympathetic interviewer, Brad Spurgeon, Wilson claimed that Carpenter had fallen asleep on the sofa while he was talking about phenomenology. This seems impossible; how could anyone fall asleep during a discussion of phenomenology?

The story of Colin Wilson is a cautionary one. If you subtract the youthful vanity and the flawed social skills, you are left with the potential plight of anyone whose passion for ideas leads them to write in too great a rush of excitement about what they love. With his chutzpah, his Kierkegaardian awkwardness, and his 'perfervid individualism', Colin Wilson perhaps captures the spirit of late-1950s existentialist rebellion better than anyone.

One of the few reviewers to show a certain sympathy to Wilson after the *Outsider* blow-up was Iris Murdoch, who considered him an ass yet wrote in the *Manchester Guardian* that she preferred Wilson's 'rashness' to the pedantic 'dryness' of more established philosophers. She too had a tendency to write in a generous spillage of words and ideas. In 1961, she wrote a kind of manifesto, 'Against Dryness', in which she urged writers to abandon the 'small myths, toys, crystals' of beautiful writing that had been fashionable, and to return to the real writer's task, which is to explore how we can be free and behave well in a complicated world, amid the rich 'density' of life.

Even when existentialists reached too far, wrote too much, revised too little, made grandiose claims, or otherwise disgraced themselves, it must be said that they remained in touch with the density of life, and that they asked the important questions. Give me that any day, and keep the tasteful miniatures for the mantelpiece.

By the 1960s, university teachers were aware of a change. The Heideggerian J. Glenn Gray, who taught philosophy at Colorado College, wrote an essay for *Harper's Magazine* in May 1965 called 'Salvation on the Campus: why existentialism is capturing the students'. He had noticed that recent students seemed more fascinated than ever by any philosopher who represented rebellion and authenticity, such as Socrates, who died for his intellectual freedom. They loved the existentialists, and especially Sartre's idea of bad faith. 'I'm sick of my own pretending,' exclaimed a student one day. The best of them were also the most likely to drop out; they would vanish in search of a more meaningful path. It worried Gray, especially when one bright young man refused all help in applying to graduate school and simply wandered off, to be last heard of drifting around the country living by casual labour.

Gray had no problem understanding the urge for freedom and for something 'real': it was he who had predicted, in the Italian village during the war, that old philosophies would offer little to the post-war world and that everything must be re-invented. Yet, when people acted on this idea almost a generation later, his impulse to celebrate was overwhelmed by concern for their future.

Gray was one of the first to note how a popularised brand of existentialism fed into the growing counter-culture. It added its terminology and transformative energy to the great social change that ensued in coming years, with the rise of student radicals, travelling hippies, the draft refusers of the Vietnam War, and all those who threw themselves into mind-expanding drugs and a free-for-all spirit of sexual experimentation. A vast and hopeful idealism pervaded these lifestyles: these people were not 'dry', Iris Murdoch might have said. Whether they slipped volumes of Camus, Beauvoir or Sartre into their pockets or not, they adopted the double Sartrean commitment: to personal freedom, and to political activism. When the student protesters occupying the Sorbonne in May 1968 cheered Sartre (alongside a few cheeky catcalls, admittedly), this was what they were acknowledging.

The student demonstrations, strikes, occupations, love-ins and be-ins of the 1960s constitute an extended historical moment to which one might point and say that existentialism had done its job. Liberation had arrived; existentialism could retire. Indeed, new philosophers were already on the scene, reacting against existentialism's personalised style of thought. New novelists turned against its literary aesthetic too: Alain Robbe-Grillet, in his 1963 manifesto *Pour*

un nouveau roman (*For a New Novel*), dismissed Sartre and Camus as
having too much of the 'human' in them. In 1966 Michel Foucault
predicted that 'man', being a relatively recent invention, might soon
be 'erased, like a face drawn in sand at the edge of the sea' – an
image that recalls Lévi-Strauss's call for studies that would 'dissolve
man'. Later, at the turn of the twenty-first century, the postmodernist
Jean Baudrillard dismissed Sartrean philosophy as a historical curiosity, like the classic 1950s films whose old-fashioned psychological
dramas and clear characterisation 'express marvellously well the –
already banal – post-Romantic death throes of subjectivity'. No one
needs this kind of 'existential garb' any more, Baudrillard wrote.
'Who cares about freedom, bad faith, and authenticity today?'

Ah, but there *were* people who cared about these things, and they
were found above all in the places where freedom and authenticity
were under threat. One such place was Czechoslovakia in and after
1968. While Parisian students were treating Sartre as a venerable relic,
young Czechs and Slovaks were reading him as though his works
had just peeled off the press. This was during the 'Prague Spring', a
period when Alexander Dubček's government tried to move towards
a more liberal and open version of Communism. Just as in Hungary
twelve years earlier, Soviet tanks and troops put a stop to the experiment. It was this act that led Sartre and Beauvoir definitively to reject
the Soviet model – only to praise people like Mao Tse-tung and Pol
Pot instead.

Even after the tanks rolled in, two of Sartre's most provocative
plays continued into production in Prague: *Dirty Hands* and *The Flies*,
both of which were anti-authoritarian. The Prague *Flies* was the latest
startling reinvention of Sartre's parable of freedom and activism.
Having begun as a story of wartime France in 1943, and found a new
audience in Germany in 1948, it now seemed all too relevant to the
citizens of post-invasion Czechoslovakia.

'Is he passé?' asked the Czech novelist Milan Kundera of Sartre in
1968. 'I have heard it said in France.' Here in Prague, he went on,
Sartre had far more to offer than writers such as Robbe-Grillet, with

his view of literature and thought as mere games. Another dissident, the playwright Václav Havel, observed that writers' words still had weight and value in Czechoslovakia: they were measured in people's lives, whereas in the West they had no substance, being too easy. Philip Roth also observed, after a later visit to Prague, that in the West 'everything goes and nothing matters', while in Czechoslovakia 'nothing goes and everything matters'. Sartrean existentialism was precisely a philosophy of *mattering*: he called on his readers to take decisions as though the whole future of humanity depended upon what they did.

It was not just Sartrean existentialism that had this moral weight; for some Czechs and Slovaks it was phenomenology. The Czech phenomenological tradition went back to the country's first modern president, Tomáš Masaryk, student of Brentano and protector of his archive. Husserl himself came from Moravia, and several of his colleagues had connections with the Czech lands. By the 1960s and 1970s, the high profile of phenomenology in Czechoslovakia was owed mostly to one of those Husserlians: Jan Patočka.

Like many others, Patočka had been swept away by his first discovery of Husserl's philosophy after hearing the great man speak in Paris in 1929. He arranged to transfer to Freiburg in 1933 – just as Sartre was going to Berlin – and became one of Husserl's circle of favourites, as well as studying with Heidegger. Husserl even gave Patočka a desktop lectern that Masaryk had originally given to him, which, as Patočka wrote, made him feel anointed as heir to a tradition. He returned to Prague and did his best to make the university a centre of phenomenological research.

When the Communist Party took over in 1948, Patočka was increasingly harassed by the authorities because his philosophy ran counter to Marxist theory. In 1972, he was forced out of active teaching at the university, and began holding private seminars at his home instead, working through texts in minute detail. His students got used to spending a whole evening on a few lines of *Being and Time*. He also gave lessons in Prague theatres to actors and writers – Václav Havel among them. Havel recalled how Patočka would bring texts alive for the group and encourage them to seek 'the meaning of things' and illumination 'of one's self, of one's situation in the world'. He spoke of his own idea of the 'solidarity of the shaken', a bond which united everyone whose life had been jolted out of unthinking 'everydayness' by some historical upheaval. Such a bond could become a basis for rebellious action. Patočka's phenomenology was dangerously political.

In fact, one could say that Patočka was only revealing the subversive tendency that had always lurked in phenomenology. Husserl's call to return to the 'things themselves' was a call to ignore ideologies such as Marxism. It was a summons to critical self-reliance, with all dogmas set aside in the *epoché*. One can even trace this anti-dogmatic spirit back to the young Franz Brentano, who refused to accept the infallibility of the Pope and was punished by losing his teaching post. Patočka refused to accept the infallibility of the Communist Party for very similar reasons. Brentano had passed the spirit of sceptical refusal to Husserl; Husserl had passed it to Patočka, and Patočka now passed it to Havel and many others.

More directly, Patočka became an activist himself. In 1976, aged nearly seventy and in fragile health, he joined Havel and others in signing the famous declaration of political opposition known as Charter 77. It could almost have been called the Philosophers' Charter: of its main representatives during the next thirteen years, almost a third (twelve out of thirty-eight) were either philosophers or former students of philosophy, many of them having studied with Patočka.

The Czech state immediately set about persecuting the charter's signatories. They brought Patočka in for questioning in Ruzyně Prison on a regular basis between January and March 1977. His interrogations were more gruelling than violent, but they would last all day, deliberately exhausting him and making no concessions to his frailties. Havel saw him once in the prisoners' waiting room where they were left to sit before interrogations – a ritual designed to heighten anxiety. Seeming quite unconcerned, Patočka talked to him about philosophy.

That same day, after interrogation, Havel was incarcerated. Patočka was freed, only to be called back again and again through subsequent months. Towards the end of this period, he wrote a 'Political Testament' in which he said, 'What is needed is for people to behave at all times with dignity, not to allow themselves to be frightened and intimidated, and to speak the truth.' It sounds so simple: again, that call to speak of things as they are, unadorned.

One day early in March, Patočka was subjected to a particularly long interrogation, lasting eleven hours. He had recently angered the regime again by contacting the visiting Dutch foreign minister, Max van der Stoel, to seek his support for Charter 77. The day after this, Patočka collapsed. He was taken to hospital, where he died on 13 March 1977.

The funeral, at the Břevnov cemetery in Prague, was attended by hundreds of people. The authorities did not prevent its taking place, but they disrupted the event in every way possible. Ivan Klíma, who was present, recalled how they sent motorcyclists to rev their engines around a nearby track and helicopters to hover overhead, so the speeches at the graveside could not be heard. Police officers in attendance turned their backs to the grave. Others ostentatiously photographed faces in the crowd.

The funeral was followed by another of those swashbuckling archive-smuggling operations that feature in the history of phenomenology. A group of former Patočka students and colleagues, led by Klaus Nellen and Ivan Chvatík together with the Polish philosopher Krzysztof Michalski, arranged for Western scholars and diplomats to sneak copies of his papers out of the country in relays, taking some each time they travelled to and from Prague. Bit by bit, the duplicate archive was reassembled in Vienna's Institute for the Human Sciences, while the originals were hidden in Prague. Patočka's memory is still preserved today by institutes in both cities. One scholar associated with the Viennese institution, Paul Ricœur, summed up his legacy thus: 'The relentless persecution of this man proves that, in the event of a people's extreme abjection, philosophical pleading for subjectivity is becoming the citizen's only recourse against the tyrant.'

This idea was also at the heart of a famous 1978 essay by Havel, 'The Power of the Powerless', dedicated to Patočka's memory. In an oppressive state, Havel wrote, people become co-opted in subtle ways. He gives an example: a greengrocer receives from his company's head office a sign bearing the standard message, 'Workers of the world, unite!' He is supposed to put it in his window, and he does so, although he cares not a bean for its message – for he knows that all kinds of inconveniences may ensue if he does not. A customer who sees the notice doesn't consciously think about it either; she has the same notice in her own office anyway. But does this mean that the sign is meaningless and harmless? No, says Havel. Each sign contributes to a world in which independence of thought and personal responsibility are quietly eaten away. The signs, in effect, emanate from the Heideggerian 'they', and they also help to keep it going. All over the country, even in the offices of the most senior figures, people simultaneously suffer from the system and perpetuate it, while telling themselves that none of it matters. It is a giant structure of bad faith and banality going all the way to the top. Everyone is 'involved and enslaved'.

For Havel, this is where the dissident must step in, to break the

pattern. The rebel demands a return to the 'here and now', Havel says
– to what Husserl would have called the things themselves. He
conducts an *epoché*, in which the cant is set aside and each person sees
what is in front of his or her eyes. Eventually, the result will be an
'existential revolution': people's relationship to the 'human order' is
overhauled and they can return to the authentic experience of things.

A revolution did come in 1989; it brought Havel to power as the
country's first post-Communist president. He would not please
everyone in this role, and the revolution was not as phenomenological
or existential as he might have hoped. At least, few thought of it that
way any longer. But there was certainly an overhaul. The phenomenological imperative to go straight to experienced reality may have had
a more lasting impact here than Sartre's more overt radicalism. Perhaps
phenomenology, even more than existentialism, is the truly radical
school of thought. Brentano, the original phenomenological rebel,
would be entitled to feel proud of the long line of influence he had.

13

Having Once Tasted Phenomenology

In which there are departures.

Forwards, always forwards! was the existentialist's cry, but Heidegger had long since pointed out that no one goes forwards forever. In *Being and Time*, he depicted Dasein as finding authenticity in 'Being-towards-death', that is, in affirming mortality and limitation. He also set out to show that Being itself is not to be found on some eternal, change-less plane: it emerges through Time and through history. Thus, both on the cosmic level and in the lives of each one of us, all things are temporal and finite.

This idea of Being or human existence as having an inbuilt expiry date never sat so well with Sartre. He accepted it in principle, but everything in his personality revolted against being hemmed in by anything at all, least of all by death. As he wrote in *Being and Nothingness*, death is an outrage that comes to me from outside and wipes out my projects. Death cannot be prepared for, or made my own; it's not something to be resolute about, nor something to be incorporated and tamed. It is not one of my possibilities but 'the possibility that there are for me no longer any possibilities'. Beauvoir wrote a novel pointing out that immortality would be unbearable (*All Men Are Mortal*), but she too saw death as an alien intruder. In *A Very Easy Death*, her 1964 account of her mother's last illness, she showed how death came to her mother 'from elsewhere, strange and inhuman'. For Beauvoir, one cannot have a relationship with death, only with life.

The British philosopher Richard Wollheim put all this another way. Death, he wrote, is the great enemy not merely because it deprives us of all the future things we might do, and all the pleasures we might experience. It takes away the ability to experience anything *at all*, ever. It puts an end to our being a Heideggerian clearing for things to emerge into. Thus, as Wollheim says, 'It deprives us of phenomenology, and, having once tasted phenomenology, we develop a longing for it which we cannot give up.' Having had experience of the world, having had intentionality, we want to continue it forever, because that experience of the world is *what we are*.

Unfortunately, this is the deal we get. We can taste phenomenology only because, one day, it will be taken from us. We clear our space, then the forest reclaims it again. The only consolation is to have had the beauty of seeing light through the leaves at all: to have had something, rather than nothing.

Some of the most likeable people to have made their appearance in the sparkling, tinkling, bustling and quarrelsome existentialist café of our story were also the first to leave it.

Boris Vian was only thirty-nine when he died, on 23 June 1959, of a heart attack, which came while he was in a cinema attending a preview of a film based on his novel *I Spit on Your Graves*. He disliked the film and was just voicing a protest from his seat when he collapsed. He died on the way to the hospital.

Just over six months later, on 4 January 1960, Albert Camus was killed in a car crash with his publisher's nephew Michel Gallimard, who was driving. The car smashed into one tree and then another, twisting itself round and scattering most of its metal to one side of the tree, its engine to the other, and Camus through a rear window. In the mud a short distance away, a briefcase was found, inside which were Camus' journal and the unfinished manuscript of *The First Man*, his autobiographical novel about his childhood in Algeria.

Beauvoir heard the news about Camus from Claude Lanzmann, who phoned her at Sartre's apartment. She put down the phone, shaking, and told herself not to be upset. Come now, she said to herself: you are not even close to Camus any more. Then she looked out of Sartre's window, watching the sun set over the Saint-Germain-des-Prés church, unable either to weep properly or to feel better. What she mourned, she decided, was not the forty-six-year-old Camus who had just died, but the young freedom fighter of the war years – the friend they had lost long ago. Sartre felt this way too: for both of them, the true Camus was that of the Resistance and *The Outsider*, not the later one. They never forgave him for his political views, but Sartre wrote a generous obituary in *France-Observateur*. He summed Camus up as an heir to the great tradition of French *moralistes*, an untranslateable word which implies both a moralist in the English sense and a curious observer of human behaviour and character. He was, said Sartre, a man whose 'stubborn humanism, narrow and pure, austere and sensual, waged a dubious battle against events of these times'. When Beauvoir was interviewed by Studs Terkel for American radio in the same year, she concluded that Camus was an ethical thinker rather than a political one – but she admitted that young people could learn from both approaches.

Another untimely death occurred that year. In Paris, Richard Wright suffered a fatal heart attack on 28 November 1960, aged fifty-two. Some of his friends, as well as his daughter, wondered whether he had been assassinated by the CIA: a mysterious woman had been seen leaving his room not long before his final collapse. The US government had indeed continued to harass and obstruct him for years. But Wright had been in poor health ever since a bout of amoebic dysentery in 1957, which left him with liver problems. These were not helped by his taking bismuth salts, which were supposed to be an alternative cure but instead gave him metal poisoning.

Although Wright had written little fiction in recent years, he had continued to write essays and polemics, and had also developed a love of Japanese haiku. Among his late works is a sequence of beautiful small poems about peach trees, snails, spring rain, storm clouds, snow, chickens that look smaller after being soaked by rain – and a tiny green cocklebur, caught in the curls of a black boy's hair.

A year later, on 3 May 1961, the fifty-three-year old Merleau-Ponty, looking as slim and fit as ever, died of a heart attack. He had been with friends in his family apartment on the boulevard Saint-Michel.

They chatted for a while, then Merleau-Ponty left them talking in the living room while he went into his study to finish some notes for a lecture on Descartes the next day. He never came back.

Again, Sartre found himself writing an obituary of a friend with whom he had fallen out, this time in a special issue of *Les Temps modernes*. Again, his obituary was thoughtful and generous, and it became the source of much of what we know about their friendship and disagreements. He mentioned that he and Merleau-Ponty had bumped into each other a short time earlier, when Sartre was giving a talk at the École normale supérieure. Sartre was touched that Merleau-Ponty had come to hear him, and afterwards hoped that they would keep in contact. But Sartre's own reactions were slowed (he was groggy with a case of flu, he said) and Merleau-Ponty was taken aback; 'he hadn't said a word about feeling disappointed, but for a split second, it crossed my mind that his face had saddened'. Sartre felt optimistic all the same: '"Everything is just as it was," I told myself. "Everything will begin anew."' A few days later, he heard that Merleau-Ponty was dead.

Merleau-Ponty's body lies in his family grave in Père-Lachaise cemetery, together with his mother and his wife Suzanne, who died in 2010. It is on the other side of Paris from Montparnasse, where Sartre's and Beauvoir's grave is. Merleau-Ponty can be found in one of the cemetery's quietest and least frequented corners, surrounded by trees.

One philosopher who had expected to die of a heart attack at a young age, but did not, was Karl Jaspers. On marrying, he had warned Gertrud that they could not expect long together, perhaps a year or so. In fact, he lived to eighty-six, and died on 26 February 1969 – Gertrud's birthday. Heidegger sent her a telegram afterwards with the simple words: 'In remembrance of earlier years, in honor and sympathy.' She wrote back on the same day, 'Thinking likewise of the earlier years, I thank you.' She lived until 1974.

Perhaps the best way to mark Karl Jaspers' passing is to revisit a radio talk he gave about his life, as part of a series in 1966–7. He spoke of his childhood by the North Sea, and especially about holidays with his parents in the Friesian islands. On the island of Norderney one evening, his father took his hand as they walked to the water's edge. 'The tide was out, our path across the fresh, clean sand was amazing, unforgettable for me, always further, always further, the water was so low, and we came to the water, there lay the jellyfish, the starfish – I was bewitched,' said Jaspers. From then on, the sea always made him think of the scope of life itself, with nothing firm or whole, and everything in perpetual motion. 'All that is solid, all that is gloriously ordered, having a home, being sheltered: absolutely necessary! But the fact that there is this other, the infinity of the ocean – that liberates us.' This, Jaspers went on, was what philosophy meant to him. It meant going beyond what was solid and motionless, towards that larger seascape where everything was in motion, with 'no ground anywhere'. It was why philosophy had always, for him, meant a 'different thinking'.

Four years after the death of Jaspers came that of another philosopher who had written about human life as a constant journey beyond the familiar: Gabriel Marcel, who died on 8 October 1973. For him, as for Jaspers, human beings were essentially vagabonds. We can never own anything, and we never truly settle anywhere, even if we stay in one place all our lives. As the title of one of his essay collections has it, we are always *Homo viator* – Man the Traveller.

Hannah Arendt died of a heart attack on 4 December 1975, aged sixty-nine, leaving a manuscript of Sartrean dimensions which her friend Mary McCarthy edited for posthumous publication as *The Life of the Mind*. Arendt never quite resolved the puzzle of Heidegger. Sometimes she condemned her former lover and tutor; at other times she worked to rehabilitate his reputation or to help people understand him. She met him a few times when she visited Europe, and tried (but failed) to help him and Elfride sell the manuscript of *Being and Time* in America to raise cash. Elements of his work always remained central to her own philosophy.

In 1969, she wrote an essay which was published two years later in the *New York Review of Books* as 'Martin Heidegger at Eighty'. There, she reminded a new generation of readers of the excitement his call to thinking had generated, back in the 'foggy hole' of Marburg in the 1920s. Yet she also asked how he could have failed to think appropriately himself in 1933 and thereafter. She had no answer to her own question. Just as Jaspers had once let Heidegger off lightly by calling him a 'dreaming boy', so Arendt now ended her assessment with an over-generous image: that of the Greek philosopher Thales, an unworldly genius, who fell into a well because he was too busy looking at the stars to see the danger in front of him.

Heidegger himself, although seventeen years older than Arendt, outlived her by five months, before dying peacefully in his sleep on 26 May 1976, aged eighty-six.

For over forty years, he had nursed his belief that the world had treated him badly. He had continued to fail to respond to his followers' hopes that he would one day condemn Nazism in unambiguous terms. He acted as though he was unaware of what people needed to hear, yet his friend Heinrich Wiegand Petzet reported that Heidegger knew very well what was expected: it just made him feel more misunderstood.

He did not let his resentments put him off his work, which continued to lead him up and down the mountain pathways of his thoughts in his late years. He spent as much time as possible at Todtnauberg, receiving visits from pilgrims and sometimes from more critical visitors. One such encounter was with the Jewish poet and concentration-camp survivor Paul Celan, who gave a reading in Freiburg in July 1967 while on temporary release from a psychiatric clinic. The venue was the same auditorium where Heidegger had given his Nazi rectorial address.

Heidegger, who admired Celan's work, tried to make him feel welcome in Freiburg. He even asked a book-dealer friend to go around all the bookshops in the city making sure they put Celan titles in their windows so the poet would see them as he walked through town. This is a touching story, especially as it is the single documented example I have come across of Heidegger actually doing something nice. He attended the reading, and the next day took Celan up to the hut. The poet signed the guest book, and wrote a wary, enigmatic poem about the visit, called simply 'Todtnauberg'.

Heidegger liked receiving travellers, but had never been a *Homo viator* himself. He was disdainful about mass tourism, which he considered symptomatic of the modern 'desert-like' way of being, with its demand for novelty. In later life, however, he became fond of taking holidays in Provence. He agonised over the question of whether he should visit Greece – an obvious destination, given his long obsession with its temples, its rocky outcrops, and its Heraclitus and Parmenides and Sophocles. But that was why he was nervous: too much was at stake. In 1955, he arranged to go with his friend Erhard Kästner. Train and boat tickets were booked, but at the last minute Heidegger cancelled. Five years later the two men planned another trip, and again Heidegger pulled out. He wrote to warn Kästner that this was probably how things would go on. 'I will be allowed to think certain things about Greece without seeing the country . . . The necessary concentration is best found at home.'

In the end, he did go. He took an Aegean cruise in 1962, with Elfride and a friend called Ludwig Helmken – a lawyer and politician of the centre right who had a past at least as embarrassing as Heidegger's, since he'd joined the Nazi Party in 1937. Their cruise sailed from Venice down the Adriatic, and then took in Olympia, Mycenae, Heraklion, Rhodes, Delos, Athens and Delphi, before returning to Italy.

At first, Heidegger's fears were confirmed: nothing in Greece satisfied him. Olympia had turned into a mass of 'hotels for the American tourists', he wrote in his notebook. Its landscape failed to 'set free the Greek element of the land, of its sea and its sky'. Crete and Rhodes were little better. Rather than traipse around in a herd of holiday makers, he became more inclined to stay on the boat reading Heraclitus. He hated his first glimpse of smoggy Athens, although he enjoyed being driven by a friend up to the Acropolis in the early morning before the crowds arrived with their cameras.

Later, after lunch and a folk-dance performance at the hotel, they went to the Temple of Poseidon on Cape Sounion – and at last Heidegger found the Greece he was looking for. Gleaming white ruins stood firm on the headland; the bare rock of the cape lifted the temple towards the sky. Heidegger noted how 'this single gesture of the land suggests the invisible nearness of the divine', then observed that, even though the Greeks were great navigators, they 'knew how to inhabit and demarcate the world against the barbarous'. Even now, surrounded by sea, Heidegger's thoughts naturally turned to imagery of enclosing, bounding and holding in. He never thought of Greece in terms of trade and openness, as Husserl had done. He also continued to be annoyed by the encroachments of the modern world, with the other tourists' infernal clicking cameras.

Reading Heidegger's account of the cruise, we get a glimpse of how he responded when the world failed to fit his preconceptions. He sounds resentful, and selective in what he is prepared to see. When Greece surprises him, he writes himself further into his private vision of things; when it fits that vision, he cautiously grants approval. He was right to have been nervous of making the trip: it did not bring out the best in him.

There was one other late moment of surprise and beauty. As the ship sailed out of the bay of Dubrovnik on its way back to Italy, a pod of dolphins swam up at sunset to play around the ship. Heidegger was enchanted. He recalled a cup he had seen in Munich's museum of antiquities, attributed to Exekias and dating from around 530 BC, on the sides of which Dionysus was depicted sailing on a vessel entwined with grapevines as dolphins cavorted in the sea. Heidegger rushed for his notebook – but as he wrote about the image, the usual language of enclosure took over. As the cup 'rests within the boundaries' of its creation, he concluded, 'so too the birthplace of Occident and modern age, secure in its own island-like essence, remains in the recollective thinking of the sojourn'. Even the dolphins had to be gathered into a homeland.

One never finds Jaspers' open sea in Heidegger's writing; one does not encounter Marcel's endlessly moving traveller, or his 'stranger met by chance'. When an interviewer from the magazine *Der Spiegel* asked

Heidegger in 1966 what he thought of the idea that humans might one day travel to other planets, leaving Earth behind – because 'where is it written that man's place is here?' – Heidegger was appalled. He replied: 'According to our human experience and history, at least as far as I see it, I know that everything essential and everything great originated from the fact that man had a home and was rooted in a tradition.'

For Heidegger, all philosophising is about homecoming, and the greatest journey home is the journey to death. In a conversation with the theology professor Bernhard Welte towards the end of his life, he mentioned his wish to be buried in the Messkirch church cemetery, despite the fact that he had long since left the faith. He and Welte both said that death meant above all a return to the soil of home.

Heidegger had his wish. He now lies in the Catholic graveyard on the outskirts of Messkirch. His grave is secular, bearing a small star in place of a cross, and he shares it with Elfride, who died in 1992. Two other Heidegger family graves lie to left and right of them, with crosses. The effect of the three monuments together, with Martin's and Elfride's larger than the others, is oddly reminiscent of a Calvary.

On the day I visited, daffodils had been freshly planted on all three graves, with handfuls of small pebbles on Martin's and Elfride's headstone. Sticking up perkily from the soil between their stone and that of Martin's parents was a little stone cherub – a dreaming boy, cross-legged, with his eyes closed.

One of the graves beside Martin Heidegger's belongs to his younger brother, Fritz, who had protected Martin's manuscripts during the war and, along with Elfride, helped him with secretarial work and other support throughout life.

Fritz had done what Heidegger had only philosophised about: he stayed close to home, living in Messkirch and working at the same bank all his life. He also remained within the family religion. Locals knew him as a lively and humorous man who, despite a stutter, was a regular star of Messkirch's annual *Fastnacht* week or 'Week of

Fools' – a festival just before Lent marked by speeches filled with hilarious word-play in the local dialect.

Some of this wit comes across in Fritz's remarks to his brother. He would joke about 'Da-da-dasein', poking fun at Martin's terminology as well as at his own speech impediment. Never claiming to understand philosophy, he used to say that Martin's work would only make sense to the people of the twenty-first century, when 'the Americans have long set up a huge supermarket on the moon'. Still, he diligently typed his brother's writings, a great help for a philosopher who was uncomfortable with typewriters. (Heidegger felt that typing spoiled writing: 'It withdraws from man the essential rank of the hand.') Along the way, Fritz would gently suggest amendments. Why not write in shorter sentences? Should not each sentence convey one single clear idea? No response from his brother is recorded.

Fritz Heidegger died on 26 June 1980, his life relatively unsung until recent years, when he caught biographers' interest as a kind of anti-Martin – a case study in *not* being the twentieth century's most brilliant and most hated philosopher.

During the 1970s, meanwhile, Sartre's faculties had gone into a long, frustrating decline, affecting his ability to work. His papers include a brief undated sheet (possibly written shortly after the moon landings of July 1969, since it begins with the two words, 'The moon') in which he records the sad fact that he has written nothing for five months. He lists the projects he still wants to finish: the Flaubert book, a biographical essay on Tintoretto, the *Critique of Dialectical Reason*. But he does not feel like writing, and is afraid that he never will again. For Sartre, not writing was like not living. He wrote: 'For years, I haven't finished anything. I don't know why. Yes I do: the Corydrane.'

Long-term addictions to Corydrane and alcohol did cause difficulties, but his writing also stalled because, after years of getting by with monocular vision, he was now going blind in the good eye. He could still watch television, seeing moving shadows and listening to the dialogue. In 1976, he saw a long programme about that very interesting subject, Jean-Paul Sartre. Based on interviews filmed a few years later, *Sartre par lui-même* (*Sartre By Himself*) was marked by an extra interview with Michel Contat to coincide with its broadcast. Sartre told Contat that not being able to write had taken away his reason for existence, but that he refused to be sad about it.

Other health problems accumulated; he had strokes, memory lapses, problems with his teeth. There were moments when he seemed to drift away entirely. During one fugue, Beauvoir asked him what he was thinking about. He replied, 'Nothing. I'm not here.' He had always described consciousness as a nothingness, but in fact his head had always been crowded with words and ideas. He had pushed work *out* of himself every day, as though he were full and needed unloading. Now, although still replete with things to say, he was running out of the energy with which to say them. Those who cared for him began to secretly hope that he would have a quick, easy death – a Camus-style death, as his friend Olivier Todd put it. The slow disintegration was too hard to watch: 'Sartre, *petit père*, don't do this to us!' wrote Todd. Still Sartre battled on, a stubborn small figure at the levers of his vast public persona.

In his last months, partners, lovers and disciples tended him in relays: Simone de Beauvoir, his young companion Arlette Elkaïm-Sartre (whom he had adopted as a daughter, to give her legal rights), and his long-time lover Michelle Vian. He also had a new young secretary and assistant, Benny Lévy, who helped with his writing and may have exerted an undue influence on him – at least, that was what some believed. Lévy was a man of strong opinions, a former Maoist now turned anti-Communist, and passionate about his Jewish identity. He was not the sort to efface himself as an invisible amanuensis.

A series of conversations between him and Sartre appeared in *Le nouvel observateur* in the last weeks of Sartre's life and were later published separately as *L'espoir maintenant* (*Hope Now*). They show a Sartre who is unusually apologetic – about his earlier pro-Soviet and Maoist views, about his 1946 book on anti-Semitism (which Lévy considered flawed), and about his earlier fascination with violence. This new Sartre looks more benignly on religious faith, although he is still not a believer. He admits to being a daydreamer in matters of politics. He sounds chastened and defeated. Some of those close to Sartre thought *Hope Now* showed no genuine change of thinking, but only the weakness of a man whose illness and disabilities were making him vulnerable. In the interview, perhaps anticipating such objections, Lévy asks whether Sartre's ideas have been affected by their relationship. Sartre doesn't deny it, but says that now he has to work in partnership or not at all. At first he considered it a lesser evil, compared to not working, but now he sees it as something positive, 'a thought created by two people'.

He was used to writing in a close partnership with Simone de Beauvoir, but now Beauvoir was foremost among those who thought Lévy was influencing Sartre too much. Raymond Aron also remarked that the ideas in *Hope Now* were so reasonable that even he could have agreed with them – a sure sign, he implied, that they were not the real Sartre.

This last stage in Sartre's life remains an enigma. Praising peaceful relationships and non-violence, he seems to be saying sensible and appealing things – yet something is missing in the new vanilla Sartre. *Hope Now* can be read as a reminder of what had been so exciting (as well as shocking) in his earlier work – mistakes, crashing insensitivity, belligerence, graphomania and all. But perhaps I am doing what he and Beauvoir tended to do with Camus: mourning an old version while dismissing an updated version as a mistake. Perhaps it was the knowledge of his own decline that was making him look more mildly on the world.

In any case, if anything demonstrates the truth of Simone de Beauvoir's vision of human life as an unresolvable, ambiguous drama of freedom and contingency, it is the last years of Sartre. As one traces his decline, one sees a blazing, garrulous figure gradually turn into his own ghost, stripped of vision and to some extent of hearing, of his pipe, his writing, his engagement with the world – and finally, as Wollheim would say, of his phenomenology. All this was out of his control. Yet he never let himself become solidified as a statue: he kept changing his thoughts until the very last moment.

During the night of 19 March 1980, when he was – unusually – left alone for a few hours, he collapsed, struggling for breath. He was taken to hospital, where he lived on for almost another month. Even in this final illness, he was chased by journalists who tried to get into his room by posing as nurses, and by photographers who picked him out through the window with zoom lenses from the roof opposite. On the evening of 14 April, suffering kidney failure and gangrene, he slipped into a coma. The next day he died.

Beauvoir was devastated, but her intellectual honesty forbade changing her lifelong conviction that death was the end: an intrusion and an abomination, with no part in life, and no promise of anything beyond. She wrote: 'His death does separate us. My death will not bring us together again. That is how things are. It is in itself splendid that we were able to live our lives in harmony for so long.'

On leaving the École normale supérieure back in 1929, Sartre and Aron had made a deal that whoever outlived the other would write his obituary for the school alumni magazine. Aron survived Sartre, but did not write the obituary. He did write about Sartre in L'express, explaining why he had elected not to stick to their deal: too much time had passed, and he considered that the commitment no longer stood. He also commented in an interview that, although Sartre had written 'touching articles' about Camus and Merleau-Ponty on their deaths, he doubted that he would have done the same for himself, had their deaths occurred that way round. It's not clear why he believed this. True, their relationship had declined more sharply than the others, mainly because their politics were more markedly divergent. But Sartre was unfailingly generous with his words, and despite everything, I suspect he would have found something appreciative to say about Aron in an obituary.

In fact, Aron very nearly had predeceased Sartre, suffering a heart attack in 1977. He survived, but never again felt fully well. The second attack came on 17 October 1983, just as he was leaving court after giving evidence for his friend Bertrand de Jouvenel, whom a journalist had accused of harbouring Nazi sympathies during the war. Aron took the stand to argue not only that the accusation was false, but

that it was ahistorical, failing to take into account the moral complexities of French life under Occupation. He left the building, collapsed,
and died instantly.

Simone de Beauvoir lived six years after Sartre's death, almost to the
hour.

During those years, she continued to head the editorial board of
Les Temps modernes, which met at her home. She read manuscripts,
wrote letters and helped younger writers, including many feminists.
One of these, the American Kate Millett, visited her annually in the
Paris apartment, which she described as filled with books, photographs
of friends ('Sartre, Genet, Camus and everybody'), and 'these funny
sort of fifties-type sofas with velvet cushions that were probably all
the rage the year she got it and decorated it'. Beauvoir, commented
Millett, was distinguished by an absolute integrity, and by 'such an
unlikely thing, a moral authority'.

Just as Sartre had adopted Arlette Elkaïm-Sartre, so Beauvoir
adopted her companion and heir, Sylvie Le Bon Beauvoir, who looked
after her together with Claude Lanzmann and other friends. Beauvoir
was afflicted by cirrhosis of the liver, not unconnected with years of
heavy drinking. Complications of this disease led to her being hospi-
talised on 20 March 1986; after several weeks recovering from surgery
and struggling with congestion of the lungs, she slipped into a coma
and died on 14 April 1986.

She was buried next to Sartre in Montparnasse cemetery. As had
happened with him, her body was put in a smaller coffin inside a large
one so that it could be taken for cremation later. Thousands of people
watched the hearse process through the streets, piled high with flowers
as Sartre's had been. It was a less grand occasion than Sartre's, but
the throng of mourners was still large enough to create an obstruc-
tion at the cemetery entrance. Guards shut the gates, fearing that too
many people would crowd in; some climbed over the barriers and
wall. Inside, at the graveside, Lanzmann read a passage from the last
pages of her third volume of autobiography, *Force of Circumstance*,
reflecting on death, life and loss. She had written:

I think with sadness of all the books I've read, all the places I've seen, all the knowledge I've amassed and that will be no more. All the music, all the paintings, all the culture, so many places: and suddenly nothing. They made no honey, those things, they can provide no one with any nourishment. At the most, if my books are still read, the reader will think: There wasn't much she didn't see! But that unique sum of things, the experience that I lived, with all its order and its randomness – the Opera of Peking, the arena of Huelva, the *candomblé* in Bahía, the dunes of El-Oued, Wabansia Avenue, the dawns in Provence, Tiryns, Castro talking to five hundred thousand Cubans, a sulphur sky over a sea of clouds, the purple holly, the white nights of Leningrad, the bells of the Liberation, an orange moon over the Piraeus, a red sun rising over the desert, Torcello, Rome, all the things I've talked about, others I have left unspoken – there is no place where it will all live again.

At the time she wrote this summing-up, before signing off the book in March 1963, she still had twenty-three years of life to go. Beauvoir was rather given to these premature valedictory reflections. They fill her study *Old Age* in 1970, as well as the 1972 volume of her autobiography that really did turn out to be the last: *All Said and Done*.

Yet these books, ever more tinged with melancholy, also show her resplendent talent for marvelling at life. In *Old Age*, she writes of gazing at a picture of herself wearing 'one of those cloche hats and a roll collar' on the Champs-Elysées in 1929, and feeling amazed at how things that once seemed natural can now look so unfamiliar. In *All Said and Done*, she describes waking after an afternoon nap and feeling 'childish amazement – why am I myself?' Every detail of an individual is unlikely – why did that particular sperm meet that particular egg? Why was she born female? So many things could have been different: 'I might not have met Sartre; anything at all might have happened.'

Any piece of information that a biographer can discover about a person, she adds, is a trifle compared to the rich confusion of that person's real life, with its web of relationships and its countless elements of experience. Moreover, each of these elements means something different depending on perspective: a simple statement such as 'I was born in Paris' has a different meaning for each Parisian, depending on his or her background and precise situation. Out of this elaborate perspectival network, a shared reality is woven. No one will ever make sense of this mystery, she says.

The longest-lived of our main dramatis personae here was Emmanuel Levinas, who died on 25 December 1995, some three weeks short of his ninetieth birthday. The span of his life covers most of the story of modern phenomenology, from his first discovery of Husserl in 1928 to his own late career – in which he took philosophy into such arcane territory that even his fans found him hard to understand. He became increasingly interested in traditional Jewish scholarship and the exegesis of biblical texts, as well as continuing to work on ethics and relationships with the Other.

Levinas's ideas were an influence on Benny Lévy, which may be why *Hope Now* is filled with ideas that sound Levinasian. If true, this is another of those intriguing sidelong contacts between Levinas and Sartre. They barely knew each other, and their ideas were often radically different, yet their paths crossed at significant points. Almost half a century earlier, Sartre had bought Levinas's book in Paris after the conversation about apricot cocktails in the Bec-de-Gaz bar. Then, in the mid-1930s, they both produced remarkably similar writings about nausea and being. Now, through Lévy, their ideas were brought into unexpected proximity again – perhaps without either one acknowledging or reflecting on the fact.

The English 'new existentialist' Colin Wilson lived until 5 December 2013, angry to the end, but retaining the loyalty of the many international readers who had been excited and enlightened by his books. One can leave worse legacies in the world.

He outlived two other great communicators: Hazel Barnes, Sartre's translator, who died on 18 March 2008, and Iris Murdoch, who had given English readers their first taste of existentialism.

Murdoch died on 8 February 1999, after living several years with Alzheimer's disease; her last novel, *Jackson's Dilemma*, shows signs of emerging symptoms. Around the time she was working on it, she decided to abandon a philosophical book called 'Heidegger: the Pursuit of Being', on which she'd been engaged for six years. Typescript and manuscript versions remain, as disconnected assemblies of chapters of which just a few parts have been published posthumously.

Heidegger seems to have been an enigma to her, as he was to many others. No doubt she was intrigued by him as a person; many of her novels revolve around charismatic, sometimes dangerous guru types. More importantly, his philosophy kept her attention long after she had turned away from Sartre. She was particularly taken by the Heideggerian image of the mind as a clearing in the forest, which she found beautiful (as do I).

In *Jackson's Dilemma*, her character Benet is also writing a book on Heidegger, and like Murdoch herself he is struggling with the project. He wonders whether the difficulty comes from not being able to decide what he really thinks of Heidegger. Some aspects are attractive while others repel him: the Nazism, the appropriation of Hölderlin, and the relentless 'poeticisation of philosophy, discarding truth, goodness, freedom, love, the individual, everything which the philosopher ought to explain and defend'. He questions whether he is 'fascinated by a certain dangerous aspect of Heidegger which was in fact so deeply buried in his own, Benet's, soul that he could not scrutinise or even dislodge it'. What *is* it that he thinks about when he thinks about Heidegger? Later, reading through his Heidegger notes again, he says, 'I am small and I do not understand.'

A lifelong Murdoch fan, I had previously avoided *Jackson's Dilemma*, expecting it to be a sad read because of the signs of illness. Coming to it now, I was astounded to find such an uncannily recognisable description of how I myself felt about Heidegger. Indeed, I found the whole book moving and thought-provoking. In this last novel, Murdoch gives us a glimpse into what it is like to be a mind (or a Dasein) that is losing coherence and connection, yet retains both the ability to put its experience into words and the fierce *desire* to do so – to the limits of human capability. It is the phenomenological desire shared by Sartre, Beauvoir, Merleau-Ponty and everyone in this book, including even Heidegger himself.

In the last scene of *Jackson's Dilemma*, the title character, Benet's servant Jackson, sits on a grassy bank by a bridge over a river, watching a spider building a web between blades of grass. As if merging with Benet, he too has been overtaken by the sense that everything is slipping away. Sometimes, he says, he feels a shift, or loss of breath and memory. Has he simply misunderstood what is happening? Is it a dream? 'At the end of what is necessary, I have come to a place where there is no road.'

He stands up, but as he does, he feels something: it is the spider, walking on his hand. He helps the spider back to its web, goes down to the bridge, and crosses over the river.

14

The Imponderable Bloom

In which we ponder bloom.

The famous existentialists and phenomenologists are gone now, and several generations have grown up since the young Iris Murdoch discovered Sartre in 1945 and exclaimed, 'The excitement – I remember nothing like it.' It has become harder to revive that initial thrill. We can still find a nostalgic romance in the black-and-white images of the pipe-puffing Sartre at his café table, the turbanned Beauvoir, and the brooding Camus with his collar turned up. But they will never again look as raw and dangerous as they used to.

On the other hand, existentialist ideas and attitudes have embedded themselves so deeply into modern culture that we hardly think of them as existentialist at all. People (at least in relatively prosperous countries where more urgent needs don't intervene) talk about anxiety, dishonesty and the fear of commitment. They worry about being in bad faith, even if they don't use that term. They feel overwhelmed by the excess of consumer choice while also feeling less in control than ever. A vague longing for a more 'real' way of living leads some people to – for example – sign up for weekend retreats in which their smartphones are taken away like toys from children, so that they can spend two days walking in the country landscape and reconnecting with each other and with their forgotten selves.

The unnamed object of desire here is authenticity. This theme also haunts modern entertainment, just as much as it did in the 1950s. Existential anxiety is more closely intertwined with technological anxiety than ever in films such as Ridley Scott's *Blade Runner*, the Wachowskis' *Matrix*, Peter Weir's *The Truman Show*, Michel Gondry's

Eternal Sunshine of the Spotless Mind and Alex Garland's *Ex Machina*. Existentialist heroes of more traditional kinds, wrestling with meaning and decision, feature in Sam Mendes' *American Beauty*, the Coen brothers' *A Serious Man*, Steven Knight's *Locke*, and any number of Woody Allen films, including *Irrational Man* which takes its title from William Barrett's book. In David O. Russell's *I Heart Huckabees* of 2004, rival existential detectives battle over the difference between gloomy and positive visions of life. In another part of the forest, we find the ecstatic Heideggerian films of Terrence Malick, who did postgraduate research on Heidegger and translated some of his work before turning to film-making. All these divergent styles of film revolve around questions of human identity, purpose and freedom.

Of these themes, freedom may prove to be *the* great puzzle for the early twenty-first century. In the previous century, I grew up naively assuming that I'd see a constant, steady increase in this nebulous stuff through my lifetime, both in personal choices and in politics. In some ways, this has come true. On the other hand, unforeseen by anyone, basic ideas about freedom have been assailed and disputed in radical ways, so that we are now unable to agree what it amounts to, what we need it for, how much of it can be allowed, how far it should be interpreted as the right to offend or transgress, and how much of it we are prepared to give away to remote corporate entities in exchange for comfort and convenience. What we cannot do any longer is take it for granted.

Many of our uncertainties about freedom amount to uncertainties about our fundamental being. Science books and magazines bombard us with the news that we are out of control: that we amount to a mass of irrational but statistically predictable responses, veiled by the mere illusion of a conscious, governing mind. They tell us that, when we decide to sit down, to reach for a glass of water, to vote, or to choose whom we would save in the 'trolley problem', we are not really choosing at all but responding to tendencies and associations that are beyond the reach of both reason and will.

Reading such accounts, one gets the impression that we take pleasure in this idea of ourselves as out-of-control mechanical dupes of our own biology and environment. We claim to find it disturbing, but we might actually be deriving a kind of reassurance from it – for such ideas let us off the hook. They save us from the existential anxiety that comes with considering ourselves free agents who are responsible for what we do. Sartre would call that bad faith. Moreover, recent research suggests that those who have been encouraged to think they are unfree are inclined to behave less ethically, again suggesting that we treat it as an alibi.

So, do we really want to understand our lives and manage our futures as if we had neither real freedom nor a truly human foundation for our existence? Perhaps we need the existentialists more than we thought.

Having argued myself to that point, I must immediately add that I do not think the existentialists offer some simple magic solution for the modern world. As individuals and philosophers, they were hopelessly flawed. Each one's thought featured some major aspect that should make us uncomfortable. This is partly because they were complex and troubled beings, as most of us are. It is also because their ideas and lives were rooted in a dark, morally compromised century. The political turmoil and wild notions of their times marked them, just as our own twenty-first-century turmoil is now marking us.

But that is one reason why the existentialists demand rereading. They remind us that human existence is difficult and that people often behave appallingly, yet they also show how great our possibilities are. They constantly repeat the questions about freedom and being that we constantly try to forget. We can explore the directions the existentialists indicate without needing to take them as exemplary personalities, or even as exemplary thinkers. They are *interesting* thinkers, which I believe makes them more worth our trouble.

I first found them interesting thirty years ago, and I still do now – but for different reasons. Looking back at them has been a disorienting and stimulating experience, like seeing familiar faces in a fairground mirror. Some features I had barely noticed before have become more prominent, while others, which used to seem beautiful, have acquired a grotesque cast. Writing this book has brought me surprises all the way, not least with the two colossi of the story, Heidegger and Sartre.

When I first read Heidegger in my early twenties, I fell under the Messkirch magician's spell. My whole way of seeing the world was influenced by his raw amazement that there *is* something rather than nothing, by his way of looking at landscapes and buildings, by his notion of humans as a 'clearing' in which Being emerges into the light, and more.

Reading Heidegger again, I feel the same gravitational pull. But even while I'm sliding back down into his dimly lit world of forest paths and tolling bells, I find myself struggling to get free, for reasons that have nothing – and everything – to do with his Nazism. There is something of the grave in this vegetative world. Give me the open sea of Jaspers, I now think, or the highways frequented by Marcel's travellers, filled with human encounter and conversation. Heidegger once wrote that 'To think is to confine yourself to a single thought', but I now feel that this is the very opposite of what thinking ought to be. Thinking should be generous and have a good appetite. I find life far too valuable these days to shut out most of its variety in favour of digging down into the depths – and remaining down there, as Hannah Arendt described the Heideggerian method of inquiry.

I also find myself thinking back to Arendt's and Sartre's observations about the uncanny absence in Heidegger where 'character' should be. Something is missing from his life and from his work. Iris Murdoch thought the missing thing was goodness, and therefore that his philosophy lacked an ethical centre or *heart*. Indeed, you can never say of Heidegger what Merleau-Ponty said of Sartre: 'he is good'. One could call this missing element 'humanity', in several senses. Heidegger set himself against the philosophy of humanism, and he himself was rarely humane in his behaviour. He set no store by the individuality and detail of anyone's life, least of all his own. It is no coincidence that, of all the philosophers in this book, Heidegger is the one who refused to see the point of biography. He opened an early lecture series on Aristotle by saying, 'He was born at such and such a time, he worked, and he died' – as though that were all one needed to know about a life. He insisted that his own life was uninteresting, too: a view that would be convenient for him, if true. The result, despite Heidegger's mythologising of home, is a philosophy that feels uninhabitable – to return again to Murdoch's notion of 'inhabited' thought. Heidegger's work is exhilarating, but in the end it is a philosophy in which I cannot find a place to live.

I have been surprised in a different way by the other giant in the field: Sartre – the writer who first tempted me into philosophy with *Nausea*. I knew he would be a powerful presence in my story, but I was surprised at how much I came to respect him, and even to like him.

Of course, he was monstrous. He was self-indulgent, demanding, bad-tempered. He was a sex addict who didn't even enjoy sex, a man who would walk away from friendships saying he felt no regret. He gave free rein to his obsessions with viscosity and gloopiness, and with the feeling that other people were looking at him and making judgements; he never seemed to worry that some readers might not share these idiosyncrasies. He defended a range of odious regimes, and made a cult of violence. He maintained that literature for its own sake is a bourgeois luxury, that writers *must* engage with the world, and that revising one's writing is a waste of time – all of which I disagree with. I disagree with quite a lot in Sartre.

But then there is that question of 'character' – and Sartre is full of character. He bursts out on all sides with energy, peculiarity, generosity and communicativeness. All of this is captured in an anecdote by the German historian Joachim Fest, who met him at a party in Berlin in the late 1940s. He describes how Sartre held court amid some thirty people who grilled him about his philosophy; in response, he rambled on about jazz and cinema and the novels of John Dos Passos. Someone who was present said afterwards that Sartre put him in mind of a South American peasant hacking through a jungle of phenomena, sending brightly coloured parrots flying up with their wings flashing in all directions. Fest remarked, 'Everything that he said seemed to me to be noticeably well informed and yet disordered, in part also muddled, but always touching on our sense of the times. Everyone was impressed. If I sum up my responses, I learned through Sartre that a degree of muddle-headedness can be quite fascinating.'

This is what fascinates me in Sartre too. Whereas Heidegger circled around his home territory, Sartre moved ever forwards, always working out new (often bizarre) responses to things, or finding ways of reconciling old ideas with fresh input. Heidegger intoned that one must think, but Sartre actually thought. Heidegger had his big *Kehre* – his 'turn' – but Sartre turned and turned and turned again. He was always thinking 'against himself', as he once said, and he followed Husserl's phenomenological command by exploring whatever topic seemed most difficult at each moment.

All this was true in his life as well as in his writing. He laboured tirelessly for his chosen causes, risking his own safety. He took his 'engagements' seriously – and for every unwise and damaging commitment, there was a worthwhile one, such as his campaign against the government's abuses in Algeria. He was never able successfully to toe a party line on anything, however hard he tried. Perhaps Sartre's politics are best summed up in a remark he made in 1968: 'If one rereads all my books, one will realize that I have not changed profoundly, and that I have always remained an anarchist.' He was anarchic because he would not stop using his brain. Moreover, to quote Merleau-Ponty again, he was good – or at least he *wanted* to do good. He was driven to it.

I am also more impressed now than ever by his radical atheism, so different to that professed by Heidegger, who abandoned his faith only in order to pursue a more intense form of mysticism. Sartre was a profound atheist, and a humanist to his bones. He outdid even Nietzsche in his ability to live courageously and thoughtfully in the conviction that nothing lies beyond, and that no divine compensations will ever make up for anything on this earth. For him, *this* life is what we have, and we must make of it what we can.

In one of his transcribed conversations with Beauvoir, he said to her, 'It seems to me that a great atheist, truly atheist philosophy was something philosophy lacked. And that it was in this direction that one should now endeavour to work.' Beauvoir replied, 'To put it briefly, you wanted to make a philosophy of man.'

When she then asked him whether he wanted to add any final remarks to their dialogues, he said that, on the whole, the two of them had lived without paying much attention to God. She agreed. Then he said, 'And yet we've lived; we feel that we've taken an interest in our world and that we've tried to see and understand it.' To do this freshly and (mostly) intelligently for seven decades is an achievement more than worthy of celebration.

One aspect of Heidegger's engagement with the world that really merits attention from the twenty-first-century reader is his double interest in technology and ecology. In his 1953 lecture 'The Question Concerning Technology', he argued that our technology is not merely an aggregation of clever devices: it reveals something fundamental about our existence. It therefore needs thinking through in a philo-sophical way rather than just in a technical one. We cannot understand our lives if we ask only what our machines can do, or how best to manage them, or what we should use them for. The essence of technology, he said, is 'nothing technological'. To investigate it properly is to be taken to much deeper questions about how we work, how we occupy Earth, and how we *are* in relation to Being.

Of course, Heidegger was thinking here of typewriters, celluloid movie projectors, big old automobiles and combine harvesters. Very few existentialists (or anyone else) foresaw the role computer technology would come to play in our lives, although in his 1954 book *Existentialism and the Modern Predicament*, the German author Friedrich Heinemann warned that the coming 'ultra-rapid computing machine' would raise a 'truly existential question', namely that of how human beings could remain free.

Heinemann could not have been more right. Later Heideggerians, notably Hubert Dreyfus, have written about the internet as the technological innovation that most clearly reveals what technology is. Its infinite connectivity promises to make the entire world storeable and available, but, in doing so, it also removes privacy and depth from things. Everything, above all ourselves, becomes a resource, precisely as Heidegger warned. In being made a resource, we are handed over, not just to other individuals like ourselves, but to an impersonal 'they' whom we never meet and cannot locate. Dreyfus was writing in 2001: since then, the internet has become even more intrusive and so ubiquitous that we can hardly find an angle from which to think it through: it is the very atmosphere many of us breathe all day. Yet surely we ought to be thinking about it – about what sort of beings we are or want to be in our online lives, and what sort of Being we have, or want to have.

Perhaps fortunately, so far, our computer technology just as frequently reminds us of what it *cannot* do, or at least cannot do yet. Computer systems perform poorly at navigating the rich texture of lived reality: that complex web of perceptions, movements, interactions and expectations that make up the most ordinary human experience, such as entering a café and looking around for your friend Pierre. They are not even good at distinguishing foreground shapes in a visual image. In other words, as Dreyfus and others have long recognised, computers are bad phenomenologists.

Such tasks are easy for humans because we swim in perceptual and conceptual complexity from a young age. We grow up immersed in the 'imponderable bloom' of life and relationships – a phrase borrowed from E. M. Forster's prescient 1909 science-fiction story, 'The Machine Stops'. It tells of a future humanity living in isolated pods beneath the Earth's surface. They rarely meet in the flesh, but communicate through a remote vision-phone system. A woman in her pod in Australia can talk to her son in Europe: they see each other's images on special plates which they hold in their hands. But the son complains, 'I see something like you in this plate, but I do not see you. I hear something like you through this telephone, but I do not hear you.' The simulacrum is no substitute for the real Other. As Forster glosses it, 'The imponderable bloom, declared by discredited philosophy to be the actual essence of intercourse, was ignored by the machine.'

This 'bloom' of experience and communication lies at the heart of the human mystery: it is what makes possible the living, conscious, embodied beings that we are. It also happens to be the subject to which phenomenologists and existentialists devoted most of their research. They set out to detect and capture the quality of experience *as we live it* rather than according to the frameworks suggested by traditional philosophy, psychology, Marxism, Hegelianism, structuralism, or any of the other -isms and disciplines that explain our lives away.

Of all these thinkers, the one who most directly tackled Forster's bloom was the one from whom I had initially expected nothing very dramatic: Maurice Merleau-Ponty. In *The Phenomenology of Perception*, he put together the fullest description he could of how we live from moment to moment, and thus of what we are – from the woman who ducks as she enters a room in a tall hat to the man who stands by a window watching the vibrating branch from which a bird has just flapped away. Merleau-Ponty arguably left the most lasting intellectual legacy of all, not least in his direct influence on the modern discipline of 'embodied cognition', which studies consciousness as a holistic social and sensory phenomenon rather than as a sequence of abstract processes. Merleau-Ponty gave philosophy a new direction by taking its peripheral areas of study – the body, perception, childhood, sociality – and bringing them into the central position that they occupy in real life. If I had to choose an intellectual hero in this story, it would be Merleau-Ponty, the happy philosopher of things as they are.

Someone else shared Merleau-Ponty's instinct for the ambiguity and complexity of human experience, and that was Simone de Beauvoir. Besides her work in feminism and fiction, she devoted her philosophical writing to exploring how the two forces of constraint and freedom play themselves out through our lives, as each of us slowly becomes ourselves.

This theme guides *The Second Sex* and *The Ethics of Ambiguity*, and it also runs through her multi-volumed autobiography, where she depicts herself and Sartre and countless friends and colleagues as they think, act, quarrel, meet, separate, have tantrums and passions, and generally respond to their world. Simone de Beauvoir's memoirs make her one of the twentieth century's greatest intellectual chroniclers, as well as one of its most diligent phenomenologists. Page by page, she observes her experience, expresses her astonishment at being alive, pays attention to people and indulges her appetite for everything she encounters.

When I first read Sartre and Heidegger, I didn't think the details of a philosopher's personality or biography were important. This was the orthodox belief in the field at the time, but it also came from my being too young myself to have much sense of history. I intoxicated myself with concepts, without taking account of their relationship to events and to all the odd data of their inventors' lives. Never mind lives; *ideas* were the thing.

Thirty years later, I have come to the opposite conclusion. Ideas are interesting, but people are vastly more so. That is why, among all the existentialist works, the one I am least likely to tire of is Beauvoir's autobiography, with its portrait of human complexity and of the world's ever-changing substance. It gives us all the fury and vivacity of the existentialist cafés, together with 'a sulphur sky over a sea of clouds, the purple holly, the white nights of Leningrad, the bells of the Liberation, an orange moon over the Piraeus, a red sun rising over the desert' – and all the rest of the exquisite, phosphorescent bloom of life, which reveals itself to human beings for as long as we are lucky enough to be able to experience it.

Cast of Characters

A who's who for reference.

Nelson Algren (1909–1981): Author of *The Man with the Golden Arm* and other novels of the American underbelly; Simone de Beauvoir's (mostly long-distance) lover from 1947 to 1950.

Hannah Arendt (1906–1975): German philosopher and political theorist based in the US after fleeing Germany in 1933; former student and lover of Martin Heidegger; author of *Eichmann in Jerusalem* and other works.

Raymond Aron (1905–1983): French philosopher, sociologist and political journalist; schoolmate of Jean-Paul Sartre; he studied in Germany in the early 1930s and told his friends about phenomenology.

James Baldwin (1924–1987): American author of novels and essays exploring race and sexuality; he moved to Paris in 1948 and spent much of the rest of his life in France.

Hazel Barnes (1915–2008): American translator and philosophical author who translated Sartre's *Being and Nothingness* in 1956.

William Barrett (1913–1992): American populariser of existentialist ideas; author of *Irrational Man* (1958).

Jean Beaufret (1907–1982): French philosopher who corresponded with and interviewed Martin Heidegger and popularised German existentialist ideas; his questions prompted Heidegger to write his *Letter on Humanism* (1947).

Simone de Beauvoir (1908–1986): Leading French existentialist philosopher, novelist, feminist, playwright, essayist, memoirist and political activist.

Jacques-Laurent Bost (1916–1990): French journalist who studied with Jean-Paul Sartre, co-founded *Les Temps modernes*, married Olga Kosakiewicz, and had an affair with Simone de Beauvoir.

Franz Clemens Brentano (1838–1917): German philosopher and former priest who studied psychology and became the first to explore the theory of intentionality, which became fundamental to phenomenology. Edmund Husserl studied with him in Vienna from 1884–6; Brentano's thesis on Aristotle's uses of the term 'being' also inspired Heidegger.

Sonia Brownell (later Orwell) (1918–1980): English journalist, assistant editor of *Horizon*; had an affair with Maurice Merleau-Ponty, and later married George Orwell.

Albert Camus (1913–1960): French–Algerian novelist, essayist, short-story writer, playwright and activist.

Ernst Cassirer (1874–1945): German philosopher and historian of ideas, specialising in studies of science, Kant and the Enlightenment; debated with Heidegger at a 1929 conference in Davos, Switzerland.

Jean Cau (1925–1993): French writer and journalist; Sartre's assistant from 1947.

Anne-Marie Cazalis (1920–1988): French writer and actor; one of the 'existentialist muses' of the Saint-German-des-Prés district in the late 1940s and 1950s.

Fyodor Dostoevsky (1821–1881): Russian novelist generally considered a proto-existentialist.

Hubert Dreyfus (1929–): American philosopher, professor at the University of California, Berkeley; a Heidegger specialist who also writes about technology and the internet.

Jacques Duclos (1896–1975): Acting Secretary General of the French Communist Party 1950–53; arrested in 1952 on suspicion of plotting to send messages via carrier pigeons. The 'pigeon plot' incident helped to radicalise Sartre.

Ralph Ellison (1914–1994): American writer, author of the novel *Invisible Man* (1952).

Frantz Fanon (1925–1961): Philosopher and political theorist born in Martinique; author of works on post-colonial and anti-colonial politics, notably *The Wretched of the Earth* (1961), for which Sartre wrote the foreword.

Eugen Fink (1905–1975): One of Husserl's key assistants and colleagues in Freiburg, later involved with the Husserl Archives in Louvain.

Hans-Georg Gadamer (1900–2002): German philosopher, best known for his work on hermeneutics; studied briefly with Husserl and Heidegger in Freiburg and recorded anecdotes about both.

Jean Genet (1910–1986): French thief, vagrant and prostitute turned poet, novelist and autobiographer; subject of Sartre's major work *Saint Genet* (1952), which began life as a foreword to his works.

Alberto Giacometti (1901–1966): Italian–Swiss artist, noted for his sculptures; a friend of Sartre and Beauvoir who sketched Sartre and others.

J. Glenn Gray (1913–1977): American philosopher, professor at Colorado College, and translator of Heidegger; also wrote *The Warriors*, a sociological study of men in war.

Juliette Gréco (1927–): French singer and actor; one of the 'existentialist muses' of the Saint-Germain-des-Prés district, and a friend of Merleau-Ponty, Sartre and others.

Václav Havel (1936–2011): Czech playwright and dissident; studied phenomenology with Jan Patočka, and served as president of Czechoslovakia and then the Czech Republic from 1989 to 2003.

G. W. F. Hegel (1770–1831): German philosopher whose *Phenomenology of Spirit* and dialectical theory influenced most of the existentialists.

Elfride Heidegger, née Petri (1893–1992): Wife of Martin Heidegger; bought and designed their property in Todtnauberg.

Fritz Heidegger (1894–1980): Banker in Messkirch, brother of Martin Heidegger; helped him type his manuscripts and tried to make him write in shorter sentences.

Martin Heidegger (1889–1976): German philosopher who studied with Husserl; author of *Being and Time* and many other influential works.

Friedrich Hölderlin (1770–1843): German poet admired and studied by Heidegger.

Edmund Husserl (1859–1938): Philosopher born in German-speaking Moravia; founding father of the phenomenological movement; disappointed mentor to Martin Heidegger.

Malvine Husserl, née Steinschneider (1860–1950): Wife of Edmund Husserl, also born in Moravia; helped to manage the rescue of his archive and manuscripts in 1938.

Gertrud Jaspers, née Mayer (1879–1974): Wife of Karl Jaspers and collaborator on much of his work.

Karl Jaspers (1883–1969): German existentialist philosopher, psychologist and political thinker, based at the University of Heidelberg until 1948 when he and his wife moved to Switzerland; friend of Hannah Arendt and, intermittently, of Martin Heidegger.

Francis Jeanson (1922–2009): Left-wing French philosopher, co-editor of *Les Temps modernes*; in 1952 he wrote a critical review of Camus' *The Rebel* which triggered the falling-out between Camus and Sartre.

Hans Jonas (1903–1993): German philosopher, mostly based in the US; former student of Heidegger, and author of works on technology, environmentalism and other themes.

Walter Kaufmann (1921–1980): German-American philosopher and translator, born in Freiburg; author of the popular work *Existentialism from Dostoevsky to Sartre* (1956).

Søren Kierkegaard (1813–1855): Danish proto-existentialist philosopher and contrarian of a religious bent, influential on the later existentialists.

Arthur Koestler (1905–1983): Hungarian novelist, memoirist and essayist; friend of Sartre and others, but fell out with them over politics.

Olga Kosakiewicz (1915–1983): Actor, protégée of Beauvoir and lover of Sartre; married Jacques-Laurent Bost.

Wanda Kosakiewicz (1917–1989): Actor, sister of Olga and lover of Sartre.

Victor Kravchenko (1905–1966): Soviet defector to the US, author of *I Chose Freedom* (1946), which occasioned a high-profile lawsuit and controversy in France in 1949.

Ludwig Landgrebe (1902–1991): Austrian phenomenologist who worked as Husserl's assistant and colleague in Freiburg, and then in the Husserl Archives in Louvain.

Claude Lanzmann (1925–): French film-maker best known for his nine-hour Holocaust documentary *Shoah*; lover of Simone de Beauvoir, living with her from 1952 to 1959.

Elisabeth Le Coin or Lacoin (1907–1929): Childhood friend of Simone de Beauvoir; was briefly engaged to Merleau-Ponty, but died aged twenty-one, possibly of encephalitis.

Henri Lefebvre (1901–1991): French Marxist theorist interested in the sociology of everyday life; initially critical of existentialism, then more sympathetic.

Michel Leiris (1901–1990): French writer, ethnographer and memoirist; friend of Sartre and Beauvoir. His autobiographical style helped inspire Beauvoir in writing *The Second Sex*.

Emmanuel Levinas (1906–1995): Lithuanian Jewish philosopher based mostly in France; studied with Husserl and Heidegger, then developed a very different post-existentialist philosophy based on ethics and the encounter with the Other. A short early book of his was Sartre's first primer in phenomenology in 1933.

Claude Lévi-Strauss (1908–2009): French structuralist anthropologist; friend of Merleau-Ponty, but took issue with phenomenology and existentialism.

Benny Lévy (1945–2003): Philosopher and activist; Sartre's assistant and co-author of the controversial series of interviews, *Hope Now* (1980).

Karl Löwith (1897–1973): German philosopher and historian of ideas who studied with Heidegger, and wrote memoirs of the experience.

György Lukács (1885–1971): Hungarian Marxist, often critical of existentialism.

Norman Mailer (1923–2007): American novelist and polemicist who intended to run for New York mayor as the 'Existentialist Party' candidate, but had to delay the campaign after stabbing his wife.

Gabriel Marcel (1889–1973): French Christian existentialist philosopher and playwright.

Herbert Marcuse (1898–1979): Philosopher and social theorist associated with the Frankfurt School; former student of Martin Heidegger who criticised him severely after the Second World War.

Tomáš Masaryk (1850–1937): Served four terms as president of Czechoslovakia after 1918; youthful friend of Husserl who also studied with Franz Brentano in Vienna, and later helped organise the rescue of his papers in Prague.

Albert Memmi (1920–): Tunisian Jewish novelist, essayist and post-colonial social theorist; author of *The Colonizer and the Colonized* (1957), a double work for which Sartre wrote a foreword.

Maurice Merleau-Ponty (1908–1961): French phenomenologist and essayist specialising in questions of the body, perception, childhood development and relations with others; author of *The Phenomenology of Perception* and other works, including polemical essays written at different stages of his life arguing for and against Communism.

Max Müller (1906–1994): German Catholic philosopher who studied with Heidegger in Freiburg and later became a professor there himself; he wrote an account of how Heidegger failed to protect him when he was in trouble with the Nazi regime in 1937.

Iris Murdoch (1919–1999): Anglo-Irish philosopher and novelist, an early writer on Sartre and existentialism who later turned away from it, although she worked on a study of Heidegger towards the end of her life.

Friedrich Nietzsche (1844–1900): German proto-existentialist philologist, aphorist and philosopher, influential on the later existentialists.

Paul Nizan (1905–1940): French Marxist novelist and philosopher, boyhood friend of Sartre; killed in battle during the German invasion of France.

Jan Patočka (1907–1977): Czech phenomenologist and political theorist who studied with Husserl and in turn taught many others in Prague, including Václav Havel; one of the key signatories of the dissident Charter 77, he was fatally persecuted for this by the regime.

Jean Paulhan (1884–1968): French writer and critic who left small anti-collaborationist poems around Paris during the Second World War. One of the co-founders of *Les Temps modernes* in 1945, he was more noted as long-term director of the *Nouvelle revue française*.

Heinrich Wiegand Petzet (1909–1997): German writer, the son of a shipping magnate and a friend of Heidegger who wrote a detailed memoir of the relationship in 1983, *Encounters and Dialogues with Martin Heidegger*.

Jean-Paul Sartre (1905–1980): Leading French existentialist philosopher, novelist, biographer, playwright, essayist, memoirist and political activist.

Stephen Spender (1909–1995): English socialist poet and diarist; travelled widely in Europe after the war, and took issue with Sartre on the question of political engagement.

Edith Stein (1891–1942): Philosopher born in Wrocław in Poland; worked as Husserl's assistant before leaving to complete her study of the phenomenology of empathy, and then to convert from Judaism to Catholicism and take orders as a Carmelite nun; she died in Auschwitz.

Olivier Todd (1929–): French biographer, memoirist and journalist, a friend of Sartre and biographer of Camus.

Frédéric de Towarnicki (1920–2008): Austrian-born French translator and journalist who visited Heidegger on several occasions in the 1940s and wrote accounts of their conversations.

Herman Leo Van Breda (1911–1974): Franciscan monk and philosopher who heroically organised the rescue of Husserl's archives and manuscripts from Freiburg in 1938, and then founded and managed the Husserl Archives in Louvain for many years.

Boris Vian (1920–1959): French jazz trumpeter, singer, novelist and cocktail mixer; a central figure in the post-war Saint-Germain-des-Prés scene and a friend of the existentialists. He affectionately mocked Sartre and Beauvoir in his novel *L'écume des jours* or *Mood Indigo* in 1947.

Michelle Vian, née Léglise (1920–): First wife of Boris Vian, also a part of the Sartre circle for many years.

Simone Weil (1909–1943): French ethical philosopher and political activist; died in England during the Second World War after refusing to eat or accept any physical comforts while others were suffering.

Colin Wilson (1931–2013): English novelist and author of popular works of 'new existentialist' philosophy and cultural history, notably *The Outsider* (1956).

Wols (Alfred Otto Wolfgang Schulze) (1913–1951): German painter and photographer mostly based in France and friends with some of the existentialist circle; died prematurely of illness related to alcoholism.

Richard Wright (1908–1960): American writer who lived for many years in Paris; author of works including *The Outsider* (1953), an existentialist novel of black American life.

Acknowledgements

This book would still be a heap of nothingness without the generous encouragement, advice and help of friends and experts, not to mention experts who have also become friends. To everyone involved: a heartfelt thank you.

Above all, this means people who read the manuscript in whole or in part, and who pointed me in new directions and/or saved me from disasters (although they are innocent of any disasters that remain): Jay Bernstein, Ivan Chvatík, George Cotkin, Robert Fraser, Peter Moore, Nigel Warburton, Jonathan Webber, Martin Woessner and Robert Zaretsky. I'm grateful not only for the reading, but for the many enjoyable and thought-provoking conversations along the way.

Thank you also to others who helped in crucial ways through friendly conversation, good advice, or both: Peter Atterton, Antony Beevor, Robert Bernasconi, Costica Bradatan, Artemis Cooper, Anthony Gottlieb, Ronald Hayman, Jim Holt, James Miller, Sarah Richmond, Adam Sharr, and Marci Shore.

Of all these, I'm particularly grateful to Robert Bernasconi and Jay Bernstein for having inspired me to study philosophy in the first place. I was incredibly lucky, back in the 1980s, to happen across the adventurous cross-disciplinary programme they helped to create at the University of Essex.

Very warm thanks go to Marianne Merleau-Ponty, who generously shared with me her memories of her father.

I wrote part of this book during a stay as Writer in Residence at the New York Institute of Humanities at NYU, and I am grateful to the Institute and to Eric Banks and Stephanie Steiker for their hospitality and friendship during a wonderful, productive two months.

Much of the rest of the writing was done in the British Library, London Library, Bodleian Library and the Bibliothèque Sainte-Geneviève in Paris; thank you to all those institutions and their staff. Thank you to Thomas Vongehr and Ullrich Melle at the Institute of Philosophy / Husserl Archives in Louvain, Belgium. Thank you to Ludger Hagedorn and (again) Ivan Chvatík of the CTS / Jan Patočka Archives. Thank you to Katie Giles at the University of Kingston for help with the Iris Murdoch Archives, and to Dan Mitchell at University College, London for help with the George Orwell Archives.

For insightful editing, friendship and more valuable advice than ever, I thank Jenny Uglow, who helped me look for a tree-trunk amid the twigs. I am grateful to Clara Farmer and all at Chatto & Windus, but especially to Parisa Ebrahimi, who has guided me through publication with clarity and grace. Thank you to my copy editor David Milner, and to Simone Massoni for the Chatto cover. Thank you to Anne Collins at Penguin Random House, Canada. In the US, thank you especially to my inimitable and life-enhancing publisher Judith Gurewich, especially for the sunny days' work in Boston, to my copy editor Keenan McCracken and all at Other Press, and to Andreas Gurewich for the cover.

I am grateful for the constant support and wisdom of my agent Zoë Waldie and everyone else at Rogers, Coleridge & White. Thank you also to Melanie Jackson in New York, and to everyone who has helped with publication elsewhere.

Finally, two more thank yous: one to my parents, Jane and Ray Bakewell, to whom this book is dedicated because they encouraged me to follow whatever I was curious about in life (and because they endured my 'teenage existentialist' years). The other is, as always, to Simonetta Ficai-Veltroni, who has stuck with me phenomenology and all, and that's just the beginning of it.

Notes

Publication details not given here can be found in the Select Bibliography. Where reference is not to a translated edition of a work, any translations are mine.

Abbreviations:

ASAD: Beauvoir, *All Said and Done*.
BN: Sartre, *Being and Nothingness* (Barnes translation).
BT: Heidegger, *Being and Time* (Macquarrie & Robinson translation). References are to this followed by original German edition.
FOC: Beauvoir, *Force of Circumstance*.
GA: Heidegger, *Gesamtausgabe*.
MDD: Beauvoir, *Memoirs of a Dutiful Daughter*.
PP: Merleau-Ponty, *Phenomenology of Perception* (Landes translation). References are to this followed by French edition of 2005.
POL: Beauvoir, *The Prime of Life*.

Chapter 1: Sir, What a Horror, Existentialism!

1   Existentialist pedigree: Walter Kaufmann's 1956 book *Existentialism from Dostoevsky to Sartre* took the story back to St Augustine; Maurice Friedman's *The Worlds of Existentialism* (New York: Random House, 1964) took it to Job, Ecclesiastes and Heraclitus.

1   Cocktails: Sartre later thought they were drinking beer, but his memory was unreliable by that stage: *Sartre By Himself*, 25–6. Beauvoir said it was apricot cocktails: POL, 135, from which most of the ensuing account comes.

2   'To the things themselves!': Husserl, *Logical Investigations*, I, 252. It is

partly down to Heidegger that this remark became a slogan, as
Heidegger calls it the 'maxim' of phenomenology: BT, 50/27–8.

3   'Since we could not understand': POL, 79. For speculation about other
previous encounters, see Stephen Light, *Shūzō Kuki and Jean-Paul Sartre*
(Carbondale & Edwardsville, IL: Southern Illinois University Press, 1987),
3–4, with Rybalka's introduction, xi.

4   'Destructive philosophy': Sartre's 'La légende de la vérité', *Bifur*, 8 (June
1931), had a byline describing him as 'at work on a volume of destructive philosophy'. See also POL, 79; Hayman, *Writing Against*, 85.

4   'I can tell you': *Sartre By Himself*, 26.

4   John Keats, 'On First Looking into Chapman's Homer', in *The Complete
Poems* (ed. John Barnard), 3rd edn (London: Penguin, 1988), 72. Sartre
was reading Levinas, *La théorie de l'intuition dans la phénoménologie de
Husserl* (Paris: Alcan, 1930); later edn translated by A. Orianne as *The
Theory of Intuition in Husserl's Phenomenology* (Evanston, IL: Northwestern
University Press, 1995).

5   Dockers, monks, etc.: MDD, 341.

6   'Existence precedes essence': Sartre, *Existentialism and Humanism*, 27.

7   King and queen: FOC, 98.

7   'Women swooned': 'Existentialism', *Time* (28 Jan. 1946), 16–17. On the
lecture, see George Myerson, *Sartre's Existentialism Is a Humanism: a
beginner's guide* (London: Hodder & Stoughton, 2002), xii–xiv, and Cohen-
Solal, *Sartre*, 249–52.

8   'Trolley problem': for more, see David Edmunds, *Would You Kill the Fat
Man?* (Princeton: Princeton University Press, 2013).

8   Student story: Sartre, *Existentialism and Humanism*, 39–43. There are
similarities with the situation of his friend and former pupil, Jacques-
Laurent Bost, who sought Sartre's opinion in 1937 about going to fight
in the Spanish Civil War: see Thompson, *Sartre*, 36. In his novel *The
Reprieve*, Sartre lent a similar dilemma to his character Boris, based on
Bost.

10   'There is no traced-out path': Sartre, interview with C. Grisoli, in *The
Last Chance: Roads of Freedom IV*, 15 (originally published in *Paru*, 13 Dec.
1945).

11   Sartre on Hiroshima: Sartre, 'The End of the War', in *The Aftermath of
War (Situations III)*, 65–75, this 65.

11   *Index*: J. M. De Bujanda, *Index des livres interdits, XI: Index librorum
prohibitorum* (Geneva: Droz, 2002) lists Sartre's *opera omnia*, 808 (Decr.

S. Off. 27-10-1948), and Beauvoir's *Le deuxième sexe* and *Les Mandarins*, 116 (Decr. 27-06-1956). See Thompson, *Sartre*, 78.

11 'Sickening mixture': *Les nouvelles littéraires*, quoted in 'Existentialism', *Time* (28 Jan. 1946), 16–17, this 17.

12 'If you were twenty': Cazalis, *Les mémoires d'une Anne*, 84.

12 'Sir, what a horror!': Marcel, 'An Autobiographical Essay', 48.

12 Private room: POL, 534. Enjoying the bustle of cafés: Contat & Rybalka (eds), *The Writings of Jean-Paul Sartre*, I: 149, quoting Roger Troisfontaines, *Le choix de Jean-Paul Sartre*, 2nd edn, (Paris: Aubier, 1946), which in turn quotes remarks made by Sartre in Brussels, 23 Oct. 1945.

13 'So long as they were interesting': Grégoire Leménager, 'Ma vie avec Boris Vian (par Michelle Vian)', *Le nouvel observateur* (27 Oct. 2011).

13 'Drowning victim' and 'shredded and tattered shirt': Michelle Vian, *Manual of Saint-Germain-des-Prés*, 46, 48, quoting Pierre Drouin, 'Tempète très parisienne', *Le Monde* (16–17, May 1948), and Robert de Thomasson, *Opéra* (Oct. 1947) respectively. Long hair: Gréco, *Je suis faite comme ça*, 81. Turban: POL, 504; also see Beauvoir, *Wartime Diary*, 166 (22 Nov. 1939). You can see the 'look' in the Lorientais jazz-club scenes in Jacques Becker's excellent 1949 film, *Rendezvous de juillet*.

14 Wols: FOC, 248–9.

14 Camembert: Cohen-Solal, *Sartre*, 262.

14 Singing: MDD, 335. Donald Duck: POL, 324.

14 Sartre's face: Aron, *Memoirs*, 23; Violette Leduc, *Mad in Pursuit*, tr. Derek Coltman (London: R. Hart-Davis, 1971), 45–6; Sartre, 'The Paintings of Giacometti', in *Situations* [IV], 175–92, this 184.

16 Légion d'honneur and Académie française: John Gerassi, 'The Second Death of Jean-Paul Sartre', in W. L. McBride (ed.), *Sartre's Life, Times and Vision du monde* (New York & London: Garland, 1997), 217–23, this 218. Beauvoir was offered the Légion d'honneur and rejected it in 1982: Bair, *Simone de Beauvoir*, 606.

16 'My life and my philosophy': Cohen-Solal, *Sartre*, 142 (citing Sartre's diary, 15 Jan. 1940).

16 Two million words: M. Scriven, *Sartre's Existential Biographies* (London: Macmillan, 1984), 1.

17 *Concluding Unscientific Postscript*: The full Danish title is *Afsluttende uviden-skabelig Efterskrift til de philosophiske Smuler. Mimisk-pathetisk-dialektisk Sammenskrift, Existentielt Indlæg.*

18 'One was always being pushed': Garff, *Søren Kierkegaard*, 313.

18   Horse and passion: Kierkegaard, *Concluding Unscientific Postscript*, 261.

18   'Abstraction is disinterested': ibid., 262.

18   Descartes: ibid., 265–6.

19   'Anxiety': Kierkegaard, *The Concept of Anxiety*, 61.

19   Bus stop: *Sartre By Himself*, 16.

20   'A kind of involuntary': Friedrich Nietzsche, *Beyond Good and Evil*, tr.
      R. J. Hollingdale (London: Penguin, 2003), 37 (part 1, s. 6).

21   King: 'Martin Luther King Jr. Traces His Pilgrimage to Nonviolence',
      in Arthur and Lila Weinburg (eds), *Instead of Violence* (New York:
      Grossman, 1963), 71. He read Sartre, Jaspers, Heidegger and others, as
      well as Paul Tillich, American existentialist theologian. See also: Eugene
      Wolters, 'The Influence of Existentialism on Martin Luther King, Jr.',
      Critical Theory (8 Feb. 2015), which refers to King's essay 'Pilgrimage to
      Nonviolence' and his notes in the King Archive.

22   Slogans: listed on https://libcom.org/history/slogans-68.

22   Demanded freedom: Sartre, 'Self-Portrait at Seventy', in *Sartre in the
      Seventies (Situations X)*, 3–92, this 52.

22   Sorbonne: Marguerite Duras muttered, 'I'm fed up with the star system,'
      according to Beauvoir. See ASAD, 460–62, and Cohen-Solal, *Sartre*, 462.

23   Funeral: 'Enterrement de Sartre' on YouTube: https://www.youtube.
      com/watch?v=C9UoHWWd214. See Hayman, *Writing Against*, 439;
      Cohen-Solal, *Sartre*, 522–3; Lévy, *Sartre*, 2.

24   Lanzmann: quoted in Ursula Tidd, *Simone de Beauvoir* (London:
      Routledge, 2003), 160.

25   Chestnut tree: Sartre, *Nausea*, 183–4.

27   'Shop-girl metaphysics' (*'une sorte de métaphysique pour midinette'*): Claude
      Lévi-Strauss, *Tristes Tropiques*, tr. J. & D. Weightman (London: Penguin,
      1978), 71, and in French, *Tristes Tropiques* (Paris: Plon, 1955), 63. 'To
      dissolve man': Claude Lévi-Strauss, *The Savage Mind* (London: Weidenfeld
      & Nicolson, 1966), 247.

29   'A sense of freedom': Michel Contat, interviewed for the BBC series
      Human, All Too Human (1999), episode 3: 'Jean-Paul Sartre: the road to
      freedom'.

30   'Life becomes ideas' and 'A discussion': Merleau-Ponty, *The Visible and
      Invisible*, 119.

31   'Inhabited philosophy': Murdoch, *The Sovereignty of Good* (London &
      New York: RKP, 2014), 46.

33   Label: FOC, 46.

Chapter 2: To the Things Themselves

35 Population and hikers' outfits in 1930s Freiburg: Martin S. Briggs, *Freiburg and the Black Forest* (London: John Miles, 1936), 21, 31.

36 'The City of Phenomenology' and 'For the young Germans': Levinas, 'Freiburg, Husserl, and Phenomenology', in *Discovering Existence with Husserl*, 32–46, this 32, 37. For Levinas's own discovery story, see interview in Raoul Mortley, *French Philosophers in Conversation* (London & New York: Routledge, 1991), 11–23, this 11.

36 'Real little Buddha': Sartre, *War Diaries*, 123.

36 'At Husserl's expense': ibid., 184.

36 Blond hair: memories of a former schoolmate as quoted in Andrew D. Osborn, *The Philosophy of Edmund Husserl: in its development from his mathematical interests to his first conception of phenomenology in Logical Investigations* (New York: Columbia University/International Press, 1934), 11; also see Spiegelberg, 'The Lost Portrait of Edmund Husserl', 342, quoting Husserl's daughter and reproducing images of the portrait.

36 'Watchmaker' and 'the fingers': Gadamer, *Philosophical Apprenticeships*, 35, the watchmaker comparison being quoted from a friend, Fyodor Stepun.

37 Film: *A Representation of Edmund Husserl*, film by James L. Adams (1936), available online at http://www.husserlpage.com/hus_imag.html. Taken from a video cassette produced by the Center for Advanced Research in Phenomenology, Florida Atlantic University, Boca Raton, Florida, c.1991.

37 Pocketknife: Husserl told the story to Levinas, who passed it on to S. Strasser, the editor of the *Husserliana* edn (*Hussserliana* I:xxix); it is retold in Karl Schuhmann, *Husserl-Chronik* (The Hague: Martinus Nijhoff, 1977), 2. Husserl's comment, 'I wonder whether . . .' comes from a version heard by Beauvoir and noted in her diary: Beauvoir, *Wartime Diary*, 161 (18 Nov. 1939).

37 'In the habit of falling': Andrew D. Osborn, *The Philosophy of Edmund Husserl* (New York: Columbia University/International Press, 1934), 11.

37 Brentano: Husserl, 'Recollections of Franz Brentano' (1919), in *Shorter Works*, eds P. McCormick & F. Elliston (Notre Dame, IN: University of Notre Dame Press, 1981), 342–8. Also see T. Masaryk & K. Čapek, *President Masaryk Tells his Story* (London: G. Allen & Unwin, 1934), 104–5, and Moran, *Introduction to Phenomenology*, 23–59.

38   Husserl's grief and depression: see Moran, *Introduction to Phenomenology*,
      80–81, and Kisiel & Sheehan, *Becoming Heidegger*, 360 (Husserl to
      Heidegger, 10 Sept. 1918), 401 (Husserl to Pfänder, 1 Jan. 1931).

39   Kindergarten: Borden, *Edith Stein*, 5. 'I am to stay': Stein, *Self-Portrait
      in Letters*, 6 (Stein to Roman Ingarden, 28 Jan. 1917).

39   'Most distressing': Dorion Cairns, *Conversations with Husserl and Fink*,
      ed. by the Husserl Archives in Louvain (The Hague: Martinus Nijhoff,
      1976), 11 (13 Aug. 1931).

39   '*A new way*' and 'to see what stands': Husserl, *Ideas*, 39.

40   'Give me my coffee': Moran, *Husserl*, 34, citing and translating Gerda
      Walther's account of a seminar in 1917, from Walther, *Zum anderen Ufer*
      (Remagen: Reichl 1960), 212. Heidegger, by contrast, preferred tea: see
      Walter Biemel, 'Erinnerungen an Heidegger', in *Allgemeine Zeitschrift
      für Philosophie*, 2/1 (1977), 1–23, this 10–11. For more recent philosophising
      about coffee, see Scott F. Parker & Michael W. Austin (eds), *Coffee: phil-
      osophy for everyone: grounds for debate* (Chichester: Wiley-Blackwell, 2011),
      and David Robson, 'The Philosopher Who Studies the Experience of
      Coffee' (an interview with David Berman of Trinity College, Dublin),
      BBC Future blog, 18 May 2015: http://www.bbc.com/future/
      story/20150517-what-coffee-says-about-your-mind.

42   Music and phenomenology: see, for example, Thomas Clifton, *Music
      As Heard: a study in applied phenomenology* (New Haven & London: Yale
      University Press, 1983).

42   Sacks' leg: Sacks, *A Leg to Stand On*, 91, 96. On medicine and phenom-
      enology, see works including S. K. Toombs, *The Meaning of Illness: a
      phenomenological account of the different perspectives of physician and patient*
      (Dordrecht: Kluwer, 1992), and Richard Zaner, *The Context of Self: a
      phenomenological inquiry using medicine as a clue* (Athens, OH: Ohio
      University Press, 1981). For many other applications of phenomenology,
      see Sebastian Luft and Søren Overgaard (eds), *The Routledge Companion
      to Phenomenology* (London & New York: Routledge, 2012).

44   Jaspers and Husserl letters: Jaspers, *Philosophy* I, 6–7 (1955 epilogue),
      quoting both; also see Kirkbright, *Karl Jaspers*, 68–9, citing Jaspers to
      his parents, 20 Oct. 1911.

44   '*A different thinking*': Jaspers, *Philosophy of Existence*, 12.

45   In love, something is loved: Brentano, *Psychology from an Empirical
      Standpoint*, 88.

46   'To wrest oneself' and 'in a nice warm room': Sartre, 'A Fundamental

Idea of Husserl's Phenomenology: intentionality', in *Critical Essays* (*Situations I*) 40–6, this 42–3 (originally published in 1939).

47 Sartre was already becoming aware: Sartre developed his analysis of Husserl further in *The Transcendence of the Ego*, tr. A. Brown, foreword by S. Richmond (London: Routledge, 2004) (originally published in *Recherches philosophiques* in 1934).

48 'Withdraw into himself': Husserl, *Cartesian Meditations*, 2. Also see Paul S. MacDonald, *Descartes and Husserl: the philosophical project of radical beginnings* (Albany: SUNY Press, 2000).

48 Augustine: Husserl, *Cartesian Meditations*, 157.

49 Debate and 'dear old leather sofa': Stein, *Self-Portrait in Letters*, 10–11 (Stein to Roman Ingarden, 20 Feb. 1917); also see Alasdair MacIntyre, *Edith Stein: a philosophical prologue* (London & New York: Continuum, 2006), 103–5. Her thesis: Stein, *On the Problem of Empathy*. Her doctorate was awarded in Freiburg in 1916, and the dissertation published in Halle, 1917.

49 Hamburg: Stein, *Self-Portrait in Letters*, 36 (Stein to Fritz Kaufmann, 8 Nov. 1919).

49 Converting and later career: Borden, *Edith Stein*, 6–10.

Chapter 3: The Magician from Messkirch

50 'For manifestly': BT, 19/1. The quotation is from Plato's *The Sophist*, 244A, where it appears in a discussion of the word 'to be'. Heidegger taught a lecture course on *The Sophist* at Marburg in 1924–5, attended by Hannah Arendt among others: see Heidegger, *Plato's Sophist*, tr. R. Rojcewicz & A. Schuwer (Bloomington & Indianapolis: Indiana University Press, 1997).

50 'The sky *is* blue' and 'I *am* happy': BT, 23/4 (giving 'merry'); Heidegger, *Being and Time*, tr. Stambaugh, 3 (giving 'happy').

50 Why is there anything?: Gottfried von Leibniz, 'The Principles of Nature and Grace, Based on Reason' (1714), in *Discourse on Metaphysics and Other Writings*, ed. P. Loptson, tr. R. Latta & G. R. Montgomery, rev. P. Loptson (Peterborough, ON: Broadview Press, 2012), 103–13, this 108–9 (paragraph 7).

50 'The great master of astonishment' and 'put a radiant obstacle': Steiner, *Martin Heidegger*, 158.

51 Praise: BT, 62/38; dedication: BT, 5.

51   Brentano's thesis: Heidegger, 'A Recollection (1957)', in Sheehan (ed.),
        Heidegger: the man and the thinker, 21–2, this 21. The thesis: Franz Brentano,
        On the Several Senses of Being in Aristotle, tr. Rolf George (Berkeley:
        University of California Press, 1973).

51   Heidegger siblings: Marie Heidegger, born 1891, grew up to marry a
        chimney sweep, and died in 1956. On her and on Heidegger's mother,
        see F. Schalow & A. Denker, *Historical Dictionary of Heidegger's Philosophy*,
        2nd edn (London: Scarecrow, 2010), 134. Fritz was born in 1894.

51   Bells: Heidegger, 'Vom Geheimnis des Glockenturms', in his GA, 13
        (*Aus der Erfahrung des Denkens*, 113–16); also see Heidegger, 'The Pathway',
        in Sheehan (ed.), *Heidegger: the man and the thinker*, 69–72, this 71; and
        Safranski, *Martin Heidegger*, 7. For other early memories, see Heidegger,
        'My Way to Phenomenology', tr. Stambaugh, in *On Time and Being*,
        74–82.

52   Cooper: the list is from https://en.wikipedia.org/wiki/Cooper_
        (profession).

52   Collecting wood, etc.: Heidegger, 'The Pathway', in Sheehan (ed.),
        Heidegger: the man and the thinker, 69–72, this 69.

53   Glass globe, etc.: Heidegger, *Letters to his Wife*, 5 (13 Dec. 1915).

53   Path and bench: Heidegger, 'The Pathway', in Sheehan (ed.), *Heidegger:
        the man and the thinker*, 69–72, this 69.

53   Meeting people's eyes: Löwith, *My Life in Germany*, 45.

53   'Martin?': Gadamer interviewed in *Human, All Too Human* (BBC, 1999),
        episode 2.

54   Borrowing *Logical Investigations*: Safranski, *Martin Heidegger*, 25; Ott,
        Heidegger, 57.

54   Hermann Heidegger: his letter in Heidegger, *Letters to his Wife*, 317.

55   *Symphilosophein*: Kisiel & Sheehan, *Becoming Heidegger*, 357 (Husserl to
        Heidegger, 30 Jan. 1918).

55   'O your youth': ibid., 359 (Husserl to Heidegger, 10 Sept. 1918).

55   Postscripts and chatterbox: ibid., 361 (Husserl to Heidegger, 10 Sept.
        1918).

55   Marvelling: see Ott, *Heidegger*, 181 (Husserl to Pfänder, 1 Jan. 1931).

55   'Phenomenological child': Jaspers, 'On Heidegger', 108–9.

55   'I truly had the feeling': Kisiel & Sheehan, *Becoming Heidegger*, 325
        (Heidegger to Husserl, 22 Oct. 1927).

55   'Foggy hole': Ott, *Heidegger*, 125.

55   Todtnauberg hut: see Sharr, *Heidegger's Hut*. Sharr also wrote about

Heidegger's town house: Sharr, 'The Professor's House: Martin Heidegger's house in Freiburg-im-Breisgau', in Sarah Menin (ed.), *Constructing Place: mind and matter* (New York: Routledge, 2003), 130–42.

56 Rhythm of chopping wood: Arendt & Heidegger, *Letters*, 7 (Heidegger to Arendt, 21 March 1925).

56 'One's ownmost' look: Löwith, *My Life in Germany*, 45; also see Petzet, *Encounters and Dialogues*, 12. Gadamer describes him wearing skiing clothes (to give a special lecture on skiing, in Marburg), and says the students called his usual clothes his 'existential outfit': Gadamer, *Philosophical Apprenticeships*, 49.

56 'Impenetrable': Löwith, *My Life in Germany*, 28.

57 'Because he was much more difficult': Hans Jonas, 'Heidegger's resoluteness and resolve', in Neske & Kettering (eds), *Martin Heidegger and National Socialism*, 197–203, this 198. (A radio interview.)

57 'Breathtaking swirl' and 'deep dark clouds': Gadamer, *Philosophical Apprenticeships*, 48.

57 'Little magician from Messkirch': Löwith, *My Life in Germany*, 44–5.

57 Thinking and digging: Arendt, 'Martin Heidegger at Eighty', in Murray (ed.), *Heidegger and Modern Philosophy*, 293–303, this 295–6.

57 'A ponderous device': Daniel Dennett and Asbjørn Steglich-Petersen, 'The Philosophical Lexicon', 2008 edn: http://www.philosophicallexicon.com.

57 'Masterfully staged', 'We do not Heideggerize' and 'How can Heidegger': Georg Picht, 'The Power of Thinking', in Neske & Kettering (eds), *Martin Heidegger and National Socialism*, 161–7, this 161, 165–6.

58 'Thinking has come to life': Arendt, 'Martin Heidegger at Eighty', in Murray (ed.), *Heidegger and Modern Philosophy*, 293–303, this 295.

58 'Wordlessly, expectantly': Safranski, *Martin Heidegger*, 147, quoting Hermann Mörchen's manuscript 'Aufzeichnungen'.

59 Pointing to Being: see Heidegger, *Introduction to Metaphysics*, 35. My explanation here owes much to Magda King's classic *Guide to Heidegger's Being and Time*, 16.

59 'Ontological difference': BT, 26/6. Being and beings: English doesn't have such a convenient pair of terms as German, so translators either use 'entity' for *Seiende* or distinguish between 'being' and 'Being' using the capital letter. Macquarrie & Robinson use both, while Stambaugh uses 'being' and 'beings' but often adds the German as well.

59 Vague, preliminary, non-philosophical understanding of Being: BT, 25/6; BT, 35/15.

59 'Ontical': BT, 71/45ff.

60 Corbin and *réalité humaine*: Heidegger, *Qu'est-ce que la métaphysique?*, tr. H. Corbin (Paris: Gallimard, 1938).

60 Spuds, rats: Günter Grass, *Dog Years*, tr. Ralph Manheim (London: Penguin, 1969), 324, 330 (translation amended slightly).

61 'Felt strangeness': Steiner, *Martin Heidegger*, 11.

61 Brecht: see Safranski, *Martin Heidegger*, 155.

61 'Awkwardness': BT, 63/39.

61 'Ahead-of-itself . . .': Heidegger, *Being and Time*, tr. Stambaugh, 312/327; Heidegger, *Sein und Zeit*, 327.

61 Stein: Gertrude Stein, *The Making of Americans: being a history of a family's progress* (Normal, IL & London: Dalkey Archive Press, 1995). 'I am always feeling': 373. 'Always I am feeling in each one of them': 383. 'Can be slimy, gelatinous': 349. See Janet Malcolm, *Two Lives* (New Haven & London: Yale University Press, 2007), 126. (The novel was written between 1902 and 1911, well before Heidegger.)

63 'Everydayness': BT, 37–8/16; also see BT, 69/43.

63 Being-in-the-world: BT, 78/52ff.

63 *Das Hammerding*: Heidegger, *Sein und Zeit*, 69. In translation: BT, 98/69.

63 Care and concern: BT, 83–4/56–8.

64 'Equipment': BT, 97/68 translates *das Zeug* as 'equipment', but I prefer Stambaugh's 'useful thing': Heidegger, *Being and Time*, tr. Stambaugh, 68/68.

64 'Readiness-to-hand' vs 'presence-at-hand': BT, 98–9/69–70. Stambaugh uses 'handiness' for *Zuhandenheit*: Heidegger, *Being and Time*, tr. Stambaugh, 69/69.

64 Revealing a world: BT, 149/114.

64 Heidegger's table: Heidegger, *Ontology: the hermeneutics of facticity*, 69, cited in Aho, *Existentialism*, 39.

64 *Mitsein*: BT, 149/114. *Mitwelt*: BT, 155/118.

64 'From whom, for the most part': BT, 154/118.

65 'Deficient' mode of Being-with: BT, 156–7/120.

65 Boat: BT, 154/118.

66 'States the obvious': Safranski, *Martin Heidegger*, 155.

66 Husserl's marginalia: 'Husserl's Marginal Remarks in Martin Heidegger, *Being and Time*', in Husserl, *Psychological and Transcendental Phenomen-*

ology and the Confrontation with Heidegger (1927–1931), 258–422, esp. 283 ('But that is absurd', on p. 12 of 1927 edn), 419, 422 (interrobangs, on pp. 424 and 437 of 1927 edn). On Husserl's readings, see Sheehan, 'Husserl and Heidegger', in same volume, 1–32, esp. 29. 'Nonsense!': Kisiel & Sheehan, *Becoming Heidegger*, 402 (Husserl to Pfänder, 1 Jan. 1931).

66 'Ludicrous': Kisiel & Sheehan, *Becoming Heidegger*, 372 (Heidegger to Löwith, 20 Feb. 1923). 'He lives with the mission': Heidegger & Jaspers, *The Heidegger–Jaspers Correspondence*, 47 (Heidegger to Jaspers, 14 July 1923).

66 *Encyclopaedia Britannica*: Husserl, '"Phenomenology" (Draft B of the *Encyclopaedia Britannica* Article), with Heidegger's Letter to Husserl', in Kisiel & Sheehan, *Becoming Heidegger*, 304–28. A fuller version with variant drafts: Husserl, 'The *Encyclopaedia Britannica* article (1927–28)', in Husserl, *Psychological and Transcendental Phenomenology and the Confrontation with Heidegger* (1927–1931), 35–196, including introduction by Sheehan relating the story of their collaboration. The entry, tr. C. V. Salmon, was published in *Encyclopaedia Britannica*, 14th edn (London: Encyclopaedia Britannica Co., 1929). On not expressing themselves clearly: see Heidegger, *Letters to his Wife*, 108 (Martin to Elfride Heidegger, 5 Feb. 1927), and Kisiel & Sheehan, *Becoming Heidegger*, 402 (Husserl to Pfänder, 1 Jan. 1931).

66 Husserl's hopes: Kisiel & Sheehan, *Becoming Heidegger*, 401–2 (Husserl to Pfänder, 1 Jan. 1931).

67 Heidegger's speech: Heidegger, 'For Edmund Husserl on his Seventieth Birthday' (8 April 1929), tr. Sheehan, in Husserl, *Psychological and Transcendental Phenomenology and the Confrontation with Heidegger* (1927–1931), 475–7, this 475. Husserl's speech in reply: Kisiel & Sheehan, *Becoming Heidegger*, 418–20.

68 'An appointed leader': Kisiel & Sheehan, *Becoming Heidegger*, 402 (Husserl to Pfänder, 1 Jan. 1931).

68 'Common sense': Friedrich Heinemann quotes him as saying, in 1931, 'Heidegger moves on the level of common sense' (*bewegt sich in der die natürlichen Einstellung*). Heinemann, *Existentialism and the Modern Predicament*, 48.

68 'Anthropology': Husserl, 'Phenomenology and Anthropology' (a lecture of June 1931), in Husserl, *Psychological and Transcendental Phenomenology and the Confrontation with Heidegger* (1927–1931), 485–500, this 485.

69 'The Being-just-present-at-hand . . .': BT, 103/73. German: Heidegger, *Sein und Zeit*, 73.

69   'Slumps toothlessly': Nicholson Baker, *The Mezzanine* (London: Granta, 1998), 13–14.

69   'The *obstinacy*': BT, 103–4/74. Lights up the project: BT, 105/75.

70   Chandos: Hugo von Hofmannsthal, 'The Letter of Lord Chandos', tr. Tania & James Stern, in his *The Whole Difference: selected writings*, ed. J. D. McClatchy (Princeton & Oxford: Princeton University Press, 2008), 69–79 (originally published in *Der Tag*, 18–19 Oct. 1902).

70   Breakdown: for example, Matthew Ratcliffe draws attention to the experience of James Melton, whose account of depression describes a withdrawal in which he cannot work out even how to approach a chair to sit down on it, as the world has 'lost its welcoming quality'; Heidegger might say he had no *concern* with things. See Melton's account in Gail A. Hornstein, *Agnes's Jacket* (New York: Rodale, 2009), 212–13, and Matthew Ratcliffe, 'Phenomenology as a Form of Empathy', *Inquiry* 55(5) (2012), 473–95. See also cases discussed in Oliver Sacks, *The Man Who Mistook his Wife for a Hat* (London: Picador, 2011).

71   Heidegger reading *The Magic Mountain*: Safranski, *Martin Heidegger*, 185.

71   Davos: the conference ran from 17 March to 6 April 1929, with around 300 scholars and students attending. See Cassirer and Heidegger, *Débat sur le Kantisme et la philosophie*; Gordon, *Continental Divide*; Michael Friedman, *A Parting of the Ways: Carnap, Cassirer, and Heidegger* (Chicago & La Salle, IL: Open Court, 2000), and Calvin O. Schrag, 'Heidegger and Cassirer on Kant', *Kant-Studien* 58 (1967), 87–100. See also Heidegger, *Kant and the Problem of Metaphysics*, 5th edn, tr. R. Taft (Bloomington: Indiana University Press, 1997). On the influence of Kant on Husserl and Heidegger, see Tom Rockmore, *Kant and Phenomenology* (Chicago & London: University of Chicago Press, 2011).

72   Seeing one world end: F. Poirié, *Emmanuel Lévinas: qui êtes-vous?* (Paris: La Manufacture, 1987), 79. Not everyone agrees with this stark interpretation: see Gordon, *Continental Divide*, 1.

72   'As awkward as a peasant', etc.: Toni Cassirer, *Mein Leben mit Ernst Cassirer* (Hildesheim: Gerstenberg, 1981), 181–3, tr. Peter Collier in P. Bourdieu, *The Political Ontology of Martin Heidegger* (Cambridge: Polity, 1991), 48–9. Maurice de Gandillac, who was there, explicitly compared Heidegger's appeal to that of Hitler: Gandillac, *Le siècle traversé*, 134.

72   Levinas's lampoon and regrets: Gordon, *Continental Divide*, 326–7, citing interview with Richard Sugarman, who spoke to Levinas in 1973.

72   'What Is Metaphysics?': Heidegger, 'What Is Metaphysics?', in *Basic Writings*, 81–110, this 95.

73   'The total strangeness of beings': ibid., 109. (On uncanniness, see also BT, 233/188.)

73   'Why are there beings': ibid., 112.

73   'The things of the world': Petzet, *Encounters and Dialogues*, 12.

73   Rejecting Heidegger's work and 'I arrived at the distressing conclusion': Kisiel & Sheehan, *Becoming Heidegger*, 398 (Husserl to Ingarden, 2 Dec. 1929), and 403 (Husserl to Pfänder, 1 Jan. 1931).

Chapter 4: The They, the Call

74   Heidegger after First World War: see Heidegger, *Letters to his Wife*, 55 (17 Oct. 1918).

74   Aron in Germany: Aron, *The Committed Observer*, 26.

74   Weil in Germany: Weil, 'The Situation in Germany', in *Formative Writings*, 89–147, this 97–8 (originally published in *L'ecole émancipée*, 4 Dec. 1932 to 5 March 1933).

75   Weil on revolutionary potential: ibid., 106.

75   Mail surveillance, etc.: Haffner, *Defying Hitler*, 96.

75   Beauvoir on not worrying: POL, 146.

75   Murder and oddity stories: POL, 130.

76   Rome trip: POL, 153–4.

76   'I rediscovered irresponsibility': Sartre, 'Cahier Lutèce', in *Les mots et autres écrits autobiographiques*, 907–35, this 210 (a notebook written sometime between 1952–4).

76   Beauvoir's visits: POL, 180, 184 (Feb.); POL, 191–6 (June).

76   Blood on mayonnaise: POL, 147.

76   Jaspers on his mistake: Jaspers, 'On Heidegger', 119. Beauvoir on French students: POL, 180. For others, see also Haffner, *Defying Hitler*, 156, and Fest, *Not I*, 42.

77   Raising an arm: Bruno Bettelheim, *The Informed Heart* (Harmondsworth: Penguin, 1986), 268.

77   Uncanniness, anaesthesia, yoked: Haffner, *Defying Hitler*, 112, 126.

77   Fragmentation and demagogues: Arendt, *The Origins of Totalitarianism*, 317, 478.

77   'Banality of evil': Arendt, *Eichmann in Jerusalem: a report on the banality of evil.*

77   *Think!*: see Arendt, *The Life of the Mind*, I, 5.

77   *Was heisst denken?*: the English translation renders it as *What Is Called Thinking?*

78   *Das Man*: BT, 164/126.

78   Responsibility/answerability: Stambaugh has 'responsibility', M&R 'answerability': BT, 165/127; Heidegger, *Being and Time*, tr. Stambaugh, 127/124.

78   Voice: BT, 313/268. Calls Dasein to itself: BT, 319/274. 'Not at home' form: BT, 321/276–7.

79   Schickele: quoted in Ott, *Heidegger*, 136.

79   Anti-Semitic remarks: Kisiel & Sheehan, *Becoming Heidegger*, 413 (Husserl to Dietrich Mahnke, 4–5 May 1933).

79   Arendt: her questions are not preserved, but his answer is, in Arendt and Heidegger, *Letters*, 52–3 (Heidegger to Arendt, undated but winter 1932/3).

80   Book-burning: Ott, *Heidegger*, 189, 194.

80   'Black Notebooks': Heidegger, *Überlegungen*, ed. Peter Trawny, GA, 94–6 (2014), generally referred to as the *Schwarze Hefte* (Black Notebooks), and containing his notes from 1931 to 1941. Heidegger wished them to be published last in his collected edn, and their appearance has caused much debate. See for example Richard Wolin, 'National Socialism, World Jewry, and the History of Being: Heidegger's Black Notebooks', *Jewish Review of Books* (6 Jan. 2014), Peter Trawny, 'Heidegger et l'antisémitisme', *Le Monde* (22 Jan. 2014), Markus Gabriel, 'Der Nazi aus dem Hinterhalt', *Die Welt* (13 Aug. 2014), G. Fried, 'The King is Dead: Heidegger's "Black Notebooks"', *Los Angeles Review of Books* (13 Sept. 2014), and Peter E. Gordon, 'Heidegger in Black', *New York Review of Books* (9 Oct. 2014), 26–8. For a fuller commentary by the volumes' editor, see Peter Trawny, *Freedom to Fail: Heidegger's anarchy* (Cambridge: Polity, 2015). The discovery led Professor Günter Figal, chair of the Martin Heidegger Society in Germany, to resign in Jan. 2015, saying that he no longer wished to represent Heidegger. For much earlier background and evidence on Heidegger's Nazism, see Ott, *Heidegger*, and Wolin (ed.), *The Heidegger Controversy*.

80   Rectorial address: Heidegger, 'The Self-Assertion of the German University' (27 May 1933), tr. William S. Lewis, in Wolin (ed.), *The Heidegger Controversy*, 29–39, quoted sections 34–6. Also see contemporary

newspaper reports in Guido Schneeberger, *Nachlese zu Heidegger: Dokumente zu seinem Leben und Denken* (Berne: Suhr, 1962), 49–57; and Hans Sluga, *Heidegger's Crisis: philosophy and politics in Nazi Germany* (Cambridge, MA: Harvard University Press, 1993), 1–2.

80 Declaration: Heidegger, 'Declaration of Support for Adolf Hitler and the National Socialist State', 11 Nov. 1933, tr. in Wolin (ed.), *The Heidegger Controversy*, 49–52, this 51.

80 Summer camps: Ott, *Heidegger*, 228–9, citing Heidegger's letter of 22 Sept. 1933 to university teaching staff.

81 Husserl's status: ibid., 176

81 Flowers and letter: Elfride Heidegger to Malvine Husserl, 29 April 1933. The letter survives only as a copy transcribed by Frédéric de Towarnicki in his 'Visite à Martin Heidegger', *Les Temps modernes* (1 Jan. 1946), 717–24, this 717–18, here as translated in Kisiel & Sheehan, *Becoming Heidegger*, 411–12. For the Husserls' response, see Kisiel & Sheehan, 412–13 (Husserl to Dietrich Mahnke, 4–5 May 1933), and Ott, *Heidegger*, 174–7.

81 Disappearing dedication: Ott, *Heidegger*, 173.

82 Border situations: Jaspers, *Philosophy* II, 178–9. Lived, existential situations: 159, 335–6.

82 Expecting to die young: Gens, *Karl Jaspers*, 50, citing Gertrud Jaspers to Arendt, 10 Jan. 1966. Managing energies: 24–7. Breath and pauses: 113–15.

83 Heidegger amazed: Heidegger & Jaspers, *The Heidegger–Jaspers Correspondence*, 162 (Heidegger, draft letter to Jaspers, 6 Feb. 1949).

83 'I think about your study': Arendt & Jaspers, *Hannah Arendt / Karl Jaspers Correspondence*, 29 (Arendt to Jaspers, 29 Jan. 1946).

83 'True philosophy needs *communion*' and 'Uncommunicativeness': Jaspers, *Philosophy* II, 100.

83 Letters, visits and plans: Gens, *Karl Jaspers*, 158; Heidegger & Jaspers, *The Heidegger–Jaspers Correspondence*, 39 (Jaspers to Heidegger, 6 Sept. 1922), 42 (Jaspers to Heidegger, 24 Nov. 1922).

84 Heidegger's silences: Jaspers, 'On Heidegger', 110. Uncanny feeling: Heidegger & Jaspers, *The Heidegger–Jaspers Correspondence*, 40 (Heidegger to Jaspers, 19 Nov. 1922).

84 Revolution needed: Jaspers, 'On Heidegger', 109. Views on style, and the challenge and denial: 111–14.

84 'Estranging': ibid., 112.

84 'One must get in step' and the talk: ibid., 117.

85 'It is just like 1914' and hands: ibid., 118.

85   'Now I must say to myself': Kirkbright, *Karl Jaspers*, 148, citing Gertrud
      Jaspers' letter to her parents, 29 June 1933. Heidegger's rudeness: Arendt
      & Jaspers, *Hannah Arendt/Karl Jaspers Correspondence*, 630 (Jaspers to
      Arendt, 9 March 1966).

85   'Ashamed': Heidegger & Jaspers, *The Heidegger–Jaspers Correspondence*,
      185 (Heidegger to Jaspers, 7 March 1950). Jaspers sceptical: Arendt &
      Jaspers, *Hannah Arendt/Karl Jaspers Correspondence*, 630 (Jaspers to
      Arendt, 9 March 1966).

85   'It was nice to see it': Heidegger & Jaspers, *The Heidegger–Jaspers corres-
      pondence*, 149 (Jaspers to Heidegger, 23 Aug. 1933).

86   Failing Heidegger: Jaspers, 'On Heidegger', 118–20.

86   Realising that life could not continue unaltered: Bruno Bettelheim, *The
      Informed Heart* (Harmondsworth: Penguin, 1986), 258–63.

86   Marcel and crispation: Gabriel Marcel, 'On the Ontological Mystery',
      in his *The Philosophy of Existence*, 1–31, esp. 27.

87   Staying awake: Gabriel Marcel, 'Conversations', in Marcel, *Tragic Wisdom
      and Beyond*, 217–56, this 249. He wrote something similar in *Men Against
      Humanity*, tr. G. S. Fraser (London: Harvill, 1952), 81–3.

87   *Meaning of Dasein's Being is Time*: BT, 39/17.

88   'Being-towards-Death' (*Sein zum Tode*): BT, 279/235.

88   'Anticipatory resoluteness': BT, 351/304. Giving it up: BT, 308/264.

88   Jonas: Hans Jonas, 'Heidegger's resoluteness and resolve', in Neske &
      Kettering (eds), *Martin Heidegger and National Socialism*, 197–203, this
      200–1.

89   Resigning: Ott, *Heidegger*, 240–41, and letter of resignation quoted 249.

89   Restored dedication: ibid., 173, 178.

89   Harassed by party: Heidegger, 'The Rectorate 1933/34: facts and
      thoughts', in Neske & Kettering (eds), *Martin Heidegger and National
      Socialism*, 15–32, this 30–32.

89   'The Rectorate': ibid., 17.

89   '*Dummheit*': Towarnicki, 'Le Chemin de Zähringen', 125.

89   'Dreaming boy': Heidegger & Jaspers, *The Heidegger–Jaspers
      Correspondence*, 186 (Jaspers to Heidegger, 19 March 1950).

90   Berlin academy proposals: Farías, *Heidegger and Nazism*, 197–202, citing
      Heidegger's letter to Wilhelm Stuckart, 28 Aug. 1934; also see Safranski,
      Martin Heidegger, 279–81.

90   Rome and Nazi pin: Löwith, *My Life in Germany*, 59–60.

90   Müller: Max Müller, 'Martin Heidegger: a philosopher and politics: a

conversation', in Neske & Kettering (eds), *Martin Heidegger and National Socialism*, 175–95, this 189–90. (Interview with Bernd Martin and Gottfried Schramm on 1 May 1985.)

91 Responses to Heidegger's Nazism: Heidegger's involvement was well known from the start. Sartre knew of it in 1944, as did the French occupiers in his area of Germany after the war. More was revealed by a major collection of documents published in 1962: Guido Schneeburger's *Nachlese zu Heidegger*. When I was studying Heidegger in the early 1980s, the Nazi question did not loom large, partly because of a then-prevalent view that questions of life and personality were not significant in considering the philosophy. In 1987 this changed, with the Chilean historian Victor Farías's *Heidegger y el Nazismo* (*Heidegger and Nazism*), a work condemning Heidegger's entire philosophy as contaminated by his Nazism. There ensued a 'Heidegger affair', especially in France, with some arguing that Heidegger's philosophy was unaffected by his politics, and others joining Farías's denunciation. Observing from Germany, the Freiburg historian Hugo Ott wrote 'in France a sky has fallen in – *the sky of the philosophers*' (Rockmore, *Heidegger and French Philosophy*, 155). Ott then published his own extensively documented account of Heidegger's Nazi activities in 1992, including much material from the Freiburg city archives: *Martin Heidegger: unterwegs zu seiner Biographie* (*Martin Heidegger: a political life*). The discussion subsided until a new 'Heidegger affair' in 2005 when Emmanuel Faye's *Heidegger* found further Nazi evidence in Heidegger's seminars of 1933–4, and similarly concluded that the philosophy was tainted. A still more recent Heidegger affair began in 2014 with the publication of his private notebooks from 1931 to 1946 (GA, 94–6), showing clear pro-Nazi and anti-Semitic views.

91 Selecting safe elements: for example, American philosopher Marjorie Grene attended Heidegger's lectures and read *Being and Time* in the early 1930s. She agonised over the Nazi question for sixty years, then wrote in her *Philosophical Testament* (1995) that she would have liked to dismiss Heidegger as unimportant but could not, and therefore had decided to preserve what was essential in his thought, assimilate it to a 'more adequate framework', and abandon the rest. Marjorie Grene, *A Philosophical Testament* (Chicago & La Salle, IL: Open Court, 1995), 76–9. Grene's *Heidegger* (New York: Hillary House, 1957) was one of the first books devoted to Heidegger in English.

91 'Solicitude': BT, 157–9/121–2.

92   *No* character: Arendt & Jaspers, *Hannah Arendt / Karl Jaspers Correspondence*,
     142 (Arendt to Jaspers, 29 Sept. 1949).

92   'Heidegger has no character': Sartre, 'A More Precise Characterization
     of Existentialism', in Contat & Rybalka (eds), *The Writings of Jean-Paul
     Sartre*, II, 155–60, this 156. For more on the notion of character in Sartre,
     see Webber, *The Existentialism of Jean-Paul Sartre*.

92   'The darkening of the world': Heidegger, *Introduction to Metaphysics*, 40.

92   'Thin stammering' and 'The manifold uncanny': Heidegger & Jaspers,
     The Heidegger–Jaspers Correspondence, 151 (Heidegger to Jaspers, 1 July 1935).
     This is the 'Ode on Man' chorus from Sophocles, *Antigone* V, 332–75, this
     332. Heidegger's German version is: '*Vielfältig das Unheimliche, nichts doch /
     über den Menschen hinaus Unheimlicheres ragend sich regt*' (GA, 13, 35). The
     line could be rendered more conventionally as 'Wonders are many, and
     none is more wonderful than man' (tr. R. C. Jebb) or 'Many things are
     formidable, and none more formidable than man!' (tr. Hugh Lloyd-Jones).
     The word translated as 'formidable' or 'wonderful' is *deinà* (*deinos*), also
     meaning 'terrible'; it features in Heidegger's later discussions of tech-
     nology. Heidegger's translation, 'Chorlied aus der Antigone des
     Sophocles', is in *Aus der Erfahrung des Denkens*, 35–6; he had it privately
     printed in 1943 as a birthday present for Elfride (GA, 13, 246n).

93   *Die Kehre*: This interpretation was first put forward in 1963 by William
     J. Richardson, an extraordinary American scholar who, as he said, devel-
     oped it while living 'in quasi-isolation as chaplain to a group of
     Benedictine nuns in a renovated Black Forest cloister'. William J.
     Richardson, 'An Unpurloined Autobiography', in James R. Watson (ed.),
     Portraits of American Continental Philosophers (Bloomington: Indiana
     University Press, 1999), 147, cited Woessner, *Heidegger in America*, 200.
     See Richardson, *Heidegger: through phenomenology to thought*. His inter-
     pretation has mostly prevailed since, though some do differ: see for
     example Sheehan, *Making Sense of Heidegger: a paradigm shift*.

93   Rejecting Berlin job, and ensuing quotes below: Heidegger, 'Why Do
     I Stay in the Provinces?', in Sheehan (ed.), *Heidegger: the man and the
     thinker*, 27–30; see also editor's note 30n.

93   Brender: see Walter Biemel, 'Erinnerungen an Heidegger', in *Allgemeine
     Zeitschrift für Philosophie*, 2/1 (1977), 1–23, this 14.

94   'All things become solitary and slow': Heidegger, 'The Thinker as Poet',
     in *Poetry, Language, Thought*, 1–14, this 9. The line has been inscribed as
     a sign above a bench in Todtnauberg.

95   'Personal destiny': Hannah Arendt, 'What Remains? The Language
      Remains', in P. Baehr (ed.), *The Portable Hannah Arendt* (New York:
      Penguin, 2003), 3–22, this 5–6 (an interview with Günter Gaus on West
      German TV, 28 Oct. 1964). Their escape: Young-Bruehl, *Hannah Arendt*,
      105–8.

96   Husserl not leaving Germany: Van Breda, 'Die Rettung von Husserls
      Nachlass und die Gründung des Husserl-Archivs – The Rescue of
      Husserl's *Nachlass* and the Founding of the Husserl-Archives', 47.

96   'He was a strongly monological type': Max Müller, 'Martin Heidegger:
      a philosopher and politics: a conversation', in Neske & Kettering (eds),
      Martin Heidegger and National Socialism, 175–95, this 186 (interview of 1
      May 1985).

96   Husserl's Prague letter: 'Lettre de M. le professeur Husserl: An den
      Präsidenten des VIII. internationalen Philosophen-Kongresses Herrn
      Professor Dr Rádl in Prag', in *Actes du huitième Congrès international de
      Philosophie à Prague 2–7 septembre 1934* (Prague: Comité d'organisation
      du Congrès, 1936), xli-xlv.

97   'Heroism of reason': Husserl, 'Vienna Lecture', in *Crisis*, Appendix I,
      269–99, this 290–99.

97   Publication of *Crisis*: David Carr, 'Introduction', in Husserl, *Crisis*, xvii.

97   Husserl's last words: Ronald Bruzina, *Edmund Husserl and Eugen Fink:
      beginnings and ends in phenomenology, 1928–1938* (New Haven: Yale
      University Press, 2004), 69, citing translated notes made by Husserl's
      daughter Elisabeth Husserl Rosenberg, 'Aufzeichnungen aus Gesprächen
      mit Edmund Husserl während seiner letzten Krankheit im Jahre 1938',
      in the Husserl Archives. On Husserl's illness, see also David Carr,
      'Introduction', in Husserl, *Crisis*, xvii.

97   'He died like a holy man': Malvine Husserl & Karl Schumann, 'Malvine
      Husserls "Skizze eines Lebensbildes von E. Husserl"', Husserl Studies
      5(2) (1988), 105–25, this 118.

97   Fear of desecration of grave: Van Breda, 'Die Rettung von Husserls
      Nachlass und die Gründung des Husserl-Archivs – The Rescue of
      Husserl's *Nachlass* and the Founding of the Husserl-Archives', 66.

97   Heidegger missing funeral: in a 1985 interview, Max Müller recalled that
      Heidegger 'was missing from Husserl's funeral, like most colleagues of
      his faculty, because he was ill'. Max Müller, 'Martin Heidegger: a phil-
      osopher and politics: a conversation', in Neske & Kettering (eds), *Martin
      Heidegger and National Socialism*, 175–95, this 187.

Chapter 5: To Crunch Flowering Almonds

98 Sartre proselytising for Husserl: Merleau-Ponty, 'The Philosophy of Existence', in *Texts and Dialogues*, 129–39, this 134. Beauvoir reading him: POL, 201.

99 'Like waking up': Wilson, *Dreaming to Some Purpose*, 234.

99 Sartre's drug experience: Sartre, 'Notes sur la prise de mescaline' (1935), in *Les mots, etc.*, 1,222–33; also POL, 209–10; and *Sartre By Himself*, 38.

99 Naples: Sartre, 'Foods', in Contat & Rybalka (eds), *The Writings of Jean-Paul Sartre*, II, 60–63.

100 Contingency notebook: Flynn, *Sartre: a philosophical biography*, 15. On the history of *Melancholia* and other manuscript versions in the Bibliothèque nationale, see M. Contat, 'De "Melancholia" à *La nausée*: la normalisation *NRF* de la contingence' (21 Jan. 2007), at ITEM (l'Institut des textes et manuscrits modernes): http://www.item.ens.fr/index.php?id=27113. (Revised version of article originally published in *Dix-neuf/Vingt*, 10 (Oct. 2000)

100 Pebble, doorknob, beer glass: Sartre, *Nausea*, 9–10, 13, 19. 'I must say': 9.

101 'I slumped on the bench': ibid., 190.

102 'Some of These Days': ibid., 35–8. Sartre writes that the song is sung by a 'Negress', but George Cotkin points out that it was more likely to have been the Jewish singer Sophie Tucker, whose signature tune it was: Cotkin, *Existential America*, 162.

102 'Beautiful and hard as steel': Sartre, *Nausea*, 252.

103 Ghost story: Sartre, *Words*, 95–6. Lucien: Sartre, 'The Childhood of a Leader', in *Intimacy*, 130–220, this 138.

103 Berlin tree: Gerassi, *Sartre*, 115 (interview of 23 April 1971).

103 'It's not just a question': Sartre, *Words*, 101.

103 'There is a part of everything': quoted in Francis Steegmuller, *Maupassant: a lion in the path* (London: Macmillan, 1949), 60.

104 Necessity idea from film: POL, 48.

104 Chaplin: POL, 244. Keaton: ASAD, 197.

104 'Wet with existence': Sartre, *Nausea*, 148.

104 Honey and sucking: BN, 628–9. For a note on how to translate '*le visqueux*', see BN, 625n.

105 Marcel gave him the idea: Gabriel Marcel, 'Existence and Human Freedom', in *The Philosophy of Existence*, 36.

105 Fronds of algae: Sartre and Jacques-Laurent Bost in *Sartre By Himself*, 41–2.

106 'Il y a': Levinas, *On Escape*, 52, 56, 66–7. Levinas developed the ideas further in 'Il y a', an article of 1946 incorporated into *De l'existence à l'existant (Existence and Existents)* in 1947. His friend Maurice Blanchot also used the concept.

106 'As if the emptiness were full': Levinas, *Ethics and Infinity*, tr. R. Cohen (Pittsburgh: Duquesne University Press, 1985), 48 (radio interviews with Philippe Nemo, Feb.–March 1981).

106 'As though they no longer': Levinas, *Existence and Existents*, 54.

106 Escape through art, etc.: Levinas, *On Escape*, 69, 73.

106 Observed similarities: see Jacques Rolland, 'Getting Out of Being by a New Path', in ibid., 3–48, this 15 and 103n4; and Michael J. Brogan, 'Nausea and the Experience of the "il y a": Sartre and Levinas on brute existence', *Philosophy Today*, 45(2) (Summer 2001), 144–53.

106 Reading Husserl and Heidegger too much: Sartre, *War Diaries*, 183–4. He returned to Heidegger during the war, reading it in German. Amazingly, no full French translation of *Being and Time* appeared until a privately printed one by Emmanuel Martineau in 1985, then a Gallimard publication by François Vezin in 1986. See Gary Gutting, *French Philosophy in the Twentieth Century* (Cambridge: CUP, 2001), 106n.

106 Should not accept brute Being: Levinas, *On Escape*, 73.

106 'A swelling, like a bubble': Sartre, *Witness to My Life*, 16 (Sartre to Simone Jollivet, undated letter of 1926).

107 Phenomenologists' novels not dull: Beauvoir, 'Literature and Metaphysics', in *Philosophical Writings*, 275.

107 Beauvoir encouraging suspense: POL, 106. Whodunnit: *Sartre By Himself*, 41.

107 Sartre's and Gallimard's titles: Cohen-Solal, *Sartre*, 116.

108 Heavy head: Beauvoir, *She Came to Stay*, 164.

109 'But the situation is concrete': cited by Merleau-Ponty, 'Metaphysics and the Novel', in *Sense and Non-Sense*, 26–40, this 26.

109 'Reality should no longer': POL, 365

109 'It's a table', and other remarks here: Sartre, *War Diaries*, 83–5.

109 'I'm no longer sure': MDD, 344.

110 Women in the École normale supérieure: Moi, *Simone de Beauvoir*, 49.

111 Merleau-Ponty's looks: Beauvoir, *Cahiers de jeunesse*, 362 (29 June 1927).

111 'Limpid', and mother liked him: MDD, 246–8.

111   Happy childhood: Emmanuelle Garcia, 'Maurice Merleau-Ponty: vie et œuvre', in Merleau-Ponty, *Œuvres*, 27–99, this 30, citing radio interview with Georges Charbonnier (22 May 1959). Merleau-Ponty's happy childhood is also mentioned by Beauvoir in MDD, 246 and FOC, 70.

112   'Is present, the dough': Sartre, *The Family Idiot*, I, 141.

112   'He is not violent' and 'I feel myself': Beauvoir, *Cahiers de jeunesse*, 388 (29 July 1927).

112   'A small band of the chosen' and most other remarks in this and following paragraphs: MDD, 246–8.

113   'Oh, how untormented': MDD, 260.

113   Brother: Beauvoir, *Cahiers de jeunesse*, 648 (12 May 1929).

113   'Invulnerable': Lacoin, *Zaza*, 223; MDD, 248. See the letters in Lacoin, *Zaza* for the whole story, especially 357, 363, 369.

114   Bourgeois hypocrisy: Bair, *Simone de Beauvoir*, 151–3; MDD, 359–60.

114   Haircut: Sartre, *Words*, 66.

115   'About contingency, violence': *Sartre By Himself*, 20.

115   Sartre's gang: MDD, 336.

116   Beauvoir not wanting to follow mother: POL, 77.

116   'There was a kind of balustrade': POL, 23.

117   'We dropped it': Beauvoir, *Beloved Chicago Man*, 212 (Beauvoir to Algren, 8 Aug. 1948).

117   Failures in honesty: see Todd, *Un fils rebelle*, 117; Bair, *Simone de Beauvoir*, 172.

117   Necessary and contingent loves: POL, 22.

117   'Languorous excitement' and 'feelings of quite shattering intensity': POL, 63.

118   Sartre on his sexuality: Beauvoir, *Adieux*, 316.

118   'The luminous sparkle', almond trees, lights: MDD, 7.

118   'Jackets and skirts': FOC, 245.

118   Marseilles explorations: POL, 89–90.

118   Mont Mézenc: POL, 217–18.

119   Stuck in a gorge: POL, 93.

119   Alpine fall: POL, 301.

119   Sartre climbing a hill: BN, 475–7.

119   Skiing: BN, 602–5, esp. 605 for waterskiing.

119   Books, pipes, pens: Sartre, *War Diaries*, 251.

120   'On an *evening out*': ibid., 244.

120   Tips, wads of cash: Sartre, 'Self-Portrait at Seventy', in *Sartre in the Seventies (Situations X)*, 3–92, this 68.

120   'Theirs was a new kind of relationship': Bair, *Simone de Beauvoir*, 183.

120   Sea elephant: POL, 19.

121   Beauvoir tending to lose herself: POL, 61.

121   Telling every detail of day: see Lanzmann, *The Patagonian Hare*, 265; cf. Beauvoir, *She Came to Stay*, 17, where she gives this urge to her protagonist Françoise.

121   'But Castor': Alice Schwarzer, *Simone de Beauvoir: conversations 1972–1982*, tr. M. Howarth (London: Chatto & Windus/Hogarth, 1984), 110.

121   Canadian film: Jean-Paul Sartre and Simone de Beauvoir, interviewed by Madeleine Gobeil and Claude Lanzmann, dir. Max Cacopardo, for *Radio Canada* TV broadcast, 15 Aug. 1967.

Chapter 6: I Don't Want to Eat my Manuscripts

122   'Anything rather than war!': David Schalk, *Roger Martin du Gard* (Ithaca: Cornell University Press, 1967), 139n., citing a letter of 9 Sept. 1936, as well as similar lines in a novel. See also Weber, *The Hollow Years*, 19.

123   'I have no wish': POL, 358.

123   'What is so detestable', and buildings falling: David Gascoyne, *Paris Journal 1937–1939* (London: The Enitharmon Press, 1978), 62, 71.

123   Bombs falling, and only tyranny: George Orwell, *Coming Up for Air* (London: Penguin, 1989; originally published 1939), 21, 157.

124   Stream of consciousness: Sartre credits both Woolf and Dos Passos: Sartre, 'Please Insert 1: 1945', in *The Last Chance: Roads of Freedom IV*, 22–3, this 23.

124   Omelettes: Sartre, *The Reprieve*, 192, 232.

124   'A hundred million': ibid., 277.

124   'A philosophy that was not just a contemplation': Sartre, *War Diaries*, 185.

125   Proposal to move Husserl documents to Prague: Josef Novák, *On Masaryk* (Amsterdam: Rodopi, 1988), 145.

125   Malvine Husserl and the rescue of the papers: for this and the whole account that follows, see Van Breda, 'Die Rettung von Husserls Nachlass und die Gründung des Husserl-Archivs – The Rescue of Husserl's *Nachlass* and the Founding of the Husserl-Archives', 39–69.

128   'Les cons!': Sartre ended *The Reprieve* with Daladier saying this on leaving

his plane: Sartre, *Le Sursis* (Paris: Gallimard, 1945), 350; Sartre, *The Reprieve*, 377.

128 Debates on peace: POL, 336.

129 Fink and Landgrebe: see Ronald Bruzina, *Edmund Husserl and Eugen Fink* (New Haven: Yale University Press, 2004), 522, and his 'Eugen Fink and Maurice Merleau-Ponty', in Toadvine & Embree (eds), *Merleau-Ponty's Reading of Husserl*, 173–200, this 175.

129 Husserl portrait: see Husserl, 'Recollections of Franz Brentano' (1919), in *Shorter Works*, eds P. McCormick & F. Elliston (Notre Dame, IN: University of Notre Dame Press, 1981), 342–48, and Spiegelberg, 'The Lost Portrait of Edmund Husserl', 341–2. (Husserl's daughter kept it on the wall of her apartment in Freiburg, and a photograph of it there has been used to reconstruct its appearance: see plates in Spiegelberg.)

129 Brentano papers: J. C. M. Brentano, 'The Manuscripts of Franz Brentano', *Revue internationale de philosophie*, 20 (1966), 477–82, this 479. (The author is Brentano's son.)

129 Husserl Archives: see Husserl-Archiv Leuven, *Geschichte des Husserl-Archivs = History of the Husserl Archives*, and the site http://hiw.kuleuven.be/hua/, as well as a list of *Husserliana* volumes at http://www.husserlpage.com/hus_iana.html.

129 Merleau-Ponty's visit: Van Breda, 'Merleau-Ponty and the Husserl Archives at Louvain', in Merleau-Ponty, *Texts and Dialogues*, 150–61, this 150–52; Bruzina, 'Eugen Fink and Maurice Merleau-Ponty', in Toadvine & Embree (eds), *Merleau-Ponty's Reading of Husserl*, 173–200, this 175. The whole volume is useful on the relationship of their ideas.

130 Unnoticed *Lebenswelt*: Husserl, *Crisis*, 123–4; see also D. Moran, *Husserl's Crisis of the European Sciences and Transcendental Phenomenology: an introduction* (Cambridge & New York: CUP, 2012), 178–217. Husserl's analysis has a lot in common with that of sociologists such as Max Weber and W. I. Thomas, as well as Alfred Schulz, who later wrote an eloquent essay about disruptions to the 'world' of a stranger abroad, partly based on his own experience as an émigré fleeing Nazism (Alfred Schutz, 'The Stranger: an essay in social psychology', *American Journal of Sociology*, 49(6) (May 1944), 499–507). Husserl may also have been influenced by the ethologist Jakob von Uexküll, who wrote of the *Umwelt* or environment experienced by different species. A dog, for example, has a world rich in smells but not in colours. J. von Uexküll, *Theoretical Biology* (London: Kegan Paul, 1926).

130   Proprioception: Husserl, *Crisis*, 107–8; 161–4.

130   Others: ibid., 331–2.

131   Home-world, alien-world and Greeks: Husserl, 'The Vienna Lecture', in *Crisis* (Appendix I), 269–99, especially 279–89.

132   'I know by my own experience': Marcel, 'On the Ontological Mystery', in his *The Philosophy of Existence*, 27.

133   'The largest and, as I actually believe': Dan Zahavi, 'Merleau-Ponty on Husserl: a reappraisal', in Toadvine & Embree (eds), *Merleau-Ponty's Reading of Husserl*, 3–29, this 7, quoting a letter from Husserl to Adolf Grimme, published in Husserl, ed. Iso Kern, *Zur Phänomenologie der Intersubjektivität (Husserliana* XV) (1973), lxvi.

133   *Solaris* sea: Safranski, *Martin Heidegger*, 78.

133   History took hold of them: POL, 359.

134   'Was it preferable?': POL, 372.

134   'Used to cure his chilblains': Koestler, *Scum of the Earth*, 21.

134   Journey to Paris: POL, 375; Beauvoir, *Wartime Diary*, 39 (1 Sept. 1939).

135   University of Louvain: Van Breda, 'Merleau-Ponty and the Husserl Archives at Louvain', in Merleau-Ponty, *Texts and Dialogues*, 150–61, this 152.

135   Husserl's urn: Van Breda, 'Die Rettung von Husserls Nachlass und die Gründung des Husserl-Archivs – The Rescue of Husserl's *Nachlass* and the Founding of the Husserl-Archives', 66. Destruction of the portrait: Spiegelberg, 'The Lost Portrait of Edmund Husserl', 342.

135   Edith and Rosa Stein: Borden, *Edith Stein*, 13–15.

136   Stein's papers: ibid., 16.

136   Valhalla: 'Die heilige Nazi-Gegnerin', *Süddeutsche Zeitung* (17 May 2010).

136   Burial of Malvine Husserl: Van Breda, 'Die Rettung von Husserls Nachlass und die Gründung des Husserl-Archivs – The Rescue of Husserl's *Nachlass* and the Founding of the Husserl-Archives', 66. Husserl's ashes: Herbert Spiegelberg, *The Context of the Phenomenological Movement* (The Hague: Martinus Nijhoff, 1981), 192n.10, citing information from their daughter, Elisabeth Husserl Rosenberg.

Chapter 7: Occupation, Liberation

137   Gas masks, headlights: Beauvoir, *Wartime Diary*, 42–3 (3 Sept. 1939).

137   'Sartre's pipe', and gas mask: ibid., 43–6 (3 Sept. 1939).

137   Blacking out windows: ibid., 58 (11 Sept. 1939).

138   Turning grey: Koestler, *Scum of the Earth*, 40.

138   'Foreign': Camus, *Notebooks 1935–1942*, 170 (March 1940).

138   'No future': ibid., 176 (undated, but early 1940).

138   Sartre writing all day: Beauvoir, *Adieux*, 387–8. Ping-pong: Sartre, *Quiet Moments in a War*, 97 (Sartre to Beauvoir, 6 March 1940).

138   'If the war goes on': Sartre, *Witness to My Life*, 312 (Sartre to Beauvoir, 24 Oct. 1939).

138   Sending books: Beauvoir, *Wartime Diary*, 153 (14 Nov. 1939), and Sartre, *Witness to My Life*, 409 (Sartre to Beauvoir, 15 Dec. 1939).

139   Bost: Beauvoir, *Wartime Diary*, 295 (30 June 1940).

139   'The narrow chest': Merleau-Ponty, 'The War Has Taken Place', in *Sense and Non-Sense*, 139–52, this 141.

139   Aron: Aron, *The Committed Observer*, 66.

139   Merleau-Ponty in hospital: Emmanuelle Garcia, 'Maurice Merleau-Ponty: vie et œuvre', in Merleau-Ponty, *Œuvres*, 27–99, this 43–4.

139   Beauvoir's flight from Paris: Beauvoir, *Wartime Diary*, 272–6 (10 June 1940). Return on German truck: 290 (30 June 1940).

140   'It seems to me': Guéhenno, *Diary of the Dark Years*, 51 (7 Jan. 1941).

140   Nazis in Paris: Beauvoir, *Wartime Diary*, 288 (30 June 1940).

140   'Repugnant': POL, 464.

140   Cooking: POL, 511.

140   Ski clothes in bed: POL, 474. In classes: 504.

140   'I aimed at simplification': POL, 504. Turban: see also Beauvoir, *Wartime Diary*, 166 (22 Nov. 1939).

140   Bourgeois homilies: POL, 465.

141   Reading Hegel and Kierkegaard: Beauvoir, *Wartime Diary*, 304 (6 July 1940); POL, 468–9. See also Beauvoir, *Ethics of Ambiguity*, 159.

141   Reading Heidegger: Sartre, *War Diaries*, 187 (1 Feb. 1940); Sartre, 'Cahier Lutèce', in Sartre, *Les mots, etc.*, 914; also see Cohen-Solal, *Sartre*, 153.

142   'I've begun to write': Sartre, *Quiet Moments in a War*, 234 (Sartre to Beauvoir, 22 July 1940). Her letters arrived: 234 (Sartre to Beauvoir, 23 July 1940).

142   His eyes: Sartre, *War Diaries*, 17 (17 Nov. 1939). Being blind in one eye: Sartre, 'Self-Portrait at Seventy', in *Sartre in the Seventies* (*Situations X*), 3–92, this 3. The escape: Cohen-Solal, *Sartre*, 159.

143   His own skin was the boundary, and 'On my first night': Sartre, 'The Paintings of Giacometti', in *Situations* [IV], 177–92, this 178.

143   Sartre's complaints to Beauvoir: POL, 479–80.

143   Eating her stews: POL, 503–4.

144   Lost briefcase: Cohen-Solal, *Sartre*, 166.

144   'Of not knowing what to do': Sartre, 'Merleau-Ponty', in *Situations* [IV], 225–326, this 231.

144   Paulhan's poems: Paulhan, 'Slogans des jours sombres', *Le Figaro littéraire* (27 April 1946). See Corpet & Paulhan, *Collaboration and Resistance*, 266.

144   Tricolours: Guéhenno, *Diary of the Dark Years*, 101 (17 July 1941).

144   Merleau-Ponty and Sous la botte: Cohen-Solal, *Sartre*, 164; Bair, *Simone de Beauvoir*, 251–2; Sartre, 'Merleau-Ponty', in *Situations* [IV], 225–326, this 231. School and portrait: Marianne Merleau-Ponty, personal communication.

144   Cycling holidays: POL, 490–91. On their visits to Gide, Malraux and others, interpreted as Resistance activity: Lévy, *Sartre*, 291–2.

145   Sartre somersault: POL, 491. Tooth: 495–6; 505.

145   'Gave up their seats' and 'do not go imagining': Sartre, 'Paris Under the Occupation', in *The Aftermath of War* (*Situations III*), 8–40, this 11 (originally published in *La France libre*, 1945).

145   Guéhenno refusing to give directions: Guéhenno, *Diary of the Dark Years*, 195 (22 Feb. 1943).

145   Merleau-Ponty being rude: Merleau-Ponty, 'The War Has Taken Place', in *Sense and Non-Sense*, 139–52, this 141–2.

145   Jewish friends: POL, 512, 525.

146   'You would phone': Sartre, 'Paris Under the Occupation', in *The Aftermath of War* (*Situations III*), 8–40, this 15–16.

146   'It was, precisely, a *nothingness*': POL, 535.

146   'The moment I began living': James Baldwin, 'Equal in Paris', in *The Price of the Ticket*, 113–26, this 114.

146   Meeting Genet: POL, 579–80; see also Beauvoir, *Adieux*, 272.

146   Meeting Camus: POL, 539. 'A simple, cheerful soul': 561. Funny, emotional: FOC, 61. In 2013, the discovery of a brief letter from Camus to Sartre confirmed the warmth of their early friendship: see Grégoire Leménager, 'Camus inédit: "Mon cher Sartre" sort de l'ombre', *Le nouvel observateur* (8 Aug. 2013).

147   Camus' father: see the autobiographical novel, Camus, *The First Man*, 55; Todd, *Camus*, 5–6.

147   World of absences: Camus, *The First Man*, 158.

147   'A certain number of years': Camus, *Notebooks 1935–1942*, 3 (May 1935).

148   Sun: see Camus, 'Three Interviews', in *Lyrical and Critical Essays*, 349–57,
      this 352 (interview with Gabriel d'Aubarède for *Les nouvelles littéraires*,
      10 May 1951).

148   Sun in *The Outsider*: Camus, *The Outsider*, 48, 51, 53.

149   'To the tender indifference': ibid., 111. Inspiration for the novel also came
      from Camus' experiences of travelling in Central Europe in 1937, and
      feeling disoriented because he could not speak the language or under-
      stand how to behave: see Camus, *Notebooks 1935–1942*, 45.

149   'Even within the limits': Camus, 'Preface' (1955), *The Myth of Sisyphus*,
      7. See also David Carroll, 'Rethinking the Absurd: le mythe de Sisyphe',
      in E. J. Hughes (ed.), *The Cambridge Companion to Camus* (Cambridge:
      CUP, 2007), 53–66, esp. 53–7.

149   Sisyphus: Homer, *Odyssey*, Book XI, 593–600.

150   'Weariness tinged with amazement': Camus, *Myth of Sisyphus*, 19. Why
      go on living: 11–13.

150   'One must imagine Sisyphus happy': ibid., 111.

150   'Resigned everything infinitely': Kierkegaard, *Fear and Trembling*, 45.

151   Football, 'is claiming to render', and Hume: Sartre, 'The Outsider
      Explained', in *Critical Essays*, 148–84, this 173. Sartre's example is rugby,
      but I've adapted it in honour of the fact that Camus played football.

152   'A first draft': William Barrett, 'Talent and Career of Jean-Paul Sartre',
      Partisan Review, 13 (1946), 237–46, this 244.

153   'Nothingness': BN, 48. 'Air-pocket': Gabriel Marcel, 'Existence and
      Human Freedom', in *The Philosophy of Existence*, 61.

153   Absence of Pierre: BN, 33–4.

154   Non-being of 200 francs: BN, 35.

154   No cream: the joke is online at http://www.workjoke.com/philosophers-
      jokes.html.

154   'I am nothing': BN, 48.

154   Vertigo: BN, 53, 56.

155   Gambler: BN, 56–7.

155   Alarm clock: BN, 61–2.

155   'So many guard rails': BN, 63.

155   Waiter: BN, 82.

156   'The Queer Feet': Chesterton, 'The Queer Feet', in *The Annotated
      Innocence of Father Brown* (Oxford & NY: OUP, 1988), 64–83.

156   'Lucien can't stand Jews': Sartre, 'The Childhood of a Leader', in
      Intimacy, 130–220, this 216.

156 Bad faith to portray oneself as passive creation: BN, 503.

157 'I have never had a great love': Sartre, *Existentialism and Humanism*, 48.

157 Facticity: BN, 501.

157 Extreme situations: BN, 574.

158 'About freedom': Beauvoir, *Adieux*, 184.

158 Too much of an essayist: Hayman, *Writing Against*, 198, quoting review in *Paris-Soir* (15 June 1943).

159 Why not just rest now?: Beauvoir, 'Pyrrhus and Cineas', in *Philosophical Writings*, 77–150, this 90.

159 Child and lovers: ibid., 97–8.

160 Tingling: POL, 579.

162 'The world and the future': POL, 598. For preceding events: 595–6.

162 Camus on executions: Camus, 'Neither Victims Nor Executioners', 24–43.

162 Tough decisions: Beauvoir, 'An Eye for an Eye', in *Philosophical Writings*, 237–60, esp. 257–8. On the Brasillach trial, see Alice Kaplan, *The Collaborator* (Chicago & London: University of Chicago Press, 2000).

163 'The war really divided': Sartre, 'Self-Portrait at Seventy', in *Sartre in the Seventies (Situations X)*, 3–92, this 48.

163 Ethics: BN, 645, and Sartre, *Notebooks for an Ethics*, tr. D. Pellauer (Chicago & London: University of Chicago Press, 1992) (*Cahiers pour une morale*, 1983).

163 'We are in the world': Merleau-Ponty, 'The War Has Taken Place', in *Sense and Non-Sense*, 139–52, this 147.

163 Authors must live up to their power: Sartre, *What Is Literature? and Other Essays* (Cambridge, MA: Harvard University Press, 1988), 184. For an account of how Sartre became a powerful public intellectual in this era, see Patrick Baert, *The Existentialist Moment* (Cambridge: Polity, 2015).

163 'I must answer that!': FOC, 56.

164 *Les Temps modernes* title from Chaplin: FOC, 22. On seeing it twice and loving it: POL, 244.

164 Merleau-Ponty at *Les Temps modernes*: Vian, *Manual of Saint-Germain-des-Prés*, 141.

164 *Roads of Freedom*, vol. 4: fragments were published in *Les Temps modernes* in 1949, then collected with unpublished manuscript pages to make a fourth volume, *La dernière chance*. On Sartre's claim that the final volume would have solved the enigma of freedom: Michel Contat, 'General Introduction for *Roads of Freedom*', in Sartre, *The Last Chance: Roads of Freedom IV*, 177–97, esp. 193, citing Contat's interview with Sartre,

L'express (17 Sept. 1959). Contat's introduction (195) also cites an unpublished 1974 interview in which Sartre said that Beauvoir's *The Mandarins* was 'the real ending of *Roads of Freedom* as I envisaged it as of 1950, but with another point of view'.

165   Gray in Italy: J. Glenn Gray, *The Warriors: reflections on men in battle* (Lincoln, NE: University of Nebraska Press, 1998), 19–22, (originally published in 1959).

165   'Hardly a day': Marcel, 'Testimony and Existentialism', in *The Philosophy of Existence*, 67–76, this 67 ('Underground' reconverted to 'Métro').

166   'Enormous tenderness': FOC, 93.

166   Vian's manual: Vian, *Manual of Saint-Germain-des-Prés*.

167   'The only one of the philosophers': ibid., 141. Dancing and philosophising: Gréco, *Je suis faite comme ça*, 98–9.

167   'Marseillaise existentialiste': Gréco, *Jujube*, 129; see also Cazalis, *Les mémoires d'une Anne*, 125.

167   'Over the Rainbow': Gréco, *Je suis faite comme ça*, 73.

168   McCoy: Horace McCoy, *They Shoot Horses, Don't They?*, originally published in 1935, was translated as *On achève bien les chevaux* (Paris: Gallimard, 1946).

168   Dos Passos: Sartre, 'On John Dos Passos and *1919*', in *Critical Essays* (*Situations I*), 13–31, this 30. See also his essay 'American Novelists in French Eyes', *Atlantic Monthly* (Aug. 1946), and Beauvoir's 'An American Renaissance in France', in her *'The Useless Mouths' and Other Literary Writings*, 107–12. Also see Richard Lehan, *A Dangerous Crossing: French literary existentialism and the modern American novel* (Carbondale & Edwardsville, IL: Southern Illinois University Press; London & Amsterdam: Feffer & Simons, 1973).

168   Vian and copycat crime: James Sallis, 'Introduction', Vian, *I Spit on Your Graves*, v–vi.

169   Sartre on US mechanisation and workers: Sartre, 'A Sadness Composed of Fatigue and Boredom Weighs on American Factory Workers', in *We Have Only This Life to Live: the selected essays of Jean-Paul Sartre 1939–1975*, eds Ronald Aronson & Adrian Van den Hoven (New York: NYRB, 2013), 108. Originally published in *Combat* (12 June 1945). It later emerged that the FBI watched the journalists closely too, looking for Communist sympathies or troublemaking tendencies. See Cohen-Solal, *Sartre*, 242–3.

169   Sartre never shut up: Lionel Abel, 'Sartre Remembered', in Robert

Wilcocks (ed.), *Critical Essays on Jean-Paul Sartre* (Boston: G. K. Hall, 1988), 13–33, this 15.

169 Camus on travelling: for an example, see Camus, 'Death in the Soul', in *Lyrical and Critical Essays*, 40–51, describing a disoriented stay in Prague.

170 'The morning fruit juices', and Camel: Camus, 'The Rains of New York', in *Lyrical and Critical Essays*, 182–6, this 184.

170 'A European wants to say', and lack of anguish: Camus, *American Journals*, 42–3.

170 Beauvoir posting letters, buying stamps: Beauvoir, *America Day By Day*, 25. For an American audience to see themselves through a stranger's eyes, she also published 'An Existentialist Looks at Americans', *New York Times Magazine* (25 May 1947), reprinted in *Philosophical Writings*, 299–316.

170 'Thrillings' and 'laffmovies': Beauvoir, *America Day By Day*, 36, 214.

171 'Was abundance': FOC, 25.

171 'Untouchables' and 'unseeables': Sartre, 'Return from the United States' (tr. T. Denean Sharpley-Whiting), in Gordon (ed.), *Existence in Black*, 83–9, this 84 (originally published in *Le Figaro*, 16 June 1945).

171 Beauvoir in Harlem: Beauvoir, *America Day By Day*, 1999, 44–5.

171 Gréco and Davis: Gréco, *Je suis faite comme ça*, 135.

172 'How those French boys and girls': Michel Fabre, *Richard Wright: books and writers* (Jackson & London: University Press of Mississippi, 1990), 141 (quoting journal, 5 Aug. 1947). See also Cotkin, *Existential America*, 162.

172 'The knobs': Rowley, *Richard Wright*, 336. Visa difficulties: 328–9.

172 'Women swooned': 'Existentialism', *Time* (28 Jan. 1946), 16–17; 'the prettiest Existentialist': *New Yorker*, 23 (22 Feb. 1947), 19–20. For American reception of existentialism in this era generally, see Fulton, *Apostles of Sartre*, and Cotkin, *Existential America*, especially 105–33.

172 *Partisan Review*: *Partisan Review*, 13 (1946). See Cotkin, *Existential America*, 109, and Cohen-Solal, *Sartre*, 271.

172 *New Republic*: Jean Wahl, 'Existentialism: a preface', *New Republic* (1 Oct. 1945), 442–4.

172 'Thingness of Things': Paul F. Jennings, 'Thingness of Things', *Spectator* (23 April 1948), and *New York Times Magazine* (13 June 1948). See Cotkin, *Existential America*, 102–3.

173 'Grim reminders' and 'banal and meaningless': William Barrett, 'Talent and Career of Jean-Paul Sartre', *Partisan Review*, 13 (1946), 237–46, this 244. See Cotkin, *Existential America*, 120–23.

173   'Crisis in French taste': F. W. Dupee, 'An International Episode', *Partisan Review*, 13 (1946), 259–63, this 263.

173   Gloomy image of existentialists: see, for example, Bernard Frizell, 'Existentialism: post-war Paris enthrones a bleak philosophy of pessimism', *Life* (7 June 1946); and John Lackey Brown, 'Paris, 1946: its three war philosophies', *New York Times* (1 Sept. 1946). See Fulton, *Apostles of Sartre*, 29.

173   Wright on existentialism as optimistic: Rowley, *Richard Wright*, 246, 326–7.

174   Arendt's articles: Arendt, 'French Existentialism' and 'What Is Existenz Philosophy?', both in Arendt, *Essays in Understanding*, 163–87, 188–93. Original versions published in *Partisan Review*, 13 (1) (1946) and *Nation*, 162 (23 Feb. 1946) respectively. See also Walter Kaufmann, 'The Reception of Existentialism in the United States', *Salmagundi*, 10–11, double issue on 'The Legacy of the German Refugee Intellectuals' (Fall 1969–Winter 1970).

Chapter 8: Devastation

175   Nomads: Spender, 'Rhineland Journal', *New Selected Journals*, 34 (July 1945) (ori-ginally published in *Horizon*, Dec. 1945). On German devastation, also see Victor Sebestyén, *1946: the making of the modern world* (London: Macmillan, 2014), especially 38 for homelessness figures.

175   Well over twelve million ethnic Germans: around 12.5 to 13.5 million Germans were expelled from or intimidated into leaving other European countries: see Werner Sollors, *The Temptation of Despair: tales of the 1940s* (Cambridge, MA & London: Belknap/Harvard University Press, 2014), 119; for Europe generally, see Keith Lowe, *Savage Continent: Europe in the aftermath of World War II* (London: Viking, 2012).

176   Lost eyes and 'a delicate smile': Petzet, *Encounters and Dialogues*, 193–5, this 194, translating Max Kommerell's account of visit in 1941. See same source, 45, on Heidegger's feeling misunderstood generally.

176   Fritz Heidegger: Safranski, *Martin Heidegger*, 8. Bietingen: Ott, *Heidegger*, 371.

176   Cave: Heidegger, *Letters to his Wife*, 188 (Martin to Elfride Heidegger, 15 April 1945).

177 Wildenstein: for this whole episode, see Ott, *Heidegger*, 302–5. For works on Hölderlin, see Heidegger, *Elucidations of Hölderlin's Poetry*.

178 'As we were marching' and following quotes: Heidegger, 'Evening Conversation: in a prisoner of war camp in Russia, between a younger and an older man', in *Country Path Conversations*, 132–60, this 132–3.

179 *Verwüstung* and *Wüste*: ibid., 136.

179 'Everything remains overseeable': ibid., 138–9.

179 Wait: ibid., 140.

180 Manuscript pick-up drive: this whole account is from Towarnicki, 'Le Chemin de Zähringen', 87–90, with Towarnicki's transcription and translation of the Sophocles chorus, 91–4.

181 Breakdown: Safranski, *Martin Heidegger*, 351. For dates, see Heidegger, *Letters to his Wife*, 191 (first letter dated 17 Feb. 1946). He had visitors, including his former teacher Conrad Gröber, who found him in a withdrawn state, and Towarnicki (Towarnicki, *À la rencontre de Heidegger*, 19n.) He was looked after by the psychiatrist Viktor Emil Freiherr von Gebsattel and others.

181 Sons: Heidegger, *Letters to his Wife*, 194 (Martin to Elfride Heidegger, 15 March 1946; see also ed.'s note by Gertrude Heidegger, 191). For Jörg still being away in 1949, see Heidegger & Jaspers, *The Heidegger–Jaspers Correspondence*, 165 (Heidegger to Jaspers, 5 July 1949).

181 'His living conditions': Schimanski, 'Foreword', in Heidegger, *Existence and Being*, 2nd edn (London: Vision, 1956), 9–11.

182 Challenging and storing: Heidegger, 'The Question Concerning Technology', in *The Question Concerning Technology and Other Essays*, 3–35, this 12–15.

182 'Places the seed': ibid., 15.

183 'Everything is ordered', and *deinos*: ibid., 16–17.

183 Losing ability to stand as object: ibid., 17.

183 'In the midst of objectlessness': ibid., 27.

183 'Human resources': ibid., 18.

183 'But where danger is': ibid., 28. He is quoting Hölderlin's hymn 'Patmos': 'Wo aber Gafahr ist, wächst / Das Rettende auch.' For the full poem, see Friedrich Hölderlin, *Selected Poems and Fragments*, tr. M. Hamburger, ed. J. Adler (London: Penguin, 1998), 230–31.

183 'Belongingness': Heidegger, 'The Question Concerning Technology, in *The Question Concerning Technology and Other Essays*, 3–35, this 32.

184 Heisenberg: Petzet, *Encounters and Dialogues*, 75.

184   'What seems easier' and 'rest upon itself': Heidegger, 'The Origin of the Work of Art', in *Poetry, Language, Thought*, 15–88, this 31. This work was drafted in 1935 and 1937, and published in 1950 in his collection *Holzwege*.

184   'Poetically, man dwells': Heidegger, 'Letter on Humanism', in *Basic Writings*, 213–65, this 260. The lines come from a late poem by Hölderlin, 'In lovely blue' ('In lieblicher Blaue'), in *Hymns and Fragments*, tr. R. Sieburth (Princeton: Princeton University Press, 1984), 248–53.

185   'Clearing': Heidegger, *Introduction to Metaphysics*, 219.

185   'A way for the cosmos': *Cosmos* (written by C. Sagan, A. Druyan & S. Soter, first broadcast on PBS, 1980), episode 1: 'The Shores of the Cosmic Ocean'.

185   'The landscape thinks itself in me': Merleau-Ponty, 'Cézanne's Doubt', in *Sense and Non-Sense*, 9–25, this 17.

186   Heidegger's anti-humanism and its later influence: see, among others, R. Wolin, 'National Socialism, World Jewry, and the History of Being: Heidegger's Black Notebooks', *Jewish Review of Books* (6 January 2014); Rockmore, *Heidegger and French Philosophy*; Karsten Harries, 'The Antinomy of Being: Heidegger's critique of humanism', in Crowell (ed.), *The Cambridge Companion to Existentialism*, 178–98; Mikel Dufrenne, *Pour l'homme* (Paris: Éditions du Seuil, 1968), and L. Ferry & A. Renaut, *French Philosophy of the Sixties*, tr. M. H. S. Cartani (Amherst, MA: University of Massachusetts Press, 1990).

186   Shoes: Heidegger, 'The Origin of the Work of Art', in *Poetry, Language, Thought*, 15–88, this 33–4.

187   Whose shoes: Meyer Schapiro, 'The Still Life as a Personal Object: a note on Heidegger and Van Gogh' (1968), and 'Further Notes on Heidegger and Van Gogh' (1994) in his *Theory and Philosophy of Art* (New York: G. Braziller, 1994), 135–42, 143–51. See esp. 136–8, on the shoes being Van Gogh's own, and 145, citing fellow student François Gauzi's account of Van Gogh buying old shoes at a Paris flea market – 'the shoes of a carter but clean and freshly polished. They were fancy shoes. He put them on, one rainy afternoon, and went out for a walk along the fortifications. Spotted with mud, they became interesting.' Schapiro also cites Heidegger's own marginal note of uncertainty on a 1960 edn of his own essay (150). For more, see Lesley Chamberlain, *A Shoe Story: Van Gogh, the philosophers and the West* (Chelmsford: Harbour, 2014), esp. 102–28.

188 'Standing there': Heidegger, 'The Origin of the Work of Art', in *Poetry, Language, Thought*, 15–88, this 42. For more on architecture, see Heidegger, 'Building, Dwelling, Thinking', in ibid., 145–61; and Adam Sharr, *Heidegger for Architects* (New York: Routledge, 2007).

188 *A different thinking*': Jaspers, *Philosophy of Existence*, 12.

188 'House of Being': Heidegger, 'Letter on Humanism', in *Basic Writings*, 213–65, this 259, 262.

189 'Came onto the way of thinking': Gadamer, *Philosophical Apprenticeships*, 156.

189 'Babbling' and 'Nobody is likely': Arendt & Jaspers, *Hannah Arendt/ Karl Jaspers Correspondence*, 142 (Arendt to Jaspers, 29 Sept. 1949).

189 'Is this really the way?': Herbert Marcuse and Martin Heidegger, 'An Exchange of Letters', in Wolin (ed.), *The Heidegger Controversy*, 152–64, this 161 (Marcuse to Heidegger, 28 Aug. 1947, tr. Wolin). See also Wolin, *Heidegger's Children*, 134–72.

189 'To former students', 'your letter', and 'in the most loathsome way': ibid., 163 (Heidegger to Marcuse, 20 Jan. 1948, tr. Wolin).

190 'Dismissed from the duty' and 'commandment': Jacques Derrida, 'Heidegger's Silence: excerpts from a talk given on 5 February 1988', in Neske & Kettering (eds), *Martin Heidegger and National Socialism*, 145–8, this 147–8.

190 Holocaust compared to expulsion of Germans: Herbert Marcuse and Martin Heidegger, 'An Exchange of Letters', in Wolin (ed.), *The Heidegger Controversy*, 152–64, this 163 (Heidegger to Marcuse, 20 Jan. 1948, tr. Wolin).

190 'Outside of the dimension': ibid., 164 (Marcuse to Heidegger, 12 May 1948, tr. Wolin).

191 Jasperses' names on list: Mark W. Clark, *Beyond Catastrophe: German intellectuals and cultural renewal after World War II, 1945–1955* (Lanham, MD & Oxford: Lexington, 2006), 52.

191 Jaspers to Switzerland: ibid., 72.

191 'Heidegger's mode of thinking': Ott, *Heidegger*, 32, quoting Jaspers' report on Heidegger, 22 Dec. 1945.

191 'How am I guilty?': Jaspers, *The Question of German Guilt*, 63.

191 'If it happens': ibid., 71.

192 Relearning communication: ibid., 19.

192 Language a bridge: Heidegger & Jaspers, *The Heidegger–Jaspers Correspondence*, 169 (Jaspers to Heidegger, 6 Aug. 1949). The texts sent

probably included Heidegger's 'Letter on Humanism', which contains the phrase 'the house of Being'.

192 'Advent' or 'appropriation' (*Ereignis*): Heidegger & Jaspers, *The Heidegger–Jaspers Correspondence*, 190 (Heidegger to Jaspers, 8 April 1950). *Ereignis* was one of Heidegger's pet notions of this period. See e.g. Heidegger, *Introduction to Metaphysics*, 5–6; Heidegger, *Contributions to Philosophy (From Enowning)* (Bloomington: Indiana University Press, 1999).

192 'Pure dreaming': Heidegger & Jaspers, *The Heidegger–Jaspers Correspondence*, 197 (Jaspers to Heidegger, 24 July 1952).

192 'Dreaming boy': ibid., 186 (Jaspers to Heidegger, 19 March 1950).

193 'When discussion begins': Petzet, *Encounters and Dialogues*, 65–6, citing Stroomann's *Aus meinem roten Notizbuch*. Stroomann, who remained a friend of Heidegger, later specialised in 'manager sickness'. See Josef Müller-Marein, 'Der Arzt von Bühlerhöhe', *Die Zeit* (18 April 1957).

193 'Ovation like a storm': Petzet, *Encounters and Dialogues*, 75.

194 'I quickly learned': Calvin O. Schrag, 'Karl Jaspers on his Own Philosophy', in his *Doing Philosophy with Others* (West Lafayette: Purdue University Press, 2010), 13–16, this 14.

194 It just happened that way: see Arendt & Jaspers, *Hannah Arendt/Karl Jaspers Correspondence*, 630 (Jaspers to Arendt, 9 March 1966).

194 Train time: Ott, *Heidegger*, 26–7.

194 Jaspers' seventieth birthday: Heidegger & Jaspers, *The Heidegger–Jaspers Correspondence*, 199 (Heidegger to Jaspers, 19 Feb. 1953).

194 'I would have taken hold': ibid., 200 (Jaspers to Heidegger, 3 April 1953).

194 'Enchanted in a snowstorm': ibid., 202 (Jaspers to Heidegger, 22 Sept. 1959).

195 Levinas in the camp: Lescourret, *Emmanuel Levinas*, 120; Malka, *Emmanuel Levinas*, 67, and 262 for the taunts (citing conversation with Levinas's son Michael).

195 Camp and hiding: Malka, *Emmanuel Levinas*, 238–9.

195 Levinas's family in Kaunas: Lescourret, *Emmanuel Levinas*, 126–7; Malka, *Emmanuel Levinas*, 80.

195 Levinas's reading: Malka, *Emmanuel Levinas*, 70–71; Lescourret, *Emmanuel Levinas*, 120–23.

195 Notebooks: Levinas, 'Preface', in his *Existence and Existents*, xxvii; Lescourret, *Emmanuel Levinas*, 127; Colin Davis, *Levinas, an Introduction* (Cambridge: Polity, 1996), 17.

195 Horror of ontological difference: Levinas, *Existence and Existents*, 1.

196 'Are also governed': ibid., 4.

196 Dog: Levinas, 'The Name of a Dog, or Natural Rights', in his *Difficult Freedom: essays in Judaism*, tr. S. Hand (London: Athlone Press, 1990), 152–3.

196 Buber: Martin Buber, *I and Thou*, tr. R. G. Smith, 2nd edn (London & NY: Continuum, 2004), 15.

196 Face: Levinas, *Existence and Existents*, 97–9. Also see his first main discussion of the face, in the 1946–7 lectures 'Time and the Other', in Levinas, *Time and the Other, and Additional Essays*, tr. Richard A. Cohen (Pittsburgh: Duquesne University Press, 1987), 39–94. It was never clear whether Levinas believed the face must be human, despite the dog story. When interviewers quizzed him about this, he sounded cross: 'I don't know if the snake has a face. I can't answer that question.' Peter Atterton & Matthew Calarco (eds), *Animal Philosophy* (London & New York: Continuum, 2004), 49, citing 'The Paradox of Morality: an interview with Emmanuel Levinas' (by T. Wright, P. Hughes, A. Ainley), in Robert Bernasconi & David Wood (eds), *The Provocation of Levinas* (London: Routledge, 1988), 168–80, this 171.

198 'He doesn't practise Grandpa's philosophy!': Malka, *Emmanuel Levinas*, 240.

198 Snapping: ibid., 238, quoting a conversation with Levinas's daughter. Interview transcripts with Levinas bear this out.

198 Weil in factory: she worked in 1934 in a plant making electrical parts for trams and metro trains. See Weil, 'Factory Journal', in *Formative Writings*, 149–226, and Gray, *Simone Weil*, 83.

198 Chlorophyll: ibid. 166.

198 None of us has rights: Simone Weil, *The Need for Roots* (London: Routledge & Kegan Paul, 1952), 1–5.

199 Marcel on ethics and mystery: Marcel, 'On the Ontological Mystery', in his *The Philosophy of Existence*, 8–9.

199 Red Cross: Marcel, 'An Essay in Autobiography', in ibid., 90–91.

199 Marcel on mystery: Marcel, 'On the Ontological Mystery,' in ibid., 8–9.

200 'Never allowed themselves': Sartre, *Nausea*, 173. Also see another early Sartre piece, '*Visages*' (1939), in Contat & Rybalka (eds), *Writings of Jean-Paul Sartre*, II, 67–71.

200 Toleration not enough: BN, 431. Similar points made in Sartre, *Anti-Semite and Jew*, tr. G. J. Becker (New York: Schocken, 1948), 55.

200   Heidegger's marvelling at Sartre: Towarnicki, 'Le Chemin de Zähringen',
      30. Beaufret's five articles were published in the journal *Confluences*
      (1945). On his visits, see also Towarnicki, 'Visite à Martin Heidegger',
      in *Les Temps modernes* (1 Jan. 1946), 717–24. On Beaufret and French
      reception of Heidegger in this era, see Kleinberg, *Generation Existential*,
      157–206, and Rockmore, *Heidegger and French Philosophy*.
200   Little time for reading: Towarnicki, 'Le Chemin de Zähringen', 37. Photo
      of Nietzsche: 47–8.
200   Towarnicki's attempts: ibid., 30 (Sartre) and 37 (Camus). Commissioned
      piece: 56–8.
201   'Feeling for concrete things': ibid., 61–3.
201   'Your work is dominated': Wolin, *Heidegger's Children*, 88, translating
      the letter from Towarnicki, 'Le Chemin de Zähringen', 83–5 (Heidegger
      to Sartre, 28 Oct. 1945).
201   *Dreck*: Dreyfus told this story to Bryan Magee in an interview for the
      1987 BBC TV series *The Great Philosophers*: see 'Husserl, Heidegger and
      Modern Existentialism', in Bryan Magee, *The Great Philosophers* (Oxford:
      OUP, 1987), 253–77, this 275.
201   Heidegger, 'Letter on Humanism', which would be hugely influential
      in post-existentialist French philosophy. On this and other aspects of
      Heidegger reception in France, see Janicaud, *Heidegger en France*.
201   'In our little hut': Wolin, *Heidegger's Children*, 88, translating the letter
      from Towarnicki, 'Le Chemin de Zähringen', 83–5 (Heidegger to Sartre,
      28 Oct. 1945).
201   Skiing: Towarnicki, 'Le Chemin de Zähringen', 63; cf. BN, 602–5.
202   'When we were skiing': Max Müller, 'Martin Heidegger: a philosopher
      and politics: a conversation', in Neske & Kettering (eds), *Martin Heidegger
      and National Socialism*, 175–95, this 192.
202   Berlin production: FOC, 153–4; also see Beauvoir, *Beloved Chicago Man*,
      155–63 (Beauvoir to Algren, 31 Jan.–1 Feb. 1948). Sartre may also have
      gone to Berlin less publicly in 1947; the historian Joachim Fest reports
      meeting him then at a private apartment in Charlottenburg (Fest, *Not
      I*, 265). A production of *The Flies* was put on in the French zone of
      Germany in 1947: see Lusset, 'Un episode de l'histoire . . .', 94.
202   'For the Germans': Sartre's article in *Verger*, 2 (June 1947), cited in Lusset,
      'Un episode de l'histoire . . .', 95.
203   Coats, trolleys: Beauvoir, *Beloved Chicago Man*, 158 (Beauvoir to Algren,
      31 Jan.–1 Feb. 1948). On terrible winter, which was one reason why people

were eager to go to the theatre to warm up even if they had to walk there in inadequate shoes: Lusset, 'Un episode de l'histoire . . .', 93–4.

203 Sartre's former lodgings: Sartre, 1979 interview with Rupert Neudeck, 'Man muss für sich selbst und für die anderen leben', *Merkur* (Dec. 1979).

204 'Loud approval': the debate was reported in *Der Spiegel* (7 Feb. 1948). See Lusset, 'Un episode de l'histoire . . .', 91–103; and 'Jean-Paul Sartre à Berlin: discussion autour des *Mouches*', *Verger*, I (5) (1948) 109–23. Several documents are collected here: http://www.sartre.ch/Verger.pdf.

204 Flies: W. G. Sebald, *On the Natural History of Destruction*, tr. A. Bell (London: Hamish Hamilton, 2003), 35, describing Hamburg and citing Hans Erich Nossack, *Interview mit dem Tode*, 238.

205 Sartre's lecture: FOC, 300.

205 Two second-hand reports of meeting between Sartre and Heidegger: FOC, 301; Petzet, *Encounters and Dialogues*, 81–2. Petzet says they spoke in German.

206 Sartre apologising: FOC, 301. Marcel's *La dimension Florestan* was broadcast 17 Oct. 1953, and translated into German as *Die Wacht am Sein* ('The Watch Over Being'), an allusion to the nationalistic song 'Die Wacht am Rhein'. See Marcel, 'Postface', *La dimension Florestan* (Paris: Plon, 1958), 159–62, where he says he admired Heidegger but did not like the liberties he took with language. See also Marcel, 'Conversations', in *Tragic Wisdom and Beyond*, 243, on the German translation.

206 Marcel's attacks on Sartre: Marcel, 'Being and Nothingness,' in *Homo Viator*, 166–84; Marcel, 'Existence and Human Freedom', in his *The Philosophy of Existence*, 32–66, esp. (on grace) 62–6.

206 'With infinite pity': Cau, *Croquis de mémoire*, 253–4

207 'Bouquets of roses!': ibid., 254. This story also told by Towarnicki, 'Le Chemin de Zähringen', 86.

207 'Four thousand': FOC, 301. Old Man of the Mountain: Cau, *Croquis de mémoire*, 253.

Chapter 9: Life Studies

208 Origins of *The Second Sex*: FOC, 103.

208 On collecting stories: Beauvoir, *Beloved Chicago Man*, 208 (Beauvoir to Algren, 26 July 1948).

209 On the shock of reception: FOC, 197–201, esp. Camus, FOC, 200.

210 Voting and other rights: Moi, *Simone de Beauvoir*, 187; Moi points out that Beauvoir did not leap to use her vote, and even said in 1949 that she had never voted; this may have been for political reasons, at a time when the far left advised people against legitimising the state by voting for it.

210 'One is not born': Beauvoir, *The Second Sex*, 293.

210 Being brave: ibid., 296. Fairy tales: 313, 316. Different roles: 320.

211 Clothes and fingernails: ibid., 182.

211 'Positioned in space': Iris Marion Young, 'Throwing Like a Girl: a phenomenology of feminine body comportment, motility and spatiality', in her *On Female Body Experience: 'Throwing Like a Girl' and other essays* (Oxford: OUP, 2005), 41 (originally published in *Human Studies*, 3 (1980), 137–56).

211 Self-consciousness: Beauvoir, *The Second Sex*, 354–6. Self-harming: 377.

211 Genitals: ibid., 296–7.

211 Sex: ibid., 406. Pregnancy: 409–10. Pleasure: 416.

211 Housework and 'dominated by fate': ibid., 655, 654.

211 Female writers: ibid., 760–66.

212 'I carry the weight': BN, 576.

212 Master–slave: on Beauvoir and Hegel, see Bauer, *Simone de Beauvoir, Philosophy, and Feminism*. Sartre, like many others, had been influenced by Alexandre Kojève's series of Hegel lectures in Paris in the 1930s, which emphasised the master–slave analysis.

212 Encounter in a park: BN, 277–9.

213 Keyhole: BN, 384–5.

213 Being looked at as defeated people: Sartre, 'Paris Under the Occupation', in *The Aftermath of War* (*Situations III*), 8–40, this 23.

213 'Hell is other people': Sartre, *No Exit*, in *No Exit and Three Other Plays*, tr. S. Gilbert, 1–46, this 45. For 'Hell is other people' explanation: Contat & Rybalka (eds), *The Writings of Jean-Paul Sartre*, I, 99: a preface for a Deutsche Grammophon recording of the play. For a different interpretation, in which humans make a hell for one another if friendship and trust are lacking, see Beauvoir, 'Existentialist Theater', in *'The Useless Mouths' and Other Literary Writings*, 137–50, this 142.

214 Love: BN, 388–93.

214 'Battle between two hypnotists': Conradi, *Iris Murdoch*, 271 (citing Murdoch's journal entry of 1947).

214 Self-consciousness and mirrors: Beauvoir, *The Second Sex*, 6–7.

215 Object of attraction: ibid., 166.

215 How to be a woman as existentialist problem par excellence: ibid., 17. On the philosophical importance of *The Second Sex*, see Bauer, *Simone de Beauvoir, Philosophy, and Feminism*.

215 Influenced by *Being and Nothingness*: Simons, *Beauvoir and The Second Sex*, x.

215 'It was I': Margaret A. Simons and Jessica Benjamin, 'Beauvoir Interview (1979)', in Simons, *Beauvoir and The Second Sex*, 1–21, this 10 (answering a question by Benjamin).

215 'Fundamental project': BN, 501–2. Thanks to Jay Bernstein for alerting me to this connection. For a subtle analysis of this aspect of Beauvoir's work, see Jonathan Webber, *Rethinking Existentialism* (forthcoming).

216 'Her true nature' and 'Woman's Life Today': see Moi, *Simone de Beauvoir*, xxiii. On the background to the Parshley translation and controversy over it, see Richard Gillman, 'The Man Behind the Feminist Bible', *New York Times* (2 May 1988).

217 Hazel Barnes not simplifying terms: Barnes, *The Story I Tell Myself*, 156.

218 Genet's sympathies with underdog: Genet, interview of 1975 with Hubert Fichte, in Jean Genet, *The Declared Enemy*, 118–151, this 125–6.

218 Genet supporting outsiders: White, *Genet*, 408. Also see Genet, 'Introduction to *Soledad Brother*', in *The Declared Enemy*, 49–55. An extract from his Baader–Meinhof piece was published in *Le Monde* as 'Violence and Brutality' (2 Sept. 1977), and caused a scandal: White, *Genet*, 683.

218 'If they ever win': White, *Genet*, 592.

218 Foreword commission: Andrew N. Leak, *Jean-Paul Sartre* (London: Reaktion Books, 2006), 97.

218 'Freedom alone': Sartre, *Saint Genet*, 584.

219 'You're a thief!': ibid., 17.

219 Asserting label: ibid., 23.

219 Comparison to Beauvoir: Sartre acknowledges the connection: ibid., 37.

219 Sublime elements: ibid., 558. Saint: 205.

220 Pastries in La Rochelle: *Sartre By Himself*, 10. 'No longer someone': Beauvoir, *Adieux*, 355.

220 Baudelaire: Sartre, *Baudelaire*, tr. Martin Turnell (London: Horizon, 1949), 21–3, 87, 91–3.

220 Writing *Words*: he started writing it in 1953, then left it for long periods, before publishing it in 1963 in *Les Temps modernes* and in 1964 as a separate

book. See *Sartre By Himself*, 87, and M. Contat (et al.), *Pourquoi et comment Sartre a écrit 'Les mots'* (Paris: PUF, 1996), 25.

220 'How does a man': Sartre, 'The Itinerary of a Thought' (interview, 1969), in *Between Existentialism and Marxism*, 33–64, this 63.

220 'Neurosis of literature' and 'Farewell to literature': *Sartre By Himself*, 88–9.

221 Labelled an idiot: Sartre, *The Family Idiot*, I,39.

221 Domestic animal: ibid., I:140.

221 'The acrid, vegetative abundance': ibid., I, 143.

222 A 'perpetual questioning': ibid., I, 223.

222 'With him I am at the border': Sartre, 'The Itinerary of a Thought' (interview, 1969), in *Between Existentialism and Marxism*, 33–64, this 44.

222 'Consciousness plays the trick': ibid., 39.

222 Publication of *The Family Idiot*: Sartre, 'On *The Idiot of the Family*', in *Sartre in the Seventies*, 110.

222 'I do not know how many times': ASAD, 55.

223 Translator: see Carol Cosman, 'Translating *The Family Idiot*', *Sartre Studies International*, 1 (1/2) (1995), 37–44.

223 'Feeling at his expense': Sartre, *The Family Idiot*, I, 137–8.

224 Existentialist psychoanalysis: BN, 645–6.

224 Freud screenplay: see J.-B. Pontalis, preface to Sartre, *The Freud Scenario*, viii. On this story, also see Élisabeth Roudinesco, 'Jean-Paul Sartre: psychoanalysis on the shadowy banks of the Danube', in her *Philosophy in Turbulent Times* (New York: Columbia University Press, 2008), 33–63.

224 Sartre and Huston story: Huston, *An Open Book*, 295–6; Pontalis, preface to Sartre, *The Freud Scenario*, viii. 'Suddenly in mid-discussion': Pontalis, citing and translating Sartre, *Lettres au Castor*, II, 358.

225 Manuscript in fire: Beauvoir, *Adieux*, 273; Sartre, 'On *The Idiot of the Family*', in *Sartre in the Seventies*, 122.

225 'Statue': White, *Jean Genet*, 438, citing Jean Cocteau, *Le passé défini*, II, 391.

225 'Disgust', and 'it's very enjoyable': Genet, interview with Madeline Gobeil (1964), in *The Declared Enemy*, 2–17, this 12.

225 Sartre on homosexuality: Sartre, *Saint Genet*, 79. For more on Sartre's views about homosexuality, see his interview of Feb. 1980 in Jean Le Bitoux & Gilles Barbedette, 'Jean-Paul Sartre et les homosexuels', *Le gai pied*, 13 (April 1980), 1, 11–14, tr. by G. Stambolian as 'Jean-Paul Sartre: the final interview', in M. Denneny, C. Ortled & T. Steele (eds), *The View from Christopher Street* (London: Chatto & Windus, The Hogarth Press, 1984), 238–44.

225 Genet on homosexuality: Genet, interview with Hubert Fichte (1975), in *The Declared Enemy*, 118–151, this 148.

225 'We cannot follow him': Sartre, *Saint Genet*, 77. On their arguing: White, *Jean Genet*, 441–4.

226 Ambiguity: Beauvoir, *The Ethics of Ambiguity*, 9, 127.

227 'I was in error': FOC, 76.

Chapter 10: The Dancing Philosopher

228 Merleau-Ponty irritating Beauvoir: MDD, 246. Also see Monika Langer, 'Beauvoir and Merleau-Ponty on Ambiguity', in Claudia Card (ed.), *The Cambridge Companion to Simone de Beauvoir* (Cambridge: CUP, 2003), 87–106.

229 'I am a psychological and historical structure': PP, 482/520.

231 Sensory metaphors: for more, see George Lakoff's & Mark Johnson's *Metaphors We Live By* (Chicago: University of Chicago Press, 1980) and *Philosophy in the Flesh: the embodied mind and its challenge to Western thought* (New York: Basic Books, 1999), works much influenced by Merleau-Ponty.

231 'All of us are constantly discussing': Sartre, *The Family Idiot*, I, 18.

232 Glass, blanket, bird: PP, 238/275–6.

232 Seeing an object, and stereoscopic vision: PP, 241–2/279.

232 Proprioception: PP, 93/119.

232 Knitting: PP, 108/136.

232 'I will never think': PP, 100/127.

233 'If I stand': PP, 102/129–30.

233 'Without any explicit calculation': PP, 143–4/177–8.

233 Schneider: PP, 105/132–3. His experience was studied by the gestalt psychologists Adhémar Gelb and Kurt Goldstein. An extraordinary recent case of lost proprioception overcome by sheer force of will is that of Ian Waterman. He has no proprioception below the neck, yet controls his movements using vision and deliberate muscle control alone. See Jonathan Cole, *Pride and a Daily Marathon* (London: Duckworth, 1991).

233 Phantom limbs: PP, 83/110.

234 Third arm: Oliver Sacks, *Hallucinations* (London: Picador, 2012), 270–71.

234 Leg injury: Sacks, *A Leg to Stand On*, 112. Sacks's experiences attest to how adaptable we can be. Even more extreme adjustments are described in Jean-Dominique Bauby's *The Diving Bell and the Butterfly*, tr. Jeremy

Leggatt (London: Fourth Estate, 1997), the story of his near-total loss
of movement following a massive stroke. Bauby was able to communicate only through eye-blinks, yet even then he was far from disembodied:
he still suffered an excruciating range of phantom sensations. His account
does bring us about as close to disembodiment as a conscious human
can be, and reminds us of the importance of the whole network of
bodily sensation, thought and movement for all of us.

234   Biting baby's fingers: PP, 368/409–10. Earlier work on imitation behaviour was done by gestalt psychologists and others, and was later followed
up by Jacques Lacan. On the phenomenology of social development,
see also Max Scheler, *The Nature of Sympathy*, tr. Peter Heath (London:
Routledge & Kegan Paul, 1954) (originally *Zur Phänomenologie der
Sympathiegefühl und von Liebe und Hass*, 1913).

234   Abandoning usual approach: Merleau-Ponty, 'The Child's Relations with
Others', tr. W. Cobb, in J. M. Edie (ed.) *The Primacy of Perception*
(Evanston, IL: Northwestern University Press, 1964), 96–155, this 115–16.

235   'Fold': PP, 223/260. See also Merleau-Ponty, *The Visible and the Invisible*,
196 (working notes), where he uses the same image.

235   'Starting from there': Merleau-Ponty, *The Visible and the Invisible*, 266.

235   'The hold is held': ibid., 266.

236   'It is as though our vision': ibid., 130–31.

236   'Flesh': ibid., 139.

236   '*Follow with my eyes*': ibid., 146. See also Taylor Carman, 'Merleau-Ponty
on Body, Flesh, and Visibility', in Crowell (ed.), *The Cambridge Companion
to Existentialism*, 274–88, especially 278–9.

236   'Rigorously to put into words': Emmanuelle Garcia, 'Maurice Merleau-
Ponty: vie et œuvre', in Merleau-Ponty, *Œuvres*, 27–99, this 33, citing
radio interview with Georges Charbonnier (22 May 1959).

237   'Only one emotion': Merleau-Ponty, 'Cézanne's Doubt', in *Sense and
Non-Sense*, 9–25, this 18.

237   'Not self-satisfied understanding': Merleau-Ponty, 'Reading Montaigne',
in *Signs*, 198–210, this 203.

237   'It is only a cerebral way': Stephen Priest, *Merleau-Ponty* (London:
Routledge, 2003), 8.

237   Dancing: Vian, *Manual of Saint-Germain-des-Prés*, 141; Gréco, *Je suis faite
comme ça*, 98–9.

237   English suits, morning coffee, inscribed copy, philosophy and life: all
Marianne Merleau-Ponty, personal communication.

238 'Not that they don't like him': Sartre, *Quiet Moments in a War*, 284 (Sartre to Beauvoir, 18 May 1948). Sartre reports having heard it as gossip.

238 Affair with Sonia Brownell: Merleau-Ponty, letters to Sonia Brownell, in Orwell Papers, University College London (S.109); also see Spurling, *The Girl from the Fiction Department*.

238 Plans to move to London: see Merleau-Ponty to Sonia Brownell (15 Nov. [1947]), in Orwell Papers, University College London (S.109).

239 *Meet Yourself*: see ibid., and Spurling, *The Girl from the Fiction Department*, 84. The full title of Prince Leopold Loewenstein's & William Gerhardi's book was *Meet Yourself as you really are, different from others because you combine uniquely features present in everyone: about three million detailed character studies through self-analysis* (London: Penguin, reissued in 1942). On the book, see Dido Davies, *William Gerhardie: a biography* (Oxford & New York: OUP, 1990), 290.

239 'Do Mickey Mouse?' and 'Have you ever felt?': Prince Leopold Loewenstein & William Gerhardi, *Meet Yourself as you really are, etc.*, 16, 15.

239 'Forming tirelessly': Merleau-Ponty, *The Visible and the Invisible*, 144. Sartre did of course take into account the importance of bodily experience, but he approached it differently. On this, see especially Katherine J. Morris (ed.), *Sartre on the Body* (Basingstoke: Palgrave Macmillan, 2010) and her own *Sartre* (Oxford & Malden: Blackwell, 2008).

239 'We discovered, astounded': Sartre, 'Merleau-Ponty', in *Situations* [IV], 225–326, this 298.

240 'Register of feeling': Merleau-Ponty, interview with Georges Charbonnier (May 1959), in *Parcours deux*, 235–40, this 237.

240 Animals: Heidegger, *The Fundamental Concepts of Metaphyics: world, finitude, solitude*, tr. W. McNeill & N. Walker (Bloomington: Indiana University Press, 1995), 177. On Heidegger and the body, see Kevin A. Aho, *Heidegger's Neglect of the Body* (Albany: SUNY Press, 2009).

240 'How did Dasein evolve?': Polt, *Heidegger*, 43.

240 'Ontical' matters: BT, 71/45ff.

241 Outsider subjects: in a series of radio broadcasts in 1948, Merleau-Ponty also described four major topics normally excluded from philosophy: children, animals, the mentally ill, and what were then referred to as 'primitive' people (Merleau-Ponty, *The World of Perception*).

241 'The philosopher is marked' and constant movement: Merleau-Ponty, *In Praise of Philosophy*, 4–5.

Chapter 11: Croisés comme ça

242   'Contingent' lives: Merleau-Ponty, 'Man and Adversity', in *Signs*, 224–43, this 239 (a talk given in Geneva on 10 Sept. 1951).

242   Sartre on Hiroshima: Sartre, 'The End of the War', in *The Aftermath of War (Situations III)*, 65–75, this 71–2.

242   Camus on Hiroshima: Camus, '[On the bombing of Hiroshima]', in *Between Hell and Reason*, 110–11: an untitled piece originally published in *Combat* (8 Aug. 1945).

243   Chain reaction: FOC, 103–4.

243   Radioactive suitcases: FOC, 119; Sartre, *Nekrassov*, in *Three Plays: Kean, Nekrassov, The Trojan Women*, tr. Sylvia & George Leeson (London: Penguin, [n.d.]), 131–282, this 211–12.

243   'A true international society': Camus, '[On the bombing of Hiroshima]', in *Between Hell and Reason*, 110–11, this 111.

245   Kravchenko case: Gary Kern, *The Kravchenko Case* (New York: Enigma, 2007), 452; FOC, 183; Beevor & Cooper, *Paris After the Liberation*, 338.

245   Rousset case: Tony Judt, *Postwar: a history of Europe since 1945* (London: Vintage, 2010), 214–15.

245   Sartre on the Rosenbergs: Sartre, 'Les animaux malades de la rage' ('Mad Beasts'), originally published in *Libération* (22 June 1953), and reprinted in Catherine Varlin & René Guyonnet (eds), *Le chant interrompu: histoire des Rosenberg* (Paris: Gallimard, 1955), 224–8. See Contat & Rybalka (eds), *The Writings of Jean-Paul Sartre*, I, 285 – the editors commenting, 'His wrath brought forth one of the strongest things he ever wrote.' See also Hayman, *Writing Against*, 285.

245   'An unimaginable stupidity': Arendt & Jaspers, *Hannah Arendt/Karl Jaspers Correspondence*, 220 (Jaspers to Arendt, 22 May 1953).

246   Baby vs humanity: Fyodor Dostoevsky, *The Brothers Karamazov*, tr. C. Garnett (London: Dent; New York: Dutton, 1927), II, 251.

246   'I will never again': Camus, 'Neither Victims nor Executioners', 41.

246   *The Just*: Camus, *The Just*, tr. Henry Jones, in Camus, *Caligula, etc.* 163–227.

246   'People are now planting bombs': Camus, 'The Nobel Prize Press Conference Incident, December 14–17, 1957', in *Algerian Chronicles*, 213–16, this 216n. On this, see Zaretsky, *A Life Worth Living*, 84–5.

247   'The perspective of heads of government': Merleau-Ponty, 'The Philosophy of Existence', in *Texts and Dialogues*, 129–39, a talk broadcast 17 Nov. 1959, tr. Allen S. Weiss.

247 'It seems to me' and 'injustice against one person': Spender, *New Selected Journals*, 220 (30 March 1956).

248 Yogi and commissar: Koestler, 'The Yogi and the Commissar', in *The Yogi and the Commissar, and Other Essays* (London: Hutchinson, 1965), 15–25, this 15–16. Also see his chapter 'Arthur Koestler', in Richard Crossman (ed.), *The God that Failed: six studies in communism* (London: Hamish Hamilton, 1950), 25–82.

248 Yogi and proletarian: Merleau-Ponty, 'The Yogi and the Proletarian', in *Humanism and Terror*, 149–77, this 176. Merleau-Ponty was also motivated by personal dislike of Koestler, partly because he felt Koestler had treated Sonia Brownell badly. See Merleau-Ponty to Sonia Brownell (14 Oct. [1947]), in Orwell Papers, University College London (S.109).

248 Quarrel at Vians' party: FOC, 120; Sartre, 'Merleau-Ponty', in *Situations* [IV], 225–326, this 253; see also Beauvoir, *Adieux*, 267.

249 'Impossible!' and 'It *is* possible', etc.: FOC, 118–19.

249 'He was my friend!', and account of quarrel: FOC, 149–50.

249 'When people's opinions': FOC, 151.

249 'Koestler, you know that': Spender, *New Selected Journals*, 79–80 (14 April 1950).

251 French writers in London: Sonia Brownell to Merleau-Ponty ('Sunday', undated but probably early 1948, after their Christmas together), in Orwell Papers, University College London (S.109).

251 Aron and Sartre in radio debate: Aron, *Memoirs*, 218–19; Hayman, *Writing Against*, 244–5. On their relationship, see Jean-François Sirinelli, *Deux intellectuels dans le siècle: Sartre et Aron* (Paris: Fayard, 1995).

251 Excrement letter and army officers: Beauvoir, *Beloved Chicago Man*, 97 (Beauvoir to Algren, 5 Nov. 1947), and 90–91 (Beauvoir to Algren, 25 Oct. 1947, continuation of letter of 23 Oct.).

252 'Dreary, flabby mixture', and 'what would a man be': Henri Lefebvre, excerpt from his *L'existentialisme* (1946), translated in his *Key Writings*, eds S. Elden, E. Lebas & E. Kofman (New York & London: Continuum, 2003), 9–11. Lefebvre later toned down his views and became more sympathetic to existentialism.

252 *Dirty Hands*: Sartre, *Dirty Hands*, tr. Lionel Abel, in *No Exit and Three Other Plays*, 125–241. Sartre was dismayed when the play was taken up in the US as a propaganda tool by anti-Communists, and in 1952 he declared that he would only sanction performances in countries where the local Communist Party accepted it. Thompson, *Sartre*, 78.

252 'A hyena with a fountain pen': Cohen-Solal, *Sartre*, 337. The remark was made at a peace congress in 1948.

252 'Decay and moral degeneration': Klíma, *My Crazy Century*, 69.

253 Algren and Beauvoir difficulties: FOC, 137.

253 Hallucinations and 'dwarf forests': FOC, 143.

253 War fears: FOC, 242; Sartre, 'Merleau-Ponty', in *Situations* [IV], 225–326, this 285.

254 'You must leave': FOC, 243.

254 'How to get away': Beauvoir, *Beloved Chicago Man*, 406 (Beauvoir to Algren, 31 Dec. 1950).

254 Going to US: ibid., 410 (Beauvoir to Algren, 14 Jan. 1951).

254 None of them wanting to flee Communists: FOC, 244.

254 'With that boyish air': Sartre, 'Merleau-Ponty', in *Situations* [IV], 225–326, this 279.

255 'Because brute force': ibid., 274.

255 Merleau-Ponty shocked by Korea: ibid., 275.

255 Duclos and pigeon plot: Jacques Duclos, *Mémoires IV: 1945–1952: des débuts de la IVe République au 'complot' des pigeons* (Paris: Fayard, 1971), 339–492, esp. the autopsy: 404. The experts: 400–401. Aragon's poem reproduced: 435–6. Also see Jacques Duclos, *Écrits de la prison* (Paris: Éditions sociales, 1952).

256 'After ten years' and 'In the language': Sartre, 'Merleau-Ponty', in *Situations* [IV], 225–326, this 287; also see *Sartre By Himself*, 72, and FOC, 245 (for Beauvoir on how it changed him).

256 'Write or suffocate': Sartre, 'Merleau-Ponty', in *Situations* [IV], 225–326, this 287–8. Sartre, *The Communists and Peace*. Originally published in parts in *Les Temps modernes*, 81 (July 1952); 84–5 (Oct.–Nov. 1952); 101 (April 1954).

257 Rebellion: Camus, *The Rebel*, 178, 253.

257 'So far but no further': ibid., 19.

257 Jeanson's review: Francis Jeanson, 'Albert Camus, or The Soul in Revolt', in Sprintzen & Van den Hoven (eds), *Sartre and Camus: a historic confrontation*, 79–105 this 101. Originally published in *Les Temps modernes*, 79 (May 1952).

257 'I am beginning': Camus, 'A Letter to the Editor of *Les Temps modernes*', in Sprintzen & Van den Hoven (eds), *Sartre and Camus*, 107–29, this 126. Originally published in *Les Temps modernes*, 82 (Aug. 1952).

257 Sartre's reply: Sartre, 'Reply to Albert Camus', in Sprintzen & Van den

Hoven (eds), *Sartre and Camus*, 131–61, this 131–2. Originally published in *Les Temps modernes*, 82 (Aug. 1952), following Camus' letter. Also reprinted in Sartre, *Situations* [IV], 69–105.

258 Camus's draft reply: Camus, 'In Defence of *The Rebel*', in Sprintzen & Van den Hoven (eds), *Sartre and Camus*, 205–21. Written Nov. 1952, but published posthumously as 'Défense de *L'homme révolté*', in Camus, *Essais*, 1,702–15.

258 Beauvoir: *The Rebel* a betrayal: FOC, 272.

259 'The more I accuse myself': Camus, *The Fall*, 103. On the novel, see also FOC, 362.

259 'We feel that we are being judged': Sartre, *Saint Genet*, 598.

259 Beauvoir on being judged: ASAD, 49.

259 'The enormous condescension': E. P. Thompson, *The Making of the English Working Class* (London: Gollancz, 1980), 14. The line is often quoted, but rarely in its proper context, which seems relevant here: 'I am seeking to rescue the poor stockinger, the Luddite cropper, the "obsolete" hand-loom weaver, the "utopian" artisan, and even the deluded follower of Joanna Southcott, from the enormous condescension of posterity. Their crafts and traditions may have been dying. Their hostility to the new industrialism may have been backward-looking. Their communitarian ideals may have been foolhardy. But they lived through these times of acute social disturbance, and we did not.'

259 'It is perfectly true': Kierkegaard, Notebook IV A 164; 1843 (D), in *A Kierkegaard Reader*, eds Roger Poole & Henrik Stangerup (London: Fourth Estate, 1989), 18; Sartre, *Saint Genet*, 599.

260 Not showing Merleau-Ponty the article: Sartre, 'Merleau-Ponty', in *Situations* [IV], 225–326, this 289.

260 Merleau-Ponty's lecture: Merleau-Ponty, *In Praise of Philosophy*, 4–5, 63.

260 'In a glacially cold tone' and 'I hope': Stewart (ed.), *The Debate Between Sartre and Merleau-Ponty*, 343 (Merleau-Ponty to Sartre, 8 July [1953]). Stewart's collection includes (327–54) a translation of the whole correspondence, first published in *Le magazine littéraire* (2 April 1994), and also included in 'Sartre and MP: les lettres d'une rupture', in *Parcours deux, 1951–1961*, 129–69, and Merleau-Ponty, *Œuvres*, 627–51.

260 Heat: Sartre, 'Merleau-Ponty', in *Situations* [IV], 225–326, this 197.

260 No longer 'engaged': Stewart (ed.), *The Debate Between Sartre and Merleau-*

Ponty, 327–54, this 334 (Sartre to Merleau-Ponty, undated but before Merleau-Ponty's reply dated 8 July 1953).

261 'Become 'engaged' on every event': ibid., 338–9 (Merleau-Ponty to Sartre, 8 July [1953]).

261 'For God's sake' and 'If I appeared': ibid., 351 (Sartre to Merleau-Ponty, 29 July 1953).

261 Merleau-Ponty smiling: FOC, 332.

261 'Found his security': Sartre, 'Merleau-Ponty', in *Situations* [IV], 225–326, this 232.

261 Discussing for hours: Marianne Merleau-Ponty, personal communication.

261 Editorial meetings and mutterings: Sartre, 'Merleau-Ponty', in *Situations* [IV], 225–326, this 292.

262 '*Alors, c'est fini*': Marianne Merleau-Ponty, personal communication; see also Sartre, 'Merleau-Ponty', in *Situations* [IV], 225–326, this 298.

262 Never called: Sartre, 'Merleau-Ponty', in *Situations* [IV], 225–326, this 301.

262 'Casually, with that sad gaiety': ibid., 301–302. His daughter also remembers a dark period.

262 'Light and free as air' and 'a living accord': Sartre, 'Merleau-Ponty', in *Situations* [IV], 225–326, this 300.

263 'Sartre and Ultrabolshevism': Merleau-Ponty, 'Sartre and Ultrabolshevism', in *Adventures of the Dialectic*, 95–201, especially 95–6.

263 Beauvoir's attack: Beauvoir, 'Merleau-Ponty and Pseudo-Sartreanism', in *Political Writings* 195–258. (Originally published in *Les Temps modernes*, 1955.)

263 Anti-Merleau-Ponty meeting: Roger Garaudy et al., *Mésaventures de l'anti-marxisme: les malheurs de M. Merleau-Ponty. Avec une lettre de G. Lukács* (Paris: Éditions sociales, 1956). The meeting took place on 29 Nov. 1955. See Emmanuelle Garcia, 'Maurice Merleau-Ponty: vie et œuvre', in Merleau-Ponty, *Œuvres*, 27–99, this 81.

263 'Someone was speaking': Sartre, 'Merleau-Ponty', in *Situations* [IV], 225–326, this 318–19. Marianne Merleau-Ponty also remembers their greetings as cool.

263 Amused looks: ibid., 318. For Spender's perspective, see Spender, *New Selected Journals*, 215 (26 March 1956). For Merleau-Ponty's contributions to this conference, see Merleau-Ponty, 'East–West Encounter (1956)', tr. Jeffrey Gaines, in Merleau-Ponty, *Texts and Dialogues*, 26–58.

264 'One leaves behind reveries': cited in Paul Ricœur, 'Homage to Merleau-

Ponty', in Bernard Flynn, Wayne J. Froman & Robert Vallier (eds), *Merleau-Ponty and the Possibilities of Philosophy: transforming the tradition* (New York: SUNY Press, 2009), 17–24, this 21.

264 Philosophers are awake: Merleau-Ponty, *In Praise of Philosophy*, 63.

264 'I thought that while I was being faithful': Sartre, 'Merleau-Ponty', in *Situations* [IV], 225–326, this 293.

264 *The Mandarins*: see FOC, 311; Lanzmann, *The Patagonian Hare*, 235. Both agree it was Lanzmann who suggested the title.

265 'He said first of all' and 'I want to kill', etc.: FOC, 294–6.

265 List and diagram of quarrels: Sartre, 'Relecture du Carnet I', (notebook, c. 1954), in his *Les mots, etc.*, 937–53, this 950–51.

265 'A thing is dead': Beauvoir, *Adieux*, 275.

265 'There was a side of him' and 'He was probably': Sartre, 'Self-Portrait at Seventy', in *Sartre in the Seventies (Situations X)*, 3–92, this 64.

266 'Merciless towards the failings': Aron, *The Opium of the Intellectuals*, ix.

266 Unfit to teach: Aron, *Memoirs*, 329.

266 '*Bonjour*': Todd, *Un fils rebelle*, 267–8; see also Aron, *Memoirs*, 447–9, and Hayman, *Writing Against*, 435.

266 'What do you think?': Aron, *Memoirs*, 457. The interview with Bernard-Henri Lévy was published in *Le nouvel observateur* (15 March 1976).

266 Soviet trip and articles: Cohen-Solal, *Sartre*, 348–9, citing articles published in *Libération* (15–20 July 1954). See also FOC, 316–23.

266 Delegating writing to Cau: Beauvoir, *Adieux*, 366.

267 'There's no time!' and giving up pleasures: Cau, *Croquis de mémoire*, 236, 248.

267 Bourgeois self-indulgence: see Sartre, 'On *The Idiot of the Family*', 109–32, in *Sartre in the Seventies (Situations X)*, this 111.

267 Beauvoir watching nervously: Beauvoir, *Adieux*, 174.

267 Twenty pages a day: Hayman, *Writing Against*, 1, citing Contat & Rybalka in *Le Monde* (17 April 1980).

267 Breakfast: Huston, *An Open Book*, 295.

267 Turbine: Cohen-Solal, *Sartre*, 281. Pit stop: Olivier Wickers, *Trois aventures extraordinaires de Jean-Paul Sartre* (Paris: Gallimard, 2000), 23.

267 Corydrane: FOC, 397; see also Cohen-Solal, *Sartre*, 373–4.

267 'I liked having confused, vaguely questioning ideas': Beauvoir, *Adieux*, 318.

267 'Facility' and 'It was dreadful': ibid., 174.

267 'About the plashing sound': ibid., 181. He is talking about his notebook entitled 'La Reine Albemarle', written 1951–2 based on Italian travels in Oct. 1951: Sartre, *La Reine Albemarle*, ed. Arlette Elkaïm-Sartre (Paris: Gallimard, 1991). See Sartre, *Les mots, etc.*, 1,491.

268 '*Il est bon*': Merleau-Ponty, interview with Georges Charbonnier (May 1959), in *Parcours deux*, 235–40, this 236.

268 'A sinister scoundrel' and 'I'd say, a person who's not bad': Sartre & Lévy, *Hope Now*, 63.

269 'We are now going off the air': Janet Flanner, *Paris Journal*, ed. W. Shawn, 2 vols (New York: Atheneum, 1965–71), I, 329 (4 Nov. 1956). On the Hungarian events, see Victor Sebestyén, *Twelve Days: Revolution 1956* (London: Weidenfeld & Nicolson, 2006).

269 *Les Temps modernes* special issue: *Les Temps modernes*, 12e année, 131 (Jan. 1957), 'La révolte de la Hongrie'. On their turmoil: FOC, 373.

269 *Critique* as Sartre's response: FOC, 397.

269 'The *Critique* is a Marxist work': Sartre, 'Self-Portrait at Seventy', in *Sartre in the Seventies (Situations X)*, 3–92, this 18.

270 Second volume: Sartre, *Critique of Dialectical Reason II*; see Ronald Aronson, *Sartre's Second Critique* (Chicago: University of Chicago Press, 1987).

Chapter 12: The Eyes of the Least Favoured

271 'Man and society as they truly are': Sartre, *The Communists and Peace*, 180, part 3. Originally published in *Les Temps modernes*, 101 (April 1954). On this, see Bernasconi, *How to Read Sartre*, 79, using the translation 'gaze of the least favored'.

272 Sartre ignored Stalin's prisons: Merleau-Ponty, 'Sartre and Ultrabolshevism', in *Adventures of the Dialectic*, 95–201, this 154.

272 Sartre as maverick: see Bernasconi, *How to Read Sartre*, 79.

273 'These black men': Sartre, 'Black Orpheus', tr. J. MacCombie (revised), in Bernasconi (ed.), *Race*, 115–42, this 115. Originally published as a preface to Léopold Senghor (ed.), *Anthologie de la nouvelle poésie nègre et malgache* (Paris: PUF, 1948), ix–xliv.

273 Memmi: Albert Memmi, *The Colonizer and the Colonized*, tr. Howard Greenfeld, with introduction by Sartre translated by Lawrence Hoey

(New York: Orion Press, 1965). Translation of *Portrait du colonisé précédé du portrait du colonisateur* (1957).

273 Fanon and Merleau-Ponty: FOC, 607.

273 *Black Skin, White Masks*: Fanon, *Black Skin, White Masks*, esp. 'The Lived Experience of the Black Man', 89–119. On Sartre and Fanon, see Robert Bernasconi, 'Racism Is a System: how existentialism became dialectical in Fanon and Sartre', in Crowell (ed.), *The Cambridge Companion to Existentialism*, 342–60.

274 'I don't like people', and account of meeting: FOC, 605–11; see also Lanzmann, *The Patagonian Hare*, 347–8.

274 Ollie Iselin: Macey, *Frantz Fanon*, 485.

274 'We have claims': FOC, 610.

274 Gaze of oppressed: Sartre, preface to Fanon, *The Wretched of the Earth*, 7–26, this 18–21. On Sartre and violence, see Ronald E. Santoni, *Sartre on Violence: curiously ambivalent* (University Park, PA: Pennsylvania State University Press, 2003).

275 Sartre's beliefs changed, but not extremism: Todd, *Un fils rebelle*, 17.

275 'Naturally in the course of my life': Sartre, 'Self-Portrait at Seventy', in *Sartre in the Seventies (Situations X)*, 3–92, this 65.

275 Josie Fanon: Macey, *Frantz Fanon*, 462–3, citing Josie Fanon, 'À propos de Frantz Fanon, Sartre, le racism et les Arabes', *El Moudjahid* (10 June 1967), 6.

275 'I've never had tender relationships': Beauvoir, *Adieux*, 148.

276 Beauvoir overjoyed: FOC, 315.

276 'I'm French': FOC, 397. See also 381–2.

276 'Anybody, at any time': Sartre, foreword to Henri Alleg, *La question* (1958), tr. by John Calder as *The Question* (London: Calder, 1958), 11–28, this 12. Beauvoir wrote about the torture victim Djamila Boupacha, first in *Le Monde* (3 June 1960) and then in a book co-written with Boupacha's lawyer Gisèle Halimi: *Djamila Boupacha* (1962), tr. by Peter Green as *Djamila Boupacha: the story of a torture of a young Algerian girl* (London: André Deutsch & Weidenfeld & Nicolson, 1962).

276 Death threats: FOC, 381; 626–8; David Detmer, *Sartre Explained: from bad faith to authenticity* (Chicago: Open Court, 2008), 5 ('Shoot Sartre'), 11 (de Gaulle).

277 Explosion: Cohen-Solal, *Sartre*, 451.

277 Phone calls: Lanzmann, *The Patagonian Hare*, 4.

277   Rejecting Nobel Prize: ASAD, 52–4, Cohen-Solal, *Sartre*, 447–8.

277   'Double-consciousness': W. E. B. Du Bois, *The Souls of Black Folk* (New York: Penguin, 1996), 5. See Ernest Allen Jr, 'On the Reading of Riddles: rethinking Du Boisian "Double Consciousness"', in Gordon (ed.), *Existence in Black*, 49–68, this 51.

278   Baldwin in Swiss hamlet: Baldwin, 'Stranger in the Village', in *The Price of the Ticket*, 79–90, this 81–3. Originally published in *Harper's Magazine* in 1953.

278   Responsiblity, and 'We're different': Wright, *The Outsider*, 114–15, 585.

279   He revised it: restored edn, with notes on editorial history: ibid., esp. 588–92. The notes are by Arnold Rampersad.

279   'I am getting a little sick': Rowley, *Richard Wright*, 407 (citing Ellison to Wright, 21 Jan. 1953); on how Ellison thought Wright was damaging himself, also see 409 (citing Ellison interview with A. Geller in 1963, in Graham & Singh (eds), *Conversations with Ralph Ellison*, 84). On Wright, Ellison and existentialism, see Cotkin, *Existential America*, 161–83.

280   Aswell: Rowley, *Richard Wright*, 472 (citing Ed Aswell to Wright, 24 Jan. 1956).

280   'Richard was able': James Baldwin, 'Alas, Poor Richard', in *Nobody Knows My Name: more notes of a native son* (London: Penguin, 1991), 149–76, this 174. The essay was originally published in 1961.

280   'I need to live free': Rowley, *Richard Wright*, 352, citing a remark of Wright's quoted by Anaïs Nin in *The Diary of Anaïs Nin*, IV, 212–14.

280   'Lonely outsiders': Richard Wright, *White Man, Listen!* (New York: Doubleday, 1957), dedication. On these works, see Rowley, *Richard Wright*, 440–91.

280   First International Congress: Rowley, *Richard Wright*, 477–80, especially 479. On Wright's interest in *The Second Sex*: Cotkin, *Existential America*, 169; M. Fabre, *The Unfinished Quest of Richard Wright*, 2nd edn (Urbana: University of Illinois Press, 1993), 320–21. On how Beauvoir was influenced by Wright, also see Margaret A. Simons, 'Richard Wright, Simone de Beauvoir, and *The Second Sex*', in *Beauvoir and The Second Sex*, 167–84.

281   Angie Pegg: Forster & Sutton (eds), *Daughters of de Beauvoir*, 54–9.

281   Margaret Walters: ibid., 45; also see interview with Jenny Turner, who was also influenced by the autobiographies: 33–4.

281   Kate Millett: ibid., 28–9.

281 Joyce Goodfellow: ibid., 103.

282 Frankl: For more on his life and thought, see Viktor Frankl, *Man's Search for Meaning* (London: Rider, 2004; originally published in 1946), and other works.

283 Sloan Wilson, afterword in *The Man in the Grey Flannel Suit* (London: Penguin, 2005), 278.

284 Squid, leeches, etc.: see Spencer R. Weart, *The Rise of Nuclear Fear* (Cambridge, MA & London: Harvard University Press, 2012), 106.

285 Eichmann: Arendt, *Eichmann in Jerusalem* (originally serialised in the *New Yorker* (Feb.–March 1963), then published in book form in 1963). For controversies around it, see also Bettina Stangneth, *Eichmann Before Jerusalem: the unexamined life of a mass murderer*, tr. R. Martin (London: Bodley Head, 2014); Richard Wolin, 'The Banality of Evil: the demise of a legend', *Jewish Review of Books* (Fall 2014); and Seyla Benhabib, 'Who's on Trial: Eichmann or Arendt?', *New York Times: the Stone Blog* (21 Sept. 2014). For experiments, see Stanley Milgram, 'Behavioral Study of Obedience', *Journal of Abnormal and Social Psychology*, 67 (4) (Oct. 1963), 371–8, and *Obedience to Authority: an experimental view* (New York: Harper, 1974); C. Haney, W. C. Banks & P. G. Zimbardo, 'Study of Prisoners and Guards in a Simulated Prison', *Naval Research Reviews*, 9 (1973), 1–17; Philip Zimbardo, *The Lucifer Effect* (New York: Random House, 1971).

285 'The American existentialist': Norman Mailer, 'The White Negro', in *Advertisements for Myself*, 337–58. Originally published in *Dissent* (1957). For more on Mailer and existentialism, see Cotkin, *Existential America*, 184–209.

286 'Oh, kinda playing': Wilson, *Dreaming to Some Purpose*, 244.

286 Mailer's sources: Mary Dearborn, *Mailer* (Boston: Houghton Mifflin, 1999), 58–9. The reference is to Barrett, *Irrational Man*. See Cotkin, *Existential America*, 185–6.

286 Several revolts, and 'perfervid individualism': both Kaufmann, *Existentialism*, 11.

286 Hazel Barnes: Sartre, *Being and Nothingness*, tr. Hazel Barnes, originally published 1956. At the time of writing, another translation is in preparation by Sarah Richmond. Zen: see Barnes, *An Existentialist Ethics*, 211–77.

286 *Self-Encounter*: Barnes, *The Story I Tell Myself*, 166–8. The drama was adapted from M. Unamuno's story 'The Madness of Doctor Montarco'. The TV

series *Self-Encounter: a study in existentialism* (1961) was once thought lost, but Jeffrey Ward Larsen and Erik Sween located a copy in the Library of Congress; another copy is now in the University of Colorado archives. See http://geopolicraticus.wordpress.com/2010/11/03/documentaries-worth-watching/.

287 Carnap: Rudolf Carnap, 'The Overcoming of Metaphysics Through Logical Analysis of Language' (originally published 1932), in Murray (ed.), *Heidegger and Modern Philosophy*, 23–34. Carnap especially picked on the phrase 'the nothing nothings' from Heidegger's *What Is Metaphysics?*

287 'People play cricket': Murdoch, *Sartre*, 78–9. On existentialism in the UK, see Martin Woessner, 'Angst Across the Channel: existentialism in Britain', in Judaken & Bernasconi (eds), *Situating Existentialism*, 145–79.

287 'The excitement': Conradi, *Iris Murdoch*, 216 (Murdoch to Hal Lidderdale, 6 Nov. 1945). Her encounter: her notebook 'Notes on a lecture by Jean-Paul Sartre', (Brussels, Oct. 1945) in Murdoch Archive, University of Kingston, IML 682. Her lectures: see Conradi, *Iris Murdoch*, 270. She originally intended to do a PhD on Husserl at Cambridge in 1947, but changed to Wittgenstein: see her Heidegger manuscript in Murdoch Archives (KUAS6/5/1/4), 83, and Conradi, *Iris Murdoch*, 254 (citing a Murdoch interview with Richard Wollheim, 1991).

289 'Smoking, making love': Wilson, *Dreaming to Some Purpose*, 113.

289 Publication of *The Outsider*: Carpenter, *The Angry Young Men*, 107.

289 'I think it possible' and 'It was a conclusion': Wilson, *Dreaming to Some Purpose*, 129.

289 Did not correct them: Spurgeon, *Colin Wilson*, 66–7.

289 Print runs: Carpenter, *The Angry Young Men*, 112.

289 Alice: Geoffrey Gorer, 'The Insider, by C*l*n W*ls*n', *Punch* (11 July 1956), 33–4. See Carpenter, *The Angry Young Men*, 168.

289 *TLS* letter: Carpenter, *The Angry Young Men*, 109, citing the *Times Literary Supplement* (14 Dec. 1956).

289 'I *am* the major literary genius': ibid., 169–70.

290 'I glimpsed': Wilson, *Dreaming to Some Purpose*, 3–4.

290 'I can't be bothered': Colin Wilson, *Adrift in Soho* (London: Pan, 1964), 114.

291 Falling asleep: Spurgeon, *Colin Wilson*, 36, with more on other writers who angered him with their reviews or profiles: 37–8, 47. The profile by Lynn Barber in the *Observer* (30 May 2004) makes an interesting read.

291 'Rashness': Iris Murdoch, review in the *Manchester Guardian* (25 Oct. 1957). She called him an ass in a letter to Brigid Brophy in 1962: see Murdoch, ed. A. Horner & A. Rowe, *Living on Paper: Letters from Iris Murdoch 1934–1995* (London: Chatto & Windus, 2015), 222.

291 'Small myths, toys': Murdoch, 'Against Dryness,' in *Existentialists and Mystics: writings on philosophy and literature*, ed. P. Conradi (London: Penguin, 1999), 287– 95, this 292–3.

291 'Salvation on the campus': J. Glenn Gray, 'Salvation on the Campus: why existentialism is capturing the students', *Harper's Magazine* (May 1965), 53–60. On Gray, see Woessner, *Heidegger in America*, 132–59.

292 Robbe-Grillet: Alain Robbe-Grillet, *For a New Novel*, tr. Richard Howard (NY: Grove, 1965), 64.

293 'Erased': Michel Foucault, *The Order of Things* (London: Tavistock, 1970), 387. 'To dissolve man': Claude Levi-Strauss, *The Savage Mind* (London: Weidenfeld & Nicolson, 1966), 247.

293 'Express' and 'Who cares about freedom?': Jean Baudrillard, *Impossible Exchange*, tr. C. Turner (London: Verso, 2001), 73. See Jack Reynolds and Ashley Woodward, 'Existentialism and Poststructuralism: some unfashionable observations', in Felicity Joseph, Jack Reynolds & Ashley Woodward (eds), *The Continuum Companion to Existentialism* (London: Continuum, 2011), 260–81.

293 Plays in Prague: ASAD, 358. *Dirty Hands* was staged in Nov., *The Flies* in Dec. 1968. See Contat & Rybalka (eds), *The Writings of Jean-Paul Sartre*, I, 89.

293 'Is he passé?': Antonin Liehm, *The Politics of Culture* (New York: Grove Press, 1973), 146 (interview with Milan Kundera, tr. P. Kussi; originally published 1968).

294 Words have weight: Havel, *Letters to Olga*, 306 (10 April 1982).

294 'Everything goes': Philip Roth, in George Plimpton (ed.) *Writers at Work: the Paris Review interviews*, 7th series (New York: Penguin, 1988), 267–98, this 296. (Interview by Hermione Lee, originally published in the *Paris Review* (Summer 1983–Winter 1984).

294 Becoming the heir: Kohák, *Jan Patočka*, xi, translating Patočka, 'Erinnerungen an Husserl', in Walter Biemel (ed.), *Die Welt des Menschen – die Welt der Philosophie* (The Hague: Martinus Nijhoff, 1976), vii–xix, this xv; Patočka also describes Husserl's reluctance to share him with Heidegger: x.

294 Whole evening on a few lines: Shore, 'Out of the Desert', 14–15.

294 Patočka's sessions: Paul Wilson, introduction to Havel, *Letters to Olga*, 18, citing Václav Havel, 'The Last Conversation' (1977), in *Václav Havel o lidskou identitu* (*Václav Havel on Human Identity*), ed. Vilém Pričem & Alexander Tomský (London: Rozmluvy, 1984), 198–9.

295 'Solidarity of the shaken': Patočka, *Heretical Essays in the Philosophy of History*, 134–5.

296 Charter 77: 'Charter 77 Manifesto', *Telos*, 31 (1977), 148–50. Also see Jan Patočka, 'Political Testament', *Telos*, 31 (1977), 151–2. On this, see Kohák, *Jan Patočka*, 340–47.

296 Philosophers: Aviezer Tucker, *The Philosophy and Politics of Czech Dissidence from Patočka to Havel* (Pittsburgh: University of Pittsburgh Press, 2000), 2–3.

296 Regular questioning: Michael Zantovsky, *Havel* (London: Atlantic Books, 2014), 182.

296 Havel's last meeting with Patočka: Paul Wilson, introduction to Havel, *Letters to Olga*, 18, citing Václav Havel, 'The Last Conversation' (1977), in *Václav Havel o lidskou identitu* (*Václav Havel on Human Identity*), ed. Vilém Prečan & Alexander Tomský (London: Rozmluvy, 1984), 198–9.

296 'What is needed': Patočka, 'Political Testament', *Telos*, 31 (1977), 151–2, this 151.

296 Patočka's death: Kohák, *Jan Patočka*, 3; Zantovsky, *Havel*, 183–4.

296 Patočka's funeral: Klíma, *My Crazy Century*, 350–51.

297 Patočka's papers: Shore, 'Out of the Desert', 14–15; Chvatík, 'Geschichte und Vorgeschichte'.

297 'The relentless persecution': Paul Ricœur, 'Patočka, Philosopher and Resister', tr. David J. Parent, *Telos*, 31 (1977), 152–5, this 155. Originally published in *Le Monde* (19 March 1977).

297 Greengrocer: Havel, 'The Power of the Powerless', 41–55.

297 'Here and now': ibid., 99.

298 'Existential revolution': ibid., 117–18.

Chapter 13: Having Once Tasted Phenomenology

299 'The possibility': BN, 568.

299 'From elsewhere': Beauvoir, *A Very Easy Death*, 91–2.

299 One cannot have a relationship with death: Beauvoir, *Old Age*, 492.

300 'It deprives us of phenomenology': Richard Wollheim, *The Thread of Life* (Cambridge, MA: Yale University Press, 1999), 269.

300 Camus crash and manuscript: Lottman, *Albert Camus*, 5.

301 Beauvoir and death of Camus: FOC, 496–7.

301 Sartre and death of Camus: Sartre, 'Albert Camus', in *Situations* [IV], 107–12. Originally published in *France-Observateur* (7 Jan. 1960).

301 Camus an ethical thinker: 'Simone de Beauvoir tells Studs Terkel How She Became an Intellectual and Feminist' (1960), audio interview, online at: http://www.openculture.com/2014/11/simone-de-beauvoir-talks-with-studs-terkel-1960.html.

301 Wright's death and suspicions: Rowley, *Richard Wright*, 524–5. Bismuth salts: 504.

301 Wright's haiku: some are included in Ellen Wright & Michel Fabre (eds), *Richard Wright Reader* (New York: Harper & Row, 1978), 251–4. Others are online: http://terebess.hu/english/haiku/wright.html.

301 Merleau-Ponty's death: Ronald Bonan, *Apprendre à philosopher avec Merleau- Ponty* (Paris: Ellipses, 2010), 12; Gandillac, *Le siècle traversé*, 372; Emmanuelle Garcia, 'Maurice Merleau-Ponty: vie et œuvre', in Merleau-Ponty, *Œuvres*, 27–99, this 93.

302 Sartre on Merleau-Ponty's death: Sartre, 'Merleau-Ponty', in *Situations* [IV], 225–326, this 320. Originally published as 'Merleau-Ponty vivant', in *Les Temps modernes*, 17e année, 184–5 (Oct. 1961), 304–76.

302 Jaspers warning of early death: Gens, *Karl Jaspers*, 50 (Gertrud Jaspers to Arendt, 10 Jan. 1966).

302 Heidegger and Gertrud Jaspers telegrams: ibid., 206 (Heidegger to Gertrud Jaspers, 2 March 1969; Gertrud Jaspers to Heidegger, 2 March 1969).

303 Jaspers on Norderney: Jaspers, 'Self-Portrait', 3.

303 Arendt helping the Heideggers: Woessner, *Heidegger in America*, 109–11.

304 Arendt on Heidegger: Arendt, 'Martin Heidegger at Eighty', in Murray (ed.), *Heidegger and Modern Philosophy*, 293–303, this 301. Originally published in the *New York Review of Books* (Oct. 1971).

304 Heidegger knew what was expected: Petzet, *Encounters and Dialogues*, 91.

304 Book-dealers' windows: Gerhart Baumann, *Erinnerungen an Paul Celan* (Frankfurt am Main: Suhrkamp, 1992), 58–82, this 66; James K. Lyon, *Paul Celan and Martin Heidegger: an unresolved conversation, 1951–1970* (Baltimore: Johns Hopkins University Press, 2006), 168.

305 Poem: Paul Celan, 'Todtnauberg', in *Poems of Paul Celan*, tr. Michael Hamburger (London: Anvil Press, 1988), 292–5 (in German and English).

305   'Desert-like': Heidegger, *Sojourns*, 37.

305   'I will be allowed': Safranski, *Martin Heidegger*, 401 (Heidegger to Kästner, 21 Feb. 1960).

305   'Hotels' and 'set free': Heidegger, *Sojourns*, 12, 19.

305   Athens: ibid., 36, 39–42.

306   'This single gesture' and 'knew how to inhabit': ibid., 43–4.

306   Cameras: ibid., 54.

306   Cup of Exekias: ibid., 57, and 70 n20. It is in the State Collection of Antiquities in Munich.

307   'Where is it written?' and 'According': Heidegger, '"Only a God can Save Us": *Der Spiegel*'s Interview with Martin Heidegger', in Wolin, *The Heidegger Controversy*, 91–116, this 106. The interview was published only after his death, in *Der Spiegel* (31 May 1976). The translation, by Maria P. Alter and John D. Caputo, was originally published in *Philosophy Today* XX (4/4) (1976), 267–85.

307   Conversations with Welte: Safranski, *Martin Heidegger*, 432, citing Welte, 'Erinnerung an ein spätes Gespräch', 251. On Heidegger and the theme of homecoming, see also Robert Mugerauer, *Heidegger and Homecoming: the leitmotif in the later writings* (Toronto: University of Toronto Press, 2008), and Brendan O'Donoghue, *A Poetics of Homecoming: Heidegger, homelessness and the homecoming venture* (Newcastle upon Tyne: Cambridge Scholars, 2011).

307   Fritz Heidegger and the *Fastnacht* speeches: Raymond Geuss, 'Heidegger and His Brother', in *Politics and Imagination* (Princeton & Oxford: Princeton University Press, 2010), 142–50, this 142–3. On Fritz Heidegger generally, see Zimmermann, *Martin und Fritz Heidegger*; Safranski, *Martin Heidegger*, 8–9, citing Andreas Müller, *Der Scheinwerfer: Anekdoten und Geschichten um Fritz Heidegger* (Messkirch: Armin Gmeiner, 1989), 9–11; and (esp. for 'Da-da-dasein' and 'supermarket on the moon') Luzia Braun, 'Da-da-dasein. Fritz Heidegger: Holzwege zur Sprache', in *Die Zeit* (22 Sept. 1989).

308   'It withdraws from man': Heidegger, *Parmenides*, 85, cited in Polt, *Heidegger*, 174.

308   Suggesting amendments: Safranski, *Martin Heidegger*, 8; Raymond Geuss, 'Heidegger and His Brother', in *Politics and Imagination* (Princeton & Oxford: Princeton University Press, 2010), 142–50, this 149.

308   'For years': Sartre, 'J'écris pour dire que je n'écris pas' (undated note), in *Les mots, etc*, 1,266–7.

309   *Sartre By Himself*. The film was shot in Feb.–March 1972 and first shown

at Cannes on 27 May 1976. On watching it together: Beauvoir 'A Farewell to Sartre', *Adieux*, 85. On watching TV despite near-blindness: Todd, *Un fils rebelle*, 20.

309 Refused to be sad: Sartre, 'Self-Portrait at Seventy', in *Sartre in the Seventies (Situations X)*, 3–92, this 4.

309 Strokes, memory, teeth: Hayman, *Writing Against*, 416–17.

309 'Nothing': Beauvoir, 'A Farewell to Sartre', *Adieux*, 65.

309 'Sartre, *petit père*': Todd, *Un fils rebelle*, 30.

309 Pro-Communist views, anti-Semitism book, violence: Sartre & Lévy, *Hope Now*, 63–4, 92, 100–103. The interviews were originally published in *Le nouvel observateur* (10, 17, 24 March 1980).

310 A lesser evil, 'a thought created': ibid., 73.

310 Beauvoir's opinion: Ronald Aronson, 'Introduction', ibid., 3–40, this 7.

310 Aron's opinion: ibid., 8, citing Aron, 'Sartre à "Apostrophes"', *Liberation/ Sartre* (1980), 49. Other people also had concerns; Edward Said wrote of meeting Sartre and Beauvoir in Paris in 1979, and being shocked at the extent to which Lévy spoke on Sartre's behalf over lunch. When Said asked to hear Sartre speak for himself, Lévy hesitated then said he would do it the next day. He did, but from a prepared text that Said suspected was written by Lévy. Edward Said, 'Diary: an encounter with Sartre', *London Review of Books* (1 June 2000). On the wider context of the interview and Sartre's collaboration with Lévy, see J.-P. Boulé, *Sartre médiatique* (Paris: Minard, 1992), 205–15.

311 Photographers: Hayman, *Writing Against*, 437, referring esp. to a shot clearly taken with a long-range lens in *Match*.

311 'His death does separate us': Beauvoir, 'A Farewell to Sartre', in *Adieux*, 127.

311 Aron's and Sartre's deal: Aron, *Memoirs*, 450.

311 'Touching articles': Aron, *The Committed Observer*, 146.

312 Aron's death: Stanley Hoffman, 'Raymond Aron (1905–1983)', *New York Review of Books* (8 Dec. 1983).

312 Beauvoir's work in late years: Bair, *Simone de Beauvoir*, 611–12; ASAD, 69.

312 'These funny sort' and 'such an unlikely thing': Forster & Sutton (eds), *Daughters of de Beauvoir*, 19, 17 (Kate Millett interview).

312 Cirrhosis: Bair, *Simone de Beauvoir*, 612–13.

312 Death, funeral and reading: ibid., 615–16.

313 'I think with sadness': FOC, 674.

313 'One of those cloche hats': Beauvoir, *Old Age*, 406.

313 'Childish amazement': ASAD, 9.

314 'I was born in Paris': ASAD, 10.

315 'Heidegger: the pursuit of Being': Murdoch's Heidegger manuscript
     (typed version, corrected in her hand) is in the Murdoch Archive at the
     University of Kingston, KUAS6/5/1/4; a manuscript version is at the
     University of Iowa. Parts have been published in an edition based on
     both texts by Justin Broackes: Murdoch, *Sein und Zeit*: pursuit of Being',
     in Broackes (ed.), *Iris Murdoch, Philosopher*, 93–114.

315 Clearing: Murdoch, '*Sein und Zeit*: pursuit of Being', in Broackes (ed.),
     Iris Murdoch, Philosopher, 97.

315 Benet's puzzlement: Murdoch, *Jackson's Dilemma*, 13–14.

315 'I am small': ibid., 47.

316 Jackson's last thoughts: ibid., 248–9.

Chapter 14: The Imponderable Bloom

317 On existentialism in films, see Jean- Pierre Boulé & Enda McCaffrey
     (eds), *Existentialism and Contemporary Cinema* (New York & Oxford:
     Berghahn, 2011), William C. Pamerleau, *Existentialist Cinema* (Basingstoke
     & New York: Palgrave Macmillan, 2009), and others.

318 Malick: see Thomas Deane Tucker & Stuart Kendall (eds), *Terrence Malick:
     film and philosophy* (London: Continuum, 2011), Martin Woessner, 'What Is
     Heideggerian Cinema?', *New German Critique*, 38 (2) (2011), 129–57, and Simon
     Critchley, 'Calm: on Terrence Malick's *The Thin Red Line*', *Film-Philosophy*,
     6 (38) (Dec. 2002), available online at http://www.film-philosophy.com/
     vol6-2002/n48critchley. Malick translated Heidegger's *The Essence of Reasons*
     (Evanston, IL: Northwestern University Press, 1969).

318 Out of control: for a fascinating example of this genre, see Daniel
     Kahnemann, *Thinking Fast and Slow* (New York: Farrar, Straus & Giroux,
     2011).

318 Research on belief in freedom: J. Baggini, *Freedom Regained* (London:
     Granta, 2015), 35, citing K. D. Vohs and J. W. Schooler, 'The Value of
     Believing in Free Will: encouraging a belief in determinism increases
     cheating', *Psychological Science*, 19 (1) (2008), 49–54. Subjects who had
     read a passage implying that behaviour is deterministic were more
     inclined to cheat on a task than those who had not.

320 'To think is to confine yourself': Heidegger, 'The Thinker as Poet', in *Poetry, Language, Thought*, 1–14, this 4.

320 Heidegger lacking heart: Murdoch, Heidegger manuscript (typed version, corrected in her hand), Murdoch Archives at the University of Kingston, KUAS6/5/1/4, 53.

320 'He was born': Kisiel, *Genesis*, 287, citing MS transcript of the first Aristotle lecture (1 May 1924), 1. Heidegger's life of no interest: Petzet, *Encounters and Dialogues*, 1. It must be said that Husserl also showed little interest in biographical details; in this respect, they shared a similar conception of the phenomenological enterprise.

322 'Everything that he said': Fest, *Not I*, 265.

322 'Against himself': FOC, 273. For an appreciative assessment of Sartre's dynamism, see Barnes, *An Existentialist Ethics*, 448.

323 'If one rereads all my books': this remark was quoted back to him in an interview by Michel Contat; Sartre agreed with it. Sartre, 'Self-Portrait at Seventy', in *Sartre in the Seventies (Situations X)*, 3–92, this 20.

323 'It seems to me' and 'To put it briefly': Beauvoir, *Adieux*, 436.

323 'And yet we've lived': ibid., 445.

324 'Nothing technological': Heidegger, 'The Question Concerning Technology', in *The Question Concerning Technology and Other Essays*, 3–35, this 4.

324 'Ultra-rapid computing machine': Heinemann, *Existentialism and the Modern Predicament*, 26, 28.

324 Internet: Dreyfus, *On the Internet*, 1–2. On the other hand, Don Ihde has argued that Heidegger's philosophy is not relevant to modern technologies, since Heidegger was thinking mainly of the industrial era: Don Ihde, *Heidegger's Technologies: postphenomenological perspectives* (New York: Fordham University Press, 2010), 117–20.

325 'I see something like you' and 'The imponderable bloom': E. M. Forster, 'The Machine Stops', in *Collected Short Stories* (London: Penguin, 1954), 109–46, this 110–11. Originally published in the *Oxford and Cambridge Review* (Nov. 1909).

325 'Embodied cognition': see, for example, George Lakoff & Mark Johnson, *Philosophy in the Flesh: the embodied mind and its challenge to Western thought* (New York: Basic Books, 1999), Mark Rowlands, *The New Science of the Mind* (Cambridge, MA & London: Bradford/MIT Press, 2010), and Shaun Gallagher, *How the Body Shapes the Mind* (Oxford: Clarendon Press, 2005).

Select Bibliography

*Details of other works referred to can
also be found in the Notes.*

Archival sources

Sonia Brownell & Maurice Merleau-Ponty: Correspondence (S.109) in
George Orwell Archive, University College London.
Iris Murdoch, 'Heidegger: the pursuit of Being' (KUAS6/5/1/4) and
'Notes on a lecture by Jean-Paul Sartre' (Brussels, Oct. 1945) (IML
682) in Murdoch Archive, University of Kingston.

Published works

Aho, Kevin, *Existentialism: an introduction* (Malden, MA & Cambridge:
Polity, 2014).
Arendt, Hannah, *Eichmann in Jerusalem: a report on the banality of evil*,
rev. and enl. edn (Harmondsworth: Penguin, 1977).
—— *Essays in Understanding, 1930–1954*, ed. J. Kohn (New York:
Harcourt, Brace & Co., 1994).
—— *The Life of the Mind*, ed. M. McCarthy (New York: Harcourt Brace
Jovanovich, 1977–8).
—— *The Origins of Totalitarianism* (London: André Deutsch, 1986)
(*Elemente und Ursprünge totaler Herrschaft*, 1951).
Arendt, Hannah & Heidegger, Martin, *Letters, 1925–1975*, ed. U. Ludz,
tr. A. Shields (Orlando: Harcourt, 2004) (*Briefe*, 1998).

Arendt, Hannah & Jaspers, Karl, *Hannah Arendt/Karl Jaspers Correspondence 1926–1969*, eds L. Kohler & H. Saner, tr. R. & R. Kimber (New York: Harcourt Brace Jovanovich, 1992) (*Hannah Arendt/Karl Jaspers Briefwechsel*, 1985).

Aron, Raymond, *The Committed Observer: interviews with Jean-Louis Missika and Dominique Wolton*, tr. J. & M. McIntosh (Chicago: Regnery Gateway, 1983) (*Le spectateur engagé*, 1981).

—— *Memoirs*, tr. G. Holoch (New York & London: Holmes & Meier, 1990) (*Mémoires*, 1983).

—— *The Opium of the Intellectuals*, tr. T. Kilmartin (London: Secker & Warburg, 1957) (*L'opium des intellectuels*, 1955).

Bair, Deirdre, *Simone de Beauvoir* (London: Vintage, 1991).

Baldwin, James, *The Price of the Ticket: collected non-fiction 1948–1985* (London: Michael Joseph, 1985).

Barnes, Hazel, *An Existentialist Ethics*, new edn (Chicago & London: Chicago University Press, 1978).

—— *The Story I Tell Myself: a venture in existentialist autobiography* (Chicago & London: Chicago University Press, 1997).

Barrett, William, *Irrational Man: a study in existential philosophy* (Garden City: Doubleday, 1962) (originally 1958).

Bauer, Nancy, *Simone de Beauvoir, Philosophy, and Feminism* (New York: Columbia University Press, 2001).

Beauvoir, Simone de, *Adieux: a farewell to Sartre*, tr. P. O'Brian (London: Penguin, 1985) (*La céremonie des adieux* . . . , 1981).

—— *All Said and Done*, tr. P. O'Brian (Harmondsworth: Penguin, 1977) (*Tout compte fait*, 1972).

—— *America Day By Day*, tr. C. Cosman (London: Phoenix, 1999) (*L'Amérique au jour le jour*, 1948).

—— *Beloved Chicago Man: letters to Nelson Algren 1947–64*, ed. S. Le Bon de Beauvoir (London: Phoenix, 1999). US edn entitled *A Transatlantic Love Affair* (New York: New Press, 1998). Originally published in French edn (*Lettres à Nelson Algren*, tr. S. Le Bon de Beauvoir, 1997); letters then restored to English originals in re-translation.

—— *The Blood of Others*, tr. Y. Moyse & R. Senhouse (Harmondsworth: Penguin, 1964) (*Le sang des autres*, 1945).

—— *Cahiers de jeunesse 1926–1930*, ed. S. Le Bon de Beauvoir (Paris: Gallimard, 2008).

—— *The Ethics of Ambiguity*, tr. B. Frechtman (New York: Citadel, 1968) (*Pour une morale de l'ambiguité*, 1947).

—— *Force of Circumstance*, tr. R. Howard (Harmondsworth: Penguin, 1968) (*La force des choses*, 1963).

—— *The Mandarins*, tr. L. M. Friedman (London: Harper, 2005) (*Les Mandarins*, 1954).

—— *Memoirs of a Dutiful Daughter*, tr. J. Kirkup (Harmondsworth: Penguin, 1963) (*Mémoires d'une jeune fille rangée*, 1958).

—— *Old Age*, tr. P. O'Brian (Harmondsworth: Penguin, 1977) (*La vieillesse*, 1970).

—— *Philosophical Writings*, eds M. A. Simons, M. Timmermann & M. B. Mader (Urbana & Chicago: University of Illinois Press, 2004).

—— *Political Writings*, eds M. A. Simons & M. Timmermann (Urbana, Chicago & Springfield: University of Illinois Press, 2012).

—— *The Prime of Life*, tr. P. Green (Harmondsworth: Penguin, 1965) (*La force de l'âge*, 1960).

—— *The Second Sex*, tr. C. Borde & S. Malovany-Chevallier (London: Cape, 2009) (*Le deuxième sexe*, 1949).

—— *She Came to Stay*, tr. Y. Moyse & R. Senhouse (London: Harper, 2006) (*L'invitée*, 1943).

—— *'The Useless Mouths' and Other Literary Writings*, eds M. A. Simons & M. Timmermann (Urbana, Chicago & Springfield: University of Illinois Press, 2011).

—— *A Very Easy Death*, tr. P. O'Brian (Harmondsworth: Penguin, 1969) (*Une mort très douce*, 1964).

—— *Wartime Diary*, tr. A. Deing Cordero, eds M. A. Simons & S. Le Bon de Beauvoir (Urbana & Chicago: University of Illinois Press, 2009) (*Journal de guerre*, 1990).

Beevor, Antony & Cooper, Artemis, *Paris After the Liberation: 1944–1949*, rev. edn (London: Penguin, 2004).

Bernasconi, Robert, *How to Read Sartre* (London: Granta, 2006).

—— (ed.), *Race* (Malden, MA & Oxford: Blackwell, 2001).

Biemel, Walter, *Martin Heidegger: an illustrated study*, tr. J. L. Mehta

(New York: Harcourt Brace Jovanovich, 1976) (*Martin Heidegger*, 1973).

Borden, Sarah, *Edith Stein* (London & New York: Continuum, 2003).

Brentano, Franz, *Psychology from an Empirical Standpoint*, ed. O. Kraus, tr. A. C. Rancurello, D. B. Terrell & L. McAlister (London & New York: Routledge, 1995) (*Psychologie vom empirischen Standpunkte*, 1874, 2nd edn 1924).

Broackes, Justin (ed.), *Iris Murdoch, Philosopher: a collection of essays* (Oxford & New York: OUP, 2012).

Camus, Albert, *Algerian Chronicles*, tr. A. Goldhammer (Cambridge, MA & London: Belknap/Harvard University Press, 2013) (*Chroniques algériennes*, 1958).

—— *American Journals*, ed. R. Quilliot, tr. Hugh Levick (London: Abacus, 1990) (*Journal de voyage*, 1978).

—— *Between Hell and Reason*, tr. A. de Gramont (Lebanon, NH: University Press of New England, 1991) (translation of essays originally published in *Combat*).

—— *Caligula, Cross Purpose, The Just, The Possessed*, tr. S. Gilbert & H. Jones (London: Penguin, 1984).

—— *Essais* (Paris: Gallimard, 1965).

—— *The Fall*, tr. J. O'Brien (Harmondsworth: Penguin, 1963) (*La chute*, 1956).

—— *The First Man*, tr. D. Hapgood (London: Penguin, 1996) (*Le premier homme*, 1994).

—— *Lyrical and Critical Essays*, tr. E. Conroy Kennedy, ed. P. Thody (New York: Knopf, 1969) (translations from *L'envers et l'endroit*, *Noces*, *L'été* and other sources).

—— *The Myth of Sisyphus*, tr. J. O'Brien (Harmondsworth: Penguin, 1975) (*Le mythe de Sisyphe*, 1942).

—— 'Neither Victims nor Executioners' (tr. D. Macdonald), in Paul Goodman (ed.), *Seeds of Liberation* (New York: G. Braziller, 1964), 24–43 ('Ni victimes, ni bourreaux', published in *Combat*, 1946).

—— *Notebooks 1935–1942*, tr. P. Thody (New York: Modern Library, 1965) (*Carnets 1935–1942*, 1962).

The Outsider, tr. S. Smith (Harmondsworth: Penguin, 2013) (*L'etranger*, 1942).

—— *The Plague*, tr. R. Buss (London: Allen Lane, 2001) (*La peste*, 1947).

—— *The Rebel*, tr. A. Bower (London: Penguin, 2000) (*L'homme revolté*, 1951).

Carman, Taylor, *Merleau-Ponty* (London & New York: Routledge, 2008).

Carpenter, Humphrey, *The Angry Young Men: a literary comedy of the 1950s* (London: Allen Lane, 2002).

Cassirer, Ernst & Heidegger, Martin, *Débat sur le Kantisme et la philosophie*, ed. P. Aubenque (Paris: Éditions Beauchesne, 1972).

Cau, Jean, *Croquis de mémoire* (Paris: Julliard, 1985).

Cazalis, Anne-Marie, *Les mémoires d'une Anne* (Paris: Stock, 1976).

Chvatík, Ivan, 'Geschichte und Vorgeschite des Prager Jan Patočka-Archivs', *Studia phaenomenologica* VII (2007), 163–89.

Cohen-Solal, Annie, *Album Jean-Paul Sartre: iconographie* (Paris: Gallimard, 1991).

—— *Sartre: a life*, tr. A. Cancogni (London: Heinemann, 1987) (*Sartre*, 1985).

—— *Une renaissance Sartrienne* (Paris: Gallimard, 2013).

Conradi, Peter J., *Iris Murdoch: a life* (London: HarperCollins, 2001).

Contat, Michel & Rybalka, Michel (eds), *The Writings of Jean-Paul Sartre*, tr. R. McCleary (Evanston, IL: Northwestern University Press, 1974) vol. 1: *A Bibliographical Life*, vol. 2: *Selected Prose*.

Cooper, David E., *Existentialism: a reconstruction*, 2nd edn (Oxford: Blackwell, 1999).

Corpet, O. & Paulhan, Claire, *Collaboration and Resistance: French literary life under the Nazi Occupation*, tr. J. Mehlman et al. (New York: Five Ties, 2009) (*Archives de la vie littéraire sous l'Occupation*, 2009).

Cotkin, George, *Existential America* (Baltimore, MD: Johns Hopkins University Press, 2005).

Cox, Gary, *The Sartre Dictionary* (London: Continuum, 2008).

Crowell, Steven (ed.), *The Cambridge Companion to Existentialism* (New York & Cambridge: CUP, 2012).

Dodd, James, *Crisis and Reflection: an introduction to Husserl's Crisis of the European Sciences* (Dordrecht, Boston & London: Kluwer, 2004).

Dorléac, Bertrand, *Art of the Defeat: France 1940–44* (Los Angeles: Getty Research Institute, 2008).

Dreyfus, Herbert L., *Being-in-the-world: a commentary on Heidegger's Being and Time, Divison I* (Cambridge, MA & London: MIT Press, 1991).

—— *On the Internet* (London & New York: Routledge, 2001).

—— *What Computers Still Can't Do* (Cambridge, MA & London: MIT Press, 1992).

Dreyfus, Hubert L. and Wrathall, Mark A. (eds), *A Companion to Phenomenology and Existentialism* (Oxford: Blackwell, 2006).

Ettinger, Elzbieta, *Hannah Arendt, Martin Heidegger* (New Haven & London: Yale University Press, 1995).

Fanon, Frantz, *Black Skin, White Masks*, tr. R. Philcox (New York: Grove, 2008) (*Peau noir, masques blancs*, 1952).

—— *The Wretched of the Earth*, foreword by J.-P. Sartre, tr. C. Farrington (Harmondsworth: Penguin, 1967) (*Les damnés de la terre*, 1961).

Farías, Victor, *Heidegger and Nazism*, tr. P. Burrell & G. R. Ricci, eds J. Margolis & T. Rockmore (Philadelphia: Temple University Press, 1989) (*Heidegger y el Nazismo*, 1987, originally published in French as *Heidegger et le nazisme*, 1987).

Faye, Emmanuel, *Heidegger: the introduction of Nazism into philosophy*, tr. M. B. Smith (New Haven & London: Yale University Press, 2009) (*Heidegger: l'introduction du nazisme dans la philosophie*, 2005).

Fest, Joachim, *Not I: a German childhood*, tr. M. Chalmers. (London: Atlantic Books, 2013) (*Ich nicht*, 2006).

Flynn, Thomas R., *Sartre: a philosophical biography* (Cambridge: CUP, 2014).

Forster, Penny & Sutton, Imogen (eds), *Daughters of de Beauvoir* (London: The Women's Press, 1989).

Fullbrook, Edward & Fullbrook, Kate, *Sex and Philosophy: rethinking De Beauvoir and Sartre* (London: Continuum, 2008).

Fulton, Ann, *Apostles of Sartre: existentialism in America* (Evanston, IL: Northwestern University Press, 1999).

Gadamer, Hans-Georg, *Philosophical Apprenticeships*, tr. R. R. Sullivan (Cambridge, MA: MIT Press, 1985) (*Philosophische Lehrjahre*, 1977).

Gallagher, Shaun & Zahavi, Dan, *The Phenomenological Mind*, 2nd edn (London & New York: Routledge, 2012).

Gandillac, Maurice de, *Le siècle traversé* (Paris: Albin Michel, 1998).

Garff, Joakim, *Søren Kierkegaard: a biography*, new edn, tr. B. H. Kirmmse (Princeton: Princeton University Press, 2007).

Genet, Jean, *The Declared Enemy: texts and interviews*, ed. A. Dichy, tr. Jeff Fort (Stanford: Stanford University Press, 2004) (*L'ennemi déclaré*, 1991).

Gens, Jean-Claude, *Karl Jaspers: biographie* (Paris: Bayard, 2003).

Gerassi, John, *Sartre: hated conscience of his century* (Chicago: Chicago University Press, 1989).

—— *Talking with Sartre: conversations and debates* (New Haven & London: Yale University Press, 2009).

Gille, Vincent, *Saint-Germain-des-Prés, 1945–1950* (Paris: Pavillon des Arts, 1989).

Gordon, L. (ed.), *Existence in Black: An Anthology of Black Existential Philosophy* (New York & London: Routledge, 1997).

Gordon, Peter Eli, *Continental Divide: Heidegger, Cassirer, Davos* (Cambridge, MA & London: Harvard University Press, 2010).

Gray, Francine du Plessix, *Simone Weil* (London: Weidenfeld & Nicolson, 2001).

Gréco, Juliette, *Je suis faite comme ça* (Paris: Flammarion, 2012).

—— *Jujube* (Paris: Stock, 1982).

Guéhenno, Jean, *Diary of the Dark Years, 1940–1944*, tr. D. Ball (Oxford & New York: OUP, 2014) (*Journal des années noires*, 1947).

Haffner, Sebastian, *Defying Hitler: a memoir*, tr. O. Pretzel (London: Weidenfeld & Nicolson, 2002) (*Geschichte eines Deutschen*, 2000).

Havel, Václav, *Letters to Olga*, tr. with introduction by P. Wilson (London & Boston: Faber, 1990) (*Dopisy Olze*, 1990).

—— 'The Power of the Powerless' (*Moc bezmocných*, 1978), tr. P. Wilson, in his *Living in Truth: twenty-two essays published on the occasion of the award of the Erasmus Prize to Václav Havel*, ed. Jan Vladislav (London: Faber, 1987), 36–122.

Hayman, Ronald, *Writing Against: a biography of Sartre* (London: Weidenfeld & Nicolson, 1986).

Heidegger, Martin, *Basic Writings*, ed. D. F. Krell, rev. and expanded edn (London: Routledge, 1993).

—— *Being and Time*, tr. J. Macquarrie & E. Robinson (Oxford: Blackwell, 1962) (*Sein und Zeit*, 1927).

—— *Being and Time*, tr. J. Stambaugh, rev. D. J. Schmidt (Albany: SUNY Press, 2010) (*Sein und Zeit*, 1927).

—— *Country Path Conversations*, tr. B. W. Davis (Bloomington & Indianapolis: Indiana University Press 2010) (*Feldweg-Gespräche*, 2nd edn (GA 77), 2005).

—— *Elucidations of Hölderlin's Poetry*, tr. K. Hoeller (New York: Humanity Books, 2000) (*Erläuterungen zu Hölderlins Dichtung*, (GA 4), 1981).

—— *Gesamtausgabe* (GA) (Frankfurt am Main: V. Klostermann, 1976–) (the collected edn of Heidegger's works).

—— *Introduction to Metaphysics*, tr. G. Fried & R. Polt (New Haven & London: Yale University Press, 2000) (*Einführung in die Metaphysik*, 1953).

—— *Letters to his Wife 1915–1970*, ed. G. Heidegger, tr. R. D. V. Glasgow (Cambridge & Malden, MA: Polity, 2008) (*Mein liebes Seelchen!*, 2005).

—— *Off the Beaten Track*, eds & tr. J. Young & K. Haynes (Cambridge: CUP, 2002) (*Holzwege*, 1950).

—— *On Time and Being*, tr. J. Stambaugh (New York: Harper & Row, 1972) (translation from various sources).

—— *Pathmarks*, ed. W. McNeill (Cambridge: CUP, 1998) (*Wegmarken*, 1967, rev. edn 1976).

—— *Poetry, Language,Thought*, tr. A. Hofstadter (New York: Harper, 1975) (translation from various sources).

—— *The Question Concerning Technology and Other Essays*, tr. W. Lovitt (New York: Harper, 1977) (*Die Frage nach der Technik*, 1953).

—— *Sein und Zeit*, 14th edn (Tübingen: Max Niemeyer, 1977).

—— *Sojourns: the journey to Greece*, tr J. P. Manoussakis (Albany: SUNY Press, 2005) (*Aufenthalte*, 1989).

—— *What Is Called Thinking?*, tr. J. G. Gray (New York: Harper, 1968) (*Was heisst denken?*, 1954).

—— Heidegger, Martin & Jaspers, Karl, *The Heidegger–Jaspers Correspondence (1920–1963)*, eds W. Biemel & H. Saner, tr. G. E. Aylesworth (Amherst, NY: Humanity Books, 2003) (*Briefwechsel*, 1990).

Heinemann, Friedrich, *Existentialism and the Modern Predicament*, 2nd edn (London: Adam & Charles Black, 1954).

Howells, Christina (ed.), *The Cambridge Companion to Sartre* (Cambridge: CUP, 1992).

Husserl, Edmund, *Cartesian Meditations: an introduction to phenomenology*, tr. D. Cairns (The Hague: Martinus Nijhoff, 1977) ('Cartesianische Meditationen', *Husserliana* I, 1950).

—— *The Crisis of the European Sciences and Transcendental Phenomenology*, ed. W. Biemel, tr. D. Carr (Evanston, IL: Northwestern University Press, 1970) (*Die Krisis der europäischen Wissenschaften und die transzendentale Phänomenologie*, 1954).

—— *Husserliana* (The Hague: Martinus Nijhoff; Dordrecht: Springer, 1950–). Collected edition of his works, with supplementary volumes.

—— *Ideas: general introduction to pure phenomenology*, tr. W. R. Boyce Gibson (London & New York: Routledge, 2012) (*Ideen*, 1913, 1952).

—— *Logical Investigations*, tr. J. N. Findlay (London: Routledge & Kegan Paul; New York: Humanities Press, 1970) (*Logische Untersuchungen*, 2nd edn, 1913– 21).

—— *Psychological and Transcendental Phenomenology and the Confrontation with Heidegger (1927–1931)*, eds & tr. T. Sheehan & R. E. Palmer (Dordrecht, Boston, London: Kluwer, 1997) (*Husserliana: Collected Works* VI).

Husserl-Archiv Leuven, *Geschichte des Husserl-Archivs = History of the Husserl Archives* (Dordrecht: Springer, 2007).

Huston, John, *An Open Book* (New York: Knopf, 1980; London: Macmillan, 1981).

Inwood, Michael, *A Heidegger Dictionary* (Oxford Blackwell, 1999).

Jackson, Julian, *France: The Dark Years 1940–1944* (Oxford & New York: OUP, 2001).

Janicaud, Dominique, *Heidegger en France* (Paris: Albin Michel, 2001).

Jaspers, Karl, *The Atom Bomb and the Future of Mankind*, tr. E. B. Ashton (Chicago: University of Chicago Press, 1961) (*Die Atombombe und die Zukunft des Menschen*, 1958).

—— *Basic Philosophical Writings*, eds E. Ehrlich, L. H. Ehrlich & G. B. Pepper (Amherst, NY: Humanity Books (Humanities Press), 1994).

—— 'On Heidegger', tr. Dale L. Ponikvar, *Graduate Faculty Philosophy Journal* 7 (1) (1978), 107–28. Translation of the added chapter *Notizen zu Martin Heidegger*, ed. Hans Saner, in revised edn of Jaspers, *Philosophische Autobiographie* (Munich: Piper, 1989). Also included as an insert in 'Philosophical Autobiography' (see below), 75/1–16.

—— *Philosophy*, tr. E. B. Ashton (Chicago & London: University of Chicago Press, 1969–70) (*Philosophie*, 1932).

—— *Philosophy of Existence*, tr. R. F. Grabau (Oxford: Blackwell, 1971) (*Existenzphilosophie*, 1938).

—— *The Question of German Guilt*, tr. E. B. Ashton (Westport, CT: Greenwood Press, 1978) (*Die Schuldfrage*, 1946).

—— 'Philosophical Autobiography', tr. P. A. Schilpp & L. B. Lefebre, in P. A. Schilpp (ed.) *The Philosophy of Karl Jaspers*. 2nd edn (La Salle, IL: Open Court, 1981), 5–94.

—— 'Self-Portrait', tr. E. Ehrlich, in L. H. Ehrlich & R. Wisser (eds), *Karl Jaspers Today: philosophy at the threshold of the future* (Washington DC: Center for Advanced Research in Phenomenology, 1988), 1–25 (an interview broadcast and recorded 1966/7 by Norddeutscher Rundfunk).

Judaken, Jonathan & Bernasconi, Robert (eds), *Situating Existentialism* (New York & Chichester: Columbia University Press, 2012).

Judt, Tony, *Past Imperfect: French Intellectuals 1944–1956* (Berkeley: University of California Press, 1992).

Kaufmann, Walter, *Existentialism from Dostoevsky to Sartre* (London: Thames & Hudson, 1957).

Kierkegaard, Søren, *The Concept of Anxiety*, tr. E. and H. Hong (Princeton: Princeton University Press, 1981) (*Begrebet Angest*, 1844).

—— *Concluding Unscientific Postscript to the Philosophical Crumbs*, ed. & tr. A. Hannay (Cambridge: CUP, 2009) (*Afsluttende uvidenskabelig Efterskrift til de philosophiske Smuler*, 1846).

—— *Fear and Trembling*, tr. A. Hannay (London: Penguin, 2005) (*Frygt og Baeven*, 1843).

King, Magda, *A Guide to Heidegger's Being and Time*, ed. J. Llewellyn (Albany: SUNY Press, 2001).

Kirkbright, Suzanne, *Karl Jaspers: a biography – navigations in truth* (New Haven & London: Yale University Press, 2004).

Kisiel, Theodore & Sheehan, Thomas (eds), *Becoming Heidegger: on the trail of his early occasional writings, 1910–1927* (Evanston, IL: Northwestern University Press, 2007).

Kleinberg, Ethan, *Generation Existential: Heidegger's philosophy in France, 1927–1961* (Ithaca: Cornell University Press, 2005).

Klíma, Ivan, *My Crazy Century*, tr. Craig Cravens (London: Grove, 2014) (US edn by Grove/Atlantic, 2013).

Koestler, Arthur, *Darkness at Noon* (London: Macmillan, 1941).

—— *Scum of the Earth* (New York: Macmillan, 1941).

Kohák, Erazim, *Jan Patočka: philosophy and selected writings* (Chicago & London: Chicago University Press, 1989).

Lacoin, Elisabeth, *Zaza: correspondance et carnets d'Elisabeth Lacoin (1914–1929)* (Paris: Éditions du Seuil, 1991).

Landes, Donald A., *The Merleau-Ponty Dictionary* (London: Bloomsbury, 2013).

Lanzmann, Claude, *The Patagonian Hare*, tr. F. Wynne (London: Atlantic, 2012). (*Le lièvre de Patagonie*, 2009).

Lescourret, Marie-Anne, *Emmanuel Levinas*, 2nd edn (Paris: Flammarion, 2006).

Levinas, *Discovering Existence with Husserl*, tr. & eds R. A. Cohen & M. B. Smith (Evanston, IL: Northwestern University Press, 1998) (*En découvrant l'existence avec Husserl et Heidegger*, 1949).

—— *Existence and Existents*, tr. A. Lingis, introduction by R. Bernasconi (Pittsburgh: Duquesne University Press, 2001) (*De l'existence à l'existent*, 1947).

—— *On Escape – De l'évasion*, tr. B. Bergo, with introductory essay, 'Getting Out of Being by a New Path', by J. Rolland (Stanford: Stanford University Press, 2003) (translation of essay published in *Recherches Philosophiques*, 1935).

—— *Totality and Infinity*, tr. A. Lingis (Pittsburgh: Duquesne University Press, 1969) (*Totalité et l'infini*, 1961).

Lévy, Bernard-Henri, *Sartre: the philosopher of the twentieth century*, tr. A. Brown (Cambridge: Polity, 2003) (*Le siècle de Sartre*, 2000).

Lewis, Michael & Staehler, Tanya, *Phenomenology: an introduction* (London & New York: Continuum, 2010).

Lottman, Herbert, *Albert Camus* (New York: Doubleday, 1979).

Löwith, Karl, *My Life in Germany Before and After 1933*, tr. E. King (London: Athlone Press, 1994) (*Mein Leben in Deutschland vor und nach 1939*, 1986).

Lusset, Félix, 'Un episode de l'histoire de la Mission Culturelle Française à Berlin (1946–1948): Sartre et Simone de Beauvoir à Berlin à l'occasion des representations des *Mouches* au theatre Hebbel (janvier 1948)', in Jérôme Vaillant (ed.), *La dénazification par les vainqueurs: la politique culturelle des occupants en Allemagne 1945–1949* (Lille: Presses universitaires de Lille, 1981), 91–103.

MacDonald, Paul S. (ed.), *The Existentialist Reader: an anthology of key texts* (Edinburgh: Edinburgh University Press, 2000).

Macey, David, *Frantz Fanon: a biography*, 2nd edn (London & New York: Verso, 2012) (first published in US by Picador, 2000).

Mailer, Norman, *Advertisements for Myself* (Cambridge, MA & London: Harvard University Press, 1992).

Malka, Solomon, *Emmanuel Levinas: his life and legacy*, tr. M. Kigel & S. M. Embree (Pittsburgh: Duquesne University Press, 2006) (*Emmanuel Lévinas: la vie et la trace*, 2002).

Marcel, Gabriel, 'An Autobiographical Essay', tr. Forrest Williams, in P. A. Schilpp & L. Hahn (eds), *The Philosophy of Gabriel Marcel* (La Salle, IL: Open Court, 1991), 3–68.

—— *Homo Viator: introduction to a metaphysic of hope*, tr. E. Craufurd (London: Gollancz, 1951) (*Homo Viator*, 1944).

—— *The Philosophy of Existence*, tr. M. Harari (London: Harvill, 1948) (translation of various works).

—— *Tragic Wisdom and Beyond: including conversations between Paul Ricœur and Gabriel Marcel*, tr. S. Jolin & P. McCormick (Evanston, IL: Northwestern University Press, 1973) (*Pour une sagesse tragique et son au-delà*, 1968).

Merleau-Ponty, Maurice, *Adventures of the Dialectic*, tr. J. Bien (Evanston, IL: Northwestern University Press, 1973) (*Les aventures de la dialectique*, 1955).

SELECT BIBLIOGRAPHY 415

—— *Humanism and Terror: the Communist problem*, tr. J. O'Neill (New Brunswick & London: Transaction, 2000) (*Humanisme et terreur*, 1947).

—— *In Praise of Philosophy*, tr. J. Wild & J. M. Edie (Evanson, IL: Northwestern University Press, 1963) (*Éloge de la philosophie*, 1953).

—— *La phénomenologie de la perception* (Paris: Gallimard, 2005).

—— *Œuvres*, ed. C. Lefort (Paris: Gallimard, 2010).

—— *Parcours deux, 1951–1961* (Paris: Verdier, 2000).

—— *Phenomenology of Perception*, tr. D. Landes (London & New York: Routledge, 2012) (*La phénomenologie de la perception*, 1945).

—— *Sense and Non-Sense*, tr. H. L. Dreyfus & P. A. Dreyfus (Evanston, IL: Northwestern University Press, 1964) (*Sens et non-sens*, 1948).

—— *Signs*, tr. & ed. R. C. McCleary (Evanston, IL: Northwestern University Press, 1964) (*Signes*, 1960).

—— *Texts and Dialogues*, eds H. J. Silverman & J. Barry Jr, tr. M. Smith et al. (New Jersey & London: Humanities Press, 1992).

—— *The Visible and the Invisible: followed by working notes*, ed. C. Lefort, tr. A. Lingis (Evanston, IL: Northwestern University Press, 1968) (*Le visible et l'invisible*, 1964).

—— *The World of Perception*, tr. O. Davis (London & New York: Routledge, 2008) (*Causeries 1948*, 2002).

Moi, Toril, *Simone de Beauvoir: the making of an intellectual woman* (Oxford & Cambridge, MA: Blackwell, 1994).

Moran, Dermot, *Edmund Husserl: founder of phenomenology* (Cambridge: Polity, 2005).

—— *Introduction to Phenomenology* (London & New York: Routledge, 2000).

Murdoch, Iris, *Jackson's Dilemma* (London: Chatto & Windus, 1995).

—— *Metaphysics as a Guide to Morals* (London: Chatto & Windus, 1992).

—— *Sartre: romantic rationalist* (Harmondsworth: Penguin, 1989).

—— '*Sein und Zeit*: pursuit of Being' (ed. Broackes), in J. Broackes (ed.), *Iris Murdoch, Philosopher: a collection of essays* (Oxford & New York: OUP, 2012), 93–114.

Murray, Michael (ed.), *Heidegger and Modern Philosophy* (New Haven: Yale University Press, 1978).

Neske, Günther & Kettering, Emil (eds), *Martin Heidegger and National Socialism: questions and answers*, tr. Lisa Harries (New York: Paragon, 1990).

Ott, Hugo, *Heidegger: a political life*, tr. Allan Blunden (London: Fontana, 1994) (*Martin Heidegger: unterwegs zu seiner Biographie*, 1988).

Patočka, Jan, *Heretical Essays in the Philosophy of History*, tr. E. Kohák, ed. J. Dodd, foreword by P. Ricœur (Chicago: Open Court, 1996) (*Kacířské eseje o filosofii dějin*, 1975).

Petzet, H. W., *Encounters and Dialogues with Martin Heidegger 1929–1976*, tr. P. Emade & K. Maly (Chicago & London: University of Chicago Press, 1993) (*Auf einen Stern zugehen: Begegnungen und Gespräche mit Martin Heidegger*, 1983).

Polt, Richard, *Heidegger: an introduction* (London: UCL Press, 1999).

Rée, Jonathan, *Heidegger* (London: Routledge, 1999).

Richardson, William J., *Heidegger: through phenomenology to thought*, foreword by M. Heidegger, 3rd edn (The Hague: Martinus Nijhoff, 1973).

Rockmore, Tom, *Heidegger and French Philosophy: humanism, anti-humanism, and Being* (London: Routledge, 1995).

Rowley, Hazel, *Richard Wright: the life and times* (Chicago: University of Chicago Press, 2008).

Sacks, Oliver, *A Leg to Stand On* (London: Picador, 1986).

Safranski, R., *Martin Heidegger: between good and evil* (Cambridge, MA: Harvard University Press, 1998) (*Ein Meister aus Deutschland: Heidegger und seine Zeit*, 1994).

Sartre, Jean-Paul, *The Aftermath of War (Situations III)*, tr. C. Turner (London, New York & Calcutta: Seagull, 2008) (*Situations III*, 1949).

—— *The Age of Reason*, tr. E. Sutton (Harmondsworth: Penguin, 1961) (*Roads of Freedom I*) (*L'âge de raison*, 1945).

—— *Being and Nothingness*, tr. H. Barnes (London: Routledge, 2003) (*L'être et le néant*, 1943).

—— *Between Existentialism and Marxism*, tr. J. Matthews, new edn (London: Verso, 2008) (a selection of essays from *Situations VIII* and *IX*, and an interview, 'Itinerary of a Thought').

— *The Communists and Peace. With an answer to Claude Lefort*, tr. I.

Cléphane (London: Hamish Hamilton, 1969) (*Les communistes et la paix*, published in *Les Temps modernes* in three parts: 81 (July 1952), 84–5 (Oct.–Nov. 1952), 101 (April 1954), and reprinted in *Situations VI: problemes du Marxisme*, 1964).

—— *Critical Essays (Situations I)*, tr. C. Turner (London, New York & Calcutta: Seagull, 2010) (*Situations I*, 1947).

—— *Critique of Dialectical Reason. Volume I: Theory of Practical Ensembles*, tr. A. Sheridan-Smith, ed. J. Rée, introduction by F. Jameson (London: Verso, 2004) (*Critique de la raison dialectique. I. Théorie des ensembles pratiques*, 1960).

—— *Critique of Dialectical Reason. Volume II (Unfinished)*, ed. A. Elkaïm-Sartre, tr. Q. Hoare (London & New York: Verso, 2006) (*Critique de la raison dialectique. II*, 1985).

—— *L'être et le néant* (Paris: Gallimard, 1943).

—— *Existentialism and Humanism*, tr. P. Mairet (London: Methuen, 2007) (*L'existentialisme est un humanisme*, 1946).

—— *The Family Idiot*, tr. C. Cosman (Chicago: University of Chicago Press, 1981–93) (*L'idiot de la famille*, 1971–2).

—— *The Freud Scenario*, ed. J.-B. Pontalis, tr. Q. Hoare (London: Verso, 1985) (*Le scenario Freud*, 1984).

—— *Imagination: a psychological critique*, tr. F. Williams (London: Cressett; Ann Arbor: University of Michigan Press, 1962) (*L'imagination*, 1936).

—— *The Imaginary*, rev. A. Elkaïm-Sartre, tr. J. Webber (London & New York: Routledge, 2004) (*L'imaginaire*, 2nd edn, 1986, 1st edn 1940).

—— *Intimacy*, tr. L. Alexander (London: Panther, 1960) (*Le mur*, 1948).

—— *Iron in the Soul*, tr. Eric Sutton (Harmondsworth: Penguin, 1963) (*Roads of Freedom III*) (*La mort dans l'âme*, 1949).

—— *The Last Chance: Roads of Freedom IV*, tr. C. Vasey (London & New York: Continuum, 2009) (*La dernière chance*, 1981).

—— Sartre, *Les mots et autres écrits autobiographiques*, eds J.-F. Louette, G. Philippe & J. Simont (Paris: Gallimard, 2010).

—— *Nausea*, tr. R. Baldick (Harmondsworth: Penguin, 1965) (*La nausée*, 1938).

—— *No Exit and Three Other Plays*, tr. S. Gilbert & L. Abel (New York: Vintage, 1989) (translation of *Huis clos*, 1944, and other works).

—— *Quiet Moments in a War: the letters of Jean-Paul Sartre to Simone de Beauvoir 1940–1963*, ed. S. de Beauvoir, tr. L. Fahnestock & N. MacAfee (New York: Scribner's, 1993) (*Lettres au Castor II*, 1983).

—— *The Reprieve*, tr. E. Sutton (Harmondsworth: Penguin, 1963) (*Roads of Freedom II*) (*Le sursis*, 1945).

—— *Saint Genet: actor and martyr*, tr. B. Frechtman (New York: Pantheon, 1963) (*Saint Genet, comédien et martyr*, 1952).

—— *Sartre By Himself: a film directed by Alexandre Astruc and Michel Contat*, tr. R. Seaver (New York: Urizen, 1978) (*Sartre par lui-même*, 1977).

—— *Sartre in the Seventies: interviews and essays*, tr. P. Auster and L. Davis (London: André Deutsch, 1978) (*Situations X*, 1976). Published in the US as *Life/Situations* (New York: Pantheon, 1977).

—— *Situations* [IV], tr. B. Eisler (London: Hamish Hamilton, 1965) (*Situations IV*, 1964). Also translated as *Portraits* (*Situations IV*), tr. C. Turner (London, New York & Calcutta: Seagull, 2009).

—— *War Diaries*, tr. Q. Hoare (London: Verso, 1984) (*Les carnets de la drôle de guerre*, 1983).

—— *Witness to My Life: the letters of Jean-Paul Sartre to Simone de Beauvoir, 1926–1939*, ed. S. de Beauvoir, tr. L. Fahnestock & N. MacAfee (Harmondsworth: Penguin, 1994) (*Lettres au Castor I*, 1983).

—— *Words*, tr. I. Clephane (Harmondsworth: Penguin, 1967) (*Les mots*, 1963).

Sartre, J.-P. and Lévy, Benny, *Hope Now: the 1980 interviews*, tr. A. Van den Hoven; introduction by R. Aronson (Chicago: University of Chicago Press, 1996) (*L'espoir maintenant*, 1991).

Sepp, Hans Rainer (ed.), *Edmund Husserl und die phänomenologische Bewegung. Zeugnisse in Text und Bild* (Freiburg: Karl Alber, 1988).

Sharr, Adam, *Heidegger's Hut* (Cambridge, MA & London: MIT Press, 2006).

Sheehan, Thomas (ed.), *Heidegger: the man and the thinker* (New Brunswick & London: Transaction, 2010).

—— *Making Sense of Heidegger: a paradigm shift* (London & New York: Rowman & Littlefield, 2015).

Shore, Marci, 'Out of the Desert,' *Times Literary Supplement* (2 Aug. 2013), 14–15.

Simons, Margaret A., *Beauvoir and The Second Sex: feminism, race, and the origins of existentialism* (Lanham, MD: Rowman & Littlefield, 1999).

Spender, Stephen, *New Selected Journals 1939–1995*, eds L. Feigel & J. Sutherland, with N. Spender (London: Faber, 2012).

Spiegelberg, Herbert, 'The Lost Portrait of Edmund Husserl by Franz and Ida Brentano', in Robert B. Palmer & Robert Hamerton-Kelly (eds), *Philomathes: studies and essays in the humanities in memory of Philip Merlan* (The Hague: Martinus Nijhoff, 1971), 341–5.

—— *The Phenomenological Movement: a historical introduction*, 3rd edn, with the collaboration of Karl Schuhmann (The Hague: Martinus Nijhoff, 1982).

Sprintzen, David A. & Van den Hoven, Adrian (eds), *Sartre and Camus: a historic confrontation* (Amherst, NY: Humanity Books, 2004).

Spurgeon, Brad, *Colin Wilson: philosopher of optimism* (Manchester: Michael Butterworth, 2006).

Spurling, Hilary, *The Girl from the Fiction Department: a portrait of Sonia Orwell* (London: Hamish Hamilton, 2002).

Stein, Edith, *On the Problem of Empathy*, 3rd edn, tr. W. Stein (Washington DC: Institute of Carmelite Studies Publications, 1989) (*Collected Works, III*) (*Zum Problem der Einfühlung*, 1917).

—— *Self-Portrait in Letters, 1916–1942*, tr. J. Koeppel (Washington DC: Institute of Carmelite Studies Publications, 1993) (*Collected Works V*) (*Selbstbildnis in Briefen*, 1976–7).

Steiner, George, *Martin Heidegger* (Harmondsworth: Penguin, 1978).

Stewart, Jon (ed.), *The Debate Between Sartre and Merleau-Ponty* (Evanston, IL: Northwestern University Press, 1998).

Les Temps modernes (Paris, 1 Oct. 1945–).

Thompson, Kenneth A., *Sartre: his life and works.* (New York & Bicester: Facts on File, 1984).

Toadvine, Ted & Embree, Lester (eds), *Merleau-Ponty's Reading of Husserl* (Dordrecht, Boston & London: Kluwer, 2002).

Todd, Olivier, *Albert Camus: une vie* (Paris: Gallimard, 1995).

—— *Albert Camus: a life*, tr. B. Ivry (London: Chatto & Windus, 1997) (an abridged and edited version of *Albert Camus*, 1995).

—— *Un fils rebelle* (Paris: B. Grasset, 1981).

Towarnicki, Frédéric de, 'Le Chemin de Zähringen', in his *À la rencontre de Heidegger: souvenirs d'un messager de le Forêt-noire* (Paris: Gallimard, 1993), 13–128.

Van Breda, Herman Leo, 'Die Rettung von Husserls Nachlass und die Gründung des Husserl-Archivs – The Rescue of Husserl's *Nachlass* and the Founding of the Husserl-Archives', tr. D. Ulrichs & B. Vassillicos, in *Geschichte des Husserl-Archivs = History of the Husserl Archives* (Dordrecht: Springer, 2007), 39–69 (Van Breda's account first published in 1959).

Vian, Boris, *I Spit on Your Graves*, tr. B. Vian & M. Rosenthal, introduction by J. Sallis (Edinburgh: Canongate, 2001) (*J'irais cracher sur vos tombes*, 1948).

—— *Manual of Saint-Germain-des-Prés* (New York: Rizzoli, 2005).

—— *Mood Indigo*, tr. J. Sturrock (New York: Grove Press, 1968) (*L'écume des jours*, 1947).

Webber, Jonathan, *The Existentialism of Jean-Paul Sartre* (New York & London: Routledge, 2009).

Weber, Eugen, *The Hollow Years: France in the 1930s* (New York & London: W. W. Norton, 1994).

Weil, Simone, *Formative Writings 1929–41*, eds & tr. D. Tuck McFarland & W. Van Ness (Abingdon & New York: Routledge, 1987).

White, Edmund, *Genet*, corrected edn (London: Picador, 1994).

Wilson, Colin, *Dreaming to Some Purpose* (London: Century, 2004).

—— *The Outsider* (London: Gollancz, 1956).

Woessner, Martin, *Heidegger in America* (Cambridge: CUP, 2011).

Wolin, Richard, *Heidegger's Children: Hannah Arendt, Karl Löwith, Hans Jonas, and Herbert Marcuse* (Princeton & Oxford: Princeton University Press, 2001).

—— (ed.), *The Heidegger Controversy* (Cambridge, MA: MIT Press, 1993).

Wright, Richard, *The Outsider: the restored text established by the Library of America*, with notes by A. Rampersad (New York & London: Harper, 2008).

Young-Bruehl, Elisabeth, *Hannah Arendt: for love of the world*, 2nd edn (New Haven & London: Yale University Press, 2004).

Zaretsky, Robert, *A Life Worth Living: Albert Camus and the quest for meaning* (Cambridge, MA & London: Belknap/Harvard University Press, 2013).

Zimmermann, Hans Dieter, *Martin und Fritz Heidegger: Philosophie und Fastnacht*, 2nd edn (Munich: C. H. Beck, 2005).

List of Illustrations

Index